PELICAN BOOKS
British Society 1914–45

John Stevenson was born in Warrington in 1946 and read history
at Worcester College, Oxford. After postgraduate research at
Nuffield College he lectured in history at Oriel College, Oxford.
Since 1976 he has taught at the University of Sheffield, where
he is a Reader in history. His previous books include *Social
Conditions in Britain between the Wars*; *The Slump: Society and
Politics during the Depression* (with Chris Cook); *Popular Disturbances in England, 1700–1870* and *The Longman Handbook of Modern
British History, 1714–1980* (with Chris Cook). He is currently
working on a study of the life and times of William Cobbett and
a major new social history of Britain.

THE PELICAN SOCIAL HISTORY OF BRITAIN
General Editor: J. H. Plumb

Already published:
Roy Porter: *English Society in the Eighteenth Century*
Arthur Marwick: *British Society Since 1945*
Joyce Youings: *Sixteenth-Century England*

Titles in preparation:
V. A. C. Gatrell: *Britain 1800–1870*
José Harris: *Britain 1870–1914*

John Stevenson

British Society 1914–45

Penguin Books

Penguin Books Ltd, Harmondsworth, Middlesex, England
Viking Penguin Inc., 40 West 23rd Street, New York, New York 10010, U.S.A.
Penguin Books Australia Ltd, Ringwood, Victoria, Australia
Penguin Books Canada Ltd, 2801 John Street, Markham, Ontario, Canada L 3 R 1 B 4
Penguin Books (N.Z.) Ltd, 182–190 Wairau Road, Auckland 10, New Zealand

First published 1984
Published simultaneously by Allen Lane
Reprinted 1986

Filmset in Monophoto Bembo by
Northumberland Press Ltd, Gateshead
Made and printed in Great Britain by
Richard Clay (The Chaucer Press) Ltd, Bungay, Suffolk

For Jackie

Contents

Editorial Foreword

Historians respond to the problems of their time almost without being conscious of the process, and the focus of their study changes with the changing times. In the nineteenth century all countries of Europe and America were preoccupied with the origins of national identity, with the need to forge a living past that would give meaning not only to the present but also to the future: Ranke, Macaulay, Michelet, Bancroft and other great historians of the nineteenth century were so preoccupied. As Britain's national identity seemed to be inexorably involved with the evolution of constitutional rights, with liberty, freedom and, particularly, democracy, it is not surprising that an ever growing number of professional historians should devote all their skills and interests to constitutional, legal and political history and that these subjects should dominate university syllabuses when they were first designed in the late nineteenth century.

The First World War, the Great Depression, and the economic disasters which followed gave great impetus to the study both of diplomatic and economic history, the one generally attracting the conservative, the other the radical historians in the 1920s and 1930s. After the Second World War interest in diplomatic history faded first or, rather, transmogrified itself into International Relations and Strategic Studies. Economic history drifted into a professional morass and developed a confused identity – the quantifiers and the econometricians moved in and so did the sociologists, especially American sociologists, hoping to establish an ideology which would refute the Marxist interpretation which had flourished within the realm of economic history.

But the problems of Western industrial society have become much more complex since the Second World War. Fantastic economic growth, and it has been fantastic this last thirty years, has created its own social tensions and, even more important, the very nature of highly industrialized society, apart from its growth, has created new conflicts. Institutions which have lasted for ten thousand years, not only in the West but also in the East, have suddenly seemed to be in jeopardy. In the last two decades there has been a mushrooming of interest amongst historians in the problems of demography, of the nature of the family, of the position of women, children, slaves, and servants, of the uses of leisure, of the influence of printing, of the expansion of the arts, of the importance of the images society creates for itself, and of the interpretation of class not in economic but in social terms. A new panorama of social history has spread before the eyes of scholars and led them to subjects which historians of previous generations would have thought of interest only to antiquarians.

Naturally other forms of history are not dead, even though some of them are corpse-like, but there can be little doubt that the historical imagination, for better or worse, has become intoxicated with social history: for example, the volume of work on death in the last ten years is prodigious and it is matched by the quantity of studies on childhood or marriage.

The danger of social history, which in spite of its present explosion has, in some of its aspects, long roots reaching back through G. M. Trevelyan to Macaulay and Sir Walter Scott, has been the tendency to drift into descriptive history, of how people lived and spent their days with little or no attempt to analyse why their lives, their beliefs, their activities were what they were. Also, the evidence social historians, even very good ones, used in the past, was impressionistic – diaries, letters, personal memories, together with material collected from folk-lorists and antiquarians. Naturally, most of this evidence related to the literate class, always, until very recent times, a modest segment of the nation.

In order to give this material greater rigour, sociological theory, either of Marxist or capitalist bent, has been used and, often, in discussion of death, birth, education of children, or the position of women, it has been infused with modern psychological analysis. Although this has given rise to some nonsense, particularly in the history of childhood, it has given the subject, on the whole, greater intellectual weight.

As with economic history, there has also been a powerful movement which has attempted to quantify the evidence of the past in order to give a statistical basis for some of the fundamental questions of social history – average size and nature of the family, whether nuclear or extended; the age of marriage for men and women; death rates and ages at death; even an attempt has been made to quantify literacy. Huge mountains of data have been assembled and computers have hummed away merrily at great expense but the results remain extremely tentative. Before the nineteenth century record-keeping was erratic and its reliability was not easy to test. There is, too, one unknown factor of great importance – how many of the population were ever recorded at all, neither their births, marriages, nor deaths? Indeed, most of the results obtained are easy to criticize and must be treated with considerable scepticism. Even so, generalizations about the family and about its size, about marriage, about bastardy, about age of death, all are firmer than they were and, because they are, help us to understand the life of the country in greater depth.

Although statistics may give shadow and depth to the picture, they cannot paint it, and social history still depends upon a great range of records. Formerly, it depended most of all on letters, diaries and imaginative literature but, although these are still of the greatest value, more attention has now been given to artefacts: to the study of houses and gardens, to newspapers, bills, and trade cards, to carriages, instruments, games and toys, indeed to everything that may throw a light on the way life was lived or the way it hurried towards its future or clung to its past. By extending its range and its depth, by encompassing a multiplicity of scenes, social history has become a far more complex and intellectually exciting discipline than it was.

Over the last ten years the flow of monographs and articles on the social history of England has increased, mushroomed like an atomic explosion, and the time is more than ripe for an attempt at synthesis.

J. H. Plumb

Preface

Some words of explanation are appropriate at the outset about any study which attempts to squeeze as many quarts into pint pots as this one does; indeed I am only too conscious of aspects of these years which have been either left out altogether or given rather cursory treatment. In terms of geographical coverage, this book is primarily a social history of mainland Britain rather than of the United Kingdom of Great Britain and Northern Ireland. Where relevant however, I have attempted to indicate some of the principal areas in which Ulster shared in, differed from or impinged upon the experience of Great Britain as a whole. Scotland and Wales have been generally discussed as part of the overall British experience rather than as separate entities, though again I have tried to emphasize the most important lines of distinctive development where applicable. Fortunately, it is possible for this period to point to a number of excellent histories of Wales and Scotland with which the reader can correct any tendency towards too anglocentric a view. Two other aspects require mention. The rise of the labour movement and some of the more emotive causes of this era, such as the suffrage question and the peace movement, straddle uneasily the boundary between political history and a broadly conceived social history. I have not attempted to do full justice to some of these issues, partly because they are already well covered in other places and also because my main concern here is with social rather than political significance. Similarly, the intellectual, artistic and scientific achievements of these years are considered primarily in so far as they reflect wider social issues. Again, far more detailed and expert accounts of these developments can be found elsewhere which assess their importance within their own spheres.

Another consequence of writing a book of this kind is the accumulation of large debts to many other writers and scholars. Unfortunately, in a format which precludes the use of a detailed set of references or footnotes I have only been able to give a limited indication in the text and in the guide to further reading of the full extent of my dependence upon the work and insights of others. To those who feel that the contributions have not been adequately signposted or their exact nuances faithfully reproduced I can only offer my apologies and plead the pressures of condensing a vast array of material into a reasonable length. I am, however, particularly conscious of the benefits I have been able to receive from reading the work of my research pupils Kate Mourby and David Round on the effect of unemployment on particular communities during the inter-war years and from my reading of Dr Mark Pegg's thesis on the social impact of radio broadcasting before the Second World War. Patrick Renshaw kindly allowed me access to an unpublished article on the Labour movement in the 1920s and I am especially grateful to Chris Cook, Edgar Jones and Howard Robinson for their interest and support over a number of years. Mr William Day and Mr Bernard Taylor have also both assisted me with their detailed recollections of these years. I benefited considerably from the opportunity to present some of my ideas about this period at a Beaverbrook seminar at the Institute of Historical Research in 1981 and the criticisms made there. The burdens of writing a book are inevitably shared with others and I am grateful to both colleagues and friends for the interest and sympathy with which they have borne being lectured at on whatever aspect of the period happened to preoccupy me at the time. The General Editor of this series, Professor J. H. Plumb, gave perceptive advice in the early stages of the work, and I must also thank Peter Carson of Penguin for his patience during the book's over-lengthy completion. My thanks also go to Pat Holland, Sue Hill, Lynda Harrison, Sandra Joyce and Muriel Shingler, who carried out the typing of the manuscript.

Introduction

In 1900 a journalist in a medium-sized industrial town in north-west England ventured on a historical odyssey. Indulging in the current fashion for imaginative time travel, he pictured his ancient community at various stages in its past: Roman camp, Norman stronghold, medieval market, Civil War battle site. Coming nearer to his own day he spanned the transition from eighteenth-century market town to the industrial hubbub of the present. Then, leaping into the future, he attempted to visualize the town fifty years on, in 1950, to see what changes the next half century might bring. He was impressed. Everything was now 'a model of cleanliness and good arrangement'. Well-built works and houses, interspersed with parks and flowerbeds, had replaced the squalor and sordidness of the slums, while new suburbs stretched out into the surrounding countryside. The streets were now wide and spacious, the air cleared of the 'sulphurous smoke' which hung over the Victorian town, and its once grossly polluted river crystal-clear and teeming with fish. A municipal 'Electrical Lighting Station' provided light and heat to the town and to its trams and factories. The infirmary, hospitals and convalescent homes were run by the municipality, 'for it was rightly felt that men's infirmities should not be left for their alleviation to the fluctuating chances of the public charity'. 'The town was so healthy and accidents were now so rare that both the convalescent home and the larger Hospital which overlooked the Park were seldom full, and often empty; whilst fevers and other contagious diseases had been almost absolutely banished by the increasing attention which was paid to every sanitary detail, and the wonderful discoveries which had done much to reduce them,

all over the country, to a minimum.' The ancient parish church
he found 'packed from end to end', while the nonconforming
churches had been 'wise enough to federate amongst themselves', and latterly with the 'Mother Church'. A university
extension college had been established to which 'the humblest
scholar in our elementary schools could enter and it could rival
Oxford in the fame of its degrees and the extent and the pro-
fundity of its many sided learnings'. New shops and works had
arisen on every side, many Corporation-owned, for 'all over
the country ... national and municipal enterprise was gradually
superseding that of individual firms or companies'. With the
rateable value so increased even the rate-payers had ceased to
protest, though most 'had early begun to see that happiness
and high rates were better than misery and low ones'. Nor
had less lofty things been forgotten: cricket and football still
flourished on the new playing fields and the Corporation
Brewery supplied beer in municipally run public houses, 'absolutely pure', 'brewed, as in the good old days, from simple
hops and malt'. Not only beer, but tea and coffee, and 'the best
of everything'.

A quaint and fanciful glimpse into the future, perhaps,
certainly one which might have been disappointed to a degree
by the reality of Britain in 1950. But not totally. With its vision
of continued economic growth, social and environmental
improvement, the beneficial impact of technical advance, and
of municipal and national progress, it reflected not only the
preoccupations of many in the years before 1914, but also offers
as useful a yardstick as any to the changes wrought in British
society during the first half of the twentieth century. In spite
of two world wars and a severe economic depression there was
material progress; economic growth brought higher living
standards, better housing and improved social amenities. Many
diseases had been conquered and social welfare extended,
though much more decisively by national rather than municipal
provision. The churches were less full than anticipated, though
a measure of Christian unity had been achieved. If no university
extension college had been founded in this town, they had been

elsewhere, and there was free entry into secondary education and state scholarships to university. Sport flourished, indeed enjoyed record attendances, while the pubs remained important centres of social life, though, thankfully, Corporation beer had yet to come. There were, however, important elements which were missing. By 1950, war memorials in almost every town and village in the country bore witness to two world wars whose economic and social repercussions must rank as some of the most important influences upon the development of British society in the twentieth century. The growth of technology conceived in terms of economic and municipal progress barely anticipated the impact of the private motor car, the cinema and radio. Also hidden from view were the profound effects of changes in the birth rate, in relations between the sexes, in fashions and culture which were to do so much to influence British society in the half century after 1900. A confident belief in 'progress' failed to appreciate the full nature of the challenges in intellectual life and science which the twentieth century would bring.

None the less, the partial accuracy of this turn of the century vision confirms that social history does not divide itself into self-contained packages. Any particular segment reflects the ultimate historical platitude that all ages are ages of transition. This was as true of the first half of the twentieth century as of any other period. Some of the most significant features of social change, such as the growth of mass consumerism, demographic change, growing state intervention, the rise of leisure, the improved status of women and children, and the decline of organized religion, have their origins in the period before 1914, frequently before 1900. The point is reinforced by the demographic fact that at any point up to 1945 British society was still in large part made up of people whose habits and assumptions had been formed in the late-Victorian and Edwardian era. Any understanding of British society between 1914 and 1945 involves recognizing that it was an end as much as a beginning, in which the concerns of the years before 1914 have as important a part to play as those which foreshadowed the society which emerged after 1945.

While a proper appreciation of the continuities with the years before 1914 is essential to an understanding of this period, there is the additional difficulty involved in writing what is essentially recent history. Even forty years after the end of the Second World War it is still difficult to put into proper perspective the ideas and assumptions which emerged in these years to form part of the post-war consensus in many areas. This period saw the growing involvement of the state in the provision of social welfare and in the management of the economy. As a process, it was hesitant, going faster at some times than others, but clearly recorded by an overall increase in state spending, an expanding bureaucracy and a wider responsibility in almost every sphere of social and economic policy. In the light of post-war developments, notably the creation of the Welfare State and a wider economic role by governments, it is often hard to resist the view that state intervention was broadly speaking 'progressive' and, therefore, desirable. Allied with the fashion for Keynesian economics, it becomes all too easy to regard opponents of deficit financing, public works, comprehensive social welfare and free secondary education as blinkered and unimaginative. But intellectual fashions change, the state intervention and expenditure which members of one generation came to regard as the very touch-stone of progressive government is now regarded by others, no less convinced, as less desirable, even harmful. No doubt, these views will be modified and challenged in their turn. The point of importance, however, is not the rights and wrongs of Keynesian economics or the efficacy and morality of state intervention as a cure for economic and social ills, but rather that we must beware applying to the past criteria which are themselves historical phenomena.

In the following pages, I have attempted to analyse some of the most important aspects of British social history between 1914 and 1945, including the effects of both world wars. I have opened with a consideration of the principal features of British society before 1914, followed by discussion of the Great War as both a national and a social event, then by a wider discussion of the economic and material developments which affected Britain between the wars. Demography, considered in the following chapter, is a difficult subject for the layman, but one which is of crucial importance for many of the most critical areas of social history, such as family size, living standards, the status of women and children, and attitudes to the home. The nature of the paid work which frequently dominated people's lives is considered next, along with the place of organized labour. The major features of housing, welfare, education and social policy form the central chapters of the book, while a special chapter is devoted to one of the most important issues of the inter-war years, unemployment. The social structure of Britain is considered next, followed by sections dealing with leisure, religion and culture. Finally, I have attempted a brief survey of the repercussions of the Second World War to provide a link with the succeeding volume in this series.

1. *Britain in 1914*

On the eve of the Great War, almost a hundred and fifty years of population increase, urbanization and economic growth had transformed Britain into a primarily urban and industrial society. In the course of the nineteenth century, the population of Great Britain quadrupled and was to increase still further in the years preceding the Great War. The official census of 1911 revealed that the total population of the United Kingdom stood at just over forty-five million people, compared with only twenty-seven million at the time of the Great Exhibition of 1851. This rapid increase in population was shared, to a varying extent, by most other countries in Western Europe prior to 1914. But while population continued to grow, the rate of increase was beginning to slacken. The Registrar-General noted in 1901 that the increase over the past decade was one of the lowest in the whole century, while the next was to reveal a further levelling-out of growth. The roots of this slow-down in population growth have been traced by demographic historians to the 1880s, when birth rates began to fall from the very high levels they had reached in the earlier part of the century. Viewed in retrospect, the late-Victorian era marked the beginning of one of those long swings in demographic trends which are easier to record than to explain. Although the total population continued to increase, the rate of growth had begun a decline which was to continue during the Edwardian era and become more pronounced between the wars.

One result of this process was that, even before the Great War cut a swathe through the younger generations, Britain had an ageing population. In 1841 just under half the population was under twenty, by 1911 less than a third. The effects of the

demographic changes were emphasized by the tide of emigration which rose to a flood in the years just before the war.
Between 1901 and 1910 the annual average rate of emigration
was running at 284,000 and was to rise to 464,000 in 1911–13,
and the majority of emigrants tended to be the younger, unattached portion of the population. Indeed, the census report
of 1911 had warned of the military and economic dangers
inherent in the declining proportion of 'workers at the most
economically efficient ages'. Awareness of the net loss of active,
young emigrants combined with demographic evidence about
a declining birth rate to produce a profound pessimism about
future population trends. Assuming existing rates of births and
deaths and a similar pattern of emigration, at some point in the
future the population of the United Kingdom was bound to
decline, possibly to begin a descending spiral in which each
generation would be smaller than the last. Such fears, accompanied by concern that an increasing proportion of each generation was the offspring of the lower social classes or immigrants,
were to raise the spectre of 'national deterioration' and lead in
the inter-war years to serious consideration of the prospect of
future depopulation.

But if the great population surge which had accompanied
Britain's industrial expansion appeared to be ebbing, many
of its other features continued to mould the shape of British
society. Victorian Britain had become an urban society and
urbanization continued into the Edwardian era. By 1901 it was
estimated that 78 per cent of the population of the United
Kingdom lived in towns, and between 1871 and 1901 alone
the number of towns with populations over 50,000 people had
doubled. The distribution of these urban communities reflected
the powerful forces exerted by the industrial revolution upon
the Victorian environment. A survey in 1901 estimated that
over half the towns of over 50,000 people were situated on or
near to coalfields. About a third were 'service' or commercial
centres, such as the great ports of London, Liverpool, Hull and
Southampton; another quarter or so, including some of those
sited on coalfields, were primarily metalworking towns, such

as Sheffield and Birmingham. Another quarter, concentrated in Lancashire and Yorkshire, were textile towns. Smaller groups were made up of the 'resort' towns, such as Blackpool, Bournemouth, Brighton and Bath; the naval towns, such as Portsmouth and Plymouth; and a category dependent for their livelihoods on particular industries, such as the pottery towns around Stoke on Trent, St Helens with its glass and chemical industries, and Burton with its brewing.

Dominating the urban scene were the large 'conurbations'. Greater London had grown from a population of 3,890,000 in 1871 to 7,256,000 in 1911; Manchester and South-East Lancashire from 1,386,000 to 2,328,000; and Birmingham and the West Midlands from 969,000 to 1,634,000. There was some evidence that the rate of expansion of many of the larger urban centres was beginning to slacken by the Edwardian era, but there remained areas where urban growth was still pressing ahead at a very rapid rate indeed. The late-Victorian and Edwardian 'boom towns' were places such as Belfast, whose population rose from 174,000 in 1871 to 415,000 in 1921; Glasgow, doubling in population in the same period to over a million inhabitants; and Cardiff, whose population rose fivefold to over 200,000 people by 1921.

While some industrial centres were still expanding at a great rate, the other major feature was that existing towns were beginning to spread further and further into the surrounding countryside. The word 'suburbia' had been coined in the 1890s to describe the fringe of half-urban, half-rural settlements growing up around London. In the last decades of the nineteenth century the area within six miles of the centre of London had been steadily losing population to the 'outer ring', the area comprising most of Middlesex and parts of Essex, Surrey, Kent and Hertfordshire, which made up the Metropolitan Police District. While the resident population of the City declined and that of the County of London grew from 3,830,000 to 4,522,000 between 1881 and 1911, the population of the 'outer ring' grew from 936,000 to 2,730,000. Whereasof thege rate of increase in English urban areas in the last decade of the nineteenth century was 15 per cent, burgeoning London suburbs such as East Ham grew by 193.5 per cent and Walthamstow by 105.3 per cent. The same story was being repeated in other parts of the 'outer ring', in places such as Leyton, Willesden, Croydon and Tottenham, where in 1905 Henrietta Barnett described the 'small villas side by side, their few yards of garden carefully cherished, the monotony of mediocrity unbroken by fine public buildings or large open spaces'. Foreign visitors were already beginning to remark upon the English penchant for low-density, suburban houses in preference to the flats and tenements more common on the continent.

Domestic writers, too, were already denouncing the gim-crack monotony of the suburbs and their life. In *The Suburbans*, published in 1905, one writer opined that in the suburbs:

> You will understand, as it were, intuitively, and without further ado, the cheapness and out-of-jointness of the times; you will com-prehend the why and wherefore and *raison d'être* of halfpenny journalism ... you will perceive the whizzers, penny buses, gramo-phones, bamboo furniture, pleasant Sunday afternoons, Glory Songs, modern language teas, golf, tennis, high school education, dubious fiction, shilling's worth of comic writing, picture postcards, miraculous hair-restorers, prize competitions, and all other sorts of twentieth-century clap-trap have got a market and a use, and black masses of supporters.

A similar pattern was revealing itself in most other towns and cities of the British Isles before 1914. Progressive displace-ment from the centre took the wealthier professional and business classes into the outer suburbs, the lower-middle classes and better-paid workmen into the inner suburbs, leaving the innermost districts to factories, offices, shops and slums. A provincial capital, such as Manchester, already had villas for the prosperous 'cottontots' as far afield as Wilmslow, Alderley Edge and Didsbury, while Chorlton, Withington, Fallowfield and Cheetham Hill were being colonized by solid, middle-class housing. On Merseyside, an exodus to Southport, Formby, Wallasey and West Derby was already under way, while the population of the central districts declined. The *Birmingham*

Mail in 1903 noticed a similar phenomenon: 'Like the Arab
they are folding their tents and stealing silently away in the
direction of Knowle and Solihull . . .' Also to Edgbaston, 'the
Birmingham Belgravia', which had risen from a population of
2,599 in 1881 to 16,368 by 1911. This suburban development
was already creating a distinctive pattern of urban sprawl, as
cities engulfed neighbouring villages and separate settlements
were linked by 'ribbon development' to the main urban mass.
A visitor to West Yorkshire in 1900 found 'one vast manufacturing hive, in which city verges on city, and one village
merges into another', while a citizen of Bristol in 1902 commented of his city: 'LOST, STOLEN OR STRAYED. Not heard
of for some time. When last seen was wearing well and running
uneventfully over a number of hills.'

This far-reaching development was made possible by a major
expansion in the transport network in which suburban railways
and electric trams were the agents of the suburban revolution.
'Suburbia,' as one child remembered it before 1914, 'was a
railway state . . . a state of existence within a few minutes walk
of the railway station, a few minutes walk of the shops, and a
few minutes walk of the fields.' Railway mileage continued
to grow in Edwardian Britain, rising from 13,562,000 miles in
1870 to 20,038,000 in 1914. As well as country branch lines,
much of this mileage consisted of suburban link lines and
improved fast routes. The South Manchester suburbs of Heaton
Mersey, Didsbury, Withington and Chorlton were linked by
a frequent and rapid commuter service to Manchester Central
Station by the 1880s, providing them with forty trains a day
into the centre of Manchester with an average frequency of ten
minutes during peak periods. The Liverpool–Southport line
was electrified in 1904, followed shortly by the suburban
services north of the Tyne owned by the North Eastern
Railway. Around London, the Brighton Company's lines were
being electrified from 1909 and the lines widened to accommodate heavier flows of traffic, while the termini at Victoria
and Waterloo were extended. Nor did railway development
solely serve the well-to-do. Cheap workmen's fares on the Great

Eastern Railway contributed to the growth of Walthamstow
from a population of 7,137 in 1861 to 95,131 in 1901. The first
underground railway serving the capital had been opened as
early as 1863 and the first electrically operated 'tube', the City
& South London Railway, was opened in 1890. The Central
London Railway, running from Shepherd's Bush to the Bank
Station, known – from its fare – as the 'Twopenny Tube', was
opened in 1900. By 1914 the other underground lines had gone
electric, linking places such as Finsbury, Hampstead and Clapham by rapid services to the centre of London.

Electric traction also provided quicker and cheaper tramway
services. Horse-drawn trams were already playing an important
part in urban transport by the 1890s, carrying an estimated 280
million passengers per year in London, to which could be added
an even larger number of passengers carried by horse omnibuses. The first part of the Bristol Tramway system, opened
in 1895, using American electrical equipment, transformed the
situation. By 1914 there were 2,500 miles of electrified tramway, operating in almost every large town and city. Cheaper
to operate than the horse-drawn trams and omnibuses, they
permitted reductions in fares and greatly stimulated traffic. By
1910 the number of passengers carried in London had risen to
764 million from 280 million fourteen years earlier, while the
number of trams doubled between 1904 and 1914. By the latter
date, the motor bus was also beginning to emerge as a major
contender for passenger traffic both in urban and in more lightly
populated rural areas. The breakthrough occurred in October
1910, when the London General Omnibus Company licensed
its first B-type bus, capable of carrying thirty-four passengers,
ten more than existing horse omnibuses. Twelve months later,
with new motor buses being produced at twenty per week,
the last of the horse omnibuses were withdrawn from service.
Elsewhere, British Electric Traction began actively to develop
motor services, with companies such as the Birmingham &
Midland Motor Omnibus Co. Ltd (later Midland Red) and
Crosland-Taylors (Crosville), based in Chester, beginning to
become familiar names. By 1914, motor-bus receipts were

about a third of the tramways and between them trams and motor buses dominated passenger road transport.

While the suburban railway and the electric tram contributed most to the rise of the suburbs, the motor bus was part of a more wide-ranging revolution in road transport which was to gather pace in the years after the Great War. The cheapest and most pervasive development was the bicycle. By 1900 the rear-chain-driven 'safety' bicycle with pneumatic tyres was being mass-produced, greatly reducing its cost, and spreading widely through almost every social class. The Webbs claimed that 'it was not until after 1895 that the world at large took to bicycling ... the bicycle was a comparatively cheap vehicle and its users were mostly the young people, and, to a great extent, the poorer section of the community.' Certainly the bicycle proved an important means both of getting to work and of leisure. Even more important, it represented one of the first consumer durables brought within reach of the working class by mass-production methods, methods which in the inter-war years would be applied to many more products. Moreover, several of the early cycle makers, such as Humber, Singer, Rover and William Morris, were to transfer their talents to making motor-cycles and motor vehicles.

By 1900 the essential breakthroughs had been made in the design of the internal combustion engine and manufacturers were emerging who would soon become household names. The Rolls-Royce partnership began in 1907 and Herbert Austin's Longbridge plant was employing 1,000 people by 1910 to produce a 7 h.p. car. In 1910 Henry Ford set up his first European plant in Trafford Park, Manchester, where 6,000 Model Ts were produced in 1913. By 1914 there were 389,000 road vehicles in Great Britain, 132,000 private cars, 124,000 motor-cycles, 51,000 buses, taxis and coaches, and 82,000 goods vehicles. Although the number of private horse-carriages was still greater than that of motor cars, in the larger towns and cities the bulk of private passenger transport was already motorized. A traffic census in London in 1913 revealed that only 6 per cent of all passenger vehicles were horse-drawn.

Goods traffic was still overwhelmingly horse-drawn on the
eve of the Great War – 88 per cent according to the same
London traffic census in 1913. Steam waggons had made some
inroads into road haulage as early as the 1890s, and were to
remain in production into the inter-war years, but by 1914
motor lorries were coming increasingly to the fore. Leyland
Motors, which had started life as the Lancashire Steam Motor
Company, had sales of £500,000 and other firms such as Albion
in Scotland and Dennis at Guildford were competing actively
for a steadily growing market. Although its possibilities had
yet to be fully exploited, the motor lorry was beginning to
provide a more flexible haulage and delivery service which
would have important effects on the siting of industry by
reducing its dependence on railways and canals. Even the
remote country villages and farms were becoming accessible
to the motor lorry and delivery van, bringing country areas
within the catchment area for retailers and buyers from the
neighbouring towns.

But outside the towns and the major cities, with their
growing traffic and spreading suburbs, there were still areas of
Britain only slowly being drawn into national life. In the more
rural parts of England, the traditional annual 'hiring fairs' were
held right up to 1914 in local market towns, at which farm
workers who wished to change their employer stood in an
allotted part of the street, or square, wearing the accepted signs
of their calling, such as a crook, or a tuft of wool worn in
the hat for a shepherd, a whip for a carter, a milking pail for a
dairymaid, and struck a bargain with an employer for a year's
work. In the North, gangs of Irish haymakers still plied their
seasonal trade through the farms of Cheshire, Lancashire and
South-West Scotland. In the South-West, isolated farms still
lived in a way almost untouched by the industrial revolution,
preparing almost everything for day-to-day use – bread, meat,
soap, cheese and butter – on the farm. In 1901 nine out of every
ten people in rural Cardigan had been born within the county
or just over its border. Here agriculture employed four times
as many men as any other occupation, and the language of

common speech, Welsh, classified a family's position by the size of its holding and the number of animals it could maintain – '*Lle buwch*' (a cow place), '*Ile ceffyl*' (a one-horse place) and '*Ille doubar*' (a place of two pairs). In a closely knit and inter-dependent community cottagers performed labour service at haymaking to pay for a bull to service their cows and obtain the right to plant potatoes in farm fields by '*dyled gwaith*' (work debt) or '*dyled tato*' (potato debt) performed at harvest time. In Scotland, prosperous lowland farms contrasted with the sub-sistence crofts of the Highlands, where as late as 1912 only three out of every hundred farmers owned their land and most holdings were valued at less than £50 per year in rent. Here, memories of evictions and rack-renting were still fresh, and the question of land reform, as in rural Wales, remained one of the most burning issues of the day.

This remoter, still predominantly rural, Britain was none the less yielding slowly to a more cosmopolitan culture. Compulsory national education had already penetrated the remoter districts, while the expansion of the branch lines and light railways, which accounted for so much of the last phase of railway construction in the years up to 1914, brought with it newspapers and magazines and a wider world of jobs and consumer goods. The gradual breakdown of rural isolation encouraged mobility and, for many, emigration, either overseas or to the larger towns and cities. Depopulation appeared to threaten the remoter parts of Britain. The population of western Wales and Cornwall in 1911 was lower than it had been thirty years earlier; that of the Highlands stagnant. Slowly and inexorably a national culture was seeping into the more rural parts of Britain.

Much remained, however, even with the advent of the rail-way and the imminence of the delivery van. A child growing up in the Forest of Dean in the 1920s could still consider it as 'remote and self-contained'. A surprisingly high proportion of British people in 1914 were still only one or two generations from the land. Although Britain was an urban and industrial society, to a quite remarkable degree its culture, folk memory and 'myth of itself' was still bound up with a rural past – a past which was, by the nature of things, increasingly far removed from direct experience.

The Classes of Men

In 1914 under 4 per cent of those who died in Britain accounted for nearly 90 per cent of the entire capital value bequeathed. The upper classes of Edwardian Britain had, generally, been beneficiaries of a national income which had risen by a fifth between 1900 and 1913, some of the largest increases occurring in 'unearned' income from shares and dividends. While real wages had remained only constant, if not actually falling, the already wealthy had seen an impressive increase in their accumulated capital. Moreover the Edwardian era saw something of a culmination of the process by which the traditional governing class based on the possession of land fused with the *nouveaux riches* 'plutocrats' from the city and industry. Although some snobberies remained, the process of absorbing the new men of wealth proceeded rapidly in the years prior to 1914. Between 1886 and 1914 two hundred individuals entered the nobility for the first time. More than a third represented the new wealth of the industrial revolution, such as the north-eastern armaments manufacturer Sir William Armstrong; another third derived their status from the professions, principally the law, diplomacy, colonial service and the armed forces, men such as Lord Kitchener, the victor of Omdurman; while less than a quarter came from the old landed families. Although some of the first two groups had already acquired land before taking a peerage, less than half the new peers came from a landed background. The remarkable feature of the Edwardian peerage as a whole, however, was the continued significance of the ownership and ethos of 'broad acres'. At the time of the constitutional crisis of 1911 over the power of the House of Lords, out of 570 hereditary peers, only an eleventh came from the business world. The British peerage was still in essence a territorial aristocracy only gradually being altered to accommodate new sources of money and power.

Amongst the upper classes in general, the tenacity with which the old landed classes maintained their influence in a world where agriculture accounted for an ever-diminishing proportion of the gross national product was equally striking. During the Victorian era it was almost axiomatic that money in itself brought little prestige, which could be obtained only through the acquisition of landed estates or a title. This constraint was lessening in the Edwardian era but still exercised its influence. A third of the new peers not born into landed families between 1886 and 1905 acquired landed estates, a proportion which fell to a sixth between 1906 and 1914. Sir William Armstrong, who died in 1900 possessing 16,000 acres, added to his Cragside mansion in 1893 a second seat at Bamborough Castle, which he modernized at a cost of £1¼ million. Others contented themselves with smaller country houses surrounded by sufficient land to be dignified by the title of an estate. Meanwhile, the landed classes increasingly participated in a wider range of economic activities. By 1896, 167 noblemen, a fourth of the peerage, sat on the boards of companies. Careful estate management had become essential in the period of the 'great depression' and many families had diversified their interests by selling land and buying stocks and shares. Others made, or at least sought, lucrative marriages with wealthy heiresses. When Consuelo Vanderbilt married the 9th Duke of Marlborough in 1896 her dowry from the legendary Vanderbilt millions was an estimated £2,000,000. The marriage settlement, arranged on a strictly commercial basis, brought the Duke £20,000 a year and income from a £500,000 fund. In 1900 another American heiress, Helena Zimmerman, the daughter of a railway director of Cincinnati, Ohio, became the Duchess of Manchester.

By 1914 the British upper classes had undergone a significant transformation. The old nobility retained their social prestige, but they had been joined by the new wealth of industry and commerce. An aristocracy of land was now an aristocracy of wealth. In the fashionable world of upper-class society, ancient names like the Cecils, Cavendishes and Churchills rubbed shoulders, if not always comfortably, with Harmsworths,

Chamberlains and Rothschilds. Many of the members of this class were fabulously rich. Amongst the wealthiest was the 2nd Duke of Westminster, who inherited an estate worth an estimated £14 million on the death of the 1st Duke in 1899, consisting of a financial empire spread over four continents and three hundred acres of central London, including most of Mayfair and Belgravia. The 17th Earl of Derby, 'the King of Lancashire', exercised an authority more akin to the eighteenth century than the first half of the twentieth. With an income from collieries, urban rents and agricultural estates of over £300,000 a year, from his seat at Knowsley Hall he controlled a London home and half a dozen estates, totalling some 70,000 acres, and a political and social domain whose influence stretched from the Cabinet to the humblest Liverpool or Salford slums.

The upper-middle class comprised the professional and managerial groups. The former, in particular, came to represent the backbone of solid middle-class life. The increasing complexity of late Victorian and Edwardian society had seen a rapid expansion of those engaged in professional occupations. In 1911 they numbered 796,000 men and women. Incomes in this category varied enormously. A successful barrister, like Rufus Isaacs (1860–1935), might achieve an income of up to £28,000 in a good year; a High Court judge, tied to a lower but more regular salary, might expect £5,000, while any income over £1,000 was considered safely 'comfortable' in the Edwardian era. At the margin, George Orwell (1903–50) described a childhood in a 'lower-upper-middle class' home where it was difficult to maintain the illusion of ease and comfort on an income of £400–500 per year:

People in this class owned no land, but they felt that they were landowners in the sight of God and kept up a semi-aristocratic outlook by going into the professions and the fighting services rather than into trade ... To belong to this class when you were at the £400 a year level was a queer business, for it meant that your gentility was almost always purely theoretical ... Theoretically you knew how to wear your clothes and how to order a dinner, although in practice you could never afford to go to a decent tailor or a decent restaurant. Theoretically you knew how to shoot and ride, although in practice you had no horses to ride and not an inch of ground to shoot over.

The key word here was 'gentility' – an attribute of status rather than income – for which some families paid by a constant struggle to preserve appearances. There were, in fact, families worse off than the Orwells who had to struggle harder to maintain their status on an even lower income. In 1909 one writer noted that a non-resident public school master might expect an income of £200 per annum after four years' service, reaching up to a maximum of £300 after ten years. In truth, many schoolteachers barely entered the ranks of the 'comfortable'; elementary teachers, usually earning salaries of less than £100 a year, would have been more properly classed as 'lower-middle class' but for their professional training and status.

Professional status carried with it not only a higher income, but a well-defined place in the social hierarchy, a regular salary and a pension. Moreover, even at its lower ends, two factors contributed to the well-being of the Edwardian middle class. The first was the low level of direct taxation. Levied at only 1s. 2d. in the pound in 1913, it barely dented the income of most middle-class families. The second was the availability of cheap, and still relatively plentiful, domestic service. A bank manager in Hertford earning £600 a year employed between 1897 and 1911 a housemaid at £12–16 a year and a cook at £16–20 a year, both of whom lived in; a 'knife-boy' paid a shilling a day who cleaned knives and boots and shoes, chopped wood and brought in coal for six or seven fires; a gardener employed once a week for between 2s. 6d. and 4s. 6d.; and a living-in nursemaid or governess employed before the children were sent off to boarding school. A solicitor who commuted daily from Teddington to London in 1900 employed a cook at £30 a year, a house parlourmaid at £25, a 'tweeny' or housemaid at £14 a year and a boot and knife-boy at 5s. a week. Even penurious curates and schoolmasters could afford servants when a living-in maid could be employed for £10 or £12 per year, the 'going-rate' in the years prior to 1914. Indeed, while it is the large retinues of servants in aristocratic households which attract attention, the majority of domestic servants were employed in the homes of the middle class. In 1901 Seebohm Rowntree rested his distinction between 'middle' and 'working' class on the possession of servants, since help about the house promoted the woman of the house to the status of a 'lady'. Although there were signs that the supply of those wanting to go into service was declining as other employment became available for women and talk of a 'servant problem' had begun, it remained the case that life in middle-class households without servants was virtually unthinkable. As one correspondent to the *Contemporary Review* in 1910 complained: 'No-one to cook the dinner, answer the door, attend to the children and carry out the many other requirements of an ordinary household.' A young and intelligent middle-class girl such as Vera Brittain, brought up in Edwardian Buxton and thrust into the harsh world of nursing during the Great War, was to find herself quite literally ignorant of how to perform the simplest domestic tasks, tasks which had always been performed for her by the household servants.

It is difficult to recapture the ease of circumstances and rela-tive affluence of the Edwardian upper-middle classes. It was their desire to escape the squalor and dirt of the central areas which fuelled the suburban building boom of the Edwardian era. In 1901 it was estimated that a 'snug' six-roomed villa could be rented for £25–30 a year in London, while a rent of around £100 would provide a substantial house with ten or more rooms. A model budget of the same year, for an annual income of £800, estimated outgoings on all household expenditure of £239, which included rent, rates and two living-in servants, a cook at £20 a year and a parlourmaid at £18. On this type of income the 'lady' of the house merely supervised those who actually did the work. A more expensive 'cook-housekeeper', for which wages of £25–30 might have to be paid, could even take on most of these responsibilities. Food and living at this level was ample. Naomi Jacob recorded the routine in a fairly wealthy household:

They began the day with a 'hearty breakfast', which meant a full meal. Porridge, eggs and bacon or kidneys and bacon, great platesful of home-fed ham and eggs 'topped off' with buttered toast and home-made marmalade, and many huge cups of tea ... My grandfather always ate a breakfast which consisted of chops or steaks, followed by eggs and ham, and drank a tankard – his own special silver tankard – or more of ale ... They breakfasted early, half past seven or eight being regarded as a normal time. They worked hard; at mid-day they wended their way to the town's best hotel. [Then] They lunched at half past one, alone with their wives and the elder children ... A heavy meal liable to necessitate a short sleep afterwards. A modest household had soup and a joint, because the 'made up' dishes were regarded as unsuitable for the master of the house ... A sweet of some sort followed, and later cheese – Stilton, Cheshire, Wensleydale or Cheddar. At the end of the meal the mistress of the house might say tentatively, 'Would you like a cup of tea?' Her spouse, having consumed light ale throughout the meal, usually made a sound like, 'Tea! Paff! Poo!' and retired ... Tea was a woman's meal, though the husband often 'just dropped in' to the drawing-room to do no more than drink a cup of tea, eat several slices of exquisitely thin bread and butter, a few small hot cakes and a piece of home-made plum, seed, sand, cherry, or other variety of cake ... Dinner was preceded by glasses of sherry, in our household usually served in my father's study ... Dinner, which was served at some houses as early as seven but in more 'advanced' homes at eight, was a meal of some formality. There was a rather stiffly laundered cloth – 'double damask' ... and huge table-napkins calculated to slip off the most careful knees. [There was] Soup, fish and a joint which the husband carved ... There was always a 'sweet', always cheese, and fruit 'in season'.

In 1909 C. F. G. Masterman described the principal characteristics of the middle classes as 'security', 'sedentary occupations' and 'respectability'. Like other social commentators, he was aware that what distinguished them from other groups was as much a question of style of life, habits, tastes and attitudes as it was of mere income. Nowhere were hard and fast categorizations more difficult than amongst the growing number of non-manual employees: shop assistants, clerks, shopkeepers, small proprietors and self-employed artisans, who comprised what was generally called the 'lower-middle class'. Many of the people in these occupations actually earned less than skilled

workmen, but their social standing was undoubtedly higher.
Shop assistants, still predominantly male and frequently 'living
in', were notoriously poorly paid and often worked long hours
with few holidays. But, whatever its shortcomings, regular,
clean, non-manual work, with some possibility of 'prospects',
marked the shopworker out from the mass of ordinary workmen. These distinctions were even clearer in the case of the
most typical 'black-coated' workers – the clerks. As Charles
Booth remarked:

> A clerk lives an entirely different life from an artisan – marries a
> different kind of wife – has different ideas, different possibilities and
> different limitations ... It is not by any means only a question of
> clothes, of the wearing or not wearing of a white shirt every day,
> but of differences which invade every department of life, and at every
> turn affect the family budget. More undoubtedly is expected from
> the clerk than the artisan, but the clerk's money goes further and is
> on the whole much better spent.

Mr Pooter in *The Diary of a Nobody*, published in 1892,
represented the aristocracy of 'superior clerks', earning comfortably more than the average industrial wage and with social pre-
tensions to match. Commuting daily from 'The Laurels',
Brickfield Terrace, Holloway, a six-roomed house, Mr Pooter
employed a living-in servant and a charlady, prided himself
on his 'nice little back garden which runs down to the railway',
and plaster-of-paris stags' heads in the hall – coloured brown
– to give it 'style'. Mr Pooter stood as the epitome of those
clerks 'in banks, insurance offices and other public companies,
who, while living on their salaries, reside in a fairly genteel
neighbourhood, wear good clothes, mix in respectable society,
go sometimes to the opera, shrink from letting their wives do
household work, and incur, as unavoidable, the numerous
personal expenses connected with an endeavour to maintain this
system'. At the other end of the scale were the many clerks
earning little more, or sometimes less, than an artisan but who
still expected and were expected to maintain a qualitatively
different style of life from that of the working classes. A survey
in 1909 revealed that nine out of ten railway clerks, three out

of four commercial clerks and about one in two clerks in commerce and banking earned just over 30s. per week, about the same wages as coalminers. 'Pound-a-week' clerks were not uncommon in the pre-war years, especially as compulsory elementary education provided a ready supply of young men and women to do routine office work. By 1911, 46 per cent of commercial clerks were under twenty-five and this supply of relatively cheap clerical labour was widely felt to undercut the bargaining position of all but the most specialized clerks. Moreover, 'keeping up appearances' in terms of dress and housing meant that though an adult clerk often had earnings comparable to the best-paid skilled workman, his cost of living was conventionally higher. When, in 1901, G. S. Layard published a series of family budgets, he took as an example of the lower-middle class a forty-year-old cashier, married with two children, earning £150 a year. He estimated that to live in an appropriate house in one of the 'clerks' suburbs', such as Clapham, Wandsworth or Walthamstow, would cost him a fifth of his income, while his total household expenses plus travel to and from work would take another third. After this 'terribly large but necessary slice' he would probably be unable to afford a living-in servant.

Taking the poorest clerks and shop assistants as the lowest tier of those who had some claim, however precarious, to middle-class status, the middle and upper classes and their dependants represented about a quarter of the total population of Edwardian Britain. The other three-quarters were engaged in or were the dependants of those engaged in manual work. These could be broken down into divisions which reflected degrees of skill and which were frequently paralleled by differences in income and living standards. According to the census of 1911, 28.7 per cent of the population were skilled workers, 34.3 per cent semi-skilled, 9.6 per cent unskilled and 1.8 per cent self-employed artisans. Wages and conditions of life varied considerably amongst these groups, but judged in the long term certain features stand out. Between the middle of the nineteenth century and the Edwardian era, national income had almost

quadrupled. Even with an expanding population, crude calculations of income per head revealed a rise from £28 in 1873 to
£50 in 1914. In fact, not all the increase in national income
went into wages; investments, savings, rents and profits took
a share, and wages and salaries were not evenly distributed
amongst the working population. None the less, the latter half
of the nineteenth century witnessed higher real wages for most
groups of workers. Not only did money wages rise outside years
of economic difficulty, but prices tumbled by as much as 40
per cent, principally as a result of an influx of cheap food and
staple commodities from overseas. Professor Mathias has
estimated that, even allowing for periodic unemployment, the
gain in real wages of the average urban worker was 'probably
of the order of 60 per cent or more' between 1860 and 1900.
From the mid-1890s, however, prices began to move upwards
again, so that by 1912–14 real wages were below the levels
achieved in 1899–1901. One study of London has revealed a
fall of 6 per cent in real wages between 1900–1901 and 1911–12,
and other surveys have confirmed this deterioration in the
Edwardian era.

But averages of this kind reveal little of the reality of
Edwardian working-class life. There were major differences in
the wages paid to skilled and unskilled labour, to men as
opposed to women, and between different trades and regions.
Living standards were also affected by such factors as family
size, the incidence of unemployment and the provision of
welfare services. In 1906 A. L. Bowley estimated the actual
average earnings of adult males, including both overtime and
short-time working, at 27s. a week, just over £70 a year. Wages
in textiles and agriculture tended to be below this average, but
those in coalmining, engineering and printing tended to be
higher. The biggest gap, however, lay between the wages of
skilled workers and the general mass of semi-skilled and
unskilled workers. The archetypal skilled worker was one who
had served a five- or seven-year apprenticeship, and reaped the
rewards in significantly higher wages than those who did not
have a 'trade'. The evidence of wage rates bears this out: one

estimate for 1913 placed the wages of unskilled workers in five basic industries at only 58 per cent of those of the skilled. In money terms this frequently meant a wage of upwards of 40s. a week for men such as printers, boilermakers and fitters. Although some skilled workers, such as those working on the railways or in textiles, often fell below these levels, the majority were able to enjoy a standard of living which offered some margin of comfort over subsistence and which provided a less precarious hold upon 'respectability'. The skilled worker in regular employment was in a position to afford a decent, clean home, to feed and clothe his family properly, and possibly save a little through the Post Office and Trustee Savings Bank. 'Respectability' also frequently meant church or chapel-going, temperance and the desire for self-improvement. As in the nineteenth century, it was the skilled workmen who provided the backbone of the most characteristic working-class institutions, the Friendly Societies, the cooperative movement and the chapels.

Much as the semi-skilled or unskilled workman might aspire to 'respectability', it was much more difficult to maintain on the incomes their work commanded. The average wage of just over a £1 a week might provide adequately for a single man or a newly married couple, but could cause serious hardship in the cases of families of four or more. As the semi-skilled and unskilled workers were amongst the last group to respond to the fashion for smaller families (see pp. 149–50), their income per head was frequently spread too thinly to provide an adequate standard of food and clothing. Maud Pember Reeves, whose study *Round About a Pound a Week* was published in 1913, concluded that there were two million men, eight million people in all including dependants, who existed on under 25s. a week. From her study of household budgets, she concluded that 'the great bulk of this enormous mass of people are under-fed, under-housed, and insufficiently clothed. The children among them suffer more than the adults. Their growth is stunted, their mental powers are cramped, their health is undermined.' With something approaching half their income spent

on food, these working-class families were adversely affected
by the inflation of the Edwardian years. Labourers, too, were
more vulnerable to lay-offs and short-time working, so that
actual earnings in trades such as building, dock-work and
textiles were often considerably lower than rates of pay sometimes suggested. Even if earnings were above 25s. a week, a
large family, unemployment, chronic sickness or inability to
manage could plunge a family into poverty and debt. How
precarious the position of the average working-class family was
was shown by Seebohm Rowntree's study of poverty in York
in 1899. He explained that the *majority* of the working class
could expect to experience poverty at three points in their lives,
as young children, when their own children were growing up
but too young to earn, and in old age. This 'poverty cycle'
could be escaped only by the practice of severe restraint,
principally by keeping family size low and avoiding 'wasteful'
expenditure on drink or gambling. If nothing was spent on
drink and the family remained under four children, poverty
might just be avoided for the average wage-earner. For the
lower-paid, two children would have to be the limit if poverty
was to be avoided.

As well as indicating the insecurity of living standards for
many of the semi-skilled and unskilled sections of the workforce, the investigations of Rowntree, Pember Reeves and
others presented incontrovertible evidence that large sections
of the working classes were living in poverty, even when
poverty was defined as the minimum income on which physical
efficiency could be maintained. Rowntree's study of York, a
city which was neither a 'black spot' nor particularly prosperous, was based on a particularly rigorous definition of
poverty. Describing his 'poverty line' as a 'standard of bare
subsistence rather than *living*', he depicted what it entailed:

A family living upon the scale allowed for in this estimate must
never spend a penny on railway fare or omnibus. They must never
go into the country unless they walk. They must never purchase a
halfpenny newspaper or spend a penny to buy a ticket for a popular
concert. They must write no letters to absent children, for they cannot

afford to pay the postage. They must never contribute anything to their church or chapel, or give any help to a neighbour which costs them money. They cannot save, nor can they join sick clubs or trade unions, because they cannot pay the necessary subscriptions. The children must have no pocket money for dolls, marbles or sweets. The father must smoke no tobacco, and must drink no beer. The mother must never buy any pretty clothes for herself or for her children, the character of the family wardrobe, as for the family diet, being governed by the regulation, 'Nothing must be bought but that which is absolutely necessary for the maintenance of physical health, and what is bought must be of the plainest and most economical description.' Should a child fall ill, it must be attended by the parish doctor; should it die, it must be buried by the parish. Finally, the wage-earner must never be absent from his work for a single day ... If any of these conditions are broken, the extra expenditure involved is met, and can only be met, by limiting the diet; or, in other words, by sacrificing physical efficiency.

Even with this austere minimum level of income, Rowntree still found that 10 per cent of the population fell below and lived in what he called 'primary poverty', where they earned insufficient to feed themselves adequately to maintain health. Another 18 per cent earned higher incomes but lived in poverty because they did not spend their incomes on the necessities of life. Rowntree's findings echoed those of Charles Booth in his monumental survey of social conditions in late-Victorian London. These had revealed an 'Arithmetic of Woe' in which 30.7 per cent of the population were living in actual poverty. Nor, as Rowntree had shown, was the problem confined to the large cities. A survey carried out in five towns, Reading, Northampton, Warrington, Bolton and Stanley (Co. Durham), on the eve of the Great War, revealed that approximately a quarter of the total population were living in poverty. The causes of poverty were also being identified. Old age, the loss of the principal wage-earner through illness or death, un-employment, low wages and irregular earnings, and large families made up the chief culprits. In addition, as Rowntree had demonstrated, many families who might have avoided poverty did not live according to the strict regime demanded of them. It is only possible to understand the emphasis placed by some social commentators upon the evils of drink, and, to a lesser extent, gambling, from their awareness that any expenditure by the poor upon such 'luxuries' almost literally took food from their own and their children's mouths. Realistic social investigators, however, recognized that it was both fruitless and unjust to expect the poor and low-paid to live lives of monastic virtue, especially when so many of the causes of poverty lay completely beyond the control of the people concerned.

Life for the 30 per cent of the population which lived near or below the poverty line was a constant struggle to make ends meet. A survey of 2,000 working-class households in 1904 showed that those earning under 25s. a week spent 67 per cent of their income on food, with bread, potatoes, tea and tinned milk, and the cheapest cuts of meat forming the bulk of the diet. Irregularity of earnings, particularly in casual trades such as dock-work, wrought havoc with any attempts at sensible budgeting. Food and fuel had to be bought in penny-packets rather than in bulk because there was never enough money to spend at any one time and storage of food was virtually impossible. Debt was a constant threat and many families eked out an existence only by regular recourse to the pawnshops which flourished in most working-class areas. In spite of the nineteenth-century efforts to provide basic civil amenities of sanitation and water supply, the poorest third of the population inevitably found themselves occupying the worst and cheapest housing. Over half the population of Scotland and one sixth of that of London lived in overcrowded conditions of more than two people per room. Insanitary, damp and verminous housing was commonplace. In the poorer tenements or courts of Glasgow, Liverpool and London, communal stand-taps and earth-privies were the norm. Birmingham had 40,000 houses without any drainage or water tap and 60,000 without a lavatory.

The contention of the social investigators that many of the country's population were living at levels which impaired their health and efficiency was borne out by the experience of the army recruiting sergeants in the Boer War. Forced by the

decline of the agricultural workforce to rely increasingly upon
the urban areas for recruits, the army authorities came face-to-
face with the consequences of poverty: 40 per cent of those
who took the 'King's Shilling' between 1897 and 1902 were
rejected as physically or medically unfit; this figure was as high
as 60 per cent in places such as Leeds and Sheffield. So startling
were these results that an inter-departmental committee was
set up to study 'Physical Deterioration'. Reporting in 1904 they
blamed the poor quality of recruits on poverty, bad housing,
insanitary employment conditions, excessive consumption of
alcohol and poor diet. Little had altered by 1910, however,
when 52.2 per cent of recruits were rejected, and the introduction of conscription in the middle of the First World War once
again revealed the ravages wrought by the legacy of Edwardian
social conditions. Mortality figures told a similar story. The
lowest occupational groups in 1910–12 had a much higher
mortality rate than the middle and upper classes. Deaths from
diseases closely related to poverty such as respiratory TB and
bronchitis were much greater amongst the poorest social classes
than amongst any others.

Moreover, since large families were a primary cause of
poverty, the proportion of children in poverty was even higher
than that of adults. Infant mortality, an almost infallible
barometer of health and well-being, stubbornly refused to fall
as rapidly as mortality had fallen amongst adults. In 1900 it
stood at 152 per 1,000 live births in England and Wales, as high
as it had been in the 'hungry forties'. Although some improvement took place during the Edwardian era, its incidence
remained heavily weighted amongst the poorer sections of the
population; so too did the deficiency diseases which resulted
from inadequate diet and poor housing conditions, such as
rickets, anaemia, dental decay and TB.

An Edwardian Crisis?

There were many who saw in the last years of Edwardian
Britain the end of an era. In his influential book, *The Strange*

Death of Liberal England, published in 1936, George Dangerfield
argued that the assumptions which had governed British society
and politics were increasingly being undermined by the
challenge to *laissez faire*, the rise of labour and the ready resort
to militant tactics by groups such as the suffragettes and Ulster
unionists. For Dangerfield, the years between 1910 and 1913
saw Liberal England 'reduced to ashes'. This view, however,
substantially overstates the case, even for the troubled years
prior to the Great War. The new organized strength of labour
as often led to negotiation as to mounting confrontation, while
the suffragettes too sought accommodation with the government rather than to remake the political world. Improvements
in living standards and the beginnings of social reform, while
increasing the tempo of bargaining, also brought gains which
consolidated the social fabric and gave groups such as trade-
unionists and the infant Labour Party a stake in the existing
political order. Reformism and gradualism were still more
pervasive influences than revolutionary violence.

Nor did these years witness any wholesale loss of confidence
in classical liberalism, but rather its modification to accommodate new concerns. Although under attack, the central
economic doctrine of *laissez faire*, free trade, was not abandoned
until 1932. In social policy 'new liberals' combined an acceptance of the need for increased state intervention with a continuing belief in the traditional virtues of self-help and voluntary
action. Throughout the inter-war period, much of the spirit
which informed the activities of both national and local
government remained based on values which were still recognizable as those of the late-Victorian period. Continuity was
a stronger element than discontinuity.

Finally, an emphasis on 'crisis' and on the divisions of
Edwardian society, manifest enough through any analysis of
social conditions and the pre-war political upheavals, tends to
obscure the cohesive and solidaristic aspects of British society,
represented by the dense network of clubs, churches, Scouts
Boys' Brigades, football clubs and voluntary organizations, not
to mention the still powerful social integration of firms, locali-

ties and individual communities. Superimposed upon these elements were the powerful and pervasive influences of popular patriotism and national consciousness, reinforced by the spread of popular literacy, national education and a generation or more of imperial expansion. Just how powerful these influences could be, and their ability, at least in the short term, to supersede any other divisions, were to be revealed to their fullest extent only in the summer and autumn of 1914.

2. War, Patriotism and the State

With the outbreak of the Great War in August 1914, British society entered a period when it was to be shaped for the first time by the demands of total war. As a conflict fought between major industrial powers able to call upon all the political, economic, social and cultural resources of modern nation states, the Great War had a much more profound influence upon society than the more limited conflicts of previous centuries. The duration, scale and cost of the war demanded a mobilization of national resources on a hitherto unprecedented scale, producing important developments in the social sphere, just as it did in the fields of economics and politics. With hindsight the chief difficulty is to disentangle the effects of the war from the long-term evolutions of British society. How far were changes in British society derived solely from the Great War and how many might have occurred without it? In many respects, this is an impossible question to answer definitively: for four years the war, like the great artillery bombardments on the Western Front, obliterated the landscape, destroyed familiar landmarks and created an unfamiliar environment in which the legacy of Edwardian Britain was obscured and distorted. While in comparison with some other combatants Britain was to emerge in many respects surprisingly little changed by the war, no society could emerge from such a conflict unaltered.

The Patriotic Call

The most obvious and direct impact of the war was felt in the recruitment of nearly five million men into the armed forces during the four years of the war, representing 22 per cent of the total male population. In January 1914 the British army had a paper strength of 711,000 men; four years later there were almost 4,400,000, almost half of them manning the trench line along the Western Front. Apart from the scale of the effort – one which by the end of the war was to tax the country almost to the limit of its manpower resources – the most remarkable feature of the British armies raised during the First World War is that they were primarily composed of volunteers. Almost unique amongst the combatants, Britain primarily relied upon the willingness of its citizens to come forward without direct compulsion to join the armed forces. Although conscription was introduced in 1916, the number of men conscripted accounted for only just over a third of the total manpower mobilized. In retrospect, one of the most striking features of the Great War was the readiness, indeed the enthusiasm, with which hundreds of thousands of British males, drawn from every walk of life and every geographical area, volunteered to fight for 'King and Country'.

Recruiting began almost without delay. On 5 August the House of Commons authorized an increase of the Regular Army by half a million men, and two days later Lord Kitchener, now Minister for War, appealed for the first hundred thousand volunteers to form the basis of a new army. He was met by a huge popular response which choked the recruiting stations and swamped the training system. The Central London Recruiting Office at Scotland Yard was reported to be 'a seething mass of men waiting to be enrolled', while the central streets of Birmingham were blocked by thousands of men waiting to sign up for the duration of the war. There were stories of men in remote areas walking all night to the nearest recruiting station and of cavalcades of workmen from rural farms and isolated mines and factories turning up *en masse* to enlist. No less than three-quarters of a million men flocked to the colours in August and September 1914. By the end of the year the number had risen to over a million. In effect, the recruiting of the first months of the war represented one of the most impressive mass movements ever witnessed in British history. Probably no other cause, religious, social or political, had mobilized so many different people in a common aim.

What was the explanation for this great patriotic upsurge, the evident enthusiasm of which still speaks to us in the photographs taken in the summer and autumn of 1914? In part it was a general European phenomenon: cheering crowds and patriotic enthusiasm could be found in the streets of Paris, Berlin, St Petersburg and Vienna as much as in London or Manchester. Indeed the general popularity of the war in its first months has led some historians to conclude that in a profound sense many people in Europe wanted war in 1914: a readiness to embark upon patriotic adventure which can only be explained in terms of the social and cultural development of European society in the years prior to the war. Mass, urban society seemed to generate its own powerful aspirations for commitment and activity, often as an escape from the drab routines of office and factory; nationalism and patriotism had become almost the new religion of modern industrial society, as mass education carried the heady brew of patriotic idealism into the meanest slum classroom or the remotest village school. Modern mass communications, railways, delivery vans, the telegraph, wireless and the newspapers also fostered a greater sense of nationhood. People of widely different backgrounds and outlook were being increasingly moulded by common, collective concerns of which the sense of national identity was one of the most powerful. Popular newspapers now carried news of colonial wars, imperial adventures and international crises often in language which did little to lessen the sense of popular chauvinism. Before 1914 the 'Fashoda incident', Mafeking and the Anglo-German 'naval race' had shown clearly the power of the new cheap press both to channel and stimulate public enthusiasm.

The readiness of young men to respond to the appeal of patriotism and of the majority of the rest of society to acquiesce in their response was of peculiar importance for a country which alone amongst the combatants had no conscript army. In fact, as the great imperial power, patriotism and national pride were almost part of the Edwardian psyche. A whole generation had been brought up on the boys' books of G. A. Henty, the *Boys' Own Paper*, the tales of Rider Haggard and best-selling accounts of the Boer War which promoted an image of war as both honourable and glorious. 'It was generally felt,' wrote Duff Cooper, 'that war was a glorious affair and the British always won.' Enthusiastic participation was also explicable in the context of the innocence of a generation which knew little if anything of the realities of modern war. As A. J. P. Taylor points out, 'there had been no war between the Great Powers since 1871. No man in the prime of life knew what war was like. All imagined that it would be an affair of great marches and great battles, quickly decided.' Indeed, most military experts saw the war as being speedily resolved by a once-and-for-all clash of armies on the Franco-German frontier and a decisive encounter in the North Sea, 'Trafalgar Re-Fought' (the title of a pre-war novel), between the navies of Britain and Germany. Those who thought differently were not generally believed. Kitchener, summoned before the Cabinet just after the outbreak of the war, told the assembled company that he calculated on a war lasting three years, which would require a million men. He was received in silence, the Foreign Secretary, Sir Edward Grey, commenting afterwards that he thought the prediction 'unlikely, if not incredible'.

With little knowledge of the possible length and nature of modern war the way was open for the channelling of the patriotic and public-spirited sentiments of Edwardian Britain into military service in a way which would have been difficult to envisage even a generation earlier. Traditionally the army was viewed with contempt by many respectable middle- and working-class families: 'I would rather bury you than see you in a red coat,' the mother of William Robertson, a Field Marshal in the Great War, wrote to him on receiving news of his enlistment in the army. In 1914, however, volunteering in the army called upon all the ideas and emotions summed up in the phrase 'King and Country'. There was a feverish rush to join the army before the war was over. Harold Macmillan wrote: 'The general view was that it would be over by Christmas. Our major anxiety was by hook or by crook not to miss it.'

Most telling of all was the way in which the call for recruits tapped the powerful group loyalties of Edwardian society, seen most dramatically in the 'Pals' battalions formed in the autumn of 1914 – men who enlisted with their 'pals' from the same occupations, factories, offices and clubs. No historian has noted their significance more acutely than John Keegan:

> It is the story of a spontaneous and genuinely popular mass move- ment which has no counterpart in the modern, English-speaking world and perhaps could have none outside its own time and place: a time of intense, almost mystical patriotism, and of the inarticulate elitism of an imperial power's working class; a place of vigorous and buoyant urban life, rich in differences and in a sense of belonging – to work- places, to factories, to unions, to churches, chapels, charitable organiza- tions, benefit clubs, Boy Scouts, Boys' Brigades, Sunday Schools, cricket, football, rugby, skittle clubs, old boys' societies, city offices, municipal departments, craft guilds – to any one of those hundreds of bodies from which the Edwardian Briton drew his security and sense of identity. This network of associations offered an emotional leverage on British male responses which the committees of 'raisers', middle-aged and self-appointed in the first flush of enthusiasm for the war, were quick to manipulate, without perhaps realizing its power.

In this highly perceptive passage, Keegan goes far to explain the reasons why so many rushed to the recruiting stations in the first months of the war. It was entirely characteristic that it was an aristocrat with a close acquaintance with the com- mercial and industrial towns of the North-West, Lord Derby, the 'King of Lancashire', who instigated the 'Pals' movement when, on 28 August at a crowded meeting in St George's Hall, Liverpool, he invited the clerks of the city to form their own battalion with the guarantee that those who 'joined together should serve together'. Within three days enough volunteers were found for three battalions: the clerks of the White Star shipping company formed their own platoon, those of Cunard another, with the Cotton Exchange, banks, insurance offices and commercial warehouses providing their own contingents. Once Lord Kitchener sanctioned the formation of 'Pals' battalions, the way was open for municipal authorities and individuals to participate in the movement. The response was enthusiastic. In Manchester a crowd stormed the Town Hall to demand a quicker processing of recruits. The city was to raise fifteen battalions in all, 20,000 men volunteering in the first month of the war. Hull raised four battalions which served together in the city's own brigade. Glasgow raised three: a recruiting station set up in the City Tramways depot found a complete battalion in sixteen hours, another was raised from members of the Boys' Brigade, while the Chamber of Commerce formed a 'Commercial' battalion. The Grimsby 'Chums' were raised from the town and the neighbouring parts of Lincolnshire on the initiative of the headmaster of a local school. Accrington, a small cotton town in northern Lancashire, was the smallest community to raise a complete battalion, a feat which took only ten days after the mayor, a retired army officer, set up a recruiting office in the town. Companies and smaller units were provided by towns, villages, works, clubs, offices and schools. Over three hundred battalions, about a quarter of a million men, were raised in this way; the battalion sub-titles, such as 'North-East Railway', '1st Public Works', '1st Football', and 'Church Lads', told their own story of the channels of loyalty along which the patriotic tide flowed in the first months of the war.

The departure of newly formed battalions caused massive demonstrations of popular patriotism and intense local pride. When the Sheffield City Battalion left the city for training at Cannock Chase on the morning of 13 May 1915, hundreds of people packed the early morning trams to see the troops off and to hear the Lord Mayor address the battalion *en route* for the railway station. By 7.15 a.m. the crowd in the city centre numbered several hundreds; by 7.30 a.m. thousands were jammed into the streets around the Town Hall, where a specially erected platform carried the leading civic dignitaries, including the Lord Mayor, Lady Mayoress, the Vice-Chancellor of the University, town councillors, the Mistress Cutler and the Dean of the Cathedral, 'a striking figure in his Khaki uniform as an army chaplain'. Under the headline 'Our Soldier Sons' the *Sheffield Daily Telegraph* described the scene:

> The men presented an inspiring spectacle as they swung down the roads, all in the best of physical condition and marching with a fine spring. As they passed down Glossop Road, they were met by a lady who went along the ranks distributing packets of cigarettes to the men. At the Engineers' Drill Hall, the soldiers there turned out in their honour, and a little further down they found a fire display arranged. The members of the Brigade had brought their engines and escapes and mounted them, and as the Battalion passed they sounded all the hooters of their motors in cheery salutation. Here and there could be seen some moving touches. One incident was that of a grey-haired mother marching along by the side of her son, and there were several cases in which sweethearts accompanied the procession striving hard and not always with complete success to preserve their cheerfulness.

Such scenes were being re-enacted in scores of towns and cities throughout Britain during the first year of the war. For a few months at least, the war tapped some of the most powerful currents of emotion and sentiment in society, touching high and low alike. As supplies of regular officers dried up, fresh subalterns were drawn from the Officer Training Corps set up at the universities and public schools in 1907 for just such a purpose. These provided 29,500 commissions in the first seven months of the war. Soon, however, even O T C certificates were waived and a public school or university background was sufficient to obtain a commission. In fact, both sets of institutions responded enthusiastically to the patriotic appeal. Marlborough, Eton and Charterhouse between them sent more than twelve hundred sixth-formers straight to France as Second Lieutenants. 'We have hardly any boys left who are of an age to serve,' a headmaster told *The Times Educational Supplement* at the beginning of the autumn term. In Oxford more than 2,000 applicants for commissions were interviewed in August and September by a Committee of Military Delegates sitting in an upstairs room just off the High Street. By the end of the year both Oxford and Cambridge had been emptied of undergraduates. Whatever charges had been levelled at the 'idle rich' in the years prior to 1914, there was no doubt, as Orwell noted some years later, that the traditional ruling class proved 'ready enough to get themselves killed'. Harold Macmillan used his family's influence to become gazetted to the Reserve Battalion of the Grenadier Guards, writing: 'It was privilege of the worst kind . . . But, after all, was it so very reprehensible? The only privilege I, and many others like me, sought was that of getting ourselves killed or wounded as soon as possible.' It was a fair enough statement: by the end of 1914 the dead included six peers, sixteen baronets, six knights, ninety-five sons of peers, eight-two sons of baronets and eight-four knights' sons.

Most strikingly of all, the first wave of patriotism pushed to one side – if only for a time – the divisive issues which had preoccupied the country in the weeks before the declaration of war. Ireland had appeared to be on the brink of civil war in the summer of 1914. The Northern protestants had organized and armed 80,000 men of the Ulster Volunteer Force, leaving it in no doubt that they would fight to resist the implementation of Home Rule. In the South, the Irish Volunteers had also been formed in readiness to resist any attempt to impose partition as part of the Home Rule Bill. As the Home Rule Bill moved towards its final stages, attempts at compromise had broken down and a conflict appeared inevitable. The outbreak of the war postponed current rivalries. In spite of fears from Ulstermen that the absorption of the U V F into the British army might leave the province open to the enforcement of Home Rule, when Kitchener asked their leader, Sir Edward Carson, for four battalions of the U V F for the New Army, Carson responded by offering him twelve, uniformed and equipped at Ulster's expense. Meanwhile, John Redmond, leader of the Irish Home Rulers, pledged Ireland's full support for the war and recruits from Catholic Ireland came forward in their thousands. By only one of the many ironies of the war,

Northern and Southern Irish who had been at each other's throats in the dying weeks of peace were to line up in the same order-of-battle on the first day of the Somme in 1916.

If the prospect of civil war in Ireland had been one major preoccupation in the months prior to the war, scarcely less so was the continuing wave of industrial unrest. Rates of strike action remained high in 1913–14, after a loss of over forty million working days in 1912. There were actually more stoppages in 1913 than in 1912, and the first seven months of 1914 witnessed levels of activity which promised another high total. With over four million members, almost a quarter of the workforce, the trade unions were clearly a power in the land. The spread of socialist and syndicalist ideas, not to mention strong internationalist and pacifist inclinations amongst some sections, were widely recognized as raising major issues in British society. Negotiations for the formation of the 'Triple Alliance' of railwaymen, transport workers and miners in the spring and summer of 1914 seemed to presage a new era of industrial conflict in which talk of a 'general strike' was becoming increasingly common. A five-month lock-out in the London building trades in 1914 and a series of stoppages in the engineering trades suggested that militancy was not only not spent, but was still spreading. When the Princess Royal came to lay the foundation stone at Marylebone Town Hall early in July 1914 she was interrupted by building workers singing the 'Red Flag' and the 'Marseillaise', followed by 'three cheers for social revolution, three boos for blacklegs and three boos for royalty'. It was hardly surprising then that there should have been concern in many quarters about the effects of pre-war militancy upon working-class support for the war. However a *Times* correspondent sent to assess the mood of the industrial areas at the end of August 1914 was able to report that the working classes were supporting the war 'to a man' and concluded:

The truth of the matter is that the working class through and through is as intensely national as any other class. There is no greater miscalculation of the agitator than that which credits miners and factory workers with a sort of first principle objection to war in any form. In a crisis the economic plea is swept aside by the appeal of patriotism. One would have said that if the doctrine of 'the international brotherhood of the workers' was to make headway anywhere it would be in South Wales. It is abundantly clear to-day that even the miners who hold the doctrine will not allow it to run counter to the ideal of national unity. The miners, in fact, have silently joined with the organized workers in all other parts of Britain in presenting a united front to the common enemy.

Indeed, the war utterly disrupted the more militant sections of the labour movement. Plans laid by the Second International for an international general strike in the event of a European war were swept aside by the tidal wave of patriotism. Although there were notable exceptions, such as Ramsay MacDonald and Keir Hardie, the majority of labour leaders threw their weight behind the war. On 24 August the liaison committee of the Labour Party, the General Federation of Trade Unions and the Trade Union Parliamentary Committee passed a resolution urging that 'an immediate effort be made to terminate all existing trade disputes'. This 'strike truce' proved very effective in the short term, only 161,437 days being lost in strikes, concerning a mere 21,128 workers, from October to December 1914, compared with almost five million in the first six months of the year.

Moreover, for a time, earlier conflicts within British society were subsumed by a passionate xenophobia which expressed itself not only in extensive volunteering for the armed forces but also in attacks on aliens. The first months of the war were rife with rumours of spies and saboteurs in which the sizable German and alien population in Britain came under intense suspicion and even physical attack. By early September 1914 *The Times* was carrying side by side with stories of German atrocities in Belgium ones about 'The Alien Enemy' and 'The Spy Peril'. With news of the first major casualties during the autumn and winter of 1914–15, anti-alien feeling reached new heights. With the first German use of poison gas in late April 1915, stories of prisoners being ill-treated, and the growth of submarine sinkings, popular hostility to German aliens was already running at a high level when news broke just in time for the late evening editions on Friday, 7 May, of the sinking of the *Lusitania* off the south coast of Ireland with large loss of life. By Saturday the national and provincial papers were ablaze with the story, tales of survivors, of German 'outrage', and the plight of relatives awaiting the ship's arrival in Liverpool. By the following evening there were attacks on alien premises in Liverpool, pork butchers' shops being attacked and their goods scattered or looted. Further attacks in Liverpool were followed by a spreading wave of disturbances in London, especially in the East End, and also in Manchester, Yorkshire and Scotland. The shops of Germans or people with German-sounding names were the most frequent targets, but there were also demonstrations against German workers, traders and professional men still working openly in Britain. In Manchester and Salford, crowds of up to six thousand, often composed of women, ransacked shops and demonstrated outside factories. Strikes were called in some places against the presence of German employees, while German traders were banned from the Liverpool Exchange. At London's Smithfield Market, German butchers were mobbed, one being ducked in a horse trough, his cart smashed and his horse auctioned to the crowd. The circle of targets widened to include Jews, Russians, Swiss and Chinese in riots which became as much anti-foreigner as anti-German. In London, hairdressing establishments, jewellery shops and restaurants all came under attack in violence which caused an estimated £100,000 worth of damage. The disturbances subsided with a trickle of arrests and, usually, small fines, assisted by the promise from the Prime Minister of internment for enemy aliens and the pre-emptive arrest of some of them by local Chief Constables. The '*Lusitania* riots' marked the biggest manifestation of anti-alien feeling during the war. Although worked up to a new pitch of intensity by the war, attacks on foreigners were not unknown before 1914. The extension of the rioting to attacks on the shops of Jews and other non-German shopkeepers or workers illustrated a latent xenophobia which was to surface periodically after 1915. During the war itself, German Zeppelin raids on Hull in June 1915 sparked off further attacks on German shops. Pacifist and anti-war meetings were frequently broken up with violence, while Bertrand Russell recorded how in 1917 a meeting at a Hoxton church in support of the Russian Revolution was invaded by a crowd who had been told that the meeting was of people in communication with the Germans and who would signal where their aeroplanes should drop bombs. Like air raids, conscription added a further ingredient to wartime feeling. In 1917 there were attacks on Jews in Leeds who had not been conscripted because they opposed the war. Post-war dislocation and the activities of anti-Jewish groups on the right of British politics were to bring a renewal of such attacks even after the war had ended.

The State Intervenes

In many respects the role of the state in Britain prior to 1914 was remarkably unobtrusive. Where it came into contact with ordinary people, its guise was largely local and unbureaucratic, typified more by the local 'Board School' and the corner post office than by the agencies of central government. Essentially Victorian traditions of individual responsibility, voluntary effort and local government continued to shape the character of Edwardian Britain, whose ethos, in spite of significant extensions of state action, remained ostensibly designed to leave its inhabitants free to carry on their lives without outside interference. The Great War, however, was to witness an enormous extension of the involvement of the state in the lives of ordinary citizens. The demands of total war in terms of the mobilization of resources and their efficient utilization led inexorably towards greater regulation and control by central government. From being one of the least centralized and regulated societies in Europe, Edwardian Britain was forced into the acceptance of a hitherto unprecedented degree of government control.

It would be simplistic, however, to ascribe the extension of state regulation solely to the exigencies of war. Although there were to be many who opposed the progressive encroachments of the state during the four-year conflict, ranging from the radical opponents of conscription in the No Conscription Fellowship to the trade-union syndicalists who remained suspicious of growing state interference in the running of industry, what was more striking was the extent to which the state was readily accepted as the most appropriate agency to solve the national crisis of war production and mass mobilization. Rodney Barker has spoken of 'increasingly pervasive opinion, accelerating over the previous thirty-five years' which had already ascribed a dominant role to central government for dealing with a wide range of problems. The role of the state both as a vehicle of social justice and a promoter of the national good had become a major feature of intellectual and political debate long before the outbreak of war. The coming of war was to provide a context in which the collectivist arguments were to become more firmly established. Having already won the argument for a greater involvement by the state in many areas of hitherto individual responsibility, it was increasingly difficult to deny yet further inroads by the state to meet the national crisis of the war. State intervention was to become not merely an argument in the hands of progressive thinkers, but part of the habit and assumptions of government.

The demands of war fell into two main interrelated categories: first, the mobilization of manpower for the armed forces, without starving agriculture and industry of those necessary to produce the goods and services essential to the continuance of the war and the maintenance of the domestic population; second, the organization of production to maximize the output of armaments, while maintaining the supplies of food, raw materials and consumer goods essential to the civilian population. In order to meet those needs, the state was forced to extend its control over ever-widening spheres of activity. To make good the huge losses of men on the Western Front, conscription had to be introduced for the first time in British history.

As the conflict wore on, the scarcity of resources forced the state to become involved in the management and control of industry, labour and conditions of work, as well as the provision of essential supplies.

Almost from its outset, the war saw the government making decisive inroads into normal activities. Some were entirely predictable, such as the restrictions imposed on the movement of aliens and the suspension of dealings on the Stock Exchange to prevent financial panic. Fears of a shortage of gold currency also led to the introduction of paper notes for £1 and 10s. But more telling indications of future developments lay in the government's first assumptions of responsibility in the economic sphere, notably the insurance of war risks on shipping; a largely formal take-over of the railways by the Board of Trade; and government intervention in the purchase, sale and distribution of sugar, now that Britain was cut off from her traditional supplies in Central Europe. Fears of disruption of trade also led to the first assumption of social responsibility. A Cabinet Committee on the Prevention and Relief of Distress was formed on 4 August and two days later a National Relief Fund was inaugurated, administered by an Executive Committee containing three members of the Cabinet. These emergency measures were completed on 8 August with the Defence of the Realm Act, giving the government wide powers to issue regulations 'for securing the public safety and the defence of the realm'. 'DORA' was initially designed to prevent the obtaining or relaying of information calculated to jeopardize the success of the armed forces or assist the enemy, and to protect vital centres of communications, such as railways, docks or harbours. Offenders were to be subject to military law and tried by court martial. Further additions to DORA were made later in August 1914, and further consolidation and modifications continued throughout the war. Until the House of Lords amended the Act in March 1915 it was theoretically possible for a civilian to be sentenced to death by a court martial for 'assisting the enemy' without recourse to a jury. In the later stages of the war, DORA provided the enabling legislation for a stream of regulations governing food control, air-raid precautions, early closing and a host of other measures. One of its most important results was to facilitate press censorship. Under its provisions, the War Office censored cables and foreign correspondence, and held the threat of prosecution over the publication of unauthorized news or speculation about future strategy. A system of censorship was created in which controversial items were supposed to be submitted to an Official Press Bureau, circumvention of which could lead to prosecution under DORA.

But the full implications of these measures lay in the future. The dominant mood in the first months of the war was summed up in the phrase 'Business as Usual', a slogan taken up by a number of big London stores during August 1914 to drum up sales. The first war budget, introduced by Lloyd George in November 1914, did little to disturb this frame of mind. The bulk of the population, those earning less than £160 a year, remained totally exempt from direct taxation. A doubling of income tax from 9d. in the pound to 1s. 6d. for those earning between £160 and £500, and extra duties on tea and beer, completed what was only a very limited introduction to the austerities of the later years of the war. In spite of a worrying rise in the price of some staple foodstuffs, the war had scarcely yet affected the lives of the great majority of the population. Theatres remained open, professional sport was still being played and, though the absence of those who had volunteered was missed, already the gaps were being filled by other workers, including some women. Government intervened in an *ad hoc* way to deal with particular problems, for example, in October 1914 raising the allowances for the dependants of men on active service. Even here, however, the initiative was taken by voluntary bodies, such as the Soldiers' and Sailors' Families Association, and it was not until November 1915 when a Naval and Military War Pensions Act was passed that a regular system of allowances and pensions was introduced.

During the course of 1915, however, the two related problems of manpower and war production were almost inexorably to force the government into a more active role. Within two days of the outbreak of the war an increase in the armed forces of half a million men had been authorized, followed on 15 September by another half a million. A million more were voted in November, followed by a third then a fourth million by the end of the year. Initially, all the government had to do to raise men was to channel the patriotic impulse and to cope with what was to prove an almost overwhelming flood of recruits. By Christmas 1914 over a million men had volunteered and the army in France numbered almost 250,000. By early 1915, some slackening of recruiting was noted, made more worrying by the already unprecedented losses suffered in stemming the German advance into France and stabilizing the trench line of the Western Front. In 1906, the Army Council had projected a 'wastage' rate for the BEF in the first six months of a future war at about 40 per cent. In the event, by 30 November, after only three months' fighting, casualties totalled 89,864, compared with a paper strength of the seven divisions which had landed in France of just over 84,000 Effectively, apart from regulars involved in training new recruits or convalescing from wounds, the pre-war regular army had been virtually wiped out. As the *Official History* grimly recorded: 'In the British battalions which fought at the Marne and Ypres, there scarcely remained in the colours an average of one officer and thirty men who had landed in August 1914.'

By the middle of 1915, casualties had risen to over 380,000, including 75,000 dead. Casualties on this scale soon began to threaten the build-up of the armed forces, particularly in view of the evidence that recruiting had slackened off. One of the first reactions was the progressive reduction of the physical requirements of recruits. At the outset, a volunteer had to stand five feet eight inches to get into the army, but by 11 October this had been reduced to five feet five, and was reduced again in November to five feet three inches. A Parliamentary Recruiting Committee commissioned over a hundred posters in order to encourage men to enlist, including Arthur Leete's famous

'Kitchener Wants You', with the finger pointing unwaveringly at the onlooker. All the techniques of mass advertising, developed in the pre-war generation to sell consumer goods, were now deployed in the drive for recruits. Almost no stone was left unturned in the search for something which would move men to enlist: German atrocities in Belgium, the fate of Serbia, the appeal of fellowship with those already fighting in France, and the threat of lasting shame to those who ignored the call were deployed in posters, postcards and recruiting rallies. In January 1915 posters appeared aimed directly at women: 'Women of England! Do your duty! Send your Man *Today* to Join our Glorious Army!' Married men were goaded with the reproaches of their children: 'Daddy, what did you do in the Great War?' By the autumn of 1915 fifty-four million posters had been issued and 12,000 meetings organized. Music-hall stars such as Harry Lauder undertook tours of the regions in order to drum up volunteers, while recruiting drives were organized in major cities. At one in London in 1915 small children paraded with banners such as 'My Dad's at the Front, where is yours?'.

Although the news of Neuve Chapelle and Gallipoli in the spring produced some increase in the numbers coming forward, the summer saw a marked waning of the 'willing spirit', with recruits falling to a mere 71,000 in September 1915, and widespread concern that thousands were dodging military service. At the outbreak of the war Britain had approximately five and a half million men of military age available for service, another half a million becoming available each year. By September 1915 two and a quarter million had volunteered; of the rest, a large percentage, just over 40 per cent of those examined, had proved incapable of military service and had been given the lowest health classification of C3. Another million and a half were in reserved occupations, mining, transport and agriculture. None the less, a National Registration Act in 1915 which required a return for every civilian male between fifteen and sixty-five revealed that almost two million men were still available and had not yet volunteered. Still reluctant to grasp the nettle of conscription, the Coalition Government appointed Lord Derby Director-General of Recruiting. His 'Derby Scheme' was a last attempt to find recruits short of introducing conscription. Using the National Register it required that men between eighteen and forty-one should be asked to 'attest' in age groups for military service, if and when called upon. Single men were to go first and a pledge was given that no married men would be called on until there were no more unmarried men available. There was to be no compulsion for men to 'attest', though considerable moral pressure was exerted by door-to-door canvassing and giving men who had attested an armlet to wear in order to protect them from allegations of 'shirking'. On 19 November a nation-wide system of tribunals was set up to grant exemptions for important war-workers or those with exceptional personal circumstances.

The scheme satisfied both those who disliked the idea of conscription, principally Liberals, backed by newspapers such as the *Daily News* and the *Manchester Guardian*, and pro-conscription groups who realized that if the scheme failed the case for conscription would be unanswerable. By early 1916 it was clear that the Derby Scheme had not come up to expectations: out of 2,179,231 single men of military age only 1,150,000 had attested and of 2,832,210 married men some 1,152,947. Plainly the married men could not be held to their attestations while so many single men held back. Moreover, the situation was increasingly urgent. The losses in the battles of 1915 had to be replaced, new reserves created for the fresh offensives planned for 1916, and more of the burden taken over from the French on the Western Front. However serious Britain's losses had been in the first eighteen months of the war, France was reeling from the terrible slaughter of 1914–15, which had produced over two and a quarter million casualties. It was impossible for the French to continue to hold five-sixths of the Western Front with casualties amounting to 150,000 a month, but Britain was being asked to take over more of the line, just as the flow of willing volunteers seemed to be ebbing away.

A Military Service Bill was introduced in January 1916 which embodied the principle of conscription for single men. Opposition was still voiced: Sir John Simon, the Home Secretary, called it the beginning of an 'immense change in the structure of our society' and resigned office, while fifty Liberal MPs voted against the Bill. The TUC also opposed the bill, but none of the Labour members of the Cabinet resigned. At the beginning of May a new universal conscription Bill became law, with facilities for conscientious objectors to be heard before local tribunals. Over 10,000 obtained exemption in this way, 7,000 taking up non-combatant duties, usually as ambulance men, and another 3,000 going into labour camps run by the Home Office. Many others failed to convince the tribunals and were shipped off to France either to obey orders or to face the full rigour of military law. Most contentious of all was the treatment of over a thousand men who refused to accept any kind of compulsory service. Drafted into the army against their will, they faced the imminent threat of court martial as soon as they refused to obey an order. Forty-one sent to France lived under the shadow of a death sentence for a month until they were brought back to England after a personal intervention by Lloyd George.

With the introduction of conscription the state had undoubtedly crossed a new threshold in its relationship with ordinary citizens. No less significant, however, was the willing acceptance of the majority opinion that conscription was the appropriate means to fill the ranks of the armed forces, once the initial wave of patriotic enthusiasm was past. But conscription had disappointing results for those who hoped that it would flush out hordes of 'slackers'. Enlistment fell to around 40,000 a month, as the numbers excluded on the grounds of war work and ill-health proved much greater than expected. The number entering the army in 1916 was less than 1915 and the total for the year was actually only marginally greater than in the six months of 1914 (see Table 1).

Although approximately half a million youths became eligible for conscription each year, pledges had been given that

Table 1: Army recruiting in the Great War

	Total joining the armed forces	*Regimental strength of British army on 1 October each year*
1914	1,186,357	1,327,372
1915	1,280,000	2,475,764
1916	1,190,000	3,343,797
1917	820,646	3,883,017
1918	493,562	3,838,265

no eighteen-year-olds would be sent to France. Moreover, political considerations meant that conscription could not be applied to Ireland, leaving a large reservoir of potential manpower untapped. As the dwindling recruitment figures for the last two years of the war revealed, Britain was coming perilously close to scraping the bottom of the barrel as far as manpower was concerned. The poverty and ill-health of many industrial workers in pre-war Britain was now reaping a bitter harvest in the large numbers of men who failed to reach the minimum standard for military service, still less combat. Of the two and a half million men examined by National Service Medical Boards in 1917–18, only 36 per cent were deemed fit for full military duties, and 41.4 per cent were placed in the two lowest categories, either unable 'to undergo physical exertion' or 'totally or permanently unfit for military service'. In some industrial areas, as many as 70 per cent of men were classed unfit for overseas duties. By the end of the war, almost a quarter of the total male population had served or was serving in the armed forces, representing some 58 per cent of all Scots, Welsh and English of military age. Even so, the huge losses in the great attritional battles of 1916 and 1917 meant that the size of the army was barely increasing, and in 1918, when the heaviest casualties of the war were suffered, it had actually begun to shrink. The German offensive of spring 1918 which caused 300,000 casualties almost knocked Britain out of the war. Desperate expedients had to be sought, including sending eighteen-year-olds out to France and the 'combing-out' of skilled labour. A measure of the dire straits to which the country had been reduced lay in the fact that half of the British infantry in France by autumn 1918 was under nineteen years of age. Serious injury, such as the loss of a foot or hand, was no longer sufficient to earn discharge from the army, but merely deployment in supply and labour duties behind the front. As a result, only the entry of the American forces with fresh reserves of manpower enabled the final offensive to be mounted which forced Germany to sue for peace.

The problem of military manpower was inextricably bound up with the question of war production. The role of government soon became one of balancing the seemingly insatiable appetite of the military chiefs for fresh divisions with the requirements of serving the basic needs of the home population, and providing the munitions of war required both by Britain and her allies. The war effort, simply in terms of the production of munitions, was immense. By the end of the war, Britain had manufactured over four million rifles, a quarter of a million machine guns, 52,000 aeroplanes, 2,800 tanks, 25,000 artillery pieces and over 170 million rounds of artillery shells. The build-up of forces in France resulted in 1918 in an immense army of almost two million soldiers equipped not only with rifles, machine guns, artillery and the normal provisions of war, but also almost quarter of a million horses and mules, 85,000 motor vehicles and 34,700 motor bikes. The expenditure of munitions matched the size of the forces involved. 'Attrition' demanded the piling-up of guns, shells and men in ever-increasing quantities to wear down the opponent. At the battle of the Somme in 1916, one and a half million shells from 1,537 guns hammered the German trenches in the week preceding the attack. For the Passchendaele offensive in 1917 four million shells were fired in the course of ten days at the German lines. On one day in September 1918, the British army fired off 943,000 shells, costing £3,871,000. As well as supplying the needs of her own armies, the factories of Great Britain also supplied the armies of other countries. In a real sense Britain was the 'arsenal of the Allies', with manufacturing potential far greater than France, Italy or Russia. Even with the entry of the United

States into the war in 1917, Britain remained the vital arms producer. Although the USA had immense reserves of man-power, it had only a small standing army and few munitions factories. As a result its new armies had to be equipped with British tanks, guns, steel helmets and even rifles. It was this pressure of arms production which was to keep the military participation ratio lower in Britain than in France, in order to keep production up, and was to force the government into assuming much greater control over industry and labour than had ever been envisaged in peace-time.

Initially, at least, government intervention was dictated largely by expediency, with little thought for long-term con-sequences or social implications. Particular crises were met by *ad hoc* solutions, but ones which were characterized by the ex-tension of the state's power to organize, supervise or control essential aspects of the economy. As the war progressed, however, these interventions became increasingly deliberate, part of a more considered response to the needs of total war in which all the resources of the country had to be harnessed in the pursuit of victory. In the first twelve months of the war, one of the most critical areas of government concern was the production of munitions and the problem of raising out-put from the engineering industry. Here, the engineering unions had a tradition of militancy in defence of the craft status of their skilled members and, in some areas, such as Clydeside, had begun to develop a wider set of socialist aspirations for workers' control under the influence of syndicalist ideas. Indus-trial relations were already tense on the eve of the war and a three-year wage agreement was due to terminate at the end of 1914. Disruption of war production was clearly something that the government wanted to avoid, but its main difficulties lay in obtaining the kind of increases in output that were neces-sary to maintain a long war. The production of munitions had already been impaired by almost a fifth of engineering workers volunteering for the armed forces, and the government was forced to recognize that only by a radical overhaul of working practices could output be raised, above all the acceptance by the engineering unions of the suspension of restrictive practices and the principle of 'dilution', the use of unskilled and semi-skilled workers to do work traditionally reserved for skilled craftsmen. A carrot-and-stick approach was adopted. In the first place the Defence of the Realm Act was amended to give the government power to utilize any resources deemed necessary for 'the public safety and the defence of the Realm' and this was followed by orders making strikes and restrictive practices illegal when engaged on war production. Faced with the threatened opposition of the skilled workers to these attempts to erode their position, Lloyd George and the principal union leaders met in March 1915 and formulated the 'Treasury Agreement', in which the unions accepted dilution on three conditions: that the traditional craft privileges would be restored after the end of the war; that some restrictions would be placed on profits; and that the unions would share in the direction of industry through local committees.

The 'Shells Scandal' which erupted in the press during the spring of 1915 helped to undermine the Asquith government and led in May to the formation of a Coalition Government committed to a more efficient and purposeful prosecution of the war. One result was the setting-up of the Ministry of Munitions in June 1915 under the control of Lloyd George. Its upper echelons were staffed by businessmen who were loaned by their firms for the duration of the war and who were able to coordinate business and state interests in such a way that the draconian powers which the government had at its disposal were rarely needed. For example, in theory, private property had ceased to be sacrosanct and the government had power to requisition any materials deemed necessary to the war effort, but, in practice, chose to pay a price based on the costs of production with a margin for reasonable profit. In addition, the Ministry sought to control industry by buying up available raw materials. Rather than rely upon private enterprise and the laws of supply and demand, government contractors were appointed to buy essential supplies abroad. Once this policy was embarked on, however, total control of commodities almost inevitably followed to avoid speculative price rises and interruption of normal marketing. In the case of a humble item such as jute – the 'brown paper of the wholesale trade' – now required in vast quantities for sandbags, the government not only requisitioned all available stocks in Britain but undertook the buying and control of the whole Indian jute crop. Steel, leather, wool, flax and other strategic materials soon came under direct control in this way. Such measures were not taken lightly, for, as E. M. Lloyd wrote in 1924:

> The idea that industry would have to be deliberately organized for war production encountered subconscious resistance in a Government committed to the doctrines of free trade and individualism. It is not surprising that the necessity for State intervention was only gradually admitted by Ministers who had spent the greater part of their political careers in exploding the fallacies of Protectionism on the one hand and Socialism on the other.

Accepted, however, it was, abetted not only by the businessmen recruited by Lloyd George but also by some of the leading 'New Liberals' such as Llewellyn Smith and William Beveridge, in whom the idea that the interests of the state and the community should take priority over the interests of individuals was already well entrenched. Control over the munitions industry was strengthened by the Munitions of War Act of July 1915, which incorporated the concessions outlined in the Treasury Agreement four months earlier but greatly extended state control. As well as the provisions regarding 'dilution', strikes and lock-outs were declared illegal and compulsory arbitration introduced. A category of 'controlled establishments' was created, covering any plant regarded as essential to the manufacture of munitions. In these establishments, all restrictive practices were suspended and wages and working conditions came under the direct control of the Ministry of Munitions. Manning levels, choice of operatives and organization of work were now under state control. A clause which was to cause great unrest later in the war stated that workers could be assigned to particular places of employment and would not be allowed to seek work elsewhere without a leaving certificate by their employer. By September 1915, over seven hundred of the main engineering plants were categorized as 'controlled establishments'. These powers were enforced by Munitions Tribunals who could proceed against any offences against the Act. By the end of the war the Ministry of Munitions employed a staff of 65,000 men and women, controlled over three and a half million workers, ran directly 250 factories, quarries and mines, and supervised 20,000 'controlled establishments'.

It was soon found that minor and piecemeal controls almost inevitably led the government to assuming wider responsibilities than originally envisaged. As Sidney Pollard has written: 'Some relatively minor control, to deal with an immediate issue, often had repercussions which required Government intervention further and further back, until the State found itself directing a major part of the country's industries, and controlling or licensing most of the remainder.' Moreover, the lesson learned from the munitions industry, as from recruiting, was that a more comprehensive system of control was essential if the best use was to be made of the resources available. The lesson, however, took almost three years of war to sink home. Considerable reluctance was felt to take on more powers than the immediate purpose in hand and it could always be maintained that the munitions industry was a special case. But the accession to power of Lloyd George in December 1916 and the progressively increasing demands of the war forged the way for more total control by government, with the effect that by 1917-18 the economy was established on a war footing. Lloyd George introduced a five-man War Cabinet which met virtually every day, backed by a personal secretariat housed in huts in St James's Park. Five new departments of government were created under 'Controllers', dealing with shipping, labour, food, food production and national service. The staffing was technocratic, businessmen being brought in to run the concerns, following the precedent of the Ministry of Munitions. The 'Controllers' had wide powers, though, as in the past, they preferred to work in cooperation with the industrialists, farmers, financial interests and trade unions rather than draw fully upon the almost unlimited powers conferred on them by statute. Although all British merchant ships were requisitioned, the owners were co-opted to manage them; similarly, the county committees which controlled agriculture were largely composed of the major local landowners. But however modified in practice, the role of government had been greatly extended. Following munitions, shipbuilding and ship-repairing, virtually all transport by rail, sea or canal, flour milling, agriculture, collieries and chemical industries were subject to government control.

The state also regulated food and drink. One of the earliest casualties of the war was the day-long opening hours enjoyed by the Edwardian drinker. Public houses in London were often open from 5 a.m. to past midnight and only marginally shorter licensing hours obtained in the provinces. Concern about public order, particularly in the armed forces, led at the end of August 1914 to an Act empowering local authorities to impose such restrictions on licensing hours as they felt desirable. In a 'Message to the Nation' on 24 October 1914, Lord Kitchener called for an end to 'treating', the buying of rounds for soldiers. By the end of the year, earlier closing times had been introduced by about half the local authorities in England, while the powerful temperance lobby pressed the government to take this opportunity to act against the 'demon drink'. Indeed, for a time, the crusade against drink expressed a domestic mood of high morality and self-sacrifice. In spring 1915, Lloyd George declared: 'We are fighting Germany, Austria and Drink, and, as far as I can see, the greatest of these deadly foes is Drink.' There was a vogue for 'taking the pledge', led by King George V, but it was the imperatives of war production which led to decisive action. A report on bad time-keeping in the shipbuilding, munitions and transport industries at the end of April 1915 blamed lost time on the ease with which highly paid workers could purchase beer and spirits. As a result the Defence of the Realm Act was amended to regulate the drink trade. A Central Control Board took over liquor-licensing in areas where drink was believed to be interfering with the war effort. More comprehensive was a restriction of opening hours in the middle of the day to two and a half hours and to two or three hours in the evening, introducing the afternoon 'break' which continued after the war. Orders against 'treating' were also passed, though unevenly enforced. Total control of all licensed premises was introduced at Enfield Lock in London, at Carlisle and Gretna on the Anglo-Scottish border, where important munitions factories were based, and around the naval establishments at Invergordon and Cromarty. More indirect, but almost certainly as effective, were increases in excise duty on beer and spirits and reductions in strength. Both to combat drunkenness and conserve grain, the gravity of beer was progressively reduced. Reductions in strength were followed by price increases. From an average of about 3d. a pint, prices soared to as much as 9d. and 10d. Price controls were introduced by the government in October 1917, but an excise duty of 3½d., compared with ¼d. in 1914, meant that by 1919 beer prices were more than double their pre-war level and consumption had been reduced by a half. A maximum of 70° proof was established for all spirits, while sales of bottles of spirits were restricted to certain days and hours. Heavy taxation probably did more than anything else to restrict spirit consumption: from being roughly comparable with beer, the price of a measure of spirits rose almost five times by the end of the war.

Food rationing provided another barometer of increasing government involvement. Initially the government hoped merely to act as a purchaser of food for the armed forces, taking fuller controls only where a particular shortage or difficulty was anticipated, as in the case of sugar. Just as recruiting was to be voluntary and war production largely unregulated in the first two years of the war, so the government was unwilling to abandon free market operations and step into the distribution of food. Shortages caused by U-boat sinkings and the huge demands of the armed forces forced up prices and led the government into trying various expedients before the introduction of rationing. Price controls were introduced over meat in 1917, in an attempt to control runaway prices, but by the end of the year, in the face of a real shortage, the government was forced to take over the slaughter and purchase of farm animals and bring all the concerns in the wholesale meat trade under its control. Lloyd George's creation of a Food Controller in December 1916 was a step towards greater intervention, but the first incumbent, Lord Devonport, showed little initiative. Restrictions on the sale of luxury foodstuffs and Royal Proclamations urging voluntary restrictions of consumption, read out in churches on successive Sundays, were more reminiscent of the Napoleonic wars than the increasingly complex issues facing the government by 1917. His successor, Lord Rhondda, appointed in June, proved more decisive. For example, a system of registration for sugar was organized, entitling holders of a ration card to a minimum of half a pound of sugar a week.

Concern over food supplies was increased in 1917 with the report of the Commission of Enquiry into Industrial Unrest, which found that rising prices were a major cause of strikes. Preparations for the introduction of rationing on the basis of a central register were overtaken in the winter of 1917–18 by something approaching a food panic. Although no absolute shortage of food was threatened, scarcities of individual items led to lengthening queues, hoarding and an atmosphere of growing tension on the domestic front. Queuing for food and other essential items was alleged to be forcing men to take time off from work to relieve their hard-pressed womenfolk. In order to allay the anxiety, a system of rationing was improvised on the basis of registration with particular shops. Government had in fact been anticipated in some areas by local Food Control Committees set up to deal with sugar rationing and also by local authorities in places such as Gravesend, Pontypool and Birmingham. By April 1918, meat rationing applied to the whole country, allocating at its minimum level three-quarters of a pound per individual a week. Tea, butter and margarine were the other major items brought under rationing systems, although no uniform scheme ever existed. Bread and potatoes remained unrationed but subject to price controls and, in the case of bread, produced as 'Government Bread', which included an increasing amount of adulteration with potato and bean flour. Rationing continued into the immediate post-war years as a means of dealing with the continuing shortages of essential items and the threat of labour unrest. Milk rationing was introduced only *after* the armistice, while the Ministry of Food de-controlled meat, butter and sugar as late as October 1919. Only in March 1921 was the Ministry of Food finally wound up.

Propaganda

But the influence of the state reached beyond the bounds of enforcing military service, organizing war production and controlling food and drink. Censorship and propaganda gave the government the power to manipulate opinion both at home and abroad. At the beginning of the war the only propaganda service was a Foreign Office secret department based at Wellington House to influence neutral and enemy opinion. Domestically, patriotic enthusiasm made extensive propaganda virtually superfluous in the first months of the war. None the less, press censorship had an important effect upon the picture of the war received by the public. A press starved of 'hard news' was forced into purveying rumours, atrocity stories and an almost hysterical campaign against spies and aliens. Amongst the most famous of the rumours was the 'Angels of Mons' – a miraculous vision alleged to have safeguarded the British retreat in August 1914 – fashioned in fact by the press from a fictional story which appeared in the *Evening News* for 29 September. The *Daily Mail* was guilty of reporting a completely fictitious naval battle off the coast of Holland, only one of a series of phoney stories which appeared in special editions designed to whip up circulation. The government, however, did contribute something. One of its most successful early 'plants' was that the Kaiser had referred to the BEF as a 'contemptible little army', a phrase actually devised by the War Office and ascribed to the Kaiser to stiffen the resolve of British troops.

The allegation of German atrocities was corroborated on the flimsiest evidence by a committee headed by Lord Bryce, whose report early in 1915 that the Germans had massacred civilians, violated women and carried out a systematic policy of destruction in Belgium and northern France was widely circulated at home and abroad. The sinking of the Cunard liner *Lusitania* off the southern coast of Ireland on 7 May 1915, with the loss of 1,201 men, women and children, gave British propagandists a field-day. Although it is now known that the liner was carrying contraband goods, including almost five thousand 3-inch shells and nearly five million rifle cartridges, no effort was spared to present the sinking both to British and neutral opinion as a particularly savage example of German 'frightfulness'. Captain Reginald Hall, the Director of British Naval Intelligence, had over 300,000 copies struck of a grisly commemorative medal said to have been issued by the German government. In fact, only forty-four such medals had been produced in Germany, on the private initiative of a Munich craftsman who wished to satirize Cunard's greed in allowing the ship to sail with contraband cargo through a war zone.

Growing war-weariness and the increasing strain of the war effort made control over public opinion a major concern and one of the most significant aspects of the widening scope of 'total war'. Public opinion became a crucial war material, at least as important as gun cotton or armour plate, and was in one sense the ultimate commodity which underpinned the continuation of the war and the ability of the government to demand ever greater sacrifices from the country. How crucial was soon to be revealed in the collapse of the Russian government and the eventual breakdown of Germany's domestic polity under the strain of blockade and shortage. The propaganda services were overhauled by the creation of a Department of Information (converted into a Ministry in 1918), which supervised four sub-divisions: Wellington

House; a Cinema Division; a Political Intelligence Division;
and a News Division. Wellington House continued to provide
propaganda both for domestic and foreign consumption.
Amongst a plethora of anti-German stories, probably its most
successful fabrication was the German 'Corpse-Conversion
Works', or 'Tallow Factory', originating in a deliberate mis-
translation of a German administrative order for the conversion
of animal remains into fat and oils which made it appear that
the Germans were using the corpses of allied soldiers for such
purposes. *The Times* printed the story and the Department
of Information circulated a pamphlet headed *A Corpse-
Conversion Factory* containing details of this 'act of unspeakable
savagery'. It was only seven years after the war that this
propaganda story was finally exploded in the House of
Commons.

The Cinema Division represented the harnessing of the new
mass medium to propaganda purposes. This had begun as early
as the autumn of 1914 with Lancelot Speed's cartoons in the
'Bully Boy' series aimed at discrediting the Kaiser. Propaganda
films were also prepared for foreign consumption by the end
of 1915. From 1916, however, a more concerted policy was
adopted to exploit the potential of the three thousand or more
cinemas in the country to present the case for the continuation
of the war. Full-length silent documentary films, such as the
'Battle' series produced for the Department of Information,
portrayed the action in major engagements on the Western
Front which, while conveying something of the squalor of the
battlefield, fell far short of a realistic picture of the awful carnage being wrought by modern weaponry. An official film of
the Battle of the Somme could devote loving detail to the massive artillery bombardment, the awesome mine explosions at
Beaumont Hamel, and the seemingly inexhaustible build-up
of supplies which preceded the offensive, but told little of the
hideous human cost of the actual fighting. Corpses, in this case,
were conspicuous by their absence. Propaganda trailers using
animation, silhouettes, documentary footage and re-enactment
were distributed through commercial newsreel networks and

reached massive audiences to ridicule the Germans, promote economy campaigns and boost war savings.

The Political Intelligence Division was primarily designed to gather reports on public opinion in the world at large; more important domestically was the News Division, which carried the responsibility for feeding war news through to the British public. Guided by a committee of newspaper magnates and editors, including at various times Lord Northcliffe, Beaver-brook, Robert Donald and C. P. Scott, the propaganda services succeeded in their primary tasks of both whipping up anti-German feeling and minimizing the full horrors of the war. Official reports, press coverage and film material always tended to play up the optimistic side of the war and to hide as much as possible of its true horror.

It was little wonder that servicemen on leave found the civilian view of the war grossly out of line with their first-hand experience and that a yawning gap developed between the appreciation of front-line soldiers and those at home. Viewed in retrospect, the use of propaganda can clearly be seen as yet one more ratchet on the wheel whereby the state took greater control over people's lives. It not only told them what to do, where to work, what to eat and how to spend their leisure, but also what to think. Most important of all it denied its citizens access to the diversity of information which, because it might have hindered the war effort, might also have led them to question whether the war was worth fighting. Such sentiments would be inappropriate were they not precisely those expressed by many people after the war. It was Philip Gibbs, one of the official war correspondents, who produced in 1920 one of the first and most harrowing descriptions of the Western Front under the title *Realities of War*, a book in which both title and contents sought to express the view that the true story of the war had not been told. Not least of the reasons for the mood of disillusion which spread amongst some sections of the population after the war and for the growth of pacifist sentiment was the persistent dissimulation, if not downright lying, by which the government sought, for good or ill, to keep its people at war.

3. Home Front

The consequences of the Great War upon the domestic population were complex and far-reaching. But in most cases the effects wrought by the war should not be seen in isolation from the longer-term developments of British society, for the peculiar circumstances of the war more often than not acted to emphasize processes which can be identified in Edwardian Britain. It remains a fine judgement how much in each sphere the war merely acted as a forcing-house for change and how much it qualitatively altered the shape and texture of British society. Four main effects of the war can be identified: the impact of the war on living standards, including poverty and health; the role of the war in the emancipation of women; the part played by the war in strengthening organized labour; and the collectivist and democratizing role of the war, including the stimulus to wider social reform.

Wages and Living Standards

The Great War had contradictory effects on living standards. The demands of war production meant, after an initial disruption, virtually full employment, plentiful overtime and generous production bonuses. Money wages rose dramatically; at the end of the first year of the war it was estimated that there had been an average rise of about 3s. 10d. per week; and by the end of 1916 between 6s. and 12s. a week. By July 1919 the rise in wages over July 1914 for those in full employment was considerable (see Table 2).

Table 1. Annual earnings of skilled and unskilled workers

	1914	1919
Skilled occupations		
Bricklayer	42s. 10d.	79s. 2d.
Shipyard riveter	37s. 9d.	74s. 9d.
Compositor	36s. 0d.	72s. 0d.
Unskilled		
Bricklayer's labourer	29s. 1d.	65s. 2d.
Engineering labourer	22s. 10d.	58s. 3d.
Fireman	26s. 0d.	66s. 0d.

Unskilled, low-paid workers made the greatest advances, as the demand for labour significantly narrowed the rates between skilled and unskilled. A study of four major industries suggested that the hourly or daily rates of unskilled workers as a percentage of skilled workers rose from between 50 and 66 per cent in 1913–14 to between 74 and 83 per cent by 1919. Large numbers of unskilled and semi-skilled workers were also able to enter skilled trades as 'dilutees', where trade-union concern about protecting the position of skilled craftsmen ensured that the 'dilutees' were paid at the full rates. Moreover, at a time of labour shortage the bargaining position of organized labour was immensely strengthened and there was a general tendency for both government and employers to concede wage demands in vital industries. For example, an engineers' strike on Clydeside in February 1915 added a penny to hourly rates as well as obtaining advances on piece-work payments. Similar concessions were made to the South Wales miners that summer. At least as important for the lowest-paid was the virtual elimination of unemployment and casual work which had condemned a significant portion of the workforce before 1914 to weekly earnings below the poverty line. 'Trading-up' in jobs was now possible and many of the lowest-paid jobs were deserted in favour of munitions factories and other well-paid war work. Not least amongst the groups to gain here were women, who, as employees, had been amongst the lowest paid of all workers prior to 1914, with an average wage of 11s. 7d. per week, a mere third of the male wage average. During the war almost half a million left generally low-paid domestic service and 'sweated trades' for work in factories, transport and offices. The wages of typists were reported to have almost doubled by September 1915 from £1 to 35s. per week and female munitions workers could earn over £2. Shortage of labour also resulted in a temporary reversal of the pre-war trend towards the progressive restriction of juvenile employment. Several local authorities requested a temporary suspension of the school attendance regulations which discouraged children below the age of fourteen from working and by 1917 it was officially admitted that 600,000 children under fourteen had gone to work, not counting many more unknown to the authorities.

The major offsetting factor to this rise in incomes and full employment was inflation. At the outset of the war, panic-buying of sugar, flour, bread, butter, margarine and cheese in anticipation of shortages led to near-riots in some slum districts and a rapid increase in prices. After the initial rise, prices moved steadily upwards, so that by June 1915 food prices were almost a third above their pre-war level, while a year later some items, such as sugar, imported meat, fish and eggs, had risen by between 82 and 163 per cent. By June 1918 the average weekly food bill for the 'standard' working-class family of 4.57 people had risen from under a pound a week in June 1914 to 47s. 3d. and the Board of Trade estimated that the cost of living for an unskilled workman's family during the four years had risen by 81 per cent. Overall the picture was plainly of substantial price rises, especially for food, but also in house rents, fares and taxes, substantial enough to erode much of the growth in money wages recorded during the war. Overall indices, balancing wage rates against prices, suggest a small average increase in real incomes, at least by 1920, when wage gains had been further consolidated in the aftermath of the war (see Table 3).

However, such increases depended largely upon individual circumstances. For some households, the absence of the main breadwinner in the armed forces combined with the sharp rise

Table 3: Wages, prices and earnings, 1913–20
(1930 = 100)

	Average annual wage earnings	Weekly wage rates	Retail prices	Average annual real wages
1913	52.4	53.2	63.3	82.8
1919	–	122.3	136.1	–
1920	143.7	146.8	157.6	91.2

Source: D. H. Aldcroft, *The Inter-War Economy: Britain, 1919–1939*, Batsford, 1970, pp. 352, 364.

in prices could entail real hardship. The war economy functioned unevenly, disrupting some traditional occupations, particularly in the first months when relief committees had to be set up in some of the major towns. The shipping crisis of 1917 was also responsible for producing part-time working amongst industries such as textiles which were dependent upon bulk supplies of raw materials from overseas. For others, however, the ability to obtain regular work with plentiful overtime meant new levels of prosperity. Households in which women and juveniles were able to obtain well-paid work for the first time could witness a transformation in living standards. Some evidence of this can be seen in the marked decline in pauperism noted by the middle years of the war and improvements in the standard of health. In spite of the serious shipping losses of 1917 and lengthening food queues, supplies of food remained sufficient to meet dietary needs. Moreover, just as military rations often put pounds in weight upon undernourished recruits ('meat every day!' was one recruiting slogan), factory canteens provided low-cost meals of a higher nutritional value than many had been accustomed to in peace-time. By the end of the war, a thousand canteens provided a million meals a day. *The Report of the Working Classes Cost of Living Committee* in 1918 claimed that the families of unskilled workmen were better fed at the end of the war than at the beginning and that the percentage of poorly nourished children entering school had declined by more than a half in London and by similar percentages in many other

towns, a circumstance which it regarded as a direct result of
parents of poorer children now being able to feed them to
a higher standard. Such conclusions have been confirmed by
statistical analysis of the health statistics for the Great War,
which suggest a real improvement in domestic mortality and
morbidity rates. Increased consumption of luxury items not
in short supply, such as tobacco, also suggested that there was
some greater margin of expenditure available to the population
at large. Robert Roberts, whose mother owned a corner shop
in a slum district of Salford, recalled that:

> some of the poorest in the land started to prosper as never before.
> In spite of the war, slum grocers managed to get hold of different
> and better varieties of foodstuffs of a kind sold before only in middle-
> class shops, and the once deprived began to savour strange delights ...
> One of our customers, wife of a former foundry labourer, both mak-
> ing big money now on munitions, airily inquired one Christmas time
> as to when we were going to stock 'summat worth chewin'. 'Such
> as what?' asked my father, sour-faced. 'Tins o' lobster,' she suggested,
> 'or them big jars o' pickled gherkins!'
>   Furious, the old man damned her from the shop. 'Before the war,'
> he fumed, 'that one was grateful for a bit o' bread and scrape!'

It was precisely such changes in expectation which have led
some historians to see in the Great War a significant transformation in the quality of life of the lower classes. As John
Burnett has remarked: 'If the Great Depression marks the first
important step by the working classes of England towards
material comfort, the First World War, for all its horrors and
miseries, marks the second.'

Women

The war also had important effects upon the status of women.
Although women had been widely employed in pre-war
industries and trades, the war witnessed a great expansion of
female employment. Large numbers of women were drawn
into war work, agriculture and clerical occupations to fill the
gaps created by the armed forces. Women's groups had taken

a lead in 'substituting' themselves for men who had gone to the front; in July 1915 Mrs Emmeline Pankhurst had organized a demonstration on behalf of women's 'right to serve'. After the official beginning of conscription on 2 March 1916, the government itself started a drive to fill the places of conscripts with female labour. In July 1914 there were 212,000 women employed in engineering and munition industries, but by 1918 the total was almost a million; in transport, numbers rose from 18,000 in 1914 to 117,000 in 1918; in clerical work from 33,000 to 102,000. The numbers of women employed in commerce, national and local government, and education all increased, while more than 150,000 women were absorbed into such auxiliary branches of the armed forces as the WAACS, the WRENS and the WRAF. In all, over a million women embarked for the first time upon paid work.

As in many other aspects of social development, the war only accelerated and intensified the movement towards the emancipation of women. Even before the war, women were moving into commerce and the professions. By 1914, a quarter of all clerks were women, double the number ten years earlier. At the outbreak of the war, just over three million women were employed in commerce and industry. By the last months of the war the number had reached almost five million. Many of these women, particularly the 'dilutees', were to lose their jobs with the return of the men from the armed forces, but a permanent addition had been made to the ranks of working women, for the number of employed females rose by over a quarter of a million between 1911 and 1921. The use of female labour had many repercussions. Women showed that they could perform almost every conceivable task, including the most skilled and the most arduous. Women drove trams, worked on the land, engaged in munitions work and nursed the sick. Many middle-class women who had been subject to the stifling restrictions of pre-war conventions were able to enjoy a degree of independence which their own income and a new environment brought to them and for the first time became more conscious of employment opportunities. In turn, many who had opposed female suffrage were forced to admit that women had played so vital a part in winning the war that political rights could not be denied to them any longer.

Similarly, wider employment opportunities helped to liberate working-class women from the often restrictive and narrow life of the slums. Many escaped from the poorly paid drudgery of a sweated labour and domestic service to take well-paid work in munitions factories. The number of domestic servants fell by almost a quarter in the war years, while the average wages of working women were often more than double the pre-war level. Unmarried girls found themselves earning unbelievably high wages, while many married women for the first time were in full control of the household wage-packet. Robert Roberts described the effect upon the women who used his mother's shop:

Wives in the shop no longer talked about 'my boss', or 'my master'. Master had gone to war and Missis ruled the household, or he worked close to her in a factory, turning out cases on a lathe and earning little more than she did herself. Housewives left their homes and immediate neighbourhood more frequently, and with money in their purses went foraging for goods even into the city shops, each trip being an exercise in self-education. She discovered her own rights. The pre-1914 movements for her political emancipation, bourgeois in origin and function, meant very little to the lower-class woman. In the end the consequences of war, not the legal acquisition of female rights released her from bondage.

The tangible results of this emancipation were seen in the Fourth Reform Act of July 1918, which enfranchised women over thirty. Although younger women had to wait until 1928 before attaining full equal voting rights with men, the contribution of women of all classes to the war effort had made an overwhelming case for granting them the vote. In addition, a Sex Disqualification (Removal) Act in 1919 provided that no person should be disqualified from the exercise of any public function or appointment by sex or marriage. Although many barriers remained to the complete equality of women in the professions and public service, the Act marked an important symbol of the drift of public sentiment. Women now had, in theory at least, opportunities to enter the highest ranks of the civil service, the legal profession and local government.

Organized labour

The war also had major effects upon the position of organized labour. Trade-union membership had been growing rapidly in the years prior to the war, reaching just over four million by 1914. The war saw an acceleration of unionization, the number of those belonging to trade unions rising from 4,145,000 in 1914 to 6,533,000 in 1918. The stronger bargaining power of labour was one encouragement to union organization for, as one senior official informed the Prime Minister Asquith in 1915: 'For the first time in the history of this country since the Black Death, the supply of labour has not been equal to the demand, and the working man knows it.' For many workers, union membership came as a consequence of the government's attempt to mobilize organized labour for the national effort. Employers' resistance to unionization, a major cause of disputes prior to the war, was often swept aside for the duration in industries considered vital to the war effort. The desire for uninterrupted production inevitably led the government into making concessions to unions and labour leaders, a policy which not only further strengthened organized labour but led by the end of the war towards some sections pressing claims not only for industrial but also for political demands.

The early support shown by labour leaders for the war was gradually transformed into a more formal relationship. Arthur Henderson, the new leader of the Labour Party, was made President of the Board of Education in 1915, though his main role was to advise on labour problems, with two other Labour MPs appointed to junior government office. With Lloyd George's premiership in December 1916, the new status of the representatives of labour was confirmed. Henderson was brought into the War Cabinet, two trade-union leaders, John

Hodge and George Barnes, took on the Ministry of Labour and the Ministry of Pensions, while several other MPs and trade-unionists were incorporated into government positions. While the acceptance of labour leaders into positions of responsibility undoubtedly enhanced the status both of the Labour Party and the trade unions, the effect at grass-roots level was often to open a gap between union leaders and the rank and file. Particularly in the engineering industry, the movement towards workshop and factory organization under part-time, local shop stewards was already under way. In some areas, too, this organizational development went hand in hand with syndicalist and guild socialist ideas which distrusted any central direction whether wielded by government, employers or trade unions. As causes for dispute multiplied during the war, the growth of the shop stewards' organizations often filled the gap left by the incorporation of Labour Party leaders and national union officials into the government machine. Government attempts, then, to harness the leaders of organized labour to the war effort frequently ran the risk that the leaders themselves might no longer be adequate representatives of the rank and file.

A pointer to later developments came in February 1915 with a strike by several thousand engineers on Clydeside in pursuit of a wage claim in defiance of their officials and organized by an unofficial body of shop stewards. Henry Pelling has noted how negotiations were held in a boardroom of the Treasury with representatives of the men before a gilt throne of Queen Anne, a spectacle Lloyd George was later to describe: '. . . those stalwart artisans leaning against and sitting on the steps of the throne of the dead Queen, and on equal terms negotiating conditions with the government of the day upon a question vitally affecting the conduct of a great war. Queen Anne was indeed dead.' Later in 1915 the South Wales miners struck after rejecting a wage claim arbitrated by the government and in defiance of a proclamation under the Munitions of War Act which made any strike in the South Wales coalfield illegal. In the event, the government was forced to negotiate a settlement and abandon coercion. A significant feature of the settlement was a victory for the South Wales Miners Federation in its long-running battle against the employment of non-unionists in the pits and the absorption of craft workers into the union. In effect, the Board of Trade forced the local coal-owners to accept a 'closed shop' in the coalfield for the duration of the war. The skilled engineers on Clydeside provided the most militant organization of labour during the war. The local shop stewards formed the Clyde Workers Committee with the declared objectives:

1. To obtain an ever-increasing control over workshop conditions.
2. To regulate the terms upon which the workers shall be employed.
3. To organize the workers upon a class basis and to maintain the Class Struggle, until the overthrow of the Wages System, the Freedom of the Workers, and the establishment of Industrial Democracy have been obtained.

Led by a group of revolutionary syndicalists, the C W C was soon to be linked via the National Workers Committee Movement to similar groups in other manufacturing centres. In 1917 continuing disputes about dilution, the operation of the Military Service Acts and rising prices, and a loss of confidence in the trade-union leaders, produced a wave of spontaneous and un-official strikes affecting Lancashire, the Midlands, Sheffield and London. A Joint Engineering Shop Stewards Committee was formed to negotiate directly with government and which repudiated any 'interference by the union executives of the workers in the present dispute'.

The Russian Revolutions of spring and autumn 1917 un-doubtedly gave fresh impetus to some of the more militant groups. In Glasgow there was talk of the creation of a Workers' and Soldiers' Soviet, but its meeting was prevented by the local magistrates, and one of the leading Marxist propagandists, John Maclean, was sentenced to five years' hard labour under the Defence of the Realm Act. In spite of the evident stimulus to militant activity, the primary fuel to industrial discontent re-mained concern over wage levels and job status. Militants, whatever their precise ideological stance, could obtain a follow-

ing only where there was a wide set of grievances on which
to work. Nevertheless, over five and a half million working
days were lost in 1917, more than the total for 1915 and 1916
put together. The final year of the war saw no improvement:
5,875,000 working days were lost – the highest total for any
year of the war – while the number of disputes was almost
50 per cent greater than 1919. In spite of the modification of
the Munitions of War Act, ending 'leaving certificates' and
granting pay rises from mid-1917, disputes about the operation
of conscription and a tightening of 'industrial conscription'
continued to provoke unrest, so that strikes continued right
up to the last days of the war.

By the time of the armistice, the position of organized labour
had undoubtedly strengthened considerably. Not only had
trade-union membership increased by almost two and a half
million members, but the proportion of all workers in trade
unions increased from 23 per cent in 1914 to 30 per cent four
years later. In the case of women the increase was even more
dramatic, rising from a mere 8 per cent to over 21 per cent,
reflecting the movement of women from largely unorganized
occupations such as domestic service into more fully unionized
areas such as transport and engineering. Two distinct trends
appeared to have emerged in regard to organized labour by
the end of the Great War: on the one hand, the greatly enhanced status of the unions seen in their involvement in government, including arbitration councils and wage boards and
reaching up to the highest councils of the state; on the other,
the continued unrest in certain areas of industry in which the
growth of shop-floor organization and the spread of socialist
ideas marked a significant development on the pre-war situation. Although the former tendency can be seen as at least as
important as the strikes and unrest of 'Red Clydeside' (see
pp. 99–100) and the Shop Stewards' movement, it was these
elements which most obviously flavoured industrial relations
in the last months of the war. In several industries, notably
mining and engineering, but also areas of transport, the wartime years had witnessed an often ill-tempered stalemate

between government and unions marked by temporary concessions on both sides, but clearly forshadowing fresh conflicts
once the special circumstances of the war had ended.

Reconstruction

But for the great majority of the working classes, the effects
of the Great War were to be measured in broader terms than
the gains or losses of organized labour. The sacrifices demanded
by the war, combined with the populist instincts of politicians
such as Lloyd George, undoubtedly encouraged both collectivist and democratic elements in British society. Experience of
state intervention and the need to give people something to
fight for led to talk of widespread social reform and post-war
'Reconstruction'. A Reconstruction Committee was formed
in March 1916 which was turned in July 1917 under the impact
of growing labour unrest and the first Russian Revolution into
the Ministry of Reconstruction. The Ministry worked through
a series of committees which investigated demobilization,
labour, unemployment pay and housing. Its reports provided
a series of blueprints for post-war society. A committee under
J. H. Whitley proposed the establishment of joint industrial
councils made up of representatives of employers and workers,
operating on national, district and works level to resolve peacefully industrial disputes. Reports on housing, drawing upon
the experience of model estates built both before the war and
during it for special groups such as munitions workers, paved
the way for the massive scheme of 'homes fit for heroes' inaugurated by the post-war Coalition Government. Parallel with
these developments were the creation of the Ministry of
Pensions in 1917, stimulated both by the need to provide for
the consequences of war casualties and the disruptions to civilian
employment. Similarly attention was turned to education: the
Board of Education Report for 1917–18 declared that the war
'has certainly brought a clearer and wider recognition of the
value of education, and, while showing the defects and shortcomings of our system, has produced the resolution to improve

it'. In 1917 H. A. L. Fisher, Vice-Chancellor of Sheffield University and President of the Board of Education, submitted a
proposal calling for a new Education Act and large-scale state
spending on education on the grounds of the deficiencies
revealed in the existing situation and the 'increased feeling of
social solidarity which has been created by the war'. The last
two years of the war also saw work on the creation of a
Ministry of Health, actually formed in 1919.

It could easily be supposed that these proposals were
primarily designed to win over public opinion to a continuation of the war in the dark days of 1916–18, particularly with
the growing militancy of organized labour and the creation
by 1918 of a new Labour Party programme drawn up by Sidney
Webb which called for a 'National Minimum', democratic
control of industry, including widespread nationalization, a levy
on capital and further redistributive taxation. Undoubtedly the
precarious position of Lloyd George as Premier and the inevitability of a general election influenced the collectivist
tendencies of policy statement, but the call for reconstruction
tapped deeper currents than short-term political advantage. The
pressure from the trade unions and the adoption of a full-
blooded socialist programme by the Labour Party under the
influence of Fabian ideas were significant in themselves of a
generation or more of socialist thought on the role of the
state. Moreover, amongst a broad band of opinion, state-
sponsored reconstruction in housing, health, education and
industry represented an extension of the 'New Liberalism' of
the pre-war years, but now sustained by the example of the
role of the state in managing the war effort. At the Board of
Trade, William Beveridge hailed a revolution in public administration: 'We have ... under the stress of war, made
practical discoveries in the art of government almost comparable to the immense discoveries made at the same time in
the art of flying.' Seebohm Rowntree, a member of the Reconstruction Committee, echoed his words, writing: 'We have
completely revised our notions as to what is possible or impossible. We have seen accomplished within a few brief months

or years reforms to which we should have assigned, not decades, but generations.'

The effect on attitudes towards greater state intervention and the role of planning was to be of profound significance. As Rodney Barker has written:

By the closing years of the war the pacific complement of all this military collectivism was the preparation for social reconstruction with the onset of peace, carried out by the state and pursued with the assistance of its own investigative committees. Once lodged in the realm of 'common sense' and sustained by 'practical' measures, state collectivism looked less and less like contestable belief, and became increasingly the broad starting point for argument, rather than its disputed conclusion.

While the majority of social measures prefigured in the wartime reports had to be postponed until the coming of peace, there was an extension of welfarist activity. Rent controls were introduced to ease some of the worst effects of housing shortages, serious enough to provoke a rent strike in Glasgow in 1915. Individual companies had provided pensions, sickness allowances and recreational facilities on a new scale. The Ministry of Munitions acted as a pacesetter in the setting-up of canteen facilities and special housing and their example was followed by private companies. Post-war reconstruction promised a further extension of welfare provision – it was the central issue upon which Lloyd George went to the country and secured a victory in the general election of 1918.

The financing of the war also involved some redistributive elements. The introduction of death duties and the 'People's Budget' prior to 1914 had already placed greater burdens upon the wealthy, yet neither capital nor income had been seriously eroded by taxation. The early war budgets saw only moderate increases in taxation, many of them occurring in indirect taxes, which actually hit the poorer sections of the community hardest. From September 1915, when McKenna introduced the first really effective war budget, direct taxation began to have greater impact upon the middle and upper classes. By the end of the war the 'normal' rate of taxation had increased from

1s. 2d. in the pound in 1913–14 to 6s. in 1918–19. Before the war, income tax was paid by just over a million people – those earning over £160 per year. The average workman, clerk or small shopkeeper paid no direct taxes at all. However, a lowering of the tax threshold to £130 and the effects of wartime inflation brought 7.8 million within the tax net by 1919–20. Although the war could therefore be held responsible for bringing many people into direct taxation for the first time, there was a strong movement for the burdens to be carried by those who could afford it most. Trade-union complaints about profiteering led to the introduction of an excess profits duty of 50 per cent in 1915, increased to 80 per cent in 1917, calculated on the basis of pre-war profits. As a result the percentage of incomes paid in taxes both direct and indirect had increased for all income levels by the end of the war, but especially at the higher levels. One post-war calculation is given in Table 4.

Table 4: Percentage of different incomes taken by taxation

		1913–14	1918–19
Earned:	£100	6.0	13.8
	£150	5.8	13.1
	£10,000	8.1	42.6
Unearned:	£10,000	15.1	50.3

Elsewhere, some inroads had been made into inherited wealth by the raising of death duties to 40 per cent on estates worth over £2 million by 1919. In sum, war taxation had some redistributive effects, and taxes on the higher incomes would never revert to pre-war levels, but the war had not ruined or impoverished the upper classes, it had only demanded a rather higher level of taxation than they had been accustomed to in the past.

In the political sphere the war dealt a final blow to the resistance to the introduction of democratic voting rights for men and to women. Even after the last of the nineteenth-century Reform Acts, that of 1884, only 58 per cent of the adult male population was entitled to vote in 1910. Property qualifications had been lowered, not abolished, restricting the vote to householders and lodgers paying more than £10 a year in rent. Those who owned land or business premises where they resided had two votes. By the middle years of the war it was widely recognized that full voting rights must form an ingredient in the post-war reconstruction of British society. A Speaker's Conference reported in 1917 to the effect that six months' residence should provide the basis for voting rights for men and that women should also be given the vote, though at a higher age than men. The Representation of the People Act which became law in June 1918 enfranchised more people than all the previous Reform Acts put together. The total electorate jumped from 7.5 million in 1910 to almost twenty million. When women under thirty were included in the franchise after 1928, over 90 per cent of the adult population had the vote. The recognition of the principle of 'one man, one vote' marked a belated acceptance of democratic rights, although some vestiges of the old system were to remain until 1948. A greatly expanded electorate was now to be a factor of political life.

Consequences

The impact of such a major event as the Great War upon the course of British society is difficult to assess against its longer-term evolutions. In most respects, it is clear, the war emphasized tendencies which were already evident. Greater state intervention, improvements, albeit uneven, in living standards, the growing emancipation of women, the strengthening of organized labour, the cultivation of a more collectivist and democratic polity, and the disintegration of pre-war certainties were all prefigured in Edwardian society. With the benefit of hindsight it is possible to see more clearly than contemporaries that many of the features thought of as consequences of the war were part of a longer-term process.

Immediate reactions were overshadowed by the tragedy of

the loss of almost three-quarters of a million men from the British Isles and the lasting reminder of the war in more than one and a half million serious casualties. Ten years after the armistice, almost two and a half million men were in receipt of a pension for war disabilities of some sort (approximately 40 per cent of the soldiers who had served in the war) and forty-eight special mental hospitals still tended 65,000 shell-shock victims. Soldiers whose wounds failed to heal or worsened provided a continuing call upon the medical services. In the year 1928, there were over 6,000 *new* issues of artificial limbs as a result of war wounds and the sight of blind and limbless ex-servicemen was a constant reminder in the inter-war years of the cost of the war. War deaths represented one in eight of the six million men from the British Isles who had served in the Great War. As well as representing innumerable private tragedies, the war dead accounted for just under 7 per cent of all males between fifteen and forty-nine in England and Wales in 1911. As a proportion of the total population these figures were smaller than in France or Germany but were, regardless, to give rise to the idea of a 'lost generation'. In fact the total loss was less dramatic in cold demographic terms than it appeared. Emigration had been running at a rate of almost 300,000 per year prior to 1914, and war casualties represented only two and a half times the annual outflow. As emigration had been drastically reduced by the war, it was perfectly possible to argue that the population of 1918 was actually higher than it might otherwise have been had the war not occurred.

Such calculations counted little beside the enormous sense of loss which the war produced amongst all classes. This was emphasized by the concentration of losses amongst the younger age groups of those eligible for war service. According to one estimate, 30.58 per cent of all men aged twenty to twenty-four in 1914 were killed and 28.15 per cent of those aged thirteen to nineteen. Moreover, behind the belief in a 'lost generation' was the feeling that those killed represented the flower of the generation. The 'best' – it was widely assumed – had volunteered first and had therefore suffered the highest casualties.

There was the conviction that it was the young officers, drawn from the universities, public schools and the upper classes, who had borne the brunt of the casualties, depriving the country of its future leaders. Study of military participation by social class had confirmed that at least in the first two years of the war a higher percentage of non-manual occupations enlisted. Whereas over 40 per cent of professional men joined the armed forces in 1914–16, only 25 per cent of miners did so. In part at least these discrepancies were the result of protected occupations, such as mining and engineering, which kept certain groups of manual workers out of the armed forces. It was also a consequence of the widespread poor health of the Edwardian working classes, which led to large numbers of them being turned down for military service. The result was that the population 'at risk' tended to come disproportionately from the middle and upper classes. The figures too for officer casualties were consistently higher than those of the rank and file, though the discrepancy was quite small, 15.2 per cent of all army officers dying, compared with 12.8 per cent of other ranks. There was of course no absolutely firm relationship between the loss of the 'best of the generation' and the loss of officers. None the less, the emphasis on the recruitment of 'gentlemen' into the officer corps at the outbreak of the war and the consequent commissioning of men of suitable attributes and attainments from the ranks tended to draw the officers from the existing social elites. Of the 13,403 students from Oxford who served in the war, 2,569, almost one in five, were killed. Cambridge showed virtually identical figures (13,126 served; 2,364 killed). Other universities showed higher than average casualty lists, though the proportions of those killed were usually lower than Oxbridge. Even so, in every case, the casualties amongst university graduates were far higher than the average for the total population. One group, the Oxford students who matriculated in 1913, suffered a casualty rate of 31 per cent killed. The major public schools showed similarly large casualties; of the 4,852 Etonians who served overseas in the war, 1,157 were killed, just over 20 per cent, a figure

similar to that for the other fifty-three public schools for which
data has been collected. That these casualties were disproportionately carried by the higher social classes has also been confirmed by studies of the death rate amongst the peerage, of
whom one in five of those who served died, according to
C. F. G. Masterman a death toll by violent death greater than
at any time since the Wars of the Roses.

More profound and less easy to gauge were the longer-term
cultural effects of the war. For the six million or more who
served in the armed forces, there were undoubtedly some consequences from the experience of mass soldiering. One factor
certainly was a broadening of horizons and a breaking-down
of the still powerful class barriers and provincialisms of British
society. The strong communal loyalties which had often led
groups of men to join up with their peers tended to be affected
by the common experiences of the war. Some jostling of life-
styles and background was almost inevitable. Young boys
straight from public school could, and did, find themselves in
charge of platoons of Durham miners or Manchester clerks.
Where defeat might have emphasized social divisions and produced widespread bitterness at the great sacrifice, the war had
been won. Stirrings of unrest in post-war Britain there undoubtedly were, but victory confirmed rather than destroyed
the conservatism of British society. For the common soldier,
moreover, the often startling innocence and ignorance which
preserved a kind of stoic endurance and naïve patriotism in
the darkest passages of the war was increasingly permeated by
aspects of the mass culture. Habits such as cigarette smoking,
the cinema, gambling, the use of contraceptives and the decline
of organized religion could all be in part attributed to the war.
Their exact place is often hard to identify amidst the myriad
reactions to the war, but a common experience shared by
millions of young men was bound to have subtle and far-
reaching effects upon post-war generations.

'Normalcy' or Revolution?

In spite of the upheaval created by the war, there was also an overwhelming desire to return as soon as possible to pre-war conditions. A widely articulated desire for a return to 'normalcy' conditioned the response to the post-war world. A conservative-dominated coalition government, led by Lloyd George, was unable and to some extent unwilling to continue in peace-time the draconian controls of the wartime administrative machine. The Ministry of Reconstruction set up in 1917 to investigate post-war needs and plans for them was dismantled in June 1919, just when it should have been at its peak of activity. Most other wartime ministries were also wound up, including Information, Blockade, Munitions, National Service, Food and Shipping. There were exceptions: the Ministry of Labour was retained and new ministries of Health and Transport were established. One other wartime control was extended when the Defence of the Realm Acts were made permanent under the Emergency Powers Act of 1920. This measure illustrated that the transition from war to peace had not been entirely smooth. The government had been forced by growing industrial unrest to equip itself with the powers to maintain control of essential services in defiance of trade-union militancy. Indeed for a time it appeared that the post-war period would not lead to peace, but to political upheaval.

There were several ingredients to the unrest which affected Britain in the immediate aftermath of the war. There were race riots in some of the major ports and clashes between the police and young people. The most serious, however, grew out of the grievances of troops over demobilization procedures and a mounting wave of industrial action which at times appeared to be attaining near-revolutionary proportions. Whereas the British army had escaped the widespread mutiny which affected the French army in 1917, the inadequacies of the demobilization plan provoked serious unrest at army camps both in England and France. There were disturbances at Dover, Folkestone and Calais, while in North Wales a mutiny in the Canadians' camp

at Rhyl led to fatal casualties. In February 1919 troops due to
return to France from leave four months after the war's end
demonstrated in Horse Guards Parade and had to be rounded
up by sections of the home garrison. A reorganization of
demobilization by Churchill on the basis of 'first in, first out'
went a considerable way towards pacifying the situation, as did
awarding higher pay to the troops required for occupation
duties in Germany. None the less, demobbed or demobilizing
soldiers were involved in a further series of disturbances in July
1919. The most serious occurred at Luton, where refusal to
allow an ex-servicemen's organization to hold a memorial
service for the official Peace Day celebrations on 19 July 1919
led to an attack on Luton Town Hall, where the local dignitaries
were planning a celebratory banquet. The Town Hall was set
on fire with petrol and gutted, while police and firemen were
attacked with bricks, bottles and stones. A subsequent assault
on Luton police station was ended only by a baton charge which
caused a hundred casualties. Shops were broken into and looted,
so that troops with fixed bayonets had to patrol the streets.
Similar, if less serious, disturbances clustering around the Peace
Day celebrations occurred in Wolverhampton, Salisbury,
Epsom, Coventry, Swindon and elsewhere.

In May and June 1919 there were also race riots in the
seaports, mainly directed against West Indian seamen recruited
into the merchant marine during the war. In East London,
Newport, Cardiff, Tyneside, Glasgow and Liverpool crowds
of whites attacked black people and ransacked their lodging
houses. Three people were killed in the riots in Cardiff and
another in Liverpool. There was also an undercurrent of
violence between youths and the police in London in July and
August, with serious clashes as the police attempted to 'move
on' crowds of young people gathering in the streets in several
of the London suburbs. Disturbances in Greenwich, Hammersmith, Tottenham, Edmonton, Barking and Brixton culminated in 'The battle of Wood Green' on 3 August 1919 in
which a crowd of several hundred youths attacked the police.
The most serious rioting, however, occurred in the first week

of August 1919 as a result of a strike by the Liverpool police. After the police struck on Friday night, 1 August, hundreds of shops were looted in Liverpool and Birkenhead. According to *The Times*:

the hooligans of the Scotland Road and the dock areas ... let themselves go ... In one district, rough-looking women kept close to the youths and indicated which shops were likely centres for spoil ... Later, the children of the looters ventured into the streets in droves, and sold bottles of beer and stout at a penny a time.

Troops were called in to control the crowds, eventually opening fire, killing one man and wounding another, and making 370 arrests.

The Liverpool police strike was itself the manifestation of the most serious challenge faced by the authorities in the years after the war (see pp. 100–102). The end of government controls led to rapid price increases and a series of bitter industrial disputes in which the pre-war Triple Alliance was reformed by the miners, railwaymen and transport workers. Strikes occurred in many industries, but the most seriously affected were the railways, mines and engineering works. The figures for working days lost through stoppages mounted to almost thirty-five million in 1919, to over twenty-six million in 1920, and to eighty-five million in 1921. Moreover these strikes were not only the result of economic circumstances. The labour movement had emerged immensely strengthened from the war and left-wing ideas flourished in the atmosphere of euphoria which followed the Bolshevik Revolution in Russia. A heady optimism and enthusiasm for the Russian example created a particularly politicized movement in places like Clydeside, South Wales, Sheffield, Merseyside and London. In Glasgow a general strike was called in support of the engineering workers' demand for a forty-hour week, and troops, supported by tanks, were sent in to police 'Red Clydeside'. Sympathy for Russia was shown during 1920, when dockers coordinated activity to prevent the government sending aid to the counter-revolutionary forces fighting the Bolsheviks.

'Red Clydeside' came to occupy a central place in the
mythology of the more militant sections of the labour movement between the wars, in which the events in Glasgow, cul-
minating in the Forty Hours' strike, were equated with the
wave of revolutionary unrest in Europe. The adoption of the
Bolshevik cause by some of its leaders, the attempt to set up
workers' and soldiers' councils, or 'soviets', and the appointment of the Marxist schoolmaster John Maclean as 'Soviet
Consul in Glasgow' contributed to a sense of participation in
an international revolutionary movement. The reality was
rather different. In spite of the commitment of leaders such
as MacLean and of some groups of workers, 'Red Clydeside'
betrayed as much the weakness as the strength of revolutionary
fervour. The strikes in the Clydeside area from 1915 onwards
were episodic, representing more the sectional interests and
concerns of different groups of workers than a unified and
politicized mass movement. The most consistent grievance was
over 'dilution', the attempt by the skilled workers to defend
their craft status from unskilled, often female, competition. In
early 1919 the 'revolutionary situation' dreamt of by Marxists
failed to materialize, as piecemeal concessions, force and internal conflicts undermined the work of the unofficial Clyde
Workers' Committee. Few unions were prepared to give
official backing to the Forty Hours' strike and several crucial
groups of workers, notably the tramwaymen and power
workers, refused to join in the strike call. Amongst the leaders,
too, there were divisions between moderates and extremists
over tactics. As in the past, and again at some subsequent points
up to 1945, even some of the most militant leaders were
reluctant to face up to the real implications of a revolutionary
general strike. It was a telling moment when a huge crowd
gathered in George Square on Friday, 31 January 1919, to hear
government replies to their demands, was unexpectedly charged
by the police. The response of two of the leaders, Emmanuel
Shinwell and Willie Gallacher, was not to meet violence with
violence, but to get strikers out of the square and calm the
situation down. Years later, Gallacher was to write his own

epitaph on 'Red Clydeside': 'Had we been capable of planning beforehand, or had there been an experienced revolutionary leadership of these great and heroic masses, instead of a march to Glasgow Green there would have been a march to Maryhill Barracks ... If we had gone there we could easily have persuaded the soldiers to come out, and Glasgow would have been in our hands.' There was almost certainly an element of wishful thinking in this. According to one historian, at least, the Forty Hours' strike 'would certainly have collapsed, and discredited unofficial action without any help from the government'. Another has called it 'more a portent of the future disunity of the left than a climax of wartime discontent'. The strike fizzled out as leaders were arrested, 12,000 troops were drafted in with six tanks and 100 lorries, and wages and rents were fixed by the government. The Clyde Workers' Committee never effectively recovered.

The Forty Hours' strike, however, did usher in a period of acute government concern about industrial and political unrest which lasted until the early 1920s. Cabinet minutes have revealed genuine fears of revolutionary activity and plans to use the full powers of the state against it. Preparations were made to maintain essential supplies, including the ear-marking of 40,000 lorries and 100,000 motor cars for use in the event of a strike. A draft Bill was even prepared in March 1919 to arrest trade-union leaders and prevent unions from drawing upon their strike funds, though it was never adopted. Hence while both 'Red Clydeside' and the Triple Alliance caused considerable alarm in government circles, the government remained firmly in control. Plans for post-war reconstruction were pushed ahead, partly at least with a view to undermining labour militancy, and determined use made of Emergency Powers, troops and police to maintain law and order. The collapse of the Triple Alliance, when in April 1921 the other two groups of workers failed to support the miners, brought the post-war phase of militancy and unrest almost to an end. In this, the government was aided by the ending of the post-war boom in the winter of 1920–21. Less favourable

economic conditions, namely growing unemployment and falling wages, took the steam out of union militancy. Unemployment doubled in the winter of 1920–21 and reached over two
million by the summer of 1921. Britain had entered the years
of the depression which were to provide the drab backcloth
to much of social life between the wars.

4. The Economy and Living Standards

An underlying paradox affects any interpretation of the social history of Britain between 1914 and 1945. On the other hand, the dominating impression of the era is of economic dislocation and instability: two world wars and a severe and persistent depression marked one of the most chequered periods for economic life at both national and local levels. The consequences of these events were obvious enough in the losses, upheaval and devastation caused by the wars and in the lengthening dole queues and derelict communities of the depressed areas. But alongside this catalogue of disruption and deprivation has to be placed the fact of major economic growth in Britain between these years. In spite of war and depression, economic growth permitted a rise in living standards for the majority of the population over the period as a whole. Whether measured in terms of real incomes, mass consumption or standards of health and welfare, side by side with the survival of large areas of poverty and deprivation the period witnessed a rise in material standards of living, shaping patterns of expenditure and lifestyle which were to develop still further in the affluence of the years after 1945.

War, Slump and Recovery

Britain entered the Great War as one of the most prosperous countries in the world. A century and a half of economic growth, expanding trade and the accumulation of foreign investments had led Britain to the position of being a major − if no longer the sole − workshop of the world and the hub of international trade and finance. Britain was still a leading upplier of coal, textiles, ships, iron and steel, and machinery to international markets and enjoyed a tremendous preeminence in particular fields. In 1913, the shipyards of North-East England alone produced a third of the world output of shipping. The cotton mills of Lancashire were still producing enough yarn and textiles to clothe half the world, contributing more than a quarter of the country's total exports. Britain was the second largest producer of coal in the world and its exports alone were greater than the national outputs of major powers like France and Russia. Britain's merchant fleet accounted for almost half the world tonnage, while abroad Britain was a major international creditor with a large inflow of invisible earnings from investments, shipping and insurance. With manufacturing and mining employing almost half the labour force and importing almost three-quarters of its foodstuffs and many of its raw materials, Britain's prosperity was, more than that of any other country in the world, dependent upon the fortunes of its export trades and the pattern of world trade. Britain was a wealthy industrial society – the wealthiest and the most industrialized in the world – but dependent on, and by implication vulnerable to, fluctuations in the pattern of world trade and the performance of its industries.

During the Edwardian era, the performance of the economy betrayed some signs of weakness, particularly in Britain's heavy commitment to the 'old staples' and a slow-down in economic growth. In 1914 textiles, coal, iron and steel, and shipbuilding provided three-quarters of Britain's exports and employed almost a quarter of the total working population. These traditional industries continued to dominate the economy at a time when the more recently industrializing countries, such as Germany and the United States, were beginning not only to challenge and overtake Britain's output of basic commodities such as coal and steel, but to develop new industries such as chemicals, electrical goods and skilled engineering more rapidly than Britain. Industrial inertia with capital and labour heavily concentrated in the 'old staples' and the attractiveness of overseas investment contributed to a backwardness in developing new sectors. While traditional industries remained reasonably prosperous, output lagged far behind those of Germany and the United States in many of the newer sectors. Overall, economic growth slowed down in 1900–1913 to little more than half what it had been prior to 1900. Abroad, France, Germany and the United States were all growing more rapidly than Britain, whose share of world trade had fallen from a third in 1870 to a seventh by 1914.

The Great War itself had several different effects. In terms of output it brought about a small fall in industrial production. This was hardly surprising given the mobilization of nearly six million men in the armed forces, but longer hours, the increased use of female and juvenile labour and more efficient organization permitted output in 1918 to reach 91 per cent of the level in 1913. Inevitably it was the armaments and related heavy industries which took the lion's share of production during the war. Steel, shipbuilding, engineering and other munitions-related industries boomed, while textiles, consumption industries and construction contracted. This process had some advantages. Britain was forced to develop some areas of industry which had hitherto been neglected. Chemicals, electrical goods, motor vehicles, aircraft and precision engineering were stimulated, as well as science-based industries such as radio and pharmaceuticals. Standardization, improved processes, mass production and more efficient management, including the more sophisticated use of statistics and accounting systems, also had lasting benefits. Given also the limited effects of physical destruction, apart from the loss of a fifth of the merchant shipping fleet, the country emerged from the war in terms of productive equipment relatively well.

There were costs, however, which went beyond the losses of manpower. The war involved an expenditure of £11,325 million pounds, including loans made to allies, many of which, such as those to Russia, were never to be repaid. About a third of this was raised through increased taxation, while liquidation of overseas investments raised another £500 million. But the bulk of the cost of the war was met by borrowing, both at home and overseas. 'War loans' from the public increased the National Debt from £650,000 to £8,000 million and Britain also borrowed £1,300 million from overseas, mainly from the United States. Britain was to emerge from the war a debtor nation, where before the war it had been a creditor. No less serious, the exigencies of war finance had forced the country off the Gold Standard with the adoption of paper £1 and 10s. notes which could no longer be converted directly into gold. Inflation and the post-war dislocation of the international financial system created a much more difficult climate in which Britain had to compete. Attempts to restore confidence, such as the return to the Gold Standard in 1925, simply left Britain with an over-valued currency and eroded still further her competitive position.

A more important consequence of the war was its distorting effect upon economic activity in the country. While the encouragement of some war-related industries was in the long term beneficial, the 'forcing-house' atmosphere of the war meant that industries were developed for wartime rather than peace-time needs. While normal conditions might have permitted a more gradual adjustment to new needs and markets, the war had acted as an overwhelming determinant of economic activity, with no guarantee that the industries fashioned for the war would be those most suitable for immediate post-war conditions. Moreover, at a time when Britain was already over-committed to the 'old staples', war requirements had encouraged still further investment in such areas as shipbuilding and iron and steel. Most seriously of all, the war profoundly disrupted Britain's export trade. Diversion of industrial capacity to the war effort and shortages of shipping made it difficult to supply traditional markets, cutting total exports by a half. As a result, overseas markets were lost to industrial rivals in Japan and the United States and through the substitution by traditional customers of home-produced for British goods. For the 'old staples' in particular, the inter-war years were to mark a difficult period of adjustment to much stronger competition and, ultimately, a failure to recover their pre-war position.

Initially, the ending of the war released a frantic speculative boom, fuelled by rising prices, the release of wartime profits in the form of bonus shares, and the widespread belief that pre-war conditions would return and with them the demand for British goods. There was a 'craze of speculation' in the Lancashire cotton industry, in which 42 per cent of spinning capacity changed hands in the years 1919–20 at seven times its pre-war valuation and new mills were constructed in expectation of a return to peace-time conditions. Nor was the mood confined to cotton: shipbuilding, shipping and engineering all anticipated a return to 'normalcy'. Shipbuilding capacity increased from 580 berths in 1914 to 806 by 1920, while production rose from 1,348,120 tons in 1918 to 2,055,624 in 1920. The collapse began in 1920 with an increase in government borrowing rates, a fall in prices and the beginnings of a rise in unemployment. By 1921–2 the impact of post-war trading conditions was making itself felt both in the reduction of exports and levels of production. Exports of cotton textiles in 1922 were less than half the 1913 figure; consumption of raw cotton had fallen from 2,178 million lb. in 1913 to 1,066 million lb. by 1921 and was never again to reach pre-war levels. Coal production by 1922 was down by 40 million tons on the 1913 output of 287 million tons and exports were only a third of pre-war. The effects were demonstrated in the rise of unemployment to almost two million by June 1921.

The bursting of the post-war boom saw the beginning of the contraction and dislocation of the 'old staples' which was to dominate the economic climate in the inter-war years and bring with it the problem of persistent mass unemployment. These industries were faced not only with stronger foreign competition but also with a more unsettled and sluggish international economy. Whereas world trade had grown by at least 25 per cent in every decade between 1830 and 1914, it grew by only 8½ per cent in the 1920s. Hopes of a stronger revival were dashed by the Wall Street Crash of 1929 which precipitated the most profound depression that the industrial

world had experienced for a century or more. The 'ailing
giants' of the twenties were hammered in the trough of a depression which saw world trade slump by 35 per cent between
1929 and 1933 and a major financial crisis in 1931 which forced
Britain off the Gold Standard and led the government to
introduce harsh deflationary measures. Steel output was halved
between 1929 and 1931; shipbuilding, already reduced by 1930
to half its output of the immediate post-war years, almost came
to a complete standstill in 1932, when only 133,000 tons of
shipping were built. Coal output fell by a fifth between
1929 and 1933, while cotton exports were halved in two years.
Though recovery began in 1933, world trade had still only
reached its 1929 level by the outbreak of the Second World
War. For the 'old staples' which had customarily exported 40
per cent of their output (in case of cotton 80 per cent) these
conditions were bound to be serious. In one case alone,
Britain's exports of cotton to India were reduced to a tenth
by the effects of the slump and the rise of competition from
the domestic Indian output and Japan. Overall Britain's share
of world exports fell from a seventh in 1913 to just under a
tenth by 1937.

However, this bleak picture can be exaggerated. While all
the old staples shed labour, bringing unemployment to the areas
dependent upon them, only shipbuilding and cotton showed
an absolute decline in terms of output in the years between
1914 and 1939. By the mid-1930s there were signs of modest
recovery in some of the heavy industries. Steel output rose
from its floor of 5.2 million tons in 1932 to reach 13 million
tons by 1937. New steel plants were built at Corby, Ebbw
Vale and Shotton, while at places such as Workington, Consett
and Sheffield extra capacity was opened. In shipbuilding a ruthless and often painful process of reducing capacity and subsidies for fresh building encouraged a modest revival in output
by 1937. The coal industry, too, achieved a measure of stability.
Production revived from its most depressed levels of 1932–3,
though it was to remain 16 per cent lower than in 1913. Some
export markets were never to be recaptured and competition

from electricity for domestic industry and household use made the home market more difficult than it had been before 1914. None the less, significant improvements in productivity were made, with large modern pits being opened and striking increases being made in productivity through the use of machinery. By 1939, 61 per cent of coal was cut by machinery and output per man had risen by over a third between 1924 and 1938. The textile industry also achieved a measure of stabilization after a savage reduction in production capacity. Between 1929 and 1939 spinning and weaving capacity in the cotton industry was cut by a third. In contrast, the woollen industry, never so dependent on exports, was able to achieve higher output by 1939 than it had in 1930.

If the economic history of the inter-war years had been solely that of the major industries in 1914, it would have been a story of slump and only very modest recovery. In fact, the economic history of the inter-war years was much more positive than the fortunes of the 'old staples' suggested. By 1924 Britain had regained the level of production in 1913, in spite of substantial reductions in working hours. Overall by the end of the 1930s the gross domestic product was more than half as great again as it had been in 1913 and the index of industrial production stood 75 per cent higher in 1935–8 than in 1910–13. In spite of the problems of the traditional sectors, the inter-war years were marked by substantial economic growth, representing a significant improvement on the Edwardian era and in comparison with most other European countries.

Growth was most evident in some of the newer sectors of industry. The development of the electricity supply industry was amongst the most striking. In 1926 a Central Electricity Board was set up which rationalized the large number of small, inefficient power stations and built a new generation of power stations connected through a national grid of high-voltage transmission lines. By 1933 the grid was virtually complete, giving Britain one of the most advanced systems of electricity supply in the world. The 'march of the pylons', combined with the development of small efficient electric motors, revolutionized the location of industry, releasing it from its traditional dependence upon the coalfields and allowing its dispersal away from the centres of the first industrial revolution. Output of electricity grew fourfold, in spite of the slump, between 1925 and 1939. Whereas in 1920 there had been only 730,000 electricity consumers in Britain, by the end of the 1930s there were almost nine million and new consumers were being added at a rate of about three-quarters of a million per year. Whereas in 1920 only one house in seventeen had been wired up for electricity, by 1930 the figure was one house in three and by 1939 two houses in three. By 1938 this largely new industry was employing 325,000 people, double the 1924 figure. From being a novelty prior to 1914, electricity between the wars brought an increasingly wide range of services and consumer durables to communities and homes alike: the cinema, broadcasting, the suburban train all depended on electricity; electricity also brought the first wave of electric domestic appliances: vacuum cleaners, refrigerators, cookers and radio sets.

Another source of industrial growth was the motor vehicle industry. In 1913 Britain had produced 34,000 motor vehicles of all kinds; by 1924 the figure had risen to 146,000 and by 1937 had reached 507,000. Even in the worst years of the slump from 1929 to 1933 Britain had produced more motor vehicles than in any previous year. A major industry employing almost 400,000 people had been created by the end of the 1930s. Mass production by assembly-line methods allowed the concentration of the industry in a few major centres, especially in the Midlands, at Coventry, Birmingham, Luton and Oxford, and in the London area. The first real mass-market motor car, the Austin Seven, was produced in 1921, soon followed by Morris Motors and Ford's, the British branch of the American concern. Mass production and a booming market led to a fall in prices, so that by 1935–6 a typical small 'family car' could be bought for half what it cost ten years earlier. The motor industry was part of a general development of the engineering industry, whose output, mainly consisting of motor vehicles, aircraft, cycles, electrical equipment and consumer durables, was 60 per cent higher in 1937 than it had been in 1924. Re-armament from the mid-1930s ensured a fresh flow of orders, particularly for the aircraft industry, with cities such as Coventry and Bristol becoming major centres of production.

Breakthroughs in the development of plastics and artificial fibres also contributed to growth in the chemical industry. Plastics, usually in the form of 'bakelite', became a standard material for many consumer goods, such as radio sets, while the development of 'rayon' and an increasing range of artificial fibres were adopted for the clothing industry. Giant combines, such as Imperial Chemical Industries (ICI), formed in 1926, produced a wide range of products including artificial fibres, synthetic dyes, pharmaceutical goods and fertilizers in an industry which employed 100,000 people by 1939. Perhaps the most spectacular advance was made in the construction industry through the growing demand for both private and public building. The industry grew at almost double the average rate for the economy during the inter-war period, but its fastest expansion occurred during the housing boom of the middle and late thirties, when construction and related industries employed almost a million people.

Growth in the inter-war years was not simply a matter of 'new' industries replacing old, though this played an important part. Britain was fortunate in that the demographic trends produced a population in which the fifteen to sixty-four age group who made up the potential working population were growing at a faster rate than the population as a whole. Although the number of older dependants was growing slowly, it was more than offset by the decline in young dependants resulting from a falling birth rate, with a growth in total working population both in absolute terms and as a percentage of the total population. In 1871 the fifteen to sixty-four age group represented 59 per cent of the population, by 1937 it was 69.3 per cent. A rise in the 'working population' which added more than three and a quarter million to the workforce between 1924 and 1937 meant, crudely, an increase in the proportion of 'producers' to 'consumers', facilitating a rise in national output and

in national output per head. Secondly, technological advance
had a large part to play. New processes and methods of production, many pioneered before or during the war, permitted
an increase in productivity in both traditional and new industries. Electricity transformed the physical labour of cutting
coal in modern pits as well as powering a wide range of tools
for the engineering industry. Mass production and assembly-
line methods, seen especially in the motor vehicle industry,
also increased output. Although the older industries shared some
of these increases in productivity, a major part was played by
the shift of resources from the slower-growing sectors into the
new industries, which by 1935 accounted for a fifth of national
output. Taken with other growing areas such as construction,
road transport and electricity supply, Britain experienced an
unprecedented improvement in efficiency and output per head.

Moreover, as well as increases in the economically active
portion of the population and improvements in techniques, the
inter-war years also witnessed important changes in the organization and pattern of economic activity. The rationalization
of smaller companies into large combines was one of the most
striking features of business development during the period.
Out of the mergers of the twenties and thirties emerged industrial giants like ICI, EMI, Unilever, Courtauld's and Royal
Dutch Shell. Several of these large firms were involved in trading in different countries, but in many cases the impetus to
rationalization came from the rise of mass consumer markets,
new forms of distribution through motor transport and the
economic advantages given by size and concentration. Significantly a large number of the giant concerns were involved
in the new industries, such as Nestlé's in food processing and
Dunlop in tyre-making. Factories too tended to be larger,
employing more men. Ford, for example, employed seven
thousand people at its Dagenham factory by 1932 and several
of the firms developing sites on the fringes of London built
on a similar scale, such as the Hoover factory opened at
Perivale in 1933.

As mass-production methods began to be used for the manufacture of consumer goods, important developments occurred in patterns of trading and marketing. Goods were now more usually packaged and priced by the manufacturer, rather than by the shopkeeper. Motor transport allowed direct delivery to multiple branches and the first 'mail-order' schemes were introduced. Under the impact of this 'retailing revolution', almost a thousand new 'chain stores' were built in the interwar period, showing virtually no decline with the depression. Marks and Spencer, for example, one of the most successful of the new retailers, opened 129 stores from 1931 to 1935 and extended sixty more. Turnover in the company rose from £2,493,000 in 1929 to £23,448,000 by 1939 and the company had opened or extended 258 stores. By the outbreak of the Second World War, Marks and Spencer, Lipton's, Sainsbury's and Woolworths had become household names in almost every medium-sized town, bringing with them a wider range of foodstuffs, clothing and household goods than had been available at the traditional corner shop and retailer. Many of these developments were stimulated by the progress of advertising, as mass production for a consumer market and the development of new outlets in newspapers and cinemas created a wider range of opportunities for sales promotion. By 1938 it was estimated that over £100 million were being spent on advertising of all kinds, mainly through newspapers. Even during the worst years of the depression, national and local newspapers bombarded the public with advertisements for clothing, cosmetics, cigarettes, foodstuffs and household goods of every description. Sales gimmicks of all kinds played a large part in promoting brand names into household words, with free gifts, 'sales' and special offers, such as Woolworth's famous boast of 'nothing over sixpence'. For many items credit facilities were becoming more readily available. By 1938 two-thirds of all larger purchases were made using hire-purchase agreements, bringing a wide range of household goods, such as furniture, into the reach of sections of the community who could not in the past have afforded them.

The growth of consumer industries and of different patterns

of marketing and retailing led to important developments in
the location and structure of the labour force. The service industries, such as distribution, transport and administration,
showed rapid growth throughout the inter-war period, continuing to rise even through the worst years of the slump. The
distributive trades showed the greatest increase, from 1,661,000
workers in 1920–22 to 2,436,000 in 1937–8. Job opportunities
were expanding for shopworkers, clerical staff, transport
employees and the professional and managerial 'salariat'. The
growth of 'white-collar' employment was registered in a census
of employment which found an increase in administrative staff
from 11.8 per cent in 1924 to 15.1 per cent in 1935. Many
of these posts were taken up by women, especially in the clerical
field, adding substantially to the numbers of women in employment. The overall effect was to increase the proportion of the
workforce involved in the service sector. The heavy industries
suffered a net loss of workers during the thirties, while the
service sector witnessed a rise which was to continue after the
Second World War. Even before the economic expansion of
the post-1945 period, the pattern of employment which is
traditionally associated with affluence – the transference of
workers from producing goods to providing services – was
being developed rapidly in the inter-war years.

The number of unemployed began to fall after 1933 and,
in spite of the deflationary policies of the government, an upswing in world trade, policies of cheap money, protection and
the restoration of financial confidence all contributed to rapid
economic growth in the mid-thirties which provided the basis
for a rise in living standards for those in work and
prosperity for some parts of the country. While unemployment
rates remained tragically high in some of the depressed areas,
the recovery of some parts of the economy could be seen in
the mushrooming suburbs, the factories lining the arterial roads
of the capital, the new industrial estates, and the consumer-
orientated industries of the Midlands and the South-East.
Hunger marchers from South Wales, Scotland or the North
on their way to London often recorded the bewildering ex-

perience of moving from near derelict communities where as many as three-quarters of the population were out of work into parts of the country which were experiencing almost boom conditions. One marcher from South Wales in 1936 recorded how he found Slough thronged with Welshmen who had come to seek work in the expanding light industries of the home counties. 'Thousands lined the streets,' he wrote in his diary, 'the accents were so thick I thought we were in Rhondda, with this difference, instead of silent pits, massive factories all lit up were in full go.' Another from Liverpool recorded his astonishment at encountering factories in the Midlands advertising 'vacancies'.

This recovery was not initially the result of re-armament. Most of it was based on increased consumer expenditure and concentrated in industries which met these needs – based more upon the door-to-door vacuum cleaner salesman, the car dealer and the estate agent than war-related industries. Growing international tension, however, did begin to have some effect upon the economy, particularly after 1936. Between 1933 and 1938 the British government spent £1,200 million on military expenditure, the bulk of it concentrated on naval construction and aircraft, bringing a much-needed boost to some of the more depressed sectors. To take one example, the fortunes of the shipbuilding firm Cammell Laird at Birkenhead, whose total order book in 1932 consisted of a solitary dredger, were transformed by the award in 1934 of a £3 million contract to build the 20,000-ton aircraft carrier *Ark Royal*. In the case of steel, where recovery based upon the demand for consumer goods, construction materials and motor vehicles was already under way, re-armament 'topped up' demand by 1937 to the point where the industry was working at full capacity for the first time since the Great War. In spite of attempts to contain arms spending, plans announced in 1936 to double the number of front-line aircraft and modernize the navy meant that Britain was already moving into a position where defence expenditure was playing a major role in the economy. With the Munich Crisis of 1938, followed by the German occupation of Prague and the threat to Poland, Britain was forced into a hasty re-equipment of the army in addition to the expenditure on the navy and the air force.

Thus, on the eve of the Second World War, the British economy was beginning to feel the beneficial effects both of defence spending and of a more generalized economic revival. The legacy of the inter-war years was felt both in the presence of over a million unemployed *and* in the rapid growth of the economy. Although the threat of a renewed down-turn in the economy was encountered in 1937–8 with a slight rise in the number of unemployed, defence spending was sufficient to stave off the threat of a renewed plunge into depression.

Wages and Incomes

In spite of the setbacks of two world wars and the depression, national income rose in both monetary and real terms between 1913 and 1945. Although there were contrary short-term fluctuations, real income per head increased overall by approximately a third. Crude averages of this kind, however, tell little of the actual distribution of incomes and of wealth. Not all was distributed as wages and salaries, and even that which was was not distributed equally amongst the population. That being said, the most striking feature of the period was the significant increase in real earnings for those in work: it produced the central paradox of this period, the contrast between improving living standards for a majority of the population and the survival of poverty for a significant minority.

Even by 1900 what Paul Thompson has called 'a critical transition in the standard of living' had taken place. The majority of the population now had a small margin of income above that required for bare subsistence. It was this, often small, surplus of income which encouraged so many of the developments in consumerism before the Great War, including mass advertising, the beginnings of suburban development, chain-stores and a wide range of cheap branded goods. Most of the population derived their living as wage- and salary-earners, of whom wage-earners were by far the largest group. For these people the crucial determinant of living standards was the interplay between wages, prices and employment. Average wage rates more than doubled as a result of the First World War, but were matched for many by a comparable rise in prices. After 1922 wage rates showed only minor fluctuations, generally falling during the depression and beginning to rise again in the years immediately before the Second World War. Prices, however, changed more dramatically, rising during and after the First World War, but then falling rapidly during the depression. Overall, the cost of living

Table 5: Wages, prices and real earnings, 1913–38

	Weekly wage rates	Retail prices	Average annual real wage earnings
	(1930 = 100)		
1913	52.4	63.3	82.8
1919	–	136.1	–
1920	143.7	157.6	92.2
1921	134.6	143.0	94.1
1922	107.9	115.8	93.2
1923	100.0	110.1	90.8
1924	101.5	110.8	91.6
1925	102.2	111.4	91.7
1926	99.3	108.9	91.2
1927	101.5	106.0	95.8
1928	100.1	105.1	95.2
1929	100.4	103.8	96.7
1930	100.0	100.0	100.0
1931	98.2	93.4	105.1
1932	96.3	91.1	105.7
1933	95.3	88.6	107.6
1934	96.4	89.2	108.1
1935	98.0	90.5	108.3
1936	100.2	93.0	107.7
1937	102.8	97.5	105.4
1938	106.3	98.7	107.7

Source: D. H. Aldcroft, *The Inter-War Economy: Britain, 1919–1939*, Batsford, 1970, pp. 352, 364.

index fell by more than a third between 1920 and 1938 and, crucially, during the early thirties, prices fell faster than wages, with the result that real earnings rose. As a consequence, average real incomes remained consistently higher in the inter-war years than in 1913, while during the thirties, for those in work, the fall in prices meant a substantial improvement in living standards compared with the 1920s. During the Second World War further gains in real incomes were obtained. Though wage rates rose more or less in line with prices, full employment, longer hours and bonus payments meant that by 1945 real earnings were about 20 per cent greater than they had been in 1938, described by Sidney Pollard as 'the most striking shift of incomes to wage-earners in any comparable period'. By 1945 average real earnings for those in regular employment stood more than a third higher than in 1913. Combined with virtual full employment after 1945 the Second World War continued a process by which average real incomes had risen substantially. Second, as well as gains in real wages, there was a reduction in average family size, producing a rise in the income per head in each household. This was especially important for the working classes, amongst whom the biggest falls in family size occurred between the wars. It not only permitted money to be spent in improving the quality of essential items such as housing, food and clothing, but also allowed a higher proportion of spending on non-necessities and semi-luxuries.

There were also some redistributive elements at work which favoured wage-earners. Although the number of wage-earners in the occupied population fell from 74.1 per cent in 1913 to 71.4 per cent in 1938, they continued to claim about the same portion of the national income in wages. In the long term this reflected a shift in resources, with the wage-earners gaining slightly relative to salaried groups. There was also evidence that business profits were squeezed to lower levels during the depression of the inter-war years. Even with recovery, profit margins failed to regain the level they had achieved prior to 1914, leaving a greater share for wages, salaries and taxation. The last of these, taxation, also produced a shift in resources in favour of the poorer sections of the community. Rates of taxation were raised by the Great War and remained consistently higher than before 1914. Higher taxation helped to finance an increase of spending on the social services from £101 million in 1913 to £596 million in 1938, representing an increase in the share of the gross national product from 4.1 per cent to 11.3 per cent and an increase in the amount per head from £2.2 to £12.5. Even taking price changes into account this represented a threefold increase. Although some of this increase could be said to have been paid for by the working classes themselves through National Insurance contributions and indirect taxes, a study carried out in 1945 concluded that the redistribution of income from rich to poor by central government in 1937 amounted to as much as £200–250 million, the bulk of the gain going to those with incomes under £125 a year. The total effect was to raise the incomes of the working classes by 8–14 per cent and reduce those of the upper and middle classes by 10–18 per cent. A later study suggested that the total redistributed was as high as £386 million, £274 million going to those with incomes under £125 a year, the major 'losers' being those on incomes over £2,000 a year. Whereas before 1914 the working classes were contributing in taxation more than the cost of social services from which they benefited, by 1925–6 they contributed only 85 per cent of the cost, falling to 79 per cent in 1935–6.

Both expenditure surveys and budgets suggest that the average family enjoyed an improvement in living standards during this period. According to the Ministry of Labour's budgetary inquiries the average family income in 1937–8 was more than double what it had been in 1913–14 and, at least as important, spread over a family only four-fifths the size. But the concept of the 'average family' concealed a kaleidoscope of differing circumstances and levels of income. For example, according to an analysis of incomes in 1938, the great majority of the population, some 88 per cent, had incomes less than £250 a year or £5 a week, of whom 31 per cent earned less than

£2 10s. At the other end of the scale there were half a
million people who had incomes over £685 a year and a smaller
minority, some two thousand, with annual incomes over
£20,000 per year, averaging £43,500 before tax. For most of
the inter-war years, the average industrial wage for men and
boys remained under £3 per week. These varied from under
£2 for agricultural workers to nearer £4 for those engaged
in the newspaper and printing industries. Actual earnings
depended for many workers upon the regularity of work, affected by short-time working, the amount of overtime, seasonal
lay-offs and the ever-present threat of unemployment. Many
dock workers, for example, were organized on a casual basis
with great irregularity of earnings. Nowhere were variations
clearer than in coalmining, where wages depended on the
number of shifts worked, and in turn upon the demand for
different types of coal. Wage cuts were common in some of
the basic industries both during the early 1920s and in the worst
phase of the slump between 1928 and 1933. The ability to command higher wages also varied considerably from region to
region. Wages of workers in the booming motor car and
engineering industries of the South and the Midlands might
be as high as £4 by the mid-1930s, whereas men of comparable
or higher skill in the textile or shipbuilding industries of the
North, Scotland or Wales could easily be earning less than £3
(see Table 6).

Averages also conceal the many workers who existed at or
below the average income. Agricultural workers, whose wages
averaged 31s. 8d. in 1929 and only 34s. 7d. in 1938, were one
of the largest categories, but there were many others, such as
general labourers, textile workers, some coalminers and shopworkers whose wages fell far below the average. But by far
the largest category of low-paid workers were women and
juveniles. Women's wages were on average rated at a proportion of about only half that of men, often for similar and, in
some cases, more skilled work. Average full-time earnings per
week for women and girls compared with men are shown
below in Table 7. Along with juvenile labour, women made

Table 6. Average earnings for manual workers, 1906–35
(£ per annum)

	1906	1924	1935
Skilled			
Coalface workers	112	180	149
Fitters	90	157	212
Engine drivers	119	276	258
Compositors	91	209	218
Semi-skilled and unskilled			
Pottery workers	77	171	173
Bus and tram drivers (London)	107	190	218
Agricultural labourers	48	82	89

Source: J. Burnett, *A History of the Cost of Living*, Penguin Books, 1969, pp. 300–301.

up the lowest-paid section of the workforce. Like juveniles, they were often more able to find work for the reason that they were less costly to employ than men. Wages for women in domestic service and retailing were amongst the lowest of all categories of employment, sometimes falling below £1 a week to as little as 10s. for young shop assistants.

Salaried staff, a group who made up an increasing proportion of the labour force between the wars, received a rather smaller increase in income than wage-earners, an average 71 per cent rise between 1911/13 and 1938 compared with 103 per cent for wage-earners. However, as a group, the salaried workers continued to enjoy most of the advantages which had made the step up to salaried status one of the principal aspirations of the Victorian and Edwardian period: steady earnings, more secure employment, the possibility of a small pension and

Table 7: Male and female earnings, 1924–35 (shillings per week)

	1924	1931	1935
Men and boys	58.9	57.3	56.6
Women and girls	28.4	28.0	27.2

'prospects'. None the less, the wages of the 'black-coated' workers (Table 8) showed a significant rise by the Second World
War, though generally salaried staff in private business offices
or banks fared better than government employees, whose wages
were cut during the economic crisis of 1931–2. Average weekly
salaried earnings for men tended to fluctuate around a level
of £4 per week during the inter-war years. While teachers
were an exceptional case, taking a pay cut of 11 per cent, the
majority of clerical workers managed to survive the worst of
the depression with only minor reductions of salary.

Table 8: Annual salaries of clerical workers, 1911/13–1935
(£ per annum)

	1911/13	1924	1935
Civil service clerical officer	116	284	260
Railway clerk	76	221	224
Bank clerk	142	280	368
Civil service shorthand typist	79	179	162

Source: John Burnett, *A History of the Cost of Living*, Penguin Books,
1969, p. 299.

Weekly-paid salaried and wage-earning employees earning
less than £250 per year made up the great majority of the
population. Above them were the 12 per cent or so of tax-
payers with incomes over that level. These ranged from the
reasonably prosperous professional or business man to the very
wealthy commanding personal incomes in excess of £20,000
a year. Inevitably, individual circumstances varied enormously,
but an indication of average salaries for some of the more
important professional groups is given in Table 9. The incomes of these groups rose by considerably more than the rate
of price increases. Even the lowest-paid, the clergy, kept well
ahead of the rates paid to the most highly paid skilled workers
or the average of salaried earnings.

Above the higher professionals lay the truly wealthy. An
analysis of income groupings in 1938 shows that of the top
100,000 incomes (out of 23,000,000), those over £2,000 per

Table 9: Average professional incomes 1913/14–1935/7
(£ per annum)

	1913/14	1922/4	1935/7
Barristers	478	1,124	1,090
General Practitioners	395	756	1,094
Clergy	206	332	370
Managers	200	480	440
		(1924/5)	(1938)

Source: John Burnett, *A History of the Cost of Living*, Penguin Books, 1969, p. 298.

year took 11.7 per cent of total pre-tax income. Amongst this group were two thousand incomes averaging £43,500 a year before tax. Although these figures revealed a gross disparity between the top and the bottom of the earnings league, they also reflected a significant change since the Edwardian era. Already there was some tendency for the income pyramid to broaden out in its middle and lower levels. It was a tendency which had become evident since the Great War and which was to continue after the Second World War. Even taking pre-tax income alone, the share of the top 100,000 incomes had been reduced to 5.3 per cent by 1956. Whereas the top million incomes still accounted for 27.8 per cent of total income in 1938, by 1956 this figure had been reduced to 17.4 per cent. In other words, some levelling-down of incomes was already evident by the inter-war years, but the most significant developments awaited the Second World War, when income distribution was drastically altered in favour of those earning less than £300 a year in 1938. According to one set of calculations, the real, pre-tax income of the top 100,000 fell by 64 per cent between 1938 and 1949 and of the top half a million by 37 per cent. On the eve of the Second World War, the wealthiest section of the community was on the brink of a far bigger redistribution of income than had been experienced since 1914.

Already, therefore, taxation was beginning to take a considerable proportion from the highest income groups. A composite of all taxation, including estimated shares of indirect taxes, expressed as a percentage of income for a family of two adults and three dependent children, living on an earned income of £10,000 per year (Table 10), shows this. Here the effect of the First World War is very evident, raising taxation on the highest incomes to completely new levels which, although reduced in the inter-war years, still in 1937–8 approximated to 40 per cent of pre-tax income. The top group, those two thousand earning an average of £43,500 per annum in 1938, kept only a little over a third of it after tax.

Table 10:
Percentage of income taken by
taxation on £10,000 per annum

1913–14	8.0
1918–19	42.5
1923–4	37.1
1925–6	31.2
1930–31	35.8
1937–8	39.1

Living Standards

What did these figures mean in terms of living standards for the widely divergent groups mentioned above, ranging from those with, at best, only a small margin of extra income over and above that required for bare subsistence to the almost fabulously wealthy? The most significant statistic relates to the average figures for consumer expenditure per head which, in real terms, rose from an average of £75.38 in 1910–14 to £92.76 in 1935–8, an increase of almost a quarter. There was clear evidence from the social surveys that part of this increase was accounted for by improvements in the standard of living of the working classes. While there continued to exist a hard-core of poverty, considered more fully later, the years between 1914 and 1945 also saw major advances in the position of the average family.

The rise in living standards was seen most clearly in the amount spent on extra food, raising per capita food consumption by 30–35 per cent between the wars. Not only was more food bought but also a greater variety, particularly of fresh foods, bringing with it improvements in health, reflected in both disease and mortality rates. The annual consumption of particular foods showed some remarkable increases on pre-1914 standards. Between 1909–13 and 1934 consumption of fruit rose by 88 per cent; vegetables, 64 per cent; butter and margarine, 50 per cent; and eggs, 46 per cent. Moreover, the development of new retail methods, particularly in the selling of branded, pre-packaged goods, and of food-processing ideas, many of them pioneered in America, brought a much wider range of foods, drinks and confectionery into the home. It was during the inter-war years that brand names such as Kelloggs, Heinz, Birds, Bisto and Ovaltine became standard items on the weekly shopping list. At the end of the Great War the range of canned foods available was restricted to salmon, corned beef, soup and California fruits, but thereafter firms like Heinz, Crosse and Blackwell, and Campbell vastly extended the range. By the thirties almost every kind of domestic and foreign fruit, meat, game, fish and vegetable was available in tinned form, even in country districts. 'Quick' Quaker Oats and American-style breakfast cereals, taken with milk and sugar, like the ubiquitous cornflakes or varieties of 'puffed' wheat and barley, were now being bought by even some of the poorest homes. Much as concerned social investigators and nutritional experts might lament it, the British working classes showed an almost irresistible urge to use part of their increased spending power on a plethora of sweets, snacks, savouries and processed foods. Beside the great evolutions of wages, prices and employment, not to mention those of social welfare and medicine, significant landmarks were also passed when in 1929, for the first time, a million packets of potato 'crisps' were sold and when the Nestlé company introduced 'instant' coffee to the consumer in 1932.

Cheaper food, a rise in real incomes and a fall in average

family size permitted a greater proportion of household incomes
to be spent on non-essentials. Whereas in 1914 the average
working-class family devoted 60 per cent of its income to food
and a further 16 per cent to rent and rates, by 1937–8 these
two items had fallen to 35 per cent and 9 per cent respectively.
Much of the extra income went on other items, such as fuel
and light, clothing, household goods, tobacco, newspapers,
transport, leisure and entertainment. All of these areas of expenditure showed marked development between the wars.
Evidence of the change since the Edwardian era could also be
found in the growth of small savings, particularly in the building societies, whose deposits rose from £82 million in 1920
to £717 million in 1938.

Combined with increased opportunities for leisure through
the reduction of the working week by an average of six hours
a week and the spread of paid holidays to over eleven million
people by 1939, many of them manual workers, the growth in
social welfare in areas such as pensions, housing and national
insurance, and the benefits brought by technological improvements like the widespread availability of gas, electricity, cheap
transport and household appliances, the inter-war years could be
seen as marking a very significant improvement in the material
standard of living of those sections of the working classes who
could obtain regular employment. Even in the depressed areas,
where many of these benefits passed the unemployed by, a
commentator like George Orwell could still remark on the
bizarre situation he found in Wigan and elsewhere:

Twenty million people are underfed but literally everyone in England has access to a radio. What we have lost in food we have gained
in electricity. Whole sections of the working class who have been plun-
dered of all they really need are being compensated, in part, by
cheap luxuries which mitigate the surface of life ... It is quite likely
that fish-and-chips, art-silk stockings, tinned salmon, cut-price
chocolate ... the movies, the radio, strong tea and the football pools
have between them averted revolution.

Whether or not the effects of increased consumption were as
important as Orwell suggested, they were certainly making

many lives at the lower end of the social pyramid more comfortable and varied. For many social critics, however, the development of consumerism was seen as a pernicious phenomenon, robbing the poor of the spare capital which might have alleviated temporary hardship and build up property. Thus John Hilton in *Rich Man, Poor Man* (1944) asked what had happened to the additional purchasing power obtained since the First World War:

Well a good deal of it has gone, of course, in better feeding and clothing and housing and furnishing and reading and holidaying – and quite right too. But it has also gone, along with what was already going in such directions, on pools, perms, and pints, on cigarettes, cinemas and singles-and-splashes; on turnstiles, totalizators, and twiddlems: and on all manner of two pennyworths of this and that.

But the really telling comments came from those who could contrast conditions in the inter-war years with what they had known before 1914. Thus Thomas Jones, writing of even so unpropitious an environment as Glasgow in 1932 and without neglecting its still serious problems, could claim:

Food is more varied. Fresh fruit is available all the year round. The milk supply is cleaner, and the byres have been driven beyond the city bounds. Drunkenness has diminished, and the scandalous scenes witnessed on Saturday nights in Argyll Street seem so far away and long ago ... Barefooted women and children were common in the eighties. No one sees them today. The shawl has gone and the hat has taken its place ... working girls, who then tidied themselves only for special occasions, are now always neatly dressed and are careful of their hair and teeth and finger-nails – a great change.

Indeed, changes in standards of clothing were one of the most obvious signs of improving material conditions. The barefoot and ragged children who had been a common sight in many towns and cities before 1914 had disappeared except from the very poorest districts by 1939. Boots and shoes, with their relatively high capital cost for those on or near the poverty line, represented a very accurate barometer of small, but significant changes in living standards. Although school medical officers in the thirties and studies of evacuees reported up to a fifth of children as 'deficient in footwear', most regarded this as a great improvement on what they had known in the past. More generally, the growth of real incomes, the development of new retail outlets, such as chain-stores and multiple tailors, and the use of new materials like rayon, had an effect on standards of clothing. Following his visit to Wigan and the North in the mid-1930s, George Orwell remarked that one of the greatest changes to have occurred since the Great War was the production of cheap smart clothes:

> The youth who leaves school at fourteen and gets a blind-alley job is out of work at twenty, probably for life; but for two pounds ten on the hire-purchase he can buy himself a suit which, for a little while and at a little distance, looks as though it had been tailored in Savile Row. The girl can look like a fashion plate at an even lower price.

While it was still possible to find shawls and ragged clothes in the slum districts, there was often a contrast between the older and the younger generation. Thus Helen Forrester noted that in the poor district of Liverpool where she was brought up the older women were dressed in 'dull greys and blacks, some with flowered pinafores and most of them wearing black shawls as protection against the cold wind. Their hair either hung in greasy confusion to their shoulders or was braided and pinned up in fashions I had seen in early Victorian photographs.' But she also encountered young girls from the same district: 'They were cheap labour and at the age of sixteen they would often be unemployed, like their elder sisters, but in the meantime they were frequently the most affluent members of their household, with money to spend in Woolworths on cosmetics and rhinestone jewellery. I envied them their neat, black, work dresses and, even more, their best Sunday coats and hats and high-heeled shoes.' No less important were the many basic aspects of everyday life which were being improved, particularly in household equipment, bedding, furniture and entertainment. Gas or electricity had become standard equipment in many homes and even the working classes could aspire to a better quality of life, as Sidney Pollard has remarked:

Statistics fail to take full account of the difference made by electricity instead of candles, and gas cookers instead of coal or coke ranges, as standard equipment in working-class homes; of improved housing, including indoor water and sanitation; or of radio, the cinema and newspapers within almost everybody's reach.

For many of the middle classes particularly, the inter-war years represented a period of growing affluence with better houses, a wider range of consumer goods, and the same benefits from improved technology as enjoyed by the working class. Moreover, with the smaller family sizes amongst the middle classes and a much greater margin of income over that required for subsistence, they were in a better position to take advantage of the consumer society which was developing around them. This was less of a change for the very wealthy, the higher professionals, businessmen and landowners than it was for the expanding sector of white-collar workers. It was the salaried middle class – civil servants, teachers, managers and clerks – who enjoyed the real fruits of 'affluence' between the wars. In spite of cuts during the worst phase of the economic crisis, rising real incomes released an enormous consumer demand. Just as for the unskilled labourer the period saw the raising of horizons beyond bare subsistence, so for the salaried, new aspirations towards houses, small cars, new consumer durables and increasing entertainment were opened up. Nowhere was this more evident than in the spectacular private house-building boom of the 1930s. It was demand primarily from the middle classes which fuelled the enormous suburban expansion of the inter-war years, not only creating 'semi-detached London', but a pattern of suburban growth and ribbon development which spread throughout the country. The inter-war years saw the completion of two and a half million houses for private sale, reaching a peak in the middle and late thirties when more than 350,000 houses were being completed each

year. New semi-detached houses with bathrooms and garage
could be bought for as little as £450. Mortgages were available on easy terms, with an average interest rate of around
4½ per cent and repayments which came well within the range
of most of the middle classes and a significant portion of the
better-off working classes. It was of this 'new post-war
England' which Priestley spoke in his *English Journey* of 1934
when he said: 'You need money in this England, but you do
not need much money. It is a large-scale, mass production job,
with cut prices . . .'

It was also reflected in the growth of private motoring.
Prior to the Great War, the domestic market in Britain had
not been large enough to support a mass-production car industry, but from the early 1920s car sales mushroomed. In 1914
there were only 140,000 motor vehicles of all kinds in Britain,
by 1931 the figure was 1½ million, and by 1939 three million,
two million of which were private vehicles. Between 1935 and
1939 the industry was turning out over 300,000 cars a year
at ever cheaper prices. By 1931 an Austin Seven or a Ford
Eight could be bought for not much more than £100, about
a third of a year's salary for a teacher. Indeed it was precisely
this group, the middling professions and the lower-middle class,
who could now begin to aspire to a small 'family car'. Inevitably many chose to spend their money on their children,
considerably increasing the demand for private education in
spite of a fall in the birth rate. There was an increase in the
numbers attending public schools of something like a third between the wars, while the number of schools included in the
Public Schools Yearbook rose, as well as the number of 'minor
public schools' who did not bother even to try for inclusion.
The number of families, largely middle-class, who were prepared and able to pay fees of around £250 for a boarder at
a public school or pay fees for attendance at a secondary grammar school was growing throughout the period.

Thus for a large section of the middle class, particularly the
lower-middle class, this was truly an era of 'never had it so
good'. Other elements aided this, especially low taxation and

the continuing availability of domestic service to carry out
many routine domestic chores. Rates of income tax which rose
as high as 6s. in the pound in the immediate post-war years
fell back in the years after 1923 to an average of 4s. 6d., leaving
a much higher percentage of income after tax than was to be
the case after 1945. In spite of new taxes on such things as
petrol, motor vehicles and entertainment, as well as the
maintenance of high indirect taxes on alcohol and tobacco from
the Great War, the tax structure fell most heavily upon the
relatively poor and the very rich, with those on incomes between £250 and £1,000 paying the lowest proportion of their
incomes in direct or indirect taxes. Although in almost every
case, the middle classes were paying a higher proportion of
their income in tax compared with before 1914, this was not
only lower than other groups, but considerably less than in
the years after the Second World War. A man on £500 per
year in 1938 would have paid just under 10 per cent through
direct taxation; by 1956 a man on an equivalent salary in terms
of prices, £1,400 a year, would have paid just under 15 per
cent of it in direct taxes.

A high level of income retained by the middle classes also
permitted them to retain domestic service. While many households reduced the number of servants, taking advantage of
some of the new labour-saving devices such as gas and electric
fires, washing machines, and the like, in 1931 nearly one in
every five households still had at least one full-time domestic
living in, while many more employed a 'daily' to do most of
the cleaning and cooking. Although there was always something of a shortage in the South-East, where demand outstripped supply, there was little doubt that in most comfortable
middle-class homes of the twenties and thirties, domestic service
was taken for granted. Correspondence to newspapers such
as the *Daily Mail* in the 1920s confirmed that a large section of
the population considered it the government's duty to restore
the supplies of domestic labour interrupted by the war. Indeed,
in spite of the resistance of women's groups, there were efforts
to encourage unemployed women both in the 1920s and the

1930s to train as domestic servants. Between 1920 and 1924 an extra 25,000 women were trained in this way by a government agency, the Central Committee on Women's Training and Employment, while during the 1930s both state-supported and private schemes trained and transferred thousands of young girls from the depressed areas to work in middle-class homes in the south of England. As a result the 1931 census showed a total of 1,332,224 women and 78,489 men in domestic work, a rise of 100,000 on 1911. Indeed, what we know of the reduction in the number of servants in some of the larger households makes it quite possible that by 1931 more households than ever before were enjoying some kind of domestic help. Moreover, at least as important for the whole tenor of life for the middle and upper classes was the continuing availability in so many areas of the economy of still relatively cheap labour. In spite of the wage rises enjoyed by many of the unskilled as a result of the First World War, wages were still low enough between the wars to provide a range and quality of services for those who could afford them which could not be sustained on anything like the same basis when working-class wages rose further as a result of the Second World War. For those with the money to take advantage of them, there were shops staffed with hordes of shop assistants, often hourly-paid, an entertainment industry which depended upon thousands of cheap 'extras' for its films or dozens of musicians for its dance bands, and a transport and postal system which remained as extensive as it was because of the relatively low pay of basic employees such as porters, bus conductors, delivery boys and postmen.

Talleyrand used to say that no one who had not lived before the French Revolution could know what *la douceur de la vie* was. It was a comment which many of the upper classes cited in the inter-war years when reflecting on the changes wrought by the Great War on the spacious and agreeable life of the wealthy in Victorian and Edwardian Britain. Certainly, as we have seen, the war marked the beginning of a period of much higher taxation on earned incomes and of heavy death duties on large estates. Combined with the psychological shock of the heavy casualties during the Great War, agricultural depression which reduced income from landed property, and a 30 per cent fall in business profits during the depression, there was some evidence of retrenchment by the wealthier classes. Capital assets, such as land, were sold and many country houses were left standing empty or put up for sale.

There was, however, little sign of a crisis of consumption in many of the wealthiest families, particularly those whose income came from sources other than land. The Astors still maintained thirty indoor servants in the 1930s and houses such as Cliveden, Hatfield and Knowsley continued to maintain great house parties and function as important centres of social and political life, though usually on a more restricted scale than before 1914. Nor did the conspicuous consumption of London 'high society' suggest that money was in short supply. Although writers with experience of the 1880s and 1890s might lament the loss of a six-month London 'season', with three or four balls every night and a glittering round of afternoon parties or other entertainments, and others regret the reduction in the number of great London houses thrown open every season for large social gatherings, there was still a shorter, three-month season revolving around the debutantes' presentation at Court, 'coming-out' balls and dinner parties in the remaining great houses of Mayfair and Belgravia. Some changes had certainly occurred. The 6th Duke of Portland listed only Londonderry, Apsley, Bridgwater and Holland House as private residences in the mid-thirties, compared with a dozen or more before 1914; the rest had been closed or converted, and 'restaurants, cabarets and night-clubs have risen in their place'. But even in the London of the 1930s the social round described in places like the *Diaries* of Chips Channon, the Conservative MP, still told of a dazzlingly expensive and luxurious 'high society' made up of royalty, politicians, the Anglo-American wealthy set and show-business celebrities. For example, on 25 February 1934, 'Dinner was staggering, champagne flowed and the food was excellent. We began with blinis served with Swedish schnapps, to wash down the caviare. The soup, followed by salmon, then

an elaborate chicken. Then a sweet and savoury. The candle-
light was reflected in my gold plate and the conversation was
incessant.' Weekend house parties and balls, with holidays in
the South of France, Switzerland or still further afield, continued to offer the well-to-do a culture of high extravagance,
style and pleasure which in some respects had abated little since
the Edwardian era.

The Survival of Poverty

While the social investigations carried out between the wars
demonstrated that there had been significant advances in
average living standards and levels of material comfort, even
using the most stringent standards, they also revealed that a
considerable proportion of the population remained in poverty,
with its attendant problems of poor housing and ill-health. One
survey of five towns in 1924 suggested an average figure of
11 per cent of the population living in poverty, while the *Social
Survey of Merseyside* recorded 16 per cent. In London, the *New
Survey of London Life and Labour*, published in 1934, estimated
that an average of 10 per cent of the population were in poverty,
ranging as high as 24 per cent in Poplar and the East End, but
down to as low as 4.8 per cent in Lewisham. In York in 1935–6,
on the same standard as used in 1899, Rowntree found 6.8 per
cent in 'primary' poverty with incomes insufficient to meet
physical requirements. By his improved minimum standard,
however, he found 18 per cent of the population in poverty,
representing almost a third of the working-class population.
Of these, half were in 'primary' poverty, while the rest so spent
their incomes that they had insufficient to live on. No less
striking was Herbert Tout's conclusions from a study of Bristol
in summer 1937 which found that 19.3 per cent of the population had 'insufficient income', while 10.3 per cent were in
'poverty', which ranged from 'utter destitution' to a standard
where almost any incidental expense was obtained at the price
of less to eat.

The principal causes of poverty remained those found before

1914, such as old age, chronic sickness, low pay and large families. In 1936 Seebohm Rowntree was able to compare his findings in the York of the mid-thirties to his 1899 survey. He found that illness, old age and unemployment were greater causes of poverty than in 1899, though large families, low wages and the death of the chief wage-earner were less important than before. In Bristol Tout also found a familiar set of problems, with old age, low wages and unemployment accounting for almost 70 per cent of those in poverty.

One of the most striking findings of the social investigators was that the proportion of children in poverty was much greater than the proportion of families in poverty, primarily as a result of the impact of large families on family budgets. In 1923 it was found that one child in sixteen under fourteen years of age was in a household where 'the normal means of living were insufficient'. When it came to examining the poor, it was obvious that children and poverty went hand in hand. In York in 1936, Rowntree found half of the persons in primary poverty were children under fourteen years old. He summed up the situation:

We would be labouring under a delusion if we got into our heads the idea that only 31.1 per cent of the working class population suffer from poverty. We see that 52.5 per cent of the children under one year of age, 49.7 per cent of those over one and under five, and 39.3 per cent of those over five and under fifteen are living below the mini-mum. Since everyone who grows up has at one time been aged 0–1, that means that, of the generation of workers born in 1936, 52.5 per cent will have been living below the minimum during the first part of their lives irrespective of what happens to them afterwards.

Very similar results came from Tout's survey of Bristol. In a prosperous town at the crest of the late thirties boom, one working-class child in five came from a home where income was below his poverty line and nine out of ten families with four or more children were below the level of sufficiency.

The other major group to suffer from poverty were the elderly. The introduction of old-age pensions in 1908 and their extension in 1925 guaranteed a basic income of 10s. per week

(£1 for a married couple living together). But while they had gone some way to relieving the worst aspects of old-age poverty, that is preventing the utter destitution that before 1914 had resulted in up to a half the elderly in some areas being forced to end their lives in the workhouse, the pension, on its own, fell below most of the existing poverty lines. Thus while the *New Survey of London* confirmed that the number of old people receiving poor relief in the capital had been reduced to a quarter of the number at the end of the nineteenth century, it stated starkly that: 'Any person of 65 and upwards living alone with no resources except pension would in the year 1929 fall below the poverty line . . .' Herbert Tout came to virtually identical conclusions about the elderly in Bristol. He found that if they could not find anywhere to live rent-free and had only their old-age pension on which to live, they would automatically fall below the poverty line, a view confirmed in a survey of Oxford in the late 1930s which revealed the elderly as the major group making claims for public assistance.

Besides children and the elderly, the other groups to suffer hardship most persistently were the sick, the widowed, the low-paid and the unemployed. The latter group, however, made up the largest group of poor in only one study. The problems of the chronically sick and the families which lost their male wage-earner had changed little since the years before the Great War. Prolonged illness in a working-class family, especially a large family, usually meant a bitter struggle against poverty. Moreover, it was still true that for many women widowhood meant not only the loss of a husband but also poverty. Normally, if they earned more than a small amount they forfeited their widow's pension. Frequently this condemned them to eking out a poverty-stricken existence on the pension or accepting low-paid, menial work. In Oxford it was recorded that widows were the most common claimants for poor relief after the elderly. That large numbers of low-paid workers fell below the 'poverty line' had been recognized by social investigators before 1914. Rowntree found that it remained an almost in-tractable cause of poverty and was likely to remain so while wages were paid which fell below the minimum standard needed to maintain families of any size in reasonable health. He found that there was little to distinguish the low-paid from hundreds of thousands of others in terms of skill and ability. Many were employed in occupations with a tradition of low wage rates, so that even full-time working made it difficult to support a family. A large number of unskilled trades fell below what Rowntree considered as a minimum wage and he picked out the building trades, transport, and municipal and government employment as examples. Agricultural labourers were also poorly paid, with average wages which fell several shillings below Rowntree's specially adjusted 'poverty line' for those working on the land. Average earnings for other workers were below the minimum standard because of short-time working resulting from the depression or a tradition of casual employment in the industry. In the coal industry, for example, a combination of low shift payments and short-time working brought many coalmining families in less favoured parts of South Wales, Scotland and the North-East close to, if not below, subsistence level. Instances were quoted in the House of Commons in 1931 of families with only 30s. a week to provide food, rent and clothing. Fenner Brockway interviewed a cotton worker in Lancashire who, although both he and his wife worked, was unable to bring the family income up to a sufficient level to keep themselves and their three children adequately fed. Even in the relatively prosperous sectors such as the motor vehicle industry, seasonal lay-offs and short-time working could push many families below the poverty line.

In this context, mass unemployment merely added to the number of families living in poverty. Although generally alleviated by some form of unemployment insurance, parish relief or, later, payments from the Unemployed Assistance Board, it could, depending very much upon the circumstances of families and individuals, still mean chronic hardship. Even in the worst years of the depression, however, a major conclusion of the social inquiries of the inter-war period was that the depression was not solely or even primarily responsible for the survival of poverty; rather it was the traditional problems identified before 1914. Indeed, what the social investigators revealed was that poverty was still an endemic feature of British society; much reduced since the Edwardian era certainly, but still, even on the eve of the Second World War, one which affected a significant minority of the total population. Amongst a still large section of the working classes, the almost predictable 'poverty cycle' – first identified by social investigators before the Great War – still existed, in which several million people might experience poverty at three major stages in their lives. The first was as children, because poverty was a characteristic of large families and the highest percentage of poverty in any age group was found amongst those aged under fifteen years. Once earning began there usually followed a period of relative comfort, lasting into the first years of marriage, but this was in turn followed by a period of renewed poverty while young children were being reared. Once the children were earning, a period of adequate living standards was likely to last until old age, when poverty tended to recur. The principal development to occur since the Edwardian era was that instead of poverty applying to virtually all unskilled workers it was now confined to only a portion of them, with the percentage of the population falling into poverty at each point of the cycle being significantly reduced, if far from eliminated entirely.

For those living at or below the poverty line, life could range from utter destitution to merely a mean and precarious existence in which obtaining adequate housing, food and clothing was a constant struggle. There undoubtedly existed a 'culture of poverty' in many of the slum districts of the large cities and towns, where thousands were accustomed to existing in conditions which, while falling below any recommended standard, had their own structure and values, and whose inhabitants, like those of third-world shanty towns, eked out a makeshift and precarious existence in which day-to-day survival took precedence over everything else. In many respects, it was still the world of the Edwardian 'Classic Slum', described by Robert Roberts – still, as Helen Forrester found in the Liverpool of the early 1930s, 'a matriarchal society where ferocious grand-mothers and nagging mothers reigned supreme', where strangers with odd accents or unfamiliar dress were likely to be abused or worse, and where 'making-do' was a way of life. It was in these communities that the pawnshop flourished, not as an exceptional recourse for the poor, but as a part of the weekly cycle of existing from pay-day to pay-day, and as the first recourse for ready cash when faced with emergencies. Helen Forrester's father, a bankrupt 'gentleman' and a complete child in the slums, was astonished to hear of the ways in which ends could be met:

There were agencies in the town, he was told, which would provide the odd pair of shoes or an old blanket for a child. There were regimental funds willing to provide a little help to old soldiers. He gathered other scraps of information, which were revelations to a man who had never had to think twice about the basic necessities of life. An open fire, he was assured, could be kept going almost all day from the refuse of the streets, old shoes, scraps of paper, twigs, wooden boxes, potato peelings; if one was very ill or had a broken bone, the outpatients departments of most of the local hospitals would give some medical care. Pawnbrokers would take almost anything saleable, and one could buy second-hand clothing from them. Junk yards would sometimes yield a much needed pram wheel or a piece for an old bike. One could travel from Liverpool to London by tramcar, if one knew the route, and it was much cheaper than going by train.

Given such 'street' knowledge it was not surprising that some of the poor managed to live on their wits and maintain remarkably comfortable lives in the most unpropitious circumstances. However much outsiders might lament the fact, the poor did, somehow, manage to frequent pubs, cinemas and fish and chip shops, and buy more than the odd packet of cigarettes. But it was a desperately precarious world, balanced for most on the knife-edge between making-do and complete destitution. Whatever comfort people could find in it, it was still in material terms mean and squalid, where doctors on emergency calls disinfected themselves before they left their surgeries, and experienced ones carried a powerful flash-lamp on night calls to the slums, knowing that it was more than likely their patients would have no money for the gas or electricity meter after darkness fell, where grocers would sell anything – tea, butter, margarine or meat – in ounces or pennyworths, and dirt, damp and vermin were common accompaniments to everyday life.

Undoubtedly the worst affected were those for whom the descent into poverty had occurred suddenly and for whom neither experience nor training prepared them – the broken-down door-to-door sellers found by Orwell in Wigan, sometimes from middle-class backgrounds, or Helen Forrester's father, all trying to exist in a world in which they hardly knew the first rules. But for all the poor, the statistics told a similar story. The poor had the worst housing conditions, the least adequate diet, the poorest health and the least opportunity of enjoying the amenities offered by economic growth and tech-nological progress. In 1943, the Women's Group on Public Welfare commented:

> Poverty leads to bad housing without the space, water supply, food storage, cooking facilities and private sanitation essential to good home-making. Ill-found accommodation encourages bad feeding. Slum conditions – noisy streets, crowded beds, the irritation of bugs, lice and skin diseases – murder sleep. Everything that militates against healthy living encourages skin diseases, which are often closely associ-ated with vermin. Bad feeding, inadequate sleep, insufficient air and lack of healthy exercise and recreation affect mind as well as body ... Children who are dirty, undisciplined, unhealthy and ill fed have no standards of well-being and later accept these conditions in their own offspring. Not only so, but they bring to parenthood enfeebled bodies and indifferent nerves. Battles are only the most sensational form of human wastage. Year by year dirt, poverty and disease pursue their unremitting campaign against the most defenceless; year by year an army of little soldiers fight and fall almost before they have lived, or limp on enfeebled in body and warped in mind.

These comments and the study from which they came had been prompted by the shock with which many middle-class homes had received over a million evacuee schoolchildren, infants and mothers in September 1939, the bulk of them drawn from the poorest and most congested parts of the major cities and towns. Within a context in which 'horror stories' soon became rife, the evacuees none the less provided a close-up view of the conditions which many of the poor accepted as normal: children with head lice, impetigo and scabies, often unwashed and without any knowledge of elementary hygiene. Some of the evacuees were reported as: '... not only very badly equipped, but they brought no change of clothes and the garments they wore often had to be burnt as they were verminous. In other cases, the householders had to keep the children in bed while they washed their clothes. Some children arrived sewn into a piece of calico with a coat on top and no other clothes at all.' In Lincolnshire, it was laconically reported that '... many children arrived in rags'. As regards the evacuated mothers, reports came from every reception area that in some cases bedrooms and beds were soon reduced to 'a foul condition', 'especially where the mothers drank to excess', as well as accepting 'insanitary habits' in children up to and over five years of age as a matter of course. The experience of filthy, shared outdoor toilets in slum districts was canvassed as one reason for the practice of some women of encouraging their children to defecate on newspaper and then burn it on the fire: 'Big boys and girls are sometimes found who know no other sanitary habits, and children thus trained must have found themselves at a loss when evacuated, so that their conduct startled their hosts.'

No doubt. But even allowing for a degree of exaggeration in the reports of the conditions found amongst some of the evacuees and what was an often profound and mutual culture shock which exacerbated some problems, they revealed no more than a situation which was familiar to those with experience of the 'submerged tenth' which still existed in the Britain of the inter-war years.

It was only with the Second World War that this poverty was to come close to eradication. When in 1951 Seebohm Rowntree and G. R. Lavers carried out a fresh survey into the incidence of poverty in York they found that only 2.8 per cent of the working-class population were in poverty compared with 31.1 per cent in 1936, 1.5 per cent of the total population compared with 18 per cent fifteen years earlier. Full employment, higher wages and the Welfare State had virtually eliminated the major causes of poverty found before 1939. None the less, elements of the classic cycle of poverty were still to be found. The elderly, the sick and large families were to remain social concerns well into the affluent years of the 1950s and 1960s.

5. *Population, Household and Family*

It has been said that the really important decisions in history are made by pairs of adults in bed. Indeed, the growth and decline of populations and the size of families provide some of the most fundamental ingredients of social change. Twentieth-century Britain has been no exception. By 1914 the United Kingdom bore in its populous cities and towns the imprint of the great increases in population which had been occurring for a century or more and had made it one of the most densely populated countries in the world. In the years up to 1945 population growth was to continue, but at a much slower rate than before, a tendency which indicated important changes in attitudes towards child-bearing and family size. What A. H. Halsey has called the 'basic demographic development of the twentieth century' – the adoption of a pattern of small families by all social classes – was to have profound implications not only for family size, but also living standards, the status of women and children, and attitudes towards home and family.

In the fifty years before the Great War the population of the United Kingdom almost doubled, that of England and Wales rising from 20.1 million in 1861 to 36.5 million in 1911. The two decades prior to the war witnessed the largest ever numerical increase in population, in spite of a large outflow of emigrants. These increases, however, concealed important changes in population trends, in particular the deceleration in the overall rate of growth. By the late-Victorian era, the rate of population increase was slowing down and was to decline even more rapidly in the inter-war period. The population of Great Britain in the two decades between 1921 and 1941 rose by 3,836,000. This represented a rate of increase of only about a third of that experienced in the nineteenth century and only a half of that achieved in the years immediately before the Great War. This was a momentous change, as Neil Tranter has written: 'The long period of rapid population growth which had lasted unbroken since the late eighteenth century came to an abrupt end in the second decade of the twentieth century.'

The other major feature of demographic change was the shift in population growth from the old industrial areas to the thriving communities of the South-East and Midlands. The South-East absorbed about 60 per cent of the total population increase in the country as a whole during the inter-war period and the London conurbation alone increased from 7½ million people in 1921 to almost 8½ million by 1939. It is estimated that over a million people of working age emigrated into the South-East during the inter-war period and a further net influx was registered in the Midlands. There was a corresponding fall in the population of the old industrial areas: that of Wales fell by almost 200,000 people between 1920 and 1939. The total loss by migration was about 450,000, which included the natural increase for the area. The population of South Wales fell by over 100,000 people between 1931 and 1938 alone. The bulk of the migration took place voluntarily and, typically, it was single young people who were most able and willing to make the break from their home areas. Not unnaturally the migration of the young and relatively mobile parts of the work-force led to fears that the traditional industrial areas would soon be denuded of their younger generation and that a vicious cycle of industrial decay and migration would be created until the old communities virtually ceased to exist. Some migration was assisted by a government transference scheme which helped almost 200,000 workers to migrate from the depressed areas during the thirties.

The rate of internal migration was not especially high by historic standards, certainly compared with the half-century before 1914. However, whereas much of the migration then had still consisted of rural workers moving off the land and characteristically 'short-distance' migration, this had virtually been exhausted by 1914. The internal migrations of the 1920s and 1930s tended to be more drastic, often involving people moving very considerable distances under the pressure of unemployment or the lure of more attractive opportunities. For example, the Kent coalfield was developed by miners transferred from Wales, Scotland and Durham, and the new steelworks of Corby in Northamptonshire staffed by workers brought from Scotland by the company involved, Stewart and Lloyds. Other workers from the depressed areas found work in the engineering factories and light industries of the Midlands and the South-East, in places such as Coventry, Luton, Oxford and Slough. By the mid-1930s it was estimated that the Morris Motors plant at Cowley in Oxford was recruiting half its labour force from the depressed areas. Hence, while the total movement of population was lower in total, it was often more disruptive. Many of the migrants were moving from long-settled communities like the pit villages of County Durham or South Wales for no other reason than that they were desperate to find work.

Heavy unemployment in the old industrial areas reinforced the effects of the relocation of industry to the Midlands and the South-East. The latter had been increasing its proportion of the total population since the nineteenth century, but after 1918 its share increased still more rapidly, while the Midlands was the only other region to grow more rapidly than the national average between the wars. The inter-war years brought to a virtual halt the rapid growth enjoyed by many of the older industrial areas up to 1914. After 1918, the largest increases in population were no longer in these areas, but in the centres of the 'new' industries. While the population of the old industrial areas stagnated or even declined, Coventry's doubled, Oxford's grew by a third and London continued to absorb an ever-greater share of the total population of Great Britain. Hence the character of population growth and distribution between 1914 and 1945 changed from what it had been in the nineteenth century. Its axis had shifted decisively: from the

industrial regions associated with the first industrial revolution
to those typical of the new sources of wealth and service
developing in the inter-war years.

If the changing distribution of population is comprehensible
in terms of the changing structure of the economy, a far more
complex problem surrounds the question of why population
growth as a whole slowed down, particularly as some of the
more obvious candidates to account for it can be shown to
be insufficient. For example, although emigration continued
during the inter-war years, it did so at lower levels than before
1914. During the 1920s, emigration ran at an average rate of
about 130,000 a year, less than half the pre-war level. The
balance of inflow and outflow took just over half a million
people from the country. During the 1930s there was actually
a surplus of immigrants over emigrants. Many earlier emigrants
returned to Britain during the 1930s and these combined with
refugees from Europe and significant entries of Irish nationals
to produce a net inflow between 1931 and 1941 of about
650,000. Hence while emigration was partly responsible for the
slowing down of British population growth during the late
nineteenth and early twentieth centuries, the sharp downturn
in population increase during the inter-war years was not related
to an increased outflow of emigrants. On the contrary, the net
drain on the country was much less serious in the 1920s than
before the Great War, and in the following decade the population actually gained from migration, bringing to a halt an
almost century-long process of population loss through emigration.

Nor could the slow-down in population growth be primarily
related to the losses of the Great War. A figure of 610,000
has been suggested for the total number of deaths attributable
to military service in the Great War, taking into account the
normal mortality which might have occurred amongst those
serving in the armed forces if they had stayed at home. Great
as these losses were, they have to be set against the high rates
of emigration which prevailed in the years before 1914. This
had produced a net loss of 750,000 in the years 1901–10, while

emigration was reaching ever higher levels in the years immediately before the war. At a conservative estimate, at least
half the losses in the war would have been losses through
emigration had pre-war trends continued. Given the very high
rates of emigration in 1910–14 it is possible that there were more
people living in Britain as a result of the war than would have
been the case had it not occurred. However, the war undoubtedly had some effects. The casualties represented a
peculiarly narrow age range and were almost exclusively male.
Pre-war emigration figures suggest that only six out of ten
emigrants were male, though they too tended to be drawn from
the younger sections of the population. More significant was
the reduction in the birth rate during the war years because
of the absence of so many males, falling from 24.1 per thousand
births in 1913 to 17.7 in 1918. By the last years of the war,
the population was virtually stagnant, births and deaths almost
cancelling each other out. There was some catching-up with
a post-war baby boom, but the birth rate soon resumed a course
which followed closely upon pre-war trends. None the less,
some 'loss' of potential births had occurred, on one estimate
approximately 500,000.

Nor, as was popularly believed, did the war drastically alter
the likelihood of marriage for the population as a whole. While
the number of males aged between twenty and forty fell from
155 per thousand in 1911 to 141 in 1921 and the proportion of
young women in the population increased slightly, this had less
dramatic effects than it might have had. Undoubtedly there
were some war spinsters who for reasons of personal grief or the
loss of males in their particular social group or environment
did not marry who might otherwise have done so. For some,
however, emigration might have been the cause of spinsterhood
if it had not been the war. More importantly, the percentage
of women aged over fifteen married in 1921 and 1931 was
greater than had been the case in 1911. The pre-war years had
been marked by a considerable 'excess' of women of marriage-
able age because of the massive outflow of emigrants. When
this drain of young men was checked by the Great War, possi-

bilities of more women being married were opened up and led to a greater percentage of women of all age groups marrying between the wars than before 1914.

The reduction of the rate of population increase between the wars was not therefore the result of heavy emigration or the losses incurred in the war. Its cause lay in the fall in the rate of natural increase measured in terms of the excess of births over deaths. In the two decades between 1921 and 1941 the natural increase represented a rise of 3,751,000 for Great Britain as a whole. This was almost three-quarters of a million less than the increase in the single decade 1901-11. The crucial ingredient in this declining rate of growth was a reduction in birth rate, which fell from 26.3 in 1906-10 to 19.9 in 1921-5 and to 14.9 in 1936-8. As suggested earlier, this fall was already evident before 1914 and can be observed to have begun in the 1870s. Even in late-Victorian and Edwardian Britain, high population growth was being sustained more by a rapid fall in mortality brought about by improved levels of nutrition and public health than by a high birth rate. By the eve of the Second World War, the birth rate in Great Britain was less than half what it had been fifty years earlier. Women married in the 1880s had an average of 4.6 children; by the 1900s 3.37; and by the end of the

Table 11: Birth and death rates in Great Britain, 1901-45

	Births per thousand population		Deaths per thousand population	
	England and Wales	Scotland	England and Wales	Scotland
1901-5	28.2	29.2	16.0	17.0
1906-10	26.3	27.6	14.7	16.1
1911-15	23.6	25.4	14.3	15.7
1916-20	20.0	22.8	14.4	15.0
1921-5	19.9	23.0	12.1	13.9
1926-30	16.7	20.0	12.1	13.6
1931-5	15.0	18.2	12.0	13.2
1936-40	14.7	17.6	12.2	13.6
1941-5	15.9	17.8	12.8	14.1

Source: Registrar-General's *Statistical Review of England and Wales*, and Registrar-General, Scotland, *Annual Reports*.

1920s 2.19. Whereas in 1900 one in four of all married women were in childbirth every year, thirty years later the number had fallen to only one in eight.

The Twilight of Parenthood?

The causes for the decline in births in the years up to 1945 still represent a fascinating puzzle. Initially, it might be noted that it was not a phenomenon confined to the United Kingdom. A similar decline has been noticed at much the same time in other European countries, leading to the observation that it is a hallmark of modern industrialized societies. Moreover, the onset of a decline in birth rates varied with social class and region, in some cases pre-dating the period when average rates fell. In the case of the British peerage, a group who have been subjected to special study, the fall began much earlier than the 1880s, and once under way after 1880, the pace varied markedly from one social class to another. Before the Great War the decline in birth rate was greatest amongst the upper and middle classes, less amongst skilled and semi-skilled workers, and least evident amongst unskilled workers and agricultural labourers. During the inter-war years the sharpest falls in fertility occurred in the classes which had until then maintained high birth rates. The result was that while the upper and professional classes continued to have the lowest birth rates and the working classes the highest, there had been a marked narrowing of the gap between them. Viewed in perspective the inter-war years saw the spread of fewer births and smaller families to all social classes, completing a process which had begun in the late-Victorian era. As a result the average size of families fell dramatically: between 1900–1919 and 1930 the percentage of couples with five or more children fell from 27.5 to 10.4; by 1940 it was only 9.2, a declining trend which was to continue after 1945. On the other hand the numbers of those with three or less children rose, by 1930 accounting for 81 per cent of all families. This decline in the number of children born to married couples was then the central feature of the reduced population growth in Britain between 1914 and 1945. As suggested above, there is no evidence that the number of marriages was in decline. Rather, the proportion of women of childbearing age who were married was consistently higher than it had been prior to the Great War: they were simply having fewer children. Why? One mechanism might have been that women were marrying later; there is, however, no evidence to support this hypothesis. The average age of marriage for women during the inter-war years was much the same as it had been during the previous fifty years; indeed it was falling slightly, which increased the childbearing potential of married women.

The most important factor was the practice of family limitation, whether through the use of artificial contraceptives or other means. According to one study, the proportion of married women who made deliberate efforts to limit their families rose from 19.5 per cent amongst those marrying in the mid-Victorian era to 72.1 per cent amongst those marrying between the wars. A survey carried out in 1949 estimated that, of women married between 1910 and 1919, 40 per cent used some form of birth control at some point in their marriage, while of those married between 1935 and 1939 66 per cent did so. Of course in the earlier survey only a quarter used any other method than withdrawal, whereas of the later group more than half used some form other than withdrawal. Evidence collected for the 1959 Marriage Survey produced broadly similar results, revealing that of those who had begun rearing families before 1930 some 53 per cent had used birth control at some point in their marriages, while for those marrying in the 1930s the figure had risen to 65.6 per cent.

Traditionally, abstention, induced abortion and the use of *coitus interruptus* – the withdrawal method – had been the principal method of birth control. For many working-class households these remained the most important methods of preventing children right up to the Second World War and beyond. *Coitus interruptus* meant that women had to be sure their husbands were 'careful', and it could be combined with various types of pessaries and douches which women could

use without their husband's knowledge. Even by the end of
the nineteenth century, some cheap women's magazines and
pseudo-scientific works such as *Aristotle's Masterpiece* carried
advertisements for contraceptives, often under the discreet
heading of cures for 'female ailments'. In Lancashire in the
1890s, vaginal syringes, preventative pessaries and the like could
also be bought from visiting speakers who gave 'Lectures to
Women Only'. The expense of such aids was often prohibitive,
however, and home-made pessaries of lard, margarine and
flour, cocoa butter and quinine were recorded as being in use
in working-class districts. Extended nursing of children and
attempts to establish a 'safe period' could also give women some
control over the number of births. For many, however, abstention was the only truly 'safe' method of control. It was also
the only one approved by many churchmen. In 1916 the
Anglican National Birth Rate Commission expressed its opposition to any form of birth control other than abstinence.
The Bishop of Southwark stated the conventional view that
sexual intercourse was only to be indulged in 'if the procreation
of children was intended' and that abstinence, even at the cost
of the break-up of the marriage, was better than sexual intercourse for 'mere gratification'. Undoubtedly sexual abstinence
was practised by married couples of all classes as the only reliable
way to avoid pregnancy. The strains it may have imposed, particularly where women were forced into the position of
'denying' their husbands for fear of becoming pregnant, can
only be guessed at, but that it must have produced many unhappy marriages seems only too likely judging from the letters
received by the likes of Marie Stopes.

Inevitably some women found themselves pregnant against
their wishes, and, for many, abortion offered a last line of
defence in the attempt to limit their families if other means
failed. Indeed, concentration on contraception has often led to
the importance of abortion as a means of family limitation being
ignored. This is partly because abortion remained a criminal
offence until the 1960s and is almost impossible to estimate
accurately. Abortive agents were widely advertised disguised

as medicines and restoratives in cheap papers and magazines aimed at women well before 1914. Quack and folklore remedies designed to induce miscarriage abounded and were plainly in wide use amongst the working classes even after more efficient methods of birth control had become available. Violent purgatives such as penny royal, slippery elm, compounds of aloes and iron, savin and ergot of rye were all used, while hot baths, gin and violent exertions were and remained part of the repertoire of methods employed by women to induce miscarriage. Evidence that lead produced miscarriages following an outbreak of lead poisoning in Sheffield in the 1890s led to the use of the lead compound diachylon amongst Sheffield women wishing to secure abortions. Spread almost entirely by word of mouth, its use in pills and pennyworths was being reported as far afield as Lancashire, Warwickshire and Nottingham by 1914. There is no reason to suppose that in the inter-war years the use of such methods became less widespread. Ted Willis, son of a Tottenham barrow boy, was to learn that his mother had sought to prevent his own birth:

She bought gin she could ill afford and drank it neat. She carried the tin bath in from the back yard, filled it to near boiling with water and then lowered herself into it, scalding her flesh so painfully that she was in agony for days. She ran up and down stairs until she was exhausted. And when all this failed to check my progress, she procured some gunpowder – enough to cover sixpence – mixed it with a pat of margarine, and swallowed it. This was reckoned in those days to be almost infallible, but it succeeded only in making her violently ill. In the end she reconciled herself to the inevitable, and I emerged, none the worse for those adventures, to add another dimension to her problems.

In Salford, according to Robert Roberts, the remedies included penny-royal syrup, hot soapy water and vet's abortifacients, while the older women favoured aloes and turpentine and the 'controlled fall downstairs'. During the 1920s Walter Greenwood was able to report women supping 'bottle after bottle' of penny royal to induce abortion, while the letters received by Marie Stopes, the birth-control propagandist and, incidentally, a staunch opponent of abortion, illustrated a continuing demand for abortion from all sections of the community. Where homespun remedies failed, recourse to backstreet abortionists was not uncommon, often with disastrous consequences. In spite of the illegality of abortion and the hostility of medical practitioners and churchmen, there is ample evidence that many poorer women did not regard abortion as wrong, at least if self-induced and before the third month, when women could still think of themselves as 'late' rather than pregnant. Although precise figures of the number of abortions is impossible to obtain, one estimate in 1914 was that a hundred thousand women a year took drugs to induce miscarriage, while one of the first histories of birth control, published in 1930, recorded that 'there are few mothers of large families who have not at some time attempted abortion'.

Birth Control

In this context greater knowledge about birth control and the development of more reliable forms of artificial contraception played a major part in the ability of people of all classes to control the size of their families more effectively. Crude sheaths and appliances of other kinds had been available long before the twentieth century, but it was only in the late nineteenth century that the vulcanization process made possible the production of reliable rubber contraceptive sheaths. By 1914 these were being produced in reasonably large quantities and could be obtained from barbers' shops in the larger towns or via newspaper advertisements. Their use accelerated as a result of the Great War, when they were issued to the troops in an attempt to contain an epidemic of venereal disease, and by the 1930s the largest English manufacturer was producing two million sheaths a year and many more were being imported from abroad. A more effective diaphragm for women was produced in 1919 and made more reliable after 1932 when a contraceptive jelly was introduced.

Certainly by the 1920s technical advances had made more

efficient and aesthetic forms of contraception available, opening
up the possibility of artificial birth control on a large scale.
Moreover, it is clear that information and demand for information on birth control was increasing even before reliable means
became widely available. Books and pamphlets on the subject
had begun to circulate fairly widely from the 1880s. H. A.
Allbutt's *The Wife's Handbook*, published in 1884, sold half a
million copies by 1929 and was only the most common of a
host of commercial guides to procreation and marriage which
contained discreet advice on birth control. Firms making
contraceptives and surgical appliances also produced their own
handbills, catalogues and sex manuals. The Malthusian League,
established in 1877, set out to persuade doctors to provide their
patients with advice on birth control and produced in 1913 its
own 'practical pamphlet', *Hygienic Methods of Family Limitation*.
Between 1879 and 1921 it issued some three million pamphlets
and leaflets, designed to promote a rational approach to population policy in which birth control played a crucial part.
Although a somewhat highbrow pressure group, it was the
Malthusian League which proposed in September 1919 to set
up in the East End the first British birth-control clinic – though
this was not actually established until 1922.

But by far the most important advocate of birth control and
a more open attitude to sexual matters was Dr Marie Stopes.
A fossil botanist – not a medical practitioner – she rose to
prominence in 1918 with the publication of two books, *Married
Love*, a guide to sex and marriage, and *Wise Parenthood*, which
advocated family planning as an essential feature of a happy
marriage. *Married Love* sold over 2,000 copies in the first
fortnight and over 400,000 copies by the end of 1923, while
Wise Parenthood sold over 300,000 copies by 1924. Her own
influences had been an unsuccessful, and possibly unconsum-
mated marriage, which led her to write *Married Love* as a
passionate plea for sexual fulfilment in marriage. Hints there
on birth control were taken up in *Wise Parenthood* and a later
volume, published in 1920, *Radiant Motherhood*. In spite of the
rather fulsome and elevated tone of much of her writing, Stopes

clearly met a massive public demand for birth-control advice and attracted an enormous correspondence from women of all classes. In 1921 she opened her first birth-control clinic in Holloway Road, North London, along with a Society to support it. After a slow start, it had advised 10,000 women by 1930. Further books and pamphlets based upon her own theories of parenthood and sexual happiness, as well as the cases seen at her clinics, achieved a wide circulation. In 1930 Stopes and other groups formed the National Birth Control Council, which in 1939 became the Family Planning Association, operating more than sixty birth-control clinics in Britain on the eve of the Second World War.

Only a minority of people ever read birth-control literature or attended a clinic. Books such as those of Marie Stopes tended to be aimed at a middle-class audience, while the Malthusian League was primarily concerned with the advocacy of its population theories and was tardy in giving practical advice on contraception. More important was the growing general awareness of the idea of family limitation as both respectable and practicable. The trial for obscenity of Charles Bradlaugh and Annie Besant in 1877 for republishing Charles Knowlton's *The Fruits of Philosophy*, which contained a few paragraphs on douching after intercourse, achieved widespread publicity and the inevitable effect of boosting sales from a mere 700 a year to over 125,000 in three months. A similar result was achieved by the sensational libel action in 1923 of Marie Stopes against a Catholic doctor who had accused her of 'experimenting on the poor'. Although judgement went against her she won on appeal, achieving enormous publicity for her advocacy of birth control. Amongst others birth control became a 'good cause' which appealed to social reformers and progressives who were concerned about the burdens of poverty and ill-health caused by large families. As a result, the inter-war years saw a gradual movement amongst important sections of opinion towards acceptance of birth control. The Church of England at the 1930 Lambeth Conference softened its opposition to contraception, reflecting the attitude of many of the liberal sections of the

clergy. Although remaining opposed to artificial contraceptives, in the early 1930s the Roman Catholic Church accepted
the use of the 'safe period' as a means of family limitation in
certain cases. In addition a number of Labour councils and
women's organizations, such as the National Union of Societies
for Equal Citizenship, advocated the provision of birth-control
advice in Maternity and Child Welfare Clinics. Birth control
also received very qualified official approval in 1930 when the
Minister of Health permitted existing Maternity and Child
Welfare Centres to give contraceptive advice to married
women – but only in those cases where further pregnancy
would be detrimental to health. By the end of the 1930s advice
could be given to women suffering from other than gynaeco-
logical illnesses and clinics could be set up by local authorities
and regional hospital boards in conjunction with the Family
Planning Association. From a fringe movement before 1914,
birth control had become by 1939 an increasingly recognized
part of the official public health apparatus, as well as on the
agenda for further action. Contributing to *Picture Post*'s 'A Plan
for Britain' in January 1941, Julian Huxley saw birth control
and family allowances as two principal ingredients of a social
health policy in the future, writing:

> Unwanted children, worn-out mothers, over-large families due to
> mere ignorance – these are just as bad as too few children. Child
> welfare centres should be multiplied, and every centre should have
> its own birth-control section. Then, if there is no excuse for ignorance
> on the one hand and fear of poverty from having children on the
> other, the centres will become organs of healthy family planning.

But the availability of more reliable methods of contraception
and the growing respectability of birth control supply only part
of the answer to the story of declining birth rates and smaller
families in twentieth-century Britain. The crucial question
remains *why* people chose to limit their families. The spread of
the idea of practising birth control and of the ideal of the small
family represents an important shift in social values. By the
Second World War many working-class families were moving

towards the pattern of family size adopted by the upper and middle classes a generation or more earlier. What the Titmusses called 'the democratization of fertility rates' meant that class differences were coming to lie less in the practice of contraception than in the methods used. Where the upper and middle classes tended to use what were known as 'appliance' methods – diaphragms, pessaries and sheaths – the manual working class still relied primarily on non-appliance methods, especially *coitus interruptus*. This is particularly significant because it was amongst the working classes that the fall in birth rates was most striking between the wars, but it was a fall which depended less upon the availability of new methods of contraception than upon the growing desire of all classes to limit the number of children.

A number of factors were at work in favour of family limitation by the early twentieth century. One was the decline in death rates for infants and children from the 1870s onwards. Deaths of young children, aged under four years, started to fall a little later, but became quite pronounced after 1900. In the period 1901 to 1935 the mortality rate for children under five in England and Wales fell by just under 70 per cent. High birth rates were desirable when large numbers of children died at an early age, but once more children began to survive, to become a burden on their parents, some control on the conception of children was necessary if families were not to become unmanageably large. Indeed, by the end of the nineteenth century, social investigators had already proved conclusively that large families were a cause of poverty amongst the poor and were urging them to practise family limitation. Children were also becoming more expensive: restrictions placed upon child labour and the raising of the school-leaving age meant that children were a financial drain upon their parents for much longer. That child labour remained important to supplement family incomes was shown in the inter-war years by the strenuous resistance from some parents to the progressive raising of the school-leaving age. Indeed, the experience of the Great War was that, given the opportunity, many working-class families were only too ready to send the children out to work at the earliest possible age. Amongst the middle and upper classes too, a suitable public or grammar school education – increasingly necessary to preserve social status and maintain children above the 'common ruck' – made children a more expensive item. One aspect of the 'servant problem' was that plentiful, *cheap* domestic help to rear and tend for children was becoming difficult to obtain. Living-in nannies, nurse-maids and full-time domestic help were becoming both scarcer and more expensive. The children of an upper-middle-class academic family like that recalled in Carola Oman's *An Oxford Childhood* were reared almost exclusively by a 'Nana', who in 1914 could be paid anything between £20 and £50 a year. By 1939 a good nanny might cost £100 in wages as well as 'living-in' expenses. While such increases mattered little to the very wealthy, they pressed rather more acutely upon ordinary professional and business families who were finding it more difficult to obtain living-in servants of any kind in the years up to the Second World War. Nothing perhaps more concentrated the minds of many middle-class families upon the necessity of limiting families than the difficulties of obtaining domestic help in the nursery.

More subtle pressures were at work too. The emphasis on child welfare from humanitarians and 'national efficiency' groups alike from before 1914 tended to elevate child-rearing into a more responsible and expensive business. As well as food and clothing there were medical bills, outings, holidays and an increasing range of consumer goods aimed at children, such as toys, games, comics and books. Whether changes in family size were caused by or followed on such attitudes is difficult to determine, but the spread of the idea that children were to be properly cared for – at a time when the incidental costs of having children were rising – led to the inescapable conclusion that smaller families were desirable. Evidence of these changes in attitudes can be found in some of the letters received by the Co-operative Women's Guild from working women just before the First World War. One woman, married for thirty-two years with three children, explained:

I may say that my husband and myself were quite agreed on the point of restricting our family to our means. If we had not done so, I could not possibly have reared my eldest girl. I was able to have good medical advice and give her plenty of attention day and night ... I think that it is better to have a small family and give them good food and everything hygienic than to let them take 'pot luck'.

This has led some historians to see children in the twentieth century as a 'consumer durable', competing with other desirable items for a share in household expenditure. Fear of depression and unemployment may have made people more cautious in adding to their family and ready to seize the opportunities offered by both new and more traditional forms of contraception. For others, rising living standards presented a real possibility of new standards of comfort – a modest house mortgage, a new 'council house', probably at higher rent, or a widening range of consumer goods – providing that family income was managed wisely and the number of children controlled. Choices had to be made between large families and material comfort, leading Richard Titmuss to conclude in *Parents' Revolt* that 'the acquisitive way of life must in the end mean that material things will take precedence over children'.

Closely related to this ingredient was the gradual improvement in the economic and social status of women. Opportunities for female employment greatly expanded between the wars not only as a consequence of the Great War but with the broader growth of clerical and service jobs and the development of new 'light' industries. There were six and a quarter million women at work by 1931, three-quarters of a million more than in 1911, as well as an important increase in the proportion of married women working. Increasing possibilities of gainful employment outside the home undoubtedly offered a major incentive to limiting the number of pregnancies. The average age at which women had their last child was dropping, from thirty-three years in 1890 to twenty-eight years in 1930 and to twenty-six years by 1950, leaving women a longer span in which to take up paid employment. A significant pointer in this direction was the low birth rate even before 1914 amongst

groups like the Lancashire textile workers where women provided a major portion of the labour force. Amongst this group
the incentives for restricting the number of children were
obvious and, if anything, increased during the short-time working and unemployment of the inter-war depression. By 1931
there were 812,000 women employed in the textile trades, an
increase of 40,000 on the 1911 figure, and it was reported from
Lancashire in the early 1930s that 'even when husband and
wife are both working they cannot face the prospect of a week
without wages after so many weeks of short pay'. In the
weaving districts of North-East Lancashire it was the rule that
women lost their jobs when the child was due and then had
to 'take their chance' when ready to go back. Moreover, with
few day nurseries or crèches, women had to pay between 6s.
and 12s. a week to have children looked after if they wanted
to go out to work.

But as well as these economic pressures on childbearing,
work, where obtainable, also played an important part in the
spread of birth-control knowledge. Observers of working-class
life before 1914, such as Robert Roberts and Maud Pember
Reeves, remarked upon the confined world in which many
working-class women lived their lives, bounded by home, close
kin and the immediate neighbourhood in which the sources
of new ideas and information were strictly limited. Cultural
diffusion by word of mouth could be painfully slow amongst
women who rarely moved out of the home or much beyond
a few familiar streets. It took almost twenty years for word of
the use of diachylon as an abortifacient to spread by informal
networks out of South Yorkshire – a place where industry was
male-dominated – the fifty or so miles to Lancashire and the East
Midlands by 1914. Work, particularly factory work, could offer
a wider range of experiences and contacts. On such an intimate
matter as sexual habits and birth control, this was, perhaps,
particularly important; hence in Gorton in 1914 it was reported
that the subject of birth control 'is freely talked about and
openly discussed in the workshops where young girls and
young women work, and also during the dinner hour ...' The

distribution of female employment undoubtedly played an important part in the spread of effective birth-control techniques. It was amongst the groups with predominantly male employment patterns, miners, agricultural workers and unskilled general labourers, that the highest birth rates were still being recorded in the years up to and beyond the Second World War.

No less important, however, was the impact of the feminist movement, which increasingly came to deplore the low status of women and the assumption that the sole function of married women was to produce children. Concern both for the advancement of women in society and their release from irresponsible pregnancy because of the 'tyranny' of men inspired many of the more active women in the years before and after the First World War. As early as 1911 a contributor to *Working Women and Divorce* was calling for men to 'learn respect for women and sexual self-restraint'. Hannah Mitchell, in her autobiography *The Hard Way Up*, told how she feared marriage because it soon reduced girls 'to prematurely aged women'. An unhappy marriage and her experience in childbirth led to the conclusion 'that although birth control may not be a perfect solution to social problems, it is the first and the simplest way at present for the poor to help themselves, and by far the surest way for women to obtain some measure of freedom'. For some women, then, control over their own bodies was part of a process of higher expectations, greater independence and growing self-respect, well illustrated in the comments by one of the correspondents to the Women's Co-operative Guild:

> Working-class women have grown more refined; they desire better homes, better clothes for themselves and their children, and are far more self-respecting and less humble than their predecessors. But the strain to keep up to anything like a decent standard of housing, clothing, diet, and general appearance, is enough to upset the mental balance of a Chancellor of the Exchequer. How much more so a struggling pregnant mother! Preventives are largely used. Race suicide, if you will, is the policy of the mothers of the future. Who shall blame us?

But the diffusion of higher expectations of life amongst women, particularly working-class women, was a very slow one and could hardly be said to have been completed by the outbreak of the Second World War. None the less, the incorporation of the idea of smaller families and of 'being careful' into women's conventional notions of respectability was a crucial one for the reduction in the birth rate, for management of births and contraception was, according to Richard Hoggart's observations of a working-class community in West Yorkshire in the late 1920s, primarily the woman's sphere of responsibility:

> Most non-Catholic working-class families accept contraception as an obvious convenience, but both husbands and wives are shy of clinics where advice is given, unless they are driven there by near-desperation. The husband's shyness and an assumption that this is really her affair often ensures that he expects her to take care of it, that he 'can't be bothered with it'. She has rarely been told anything before marriage, and the amount she has picked up from older girls or married women at work or nearby varies enormously. She must take what advice she can early unless there are to be more children than either she or her husband want. When she has done that her knowledge of the possibilities is likely to be limited to coitus interruptus, the best-known type of pessary, and the sheath. Husbands tend not to like sheaths – 'they take away the pleasure'; she may be embarrassed in buying either those or pessaries, and both are dear; coitus interruptus is probably the commonest practice.

These methods were by no means always effective because of domestic circumstances:

> But to use any of these methods requires a rigid discipline, a degree of sustained competence many wives are hardly capable of. She forgets just once or 'lets herself go', or a sheath is cheap and bursts, or the husband demands awkwardly after a night at the club. How often, therefore, it is assumed that any children after the first one or two were 'not intended' ... unless a miscarriage is procured, the first unintended child is likely to arrive only a year or two after the others.

Families and Households

The trends in population and family size had important effects on the size and number of households and, in turn, on social conditions in British society. Fewer children being conceived meant that households in the inter-war years were generally smaller than they had been in late-Victorian and Edwardian Britain, a trend which was to continue after the Second World War in spite of a rise in the immediate post-war birth rate (see Table 12). But this reduction in average family size was

Table 12: Mean household size,
England and Wales, 1891–1951

1891	4.6
1911	4.4
1921	4.1
1931	3.7
1951	3.2

accompanied by an increase in the number of households. The total number of 'separate occupiers', or families, in England and Wales rose from eight million in 1911 to ten million in 1931, an increase of 25 per cent, while the total population rose by only 11 per cent. The key feature in these seemingly contradictory trends was an upsurge in the proportion of the population getting married which began prior to the First World War. Although the inter-war years saw a marked variation in the number of marriages, with a high point in the immediate post-war years, with the demobilization of troops, and low points in years of economic difficulty such as 1926 and 1932, the overall trend was upwards. By the end of the 1930s the marriage rate in Great Britain as a whole was higher than it had been at any point since the mid nineteenth century. In 1901 only 34 per cent of women aged between fifteen and thirty-nine were married; by 1921 38 per cent; by 1931 41 per cent; and by 1951 almost 49 per cent.

The combination of a reduction in the size of families and an increase in the number of households had major implications for both living standards and social policy. Smaller families meant that income had to be spent on fewer people and average household income per head would have risen in the inter-war years even if real incomes had only remained constant simply because of the reduction of family size. In addition, less of the family income had to be spent on basic necessities, such as food, permitting an increase in savings and in spending on consumer goods and semi-luxuries. As many social investigators had argued, a reduction in family size was one of the principal elements in the reduction of poverty in inter-war Britain and an increase in the standard of comfort for a larger portion of the population. Against that has to be set the link between the increase in the number of households and the provision of housing. Even without changes in the number of households, higher expectations in standards of housing were already evident prior to 1914, but an increase of a quarter between 1911 and 1931 of the number of separate family units put enormous pressures upon housing. A combination of higher expectations and demographic pressure was to make housing one of the major areas of social legislation between the wars. Increasing numbers of marriages but smaller families, allowing greater spending on rent or on a mortgage, provided a major stimulus to the private house-building boom of the 1930s.

Smaller families had important other effects, particularly in regard to the health and status of women. Social investigation into the lives of the poor, and letters received by groups such as the Women's Co-operative Guild or by birth-control pioneers such as Marie Stopes, frequently revealed harrowing stories of women broken in health and spirit by pregnancy after pregnancy. Accounts of five pregnancies in five years, fourteen children by the age of thirty-seven, of sick, worn-out women, already old by their thirties, terrified of the effect of more pregnancies on their physical and material survival, testified to the nature of the situation from which many women had still to free themselves. Fewer large families and a trend towards smaller ones between the wars undoubtedly relieved some of these pressures, but they were certainly not eliminated entirely. Maternal mortality rates remained stubbornly high, particularly in the poorer parts of Britain, and large families remained a cause of family poverty well after the Second World War. But the overall reduction in family size and the use

of birth control of various types undoubtedly reduced the
incidence of desperately large families and the consequent ill-
health of women.

At least as important, as family size declined, birth tended
to become increasingly concentrated in the early years of
married life, so that married women had greater freedom to
take up work outside the home. At the beginning of the
twentieth century, a British woman aged twenty could expect
to live another forty-six years, but spend a third of this time
devoted to childbearing and maternal responsibilities; by 1930
a woman of the same age could expect another sixty years of
life and spend only a tenth of her time bearing or caring for
children. Although only about 22 per cent of married women
went out to work as late as 1951, this was double the rate
thirty years earlier and the opportunity for even this minority
to take up paid work played a significant part in raising living
standards by adding an extra income to the family. Britain was
on the way to having an increasing proportion of married
women at work, a factor to have profound effects upon living
standards and the quality of family life. Fewer children and
work outside the home, combined with rehousing, suburban-
ization and geographical mobility, contributed to the broader
emancipation of women in the first half of the twentieth
century. For some working-class women, this could mean
escape from the tightly structured communities described by
Robert Roberts in *The Classic Slum*; though their survival was
also an important factor in the stability of many older urban
areas in the larger conurbations. For other women, a longer
period free from childbearing meant more time for other
activities. An unseen revolution in which women had more
time to devote themselves to the home or to outside activities
must count as one of the results of a reduction in birth rate.

Moreover, married couples could now look forward to a
longer period living together without young children to look
after and with fewer of them. One result, according to A. H.
Halsey, was the tendency for men to be drawn into a 'more
intimate and longer spousehood'. To a degree there was a

'domestication' of men – a greater involvement by husbands in housework, home improvement and shopping. Leisure activities such as cinema-going, excursions and nights out at the pub were more likely to be shared. Although these tendencies all became more pronounced after 1945 and there were important regional and class variations, there were significant pointers in these directions before the war. Palatial cinemas and new public houses built in the 1930s with lounge bars and decent toilets were aimed not only at men but also their wives and girlfriends. Mass Observation's survey of drinking habits in the mid-thirties noted that, on a typical Saturday evening in a Fulham pub, over a third of the customers were women. Even in a northern working-class town like Bolton, they found that at the weekends in the town-centre pubs, a quarter of the clientele were women, some single girls, but most married women accompanied by their husbands. Heavy, male-only, drinking was concentrated at weekends – most married men stayed at home during the weekday evenings with their wives.

Another consequence of fewer children was a more comfortable house, in which people were becoming home-centred and 'privatized'. Such attitudes dated from well before 1914, particularly amongst the lower middle class and the labour aristocracy who could aspire to 'respectability' and a style of life which in some features at least was moulded by middle-class standards of behaviour. In that sense the adoption of a smaller family pattern was both a symptom and a cause of the increasing absorption of the working class into a pattern of life set by the middle classes. Smaller families, pride in the home, personal cleanliness and domesticity may not have been intrinsically middle-class virtues, but it was they who were first to be able to realize them in the late nineteenth century and it was, chronologically, the working class who followed them in the three or four generations from the end of the nineteenth century to the middle of the twentieth. The gradual ability to afford a wider range of material possessions and the ready acceptance of middle-class ideals of domestic comfort form part of a wider tapestry of cultural change in which smaller families played an important part.

The Place of Women

One of the clichés of modern British social history is the growing emancipation and changing place of women. The granting of political rights, especially the right to vote, increased employment opportunities, and greater freedom in the social sphere marked significant developments on the situation before 1914. Even a few years ago the analysis of these changes involved little more than a relatively straightforward description of 'improvement'. Yet few areas have received more attention in recent years than the role and place of women in society at large, and feminist writing has raised a number of issues which make the evaluation of the position of women in the first half of the twentieth century a far more complicated one than it may appear at first sight.

Undoubtedly the first part of the twentieth century saw important gains for women both in terms of political rights and greater legal, economic and social status. Although the First World War has usually been taken as marking a turning-point both in the acquisition of the right to vote and in wider opportunities for women, it is clear that the war was as much the occasion as the cause of growing female emancipation. By the end of the nineteenth century the Married Women's Property Acts of 1870 and 1882 had given women the right to keep their own wages and wealth; and by 1907 women had acquired both the right to vote and to be elected to positions in local government. The growing national movement for women's suffrage before 1914 had put women's rights on the agenda for future action as one of the most prominent political issues of the Edwardian period. Moreover, although many women, particularly middle-class women, expressed frustration with the restrictions placed upon them by social convention, there were signs of change, seen, for example, in the progress in the provision of women's education. The Girls' Public

Day School Trust opened thirty-three schools between 1872 and 1900 and the establishment of women's colleges at the universities offered greater possibilities for a worthwhile career. By 1914 there were a small number of women doctors, architects and law clerks, a much larger number of teachers, and expanding opportunities in clerical and office work, so that the number of women employed in public administration, professional occupations and commerce rose from 223,000 in 1881 to 590,000 in 1911. By 1914 there were 437,000 women trade-unionists and at a local level many working-class women had become involved in constituency parties, cooperative branches and organizations such as the Women's Co-operative Guilds. Women of all classes also formed the backbone of many of the philanthropic agencies of Victorian and Edwardian society. As well as bringing many middle-class women into contact with some of the most sordid aspects of life, poverty, disease, overcrowding, prostitution, drunkenness and domestic violence, it also produced social investigators such as Maud Pember Reeves and Beatrice Webb who could easily stand on a par with their male counterparts. There was also some evidence of a loosening of social conventions as more women went out to work and some of the fussier constraints of Victorian society were being overcome. Complaints were being registered in local newspapers as early as the 1880s about women seen smoking in public, and the writings of provincial young women like Vera Brittain about their position in the years just before 1914 already registered a growing impatience with restrictions on their freedom to go about unchaperoned, to obtain an education comparable with men and to pursue a career. In that sense the campaign for women's rights – in every sphere – formed part of the 'Progressivism' which was such a prominent feature of Edwardian society.

It is therefore perfectly possible to argue that the years between 1914 and 1945 merely saw the working-out of many of the trends evident before 1914. The granting of women's suffrage in 1918 and its extension to all women on the same basis as men in 1928 marked the most obvious example of this. Other legislation and developments also demonstrated a development of the pre-1914 situation: with the Sex Disqualification (Removal) Act of 1919, the formal legal restrictions on women entering the professions, especially the law, were finally removed, and, by the 1920s, an increasing number of women were entering public life. A notable landmark was the election to Parliament in 1918 of the first woman MP, Countess Markievicz. As a Sinn Feiner she did not take her seat, though she was soon followed by Nancy Astor, who entered Parliament in 1919. The first woman Justice of the Peace, Mrs Ada Summers, took her place in court at Stalybridge in 1920 and Miss Ivy Williams was the first woman to be called to the English Bar, in 1922. According to one estimate, by 1923 there were about 4,000 women magistrates, mayors, councillors or guardians, while in 1929 Margaret Bondfield became the first woman to be appointed a Cabinet Minister.

Legislation also continued the process of enhancing women's rights in family affairs which had begun before 1914. The Matrimonial Causes Act of 1923 relieved a wife of the necessity of proving cruelty, desertion or another 'cause' in addition to adultery as grounds for divorce, followed by the extension of the grounds for divorce by an act of 1927. In a similar way, the Guardianship of Infants Act of 1924 vested the guardianship of infant children in both parents jointly, with the courts to decide upon custody in the event of disagreement between the parents. Women's control over their property was also confirmed by the New English Law of Property of 1926, which provided that both married and single women could hold and dispose of their property, real and personal, on the same terms as men, and the Law Reform Act of 1935, which empowered a married woman to dispose of all her property as if she was single.

Equally important were the growing employment opportunities for women. Although many of the women recruited for factory work during the Great War were substituted by men with the coming of peace, the war permanently enlarged the number of women who went out to work and continued a process of breaking down sexual exclusiveness in several areas, particularly the Civil Service. By 1921 the number of women in public administration and professional and commercial occupations doubled the 1911 figure, reaching over a million, and rose to over one and a half million by 1931. All told the number of women in gainful employment rose by 234,000 between 1911 and 1921 and by another half million by 1931. In addition, many of the new light industries of the inter-war years depended upon the use of relatively cheap female labour. By 1951 the number of women employed had reached 6,961,000, compared with 5,701,000 in 1921. The Second World War itself saw an extra two million women absorbed into the workforce and another half million in the Women's Auxiliary Services. While many of these were only temporary involvements, they again left a permanently enlarged female labour force. In effect both world wars accelerated a trend which can be perceived as early as the Edwardian era, the increasing tendency for women to seek paid work outside the home.

Indeed, taking a long-term view, one of the most peculiar features of twentieth-century British employment patterns in comparison with those of other countries is the high percentage of women who go out to work. By the 1960s this was already higher than in any other European country. One reason for this phenomenon lies in the combination of often low basic wages with high consumer aspirations, particularly in terms of housing. Two incomes became essential to the maintenance of 'affluent' standards and it is possible to argue that this trend was already evident in Britain before the Second World War. Interestingly, Britain stood in this regard closer to American than European experience. Britain had approximately the same proportion of women employed by 1939 as America, but far more than almost every other European country. That Britain had such a high percentage of women at work marked an important cultural development. It also meant that in the Second World War Britain was able to call upon its reserves of woman power much more easily than, say, Germany. As Britain strained every resource for national survival, it was only in line with past experience that British women should play a greater part in the war economy than in most other countries. As a result four-fifths of the total addition to the labour force between 1939 and 1943 consisted of women who had not previously been employed or had been housewives – a transfer which could only have been accomplished without massive protest in a society already conditioned to the idea of women doing a full-time job. Significantly the United Kingdom was the only country where the government took full powers to conscript and direct women, and where unmarried women in certain age groups were in fact conscripted to work in war industries. As a result the proportion of women over fourteen employed in Britain rose from 27 per cent in 1939 to 37 per cent in 1943. That female employment in the years after 1945 was to remain higher in Britain than in most other European countries, in spite of relatively low casualties in the Second World War amongst the male population, served merely to confirm the trend of the pre-war years.

While for many women employment outside the home provided the most important source of independence, there were other forces at work too. Although the suffragette organizations lost much of their impetus after 1918, other women's organizations were developing rapidly. Co-operative Guilds and Labour Women's sections provided one focus of activity for working-class women, holding lectures and discussion groups at which topics might range from birth control to international relations. For some women in more traditional working-class areas they provided a vital window on a much wider range of issues and attitudes than was available in their home surroundings. Their vitality was shown in the way many of them served as the organizational backbone for campaigns like the Peace Ballot and the Aid to Spain movement in the 1930s. In the latter, large quantities of money and food were collected from some of the poorest parts of the country to aid the Republic. In rural areas, a Canadian idea, Women's Institutes, came to play an important role after the first was established in Anglesey in 1915. During the twenty years between the wars Women's Institutes were opened at the rate of five per week. As places where women could meet other women, organize charitable and other activities, as well as broaden their horizons through speakers and outings, they provided further evidence of the growth of women's self-help organizations. Probably the only organization to rival the 'WIs' was the Women's League of Health and Beauty, started in 1930 by Mrs Bagot Stack and her daughter Prunella. Falling in with the cult of healthy athleticism and 'keep fit', which was one of the major aspects of the leisure boom of the 1930s, thousands of women donned white sleeveless blouses and black silk shorts to perform rhythmic exercises to music in countless schools and drill halls, as well as in spectacular mass demonstrations in places like the Albert Hall, Wembley Stadium and Hyde Park. By 1939 an estimated 166,000 women had attended the classes.

But to contemporaries the most obvious changes lay in the dress and appearance of women. In contrast to the elaborate dress and ample curves of the Edwardian era, from 1919 the 'boyish' figure was 'in', with underwear designed to flatten the bosom and clothes which abolished the waistline. Hemlines rose steadily and by the mid-1920s were above the knee. Hair-styles also reflected greater freedom. The general fashion before 1914 was for long hair, only a few women in 'Bohemian' circles wearing it short. After the war, partly under the influence of war work in factories and on farms, there was an almost universal triumph for short hair, with the 'bob', 'shingle' or 'Eton crop' cuts. Both in hair-styles and clothing, women seemed to be demonstrating a new-found freedom. They were assisted in the search for lighter and less elaborate clothing by the development of artificial fibres, such as rayon and nylon, and the development of knitted and woven fabrics such as Celanese. Woollen stockings were increasingly replaced by silk and, later, 'art-silk' stockings or 'nylons'. These fabrics reduced the weight of women's underwear from pounds to a few ounces, doing away with the starched cotton petticoats and formidable corsets – at least for the young – favoured before 1914. Although fashions in both hair-styles and clothing were to change during the inter-war years, with a distinctly more glamorous and 'groomed' look in the 1930s, to be followed by a fashionable 'utility' or 'military' look in the Second World War, there were clear trends in the inter-war years towards shorter hair and much lighter clothing, particularly underwear. By the 1920s newspapers were filled with advertisements for 'lingerie' and 'undies' which would have been classed as indecent a generation earlier. With them came other developments, like the widespread use of cosmetics, particularly lipstick, which had not been considered 'respectable' before the Great War. The introduction of disposable sanitary towels, or tampons, introduced from America in the late 1920s, allowed women greater freedom of movement and enjoyment at all times – a major theme of advertisements in women's magazines from before the Second World War. The emphasis on health and freedom also interacted with fashion in the area of sport. Bathing costumes for women were becoming simpler; the short sleeves and skirt still common in the early 1920s were gradually abandoned and the 'backless' one-piece costume appeared in 1930. In tennis, long skirts, collar and tie, and full-length stockings for women players were abandoned during the 1920s and 'shorts' – introduced from America – had become common by the mid-1930s.

These changes in dress were mirrored by a loosening of the social restraints upon women. For those with experience of the situation before 1914, the change was startling. As one elderly writer in 1932 remarked: 'That a young man should ask his favourite dancing partner to come out with him for the afternoon or evening and take her to some public area, and that it should be a matter of course that he should pay for all incidental expenses and all refreshments consumed by her, would fifty years ago have seemed to us all absolutely outrageous.' By the 1920s young women of all classes could aspire to be free to go out with a boyfriend or girlfriends to cinemas or dance halls without exciting too much comment or parental opposition. Between the wars, freedom and independence were the watch-words of younger women, who could at least contemplate doing many of the jobs done by men and having most of the same liberties. In the public eye, probably no single woman did more to demonstrate the growing independence of women than the flyer Amy Johnson. The daughter of a Hull fish-merchant and graduate of Sheffield University, she took flying lessons and an engineer's licence while earning her living as a typist and solicitor's assistant in London. Her solo flight from England to Australia in 1930, followed by other record-breaking flights, attracted enormous publicity. Although much of the public attention surrounding both Amy Johnson and other female 'firsts' was distinctly patronizing, it was feasible to argue by the outbreak of the Second World War that some women at least had secured a foothold in many hitherto male-dominated areas.

Many of these changes seemed confirmed by the Second World War. Although no women were officially engaged in combat duties, some members of the Women's Auxiliary Air Force underwent virtual front-line service at radar stations and fighter bases in southern England during the Battle of Britain. Women also acted as air-ferry pilots across the Atlantic and in a host of roles, such as drivers, searchlight and anti-aircraft crews, wireless and radar operators, and fighter controllers, most of which would have been deemed unsuitable for women twenty years earlier. Moreover, with the general expansion of female employment during the war and the much greater mobility demanded of male and female labour, many more women were forced to play an independent role, living away from home, finding their own entertainment and essentially living their own lives.

But while by 1945 women had made important steps towards emancipating themselves in some directions, in certain areas very little had changed. Women remained, in spite of their more equal political, legal and economic status, something of a sub-class. While a few women arrived at the top in politics, the professions and the arts, the numbers were very small indeed compared with men. Women might possess the vote, Amy Johnson might have set a new record for a solo flight from

England to India, and women might no longer be regarded as scandalous for smoking in public, but there were still only sixty-seven women parliamentary candidates (nine elected) in the last election before the Second World War and still only eighty-seven (twenty-four elected) in 1945. While both these figures were an improvement on the situation in 1918 (seventeen candidates, one elected), women had clearly a long way to go before achieving anything approaching parity with men in political life – the number of women Cabinet Ministers before 1945 could be counted comfortably on the fingers of one hand. That this affected most other areas of public life was only too obvious to contemporary 'thinking' women. In *Women*, published in 1934, Winifred Holtby noted:

> The young probationer, scuttling down the long corridors of the hospital; the aspirant to the hotel business counting linen in the basement storeroom; the junior reporter encountering upon the stone staircase of the great newspaper building the boss of the concern, and the factory hand watching the proprietor of the works drive off to a board meeting – these leaders, these field marshals whose baton she does not, she feels, carry in her knapsack, are not women.

The situation was reflected in all fields of employment. Women were characteristically employed in what were classed as unskilled jobs, particularly in the distributive, clerical and service industries. Their wage rates were usually half those of men and their conditions of employment, in terms of training and promotion prospects, markedly inferior. Indeed one of the principal reasons why female employment expanded in many of the new light industries and service trades was precisely because they were cheaper to employ than men. Women also remained one of the least organized sections of the workforce, primarily because they were in trades which were notoriously difficult to organize. Although the total number of women in trade unions grew between the wars, it did so only slightly. By 1938 the number of women trade-unionists had risen only 100,000 (to 926,000) over the figure in 1923, and the percentage of all women employees in trade unions was only 14.7 per cent compared with 37.8 per cent of men.

Both low pay and lack of organization were symptoms of a position in which women's work was considered secondary to that of men. Moreover, male trade-unionists were often the strongest opponents of greater opportunities for women. As the 'dilution' arguments of the First World War had revealed – and an era of heavy unemployment was to emphasize – women workers were often seen as a threat both to jobs and wage levels. The comments of Barbara Drake in a Labour Research Department publication produced just after the First World War, *Women in Trade Unions*, continued to apply with great force throughout the inter-war years: 'Trade union restrictions on female labour are the common rule in organized trades. According as the men's trade unions are strong, female labour is entirely prohibited ... or women are restricted to certain inferior branches of the industry, or to low-paid work and customarily define their status as "unskilled", whatever the actual nature of the work involved.' Significantly, the only opposition to the Restoration of Pre-War Practices Act in 1918, which ended the 'dilution' agreements, came from middle-class women's organizations who saw it as a re-confirmation of women as second-class workers. The result of these attitudes, as Drake suggested, was that women tended to be unorganized and developed a 'non-union' tradition which gave employers a vested interest in securing cheap and docile female labour in preference to men.

But these attitudes on the part of male trade-unionists, while affecting a vital sphere – the possibilities of full economic independence for women – were only symptoms of a more general attitude towards women shared by most people in responsible positions in government and society, usually, of course, men, but also, more tellingly, by many women themselves. This was, in essence, that the proper sphere of women, especially married women, was in the home. Hence, legislation such as the Anomalies Act of 1931 almost assumed that married women should not be part of the labour force. The Act provided that unless a married woman had paid a certain number of contributions since marriage, she would receive no unemployment benefit however many contributions she had made while single. Married women were not normally to be regarded as part of the workforce, whatever the effects of changing patterns of family size or women's aspirations. Nor were these attitudes confined to conservatives – they would have been supported by many working-class men, and even by many of the more progressive voices of the inter-war years. In 1946, William Beveridge could write in relation to his National Insurance proposals that: '... the attitude of the housewife to gainful employment outside the home is not and should not be the same as that of the single woman ... Mothers have vital work to do in ensuring the adequate continuance of the British race.' Hence even in what were regarded as progressive occupations, such as the Civil Service (who paid women four-fifths of men's salaries), women had to leave the Service when they married. There were few married women teachers and for many an effective choice had to be made between a family or a career. Even in areas with a tradition of female employment, married women who left work to have children had virtually no prior claim to their old jobs.

Hence in spite of the widening of employment opportunities for women, particularly during the Second World War, many traditional attitudes remained. For example, the conscription of women proceeded to a limited extent during the Second World War – in practice it applied only to single women between nineteen and twenty-four. While some women in these services took up challenging roles, a majority were employed in traditional 'female' jobs – nursing, catering and clerical work. Attitudes, in fact, proved much harder to change than the franchise qualifications or the law of property. While women were primarily seen and, it must be said, largely saw themselves as mothers and homemakers, it was almost inevitable that they would play a secondary role to men in careers and public life. Though the spread of smaller families gave women more opportunity to spend a greater part of their lives at work, either before marriage or after their children had grown up, there is ample evidence that the majority of women saw paid work or a career as only a secondary part of their lives. Concerns primarily with home and family were reflected and reinforced by the highly successful women's magazines which came into their own in the inter-war years. The overwhelming emphasis of all these magazines was on romance, marriage, home and family, and the most popular combined serials, short stories, recipes, fashion tips, clothes' patterns, advice on home management, problem pages and a quasi-philosophical article (usually written by a man). *Woman*, the most successful, with three-quarters of a million sales by 1939, advertised its 'comprehensive advice service', which invited its readers to write in on 'your woes, whatever they are' and listed its specialist advisers under the headings beauty, fashion, art of living, furnishing, housekeeping, cookery and child care. This was woman's sphere with a vengeance – and it was immensely popular. The staple diet of serials and stories was love and marriage or, as Kate Caffrey pithily put it, 'stories about the problems of married couples, and the stories about how one got to be a married couple'.

An important component of these magazines and the press in general was the image of women presented in advertising. Whether aimed at the middle-class housewife or the working girl, the emphasis was on clothes and cosmetics, the 'ideal' home, and the contented well-fed family and happy husband. 'Happy and lucky is the man,' noted the new magazine *Housewife*, launched in 1939, 'whose wife is houseproud ... who likes to do things well, to make him proud of her and her children.' Both the rise in real household incomes and the growing number of women with independent incomes made them immensely important as consumers. Whether advertisers shaped or merely reflected women's roles is a moot point. There is little doubt, however, that their emphasis on appearance and domesticity did little to disturb the *status quo*. Indeed, at a time when women might theoretically aspire to a wider role in society as a result of smaller families and an increase in job opportunities, advertising insistently urged them to concentrate their free time and extra income within conventional stereotypes of a woman's place and role.

In sexual matters, women were still only emancipating themselves from a combination of ignorance and prudery. One of
the principal undertakings of such people as Marie Stopes was
to advocate sexual enjoyment and fulfilment for women at a
time when, as letters to her well into the 1930s often so painfully revealed, many women had little of either. Certainly, the
First World War and the 1920s saw the lowering of some
sexual taboos in which sexual pleasure and birth control were
espoused in progressive circles. There was also a growing
emphasis on sexual pleasure in marriage by a number of writers
and the beginning of the scientific investigation of sexuality.
Books such as Theodore van de Velde's *Ideal Marriage*, translated from the original Dutch in 1930, advocated sexual fulfilment for both partners in marriage through the conscious
application of sexual technique and, going through forty-three
printings, reached an educated readership. So too did the
Christian manual, *Threshold of Marriage*, published in 1932 for
engaged couples, which offered instruction on how both
partners could achieve orgasm and sold over half a million
copies. These changes also began to be reflected in advice
columns in women's magazines by the late 1930s, some of
which by 1939 were running articles on sexual matters and
providing booklets on family planning and marital problems
to do with sex. Fragmentary evidence from sexual inquiries
also suggested that more women growing up in the inter-war
years had some sexual experience before marriage. Whereas 19
per cent of married women born before 1904 had engaged in
pre-marital sex, this figure rose to 36 per cent of those born
in 1904–14 and to 39 per cent for those born in 1914–24. This
meant that, roughly, the proportion of women who were
virgins on marriage had fallen from about 80 to about 60 per
cent between 1918 and 1945. Similar increases were also found
in the incidence of 'petting' and non-coital sex. According to
one survey of working-class women, half found 'some pleasure'
in sex, but for only a minority was it a source of 'real pleasure'.
Whereas a third always experienced orgasm, between a third
and a quarter did so infrequently or insufficiently. Clearly

experience of sexual enjoyment varied enormously between individuals and circumstances, but at least one woman writer noted in 1931 that 'The subject of physical happiness in marriage raises a pathetically eager response in working women's meetings ... It is often news to them that they might at all share the sex enjoyment of their husbands...' Guilt, embarrassment, frustration, unhappiness and sheer ignorance were still all too common features of many women's attitude towards sex, and were far from being eliminated even by the end of the Second World War. Sex was often still something to be endured rather than enjoyed.

On the other hand, and with often cruel irony, women were expected to be sex symbols. 'Keep young and beautiful, if you want to be loved,' the theme of one popular song, neatly expressed the basic message of countless romantic songs, stories and advertisements in the inter-war years aimed at women. While much of this kind of popular culture could be dismissed as mere fantasy, there was little doubt that women were expected to conform to certain stereotypes which demanded of them constant attention to fashion and cosmetics, and a trim, healthy figure. 'What happens to girls in black stockings?' – 'Nothing,' was just one refrain in a dialogue between women and their culture which left little scope for breaking conventional sexual roles.

Women emerged after the Second World War as a kind of sub-class. Many of the high hopes of the early feminist pioneers for full equality had not been achieved. Equal pay and equal opportunities was still more talked about than practised and women had still to go a very long way before sloughing off the traditional roles and attributes assigned to them by men and willingly, in most cases, accepted by women. By the post-war years there were not a few veteran suffragettes who were ready to admit that the high ideals of the early movement had been sold out for short-term benefits. In truth, as in so many radical movements in the British context – indeed in the case of feminism one which carried to its logical conclusions had genuinely revolutionary implications for the conduct of society, economy and politics – women had accepted half a loaf as better than none. *Relative* improvements, in terms of legal status, employment opportunities and social freedoms, had been accepted by women, most of them quite unconscious of the larger issues, to the disregard of the basic inequalities from which they suffered. A measure of equality and an element of independence had been obtained but only within a culture and economy which remained male-dominated in all its important features.

6. Occupations, Work and Organized Labour

The experience of work was obviously one of the central features in the lives of the average British man or woman in this period. Occupation to a large degree determined income, place of residence and social status. In turn these largely accounted for living standards, expectations, friends and associates, and patterns of leisure and culture. Work occupied the bulk of the active time of the great majority of men and a smaller proportion of women during their years of youth and adulthood. Apart from spells of sickness or unemployment, it was perfectly feasible for someone to spend between five and six days a week for at least fifty weeks a year between the ages of fifteen and seventy working. For many, work was not only a means of earning a living, it was also what shaped the whole pattern of life, structuring the day, week and year, as well as influencing private life and leisure. Ultimately, for many, work provided a sense of identity in which people characteristically described themselves in terms of their occupation with the social and cultural resonance it implied. The experience of the unemployed who, characteristically, often felt not only material hardship but also a profound sense of personal loss and inadequacy, testified to the central role of work in personal esteem.

Occupations

Already by the Edwardian era, the great majority of the population of Great Britain were dependent upon industry and commerce for their livelihoods. Although it still employed almost two million people in 1911, agriculture accounted for less than a tenth of the working population. By this date the total occupied population of England, Wales and Scotland amounted to 18,300,000 people, 12,900,000 men and 5,400,000 women. Some of the largest categories occupying male workers reflected the enormous industrial expansion of the nineteenth century. More than a million men (1,202,000) were engaged in mining and quarrying; almost two million (1,795,000) in metal manufacture, vehicle building and engineering; and another million in textiles and clothing (1,071,000). But just as the population working in agriculture had stabilized, the proportions working in mining and other staple industries had reached a peak. Some of the most significant growth now lay in consumer industries. The food, drink and tobacco industries employed 806,000 in 1911, more than either textiles or clothing taken separately. The building and construction industry, benefiting from the rapid urbanization of the Victorian and Edwardian period, employed over a million workers (1,140,000). Transport now also involved more than a million workers (1,262,000), including all classes of railwaymen, drivers, carters and seamen. The rise of these 'service' industries was one significant feature of the Edwardian era; another was the growth of the 'black-coated' workers, involved in clerical work, serving in shops, and in the lower grades of the professions. The number engaged in 'commercial occupations' had risen from a mere 91,000 in 1851 to 739,000 by 1911. Similarly the numbers involved in professional occupations had risen to 413,000.

In the third of the Edwardian workforce which consisted of women, over two million were accounted for by domestic servants, totalling 2,127,000 in 1911. Although the number of women and girls 'in service' had almost doubled since 1851, the growth had slowed in the Edwardian period, rising by only 124,000 between 1901 and 1911. Women and girls were also strongly represented in the clothing and textile trades. There were, in fact, more women employed in the textile industry than men (870,000) and twice as many in the clothing industry as men (825,000). Women were also heavily engaged in commercial occupations, as shop assistants and the like, and

Table 13: Occupational status as a percentage of all workers in Great Britain in 1911 and 1951

	Males		Females	
	1911	1951	1911	1951
Self-employed and higher-salaried professionals	1.5	2.8	1.0	1.0
Employers and proprietors	7.7	5.7	4.3	3.2
Administrators and managers	3.9	6.8	2.3	2.7
Lower-grade professionals and technicians	1.4	3.0	5.8	7.9
Inspectors, supervisors and foremen	1.8	3.3	0.2	1.1
Clerical workers	5.1	6.0	3.3	20.3
Sales personnel and shop assistants	5.0	4.0	6.4	9.6
Skilled manual workers and self-employed artisans	33.0	30.3	24.6	12.7
Semi-skilled manual workers	29.1	24.3	47.0	33.6
Unskilled manual workers	11.5	13.8	5.1	7.9
Total per cent	100	100	100	100

in the lower grades of professional work as clerks and typists. Between them, these two categories employed another half million women. Taken together, 71 per cent of all men were occupied and 29 per cent of all women.

This occupational breakdown reveals that in 1911 over three-quarters of the working population were engaged in manual work, whether skilled, semi-skilled or unskilled. Although manual occupations were gradually declining as a proportion of the total workforce with the rise of service industries such as retailing, entertainment and clerical work, they still made up the bulk of the employed population. The lowest category of unskilled labour consisted primarily of general labourers, more typically men than women. The semi-skilled category included domestic servants, accounting for the strong representation of women workers. Women were also well represented in the category of skilled manual work, primarily in the textile spinning and weaving industries, though other trades, such as coalmining, engineering and most other skilled trades, were exclusively male preserves. Shop assistants were usually men, but the number of women employed was rising steadily. Of the great army of clerks, 21 per cent were now women compared with 13 per cent in 1901, though the higher grades of 'superior' clerks still tended to be male-dominated. Women were more prominent in the category of 'lower-grade professionals', a category which included teachers. Although some women were represented in the three higher grades, particularly as boarding-house keepers and landladies, the higher echelons of the professions, business and management were predominantly male.

The major changes in this pattern of occupations and employment were the tendency, present throughout the twentieth century and shared by other developed industrial societies, for the occupational structure to become more differentiated and more balanced. The proportion of manual workers in the population was beginning to fall. In 1911 they had made up almost three-quarters of the working population, by 1951 barely two-thirds, a trend which was to continue after 1951. At the same time the proportion of the workforce occupying the middle-ranking occupations, clerical, administrative and technical areas, was growing. This change in the occupational structure has been described as a change from one shaped liked a pyramid to one shaped like a light bulb. It was a shift, however, which affected men and women differently. In 1911 approximately the same proportion of men as women employees were involved in manual work, approximately three-quarters. Although the proportion of men in manual work did decline, the fall was very much greater amongst women, only half being in manual work by 1951, with a very distinct movement of women into non-manual areas, especially clerical work.

The growth of 'white-collar' workers has been described as the 'outstanding social change' in this period. This development was the result of two related factors: the increasing proportion of salaried workers in industry and elsewhere, and the growth of service occupations, such as retailing, local and central government and entertainment, which tended to employ salaried workers. Between 1924 and 1948 it has been estimated that the proportion of administrative staff to manual workers increased from about one in nine to one in five. According to the census returns, there was an increase of nearly 1.4 million people in salaried occupations between 1911 and 1931, of whom 650,000 were women, while the number of salaried employees in private industry rose by 1,170,000 and in public service by more than 200,000. This growing sphere of administrative and clerical work offered women in particular increased opportunities, but salaried occupations in general provided nearly all their workers with more stable incomes and higher social status. Although as a percentage of the total labour force the increase in the numbers of salaried workers was only a matter of a few per cent, they represented a crucial element in the social mobility of the period: expanding opportunities for raised status and more secure employment than existed in manual work.

Manual workers continued to make up the bulk of the workforce. Undoubtedly the flight of women from manual work was one of the striking features of the period, though the proportion of men remained more stable. Within the manual sector, however, important changes were taking place. Not only was there a fall in the numbers engaged in manufacturing, but there were major changes between different areas of industry. There was, for example, a considerable fall in the numbers involved in several of the staple industries. Employment in the coal industry fell by almost half a million, from 1,202,000 in 1911 to 702,000 in 1938; in cotton textiles from 621,500 in 1912 to 393,000 in 1938; and in the shipbuilding industry by a quarter between 1924 and 1937. But expansion of employment occurred in areas such as construction, which absorbed an extra 318,000 workers between 1920 and 1938, and in the electricity supply industry, which increased by 107,000. The biggest absolute gains in employment occurred in wholesale and retail distribution, where employment rose from 1,773,200 in 1920 to 2,438,200 in 1938, while 'miscellaneous services', including entertainment, sport, catering, dry-cleaning and personal services, such as hairdressing, rose from 2,025,400 to 2,754,800 between 1920 and 1938.

Work

The nature and variety of the experience which so shaped people's lives is difficult to portray in general terms. While the proportion of manual workers was falling, they still in 1931 made up almost 70 per cent of the workforce, overwhelmingly employed and paid on a weekly basis. On one side of this group lay the professional and salaried workers, usually paid monthly, while on the other lay the casual workers, the day labourers of the docks, the building workers, and fringe 'casuals' who took up marginal employment of many different kinds when it became available.

Conditions of work varied enormously. If one trend was evident increasingly from the late nineteenth century it was the gradual transformation of the character of manual work. New production methods meant that the size of factories was increasing and there was a growing reliance upon semi-skilled and unskilled labour. The independent craftsman was a dwindling breed, while the number of 'casuals' was beginning to fall. The general tendency which has been identified is that of a routinization of work, with fewer skilled workers, less casuals, larger concerns and more impersonal relations between employers and employees. It appears that mechanization and mass production were beginning to undermine the position of the skilled worker. For example, the crafts of the coach-builder and engineer seen in the first motor cars were increasingly overtaken by the lesser skills of the production-line worker in the new car factories. The theme was captured in film and literature. Chaplin's *Modern Times* of 1940, with its caricature of

production-line techniques, was retold from real-life experience
by Walter Greenwood in his description of the Ford works
at Trafford Park, Manchester, in the late 1920s:

When an employee of the Motor Works passed through the works'
gates to the clocking-on machines he stepped from Britain into Detroit
where Moloch, in the shape of the Main Line Assembly, held unrelent-
ing sway. Parallel tracks down the central aisles of the main shop's
length crept forward at a pre-set pace. Tributary feeder tracks at angles
conveniently placed and moving at synchronized speed delivered the
prefabricated bits and pieces to the servitors who had to be at their
stations along the lines the moment the klaxon blared its imperious
and ear-lacerating dissonance. And there the workers stayed, each
performing his repetitive operation, until the hooter screamed again
signalling the half-hour midday break and the mad rush into the street,
rain or shine, to bolt a boxed lunch and devour a cigarette before the
siren's discord recalled the hirelings to the paralysing monotony of
the endless afternoon.

Irrespective of its tone of hostility, this quotation suggests
much of the salient character of the new, mass-production
factories which were beginning to dominate some of the major
industries. In the retail and service trades, something of a similar
development can be seen in the growth of large concerns. Scale,
whatever its other compensations in terms of efficiency, viability
and higher wages, frequently meant a more impersonal work
environment. By the post-war years, sociologists were beginning to talk about the 'instrumental' approach amongst workers
in large-scale modern industry: work as a necessary means of
obtaining money through which satisfactions of other kinds –
the products of consumerism and leisure – could be obtained,
with fewer of the satisfactions possible from skill or personal
commitment. But it is almost impossible to assess with any
real degree of certainty whether most manual workers were,
in general terms, any less committed, or committed in a
different way, to their work in 1945 than in 1914. Opinions
can be cited which support either the view that attitudes were
changing a good deal, or that much stayed the same. The situation is complicated because industrial conditions varied

enormously from one part of the country to another, between
particular industries and even from plant to plant. Scotland,
for example, had seen the growth of a number of very large
engineering companies even before the First World War. The
Singer plant at Clydebank employed 10,000 in 1914 and during
the war there was a massive expansion of capacity and plant-size
in the engineering and munitions sector. The effects of the
depression, however, left the economy still dominated by small
to medium-sized concerns on the eve of the Second World
War. Out of 433 factories employing more than 250 people
in 1938, only fifty-nine employed over 1,500 people. Similar
results could be found in other areas. The large modern coal
pits of east Durham, contrasted with the much smaller, older
mines of the west. If in the new trading estates, such as Trafford
Park and the more prosperous areas of the South and Midlands,
the larger factory was becoming more common, elsewhere it
often existed side by side with older, smaller concerns. Even
some expanding areas of the economy, such as the construction
industry, were still organized on a relatively small scale. None
the less, by 1935 over one half of the workers enumerated in
the industrial census worked in plants employing 500 or more,
with the heaviest concentrations in the newer industries, such
as artificial fibres, electrical machinery, food processing and the
rubber industry.

   Although in the service sector the number of employees per
unit was usually much lower, a parallel development can be
seen in the much greater likelihood of being employed by a
large organization. On the one hand there were the expanding
public service occupations, the Civil Service, the Post Office
and local government, on the other the growth of the large
retail chains, the commercial and financial companies, and the
entertainment industry. The 'living-in' shop assistant, working
for a personal employer, was increasingly being replaced by
the employee of an organization such as Marks and Spencer
or Woolworths, the clerk or secretary belonging to one of
the big banking groups or major insurance companies. The
equivalent to mechanization and routinization for the growing

number of office workers was the establishment of standard procedures and specialization of function within the office. Bureaucratic reorganization of work carried out in both the Civil Service and banking after the First World War paralleled what was happening in manual work through the introduction of machinery. There were, however, important differences in their effects in the office as opposed to the factory. Office workers were still typically employed in relatively small units. Half of all office workers in 1949 were working in establishments where the average number of clerks or typists was twenty-six or less. Small offices or office sections of manufacturing industry provided a far less impersonal environment than the assembly line. Moreover, in contrast to factory production, rationalization of clerical and office work frequently permitted the retention of a more personal working environment by multiplying both the number of managerial and supervisory positions and the number of specialized office units. Generally these seem to have allowed the continuation of a more personal involvement by clerical staff in their work than in the factory, while the proliferation of supervisory grades permitted investment in title and status increasingly denied to the factory 'hand'. They added ever further to the attractions of office work as the factory became increasingly a place of routine, mechanized production.

In terms of actual conditions of work, an enormous disparity of experience has also to be recorded. To an extent at least, one of the most important legacies of the nineteenth century lay in government legislation to limit hours of work and protect particular groups. Concern about the 'sweated trades' in the late-Victorian and Edwardian era had led to protective legislation. Traditional concern about the employment of young people and women was also reflected in a new Factory Act in 1937, which laid down that young people under sixteen were to work no more than a forty-four hour week, and those between sixteen and eighteen, and women, not more than forty-eight hours a week. Moreover, as in the Great War, control of labour in the years 1939–45 forced a fresh appraisal of work conditions. Within a wider context of improved welfare facilities, including such things as universal free school meals and nursery facilities to encourage women to go to work, there was a vast expansion in medical and social services in the munitions factories and other essential industries. The number of whole-time and part-time factory doctors, thirty-five and seventy respectively, rose to 181 and 890 by 1944, and there was an increase from 1,500 to 8,000 in the number of industrial nurses between 1939 and 1943. The number of factory canteens rose substantially, from about 3,000 in 1940 to almost 12,000 in 1945. Factory inspectors were also empowered to appoint welfare and personnel officers in large concerns, the number rising threefold to almost 5,400 by 1944.

This rapid improvement of working conditions was in large measure a direct result of the war effort; it also provided a barometer of the level of provision in most factories and mines up to the Second World War. Except in a few enlightened firms, notably philanthropic employers like Cadbury and Son, Marks and Spencer, and the cooperative movement's manufacturing and retail side, there was often little concern for the safety and convenience of employees. While many of the more modern factories were healthier than the old, with better lighting, heating, sanitation and medical facilities, even a utilitarian works canteen or adequate washing facilities were relative luxuries for many manual workers between the wars. In many older factories and workshops conditions were still more often than not primitive and degrading. Moreover, with the spread of greater mechanization and mass-production methods there was often a price to be paid in terms of accidents and sickness. In 1931 the factory inspectorate reported the rise of 'nervous disabilities' and 'mental weariness' amongst process workers, while a very large number of deaths and injuries was commonplace, and the accident rate was virtually no better than it had been in the Edwardian era. Young and inexperienced workers were particularly vulnerable. The 1937 Factory Act attempted to strengthen and codify safety regulations and improve conditions of work as regards minimum standards of ventilation, temperature and lighting, industries with 'dangerous processes', special facilities for women workers, and training for young workers before they worked dangerous machinery. Nevertheless the number of fatal accidents in Britain between the wars was almost twice what it was in the 1960s, even though the workforce was considerably smaller. Just how dangerous British industry could still be was shown in the explosion at Gresford Colliery, near Wrexham, in September 1934 in which 264 men lost their lives. This was an exceptional catastrophe, but there was a continual toll of fatalities and accidents which rarely received much publicity. It was, however, to make workmen's compensation for death and industrial injury one of the major demands of organized labour between the wars, though it was not to be achieved until 1946.

Hours of work, however, were reduced substantially in the phase of industrial militancy in 1918–21. Generally, the working day was reduced from 9 hours, usually meaning a 54-hour week, including a lengthy Saturday work period, to 8, with a 46½–48 hour week becoming common. Some industries saw a reduction from two shifts of 12 hours to three shifts of 8 hours. Although these changes came under pressure during the depression as employers sought to cut costs and trade-union bargaining power was weakened, Sidney Pollard described the reduction in hours of work as 'perhaps the most valuable permanent gain from all the high hopes of post-war "reconstruction" '. But while trade-union agreements generally provided for a 48-hour week, it was still legal up to 1937 for women and young people to work up to 60 hours in non-textile factories and up to 600 hours' overtime per year. In some casual trades, agriculture and smaller firms existing in the twilight area of semi-legality, these terms could be and were easily abused. Rush periods in industries like clothing or light engineering often led to long hours being worked by women, youths and those desperate for work. Even the Factory Act of 1937, which reduced the legal hours of work for women and youths, still permitted employees in seasonal trades to work up to 60 hours a week for half the year. Although hours of work for young shop assistants were limited to 48 a week by the 1934 Shops Act, exceptions could be made for seasonal work. Thus in 1938 the average number of hours worked by men over twenty-one in 'principal industries' was 47.7 hours a week, for women 43.5. Significantly these were virtually the same as found twenty years later, except that men's hours of work had slightly increased because of more plentiful overtime, while those of women had been slightly reduced. Although concealing massive variations and the very considerable dis-locations caused by unemployment and short-time working, these figures suggested a typical working week of five or five and a half days. Ten- and twelve-hour shifts were still not uncommon in some industries, while split-shifts, in which workers might be called on to go to work twice to complete a day's work, were far from uncommon, particularly in indus-tries such as transport and those under severe pressure during the depression. Paid holidays came relatively slowly in Britain. Only three million people were entitled to them as late as 1938, when the Holidays with Pay Act extended paid holidays to over eleven million workers, usually of one week. On the eve of the Second World War the Agricultural Wages Boards and Trade Boards were also given power by the Act to fix holidays with pay. If voluntary agreements proved inadequate, the government proposed to bring in compulsion.

A crucial aspect of employment conditions was also governed by the extension of National Insurance to cover sickness and unemployment (see pp. 296–306). In the major area of wages, the First World War also led to greater government inter-vention to promote arbitration and wage fixing. Although it was industrial militancy which often captured the headlines in the aftermath of the war, there was a powerful undercurrent of conciliation which, in spite of its failures, never entirely sub-sided. The Whitley Report in 1917 had proposed the setting-up of joint industrial councils, made up of representatives of employers and workers, on national, district and works level, to resolve labour questions. Joint Industrial Councils were founded in a number of minor industries, though usually without the local sub-committees recommended in the Report. Their most successful application came in government-controlled areas of work, the Civil Service and the Post Office. Another result of the Whitley Report, the Industrial Courts Act of 1919, gave the Ministry of Labour power of conciliation and inquiry without power of compulsory arbitration. On the other hand the National Industrial Conference, established to provide a permanent peaceful meeting ground of capital and labour, ceased to exist in 1921. In that year, however, the Railway Act instituted an arbitration procedure. In agriculture, although the traditional hiring fair was to survive even after 1945 in some of the more remote parts of Britain, it was dealt a blow by the introduction of an Agricultural Wages Board in 1917 and by the Agricultural Wages Act of 1924. Thirty-three new Trade Boards were also set up between 1919 and 1921 to provide a compulsory system of wage fixing in industries without formal negotiating machinery. A move against this system came in 1922 with the report of the Cave committee, so that only ten new boards were created between 1922 and 1939. In all by 1939 Trade Boards covered only one and a half million workers. The Industrial Court set up in 1919 continued to operate between the wars, drawing its members from three groups, employers, employees and independents. Although the courts could only be appointed on the request of both main parties and its decisions were not binding, it made 1,700 awards between 1919 and 1934. The Industrial Court was also given further jurisdiction in specific industries between the wars, as in the Road Traffic Act of 1930, the Sugar Industry Act of 1936, the Air Navigation Act of 1936 and the Road Haulage Wages Act of 1938. A new departure in industrial legislation was undertaken in the cotton industry in 1934 following a bitter strike in the weaving trade in 1932. The Cotton Manufacturing Industry (Temporary Provisions) Act provided for statutory sanction to be given to wages arrived at by collective bargaining. Similar provisions were written into the Road Haulage Act of 1938. In 1936, the Civil Service Arbitration Tribunal was set up to deal with all Civil Service disputes.

Two major features stand out concerning the place of work in this period. First, for an increasing number of manual workers there was increasing impersonalization of work – larger firms, bigger factories, more routine and mechanized production. Whatever their other effects, these factors contributed to what has been characterized as 'low-discretion' and 'low-trust' relationships between workers and employers. The increasing demise of the small family firm, small workshop and individual craftsmen – all in evidence before 1914 – helped to encourage amongst employees the 'instrumental' approach to work. Real improvements in working conditions were often more than offset by the effects of depression and short-time working. For many workers, the inter-war years were a time of vulnerability, when every concession had to be fought for and small gains defended if possible. Second, the experience of the increased bargaining strength of labour in the wars and of greater government concern often served only to reinforce the impression, whether true or false, that little could be gained without a display of organized militancy, that concessions from employers were grudging and that a wide gap separated the interests of workers and management. In spite of the various excursions into arbitration and conciliation, there was little evidence by 1945 that the majority of manual workers could respond in anything other than a marginal way to demands for greater commitment or involvement in their work. A legacy of grievances from the nineteenth century, the experience of the depression and the often crude application of modern production and management techniques prevented any real development of attitudes beyond those already prevalent in 1914.

Organized Labour

The Great War witnessed a major expansion of trade-union membership, providing a continuation of the growth already evident by 1914. By 1920 there were 8.3 million trade-unionists, representing about 45 per cent of potential union members in the workforce. Thereafter union membership began to fall, reaching a low point of 4.4 million members in 1933, less than a quarter of the workforce. By 1939, however, this had recovered to 6.3 million and during the Second World War again climbed to near its former peak, with 7.9 million trade-union members in 1945.

The growth of the unions from before 1914 had been encouraged by their success in raising wages and improving conditions for unskilled and semi-skilled as well as for skilled workers. Trade-unionists had become an influential body of opinion, emphasized during the Great War by the efforts made to secure their cooperation in the war effort through representation in government, public authorities and arbitration tribunals. As the demands of the war increased, the power of organized labour was strengthened. Dilution agreements, wage increases and greater political concessions, such as the introduction of rationing and taxes on war profits, illustrated their strong bargaining position. These carried over into the immediate post-war period when union militancy was reinforced by rising material expectations, the impact of the Russian Revolution, the spread of socialist and Marxist ideas amongst some sections of labour, and syndicalist ideas which counselled faith in union militancy rather than political means to obtain industrial and political objectives. The effect was a mounting toll of strikes, of which there were more in the immediate post-war years than at any other time in the inter-war period, apart from the year of the General Strike (see Table 14).

The strike-wave of the years 1917–22 formed a continuation of pre-war developments. Although interrupted by the war, industrial action in the period from 1906 to the General Strike has been characterized by one writer as having four main themes: first, the recognition of trade unions by employers; second, increases in wages in the era of rising prices up to 1920; third, the attempt to integrate new categories of skilled and semi-skilled work into the existing framework of industrial relations; and fourth, the retention of gains in wages and hours of work achieved during the war and immediate post-war years.

Table 14: Working days lost in industrial disputes, 1914–45

	('000s)		
1914	9,878	1930	4,399
1915	2,953	1931	6,983
1916	2,446	1932	6,488
1917	5,647	1933	1,072
1918	5,875	1934	959
1919	34,969	1935	1,955
1920	26,568	1936	1,829
1921	85,872	1937	3,413
1922	19,850	1938	1,334
1923	10,672	1939	1,356
1924	8,424	1940	940
1925	7,952	1941	1,079
1926	162,233	1942	1,527
1927	1,174	1943	1,808
1928	1,388	1944	3,714
1929	8,287	1945	2,835

Strikes amongst engineers, railwaymen, cotton workers, York-shire miners, foundry workers and the police, to name only the most prominent, gave the post-war years a character quite different from the rest of the inter-war years. Political demands for the nationalization of the mines, railways and land, workers' control, taxes on capital, the nationalization of the banks, and improved provisions for the unemployed proved attractive in a period of heady optimism in which trade-unionists flexed the muscles developed during the war years. But from the end of 1920, many trade unions were on the defensive. Rising unemployment and depression in the staple industries undermined their bargaining power, and there was a series of bitter conflicts as employers began a counter-offensive. The largest of the post-war disputes outside the coal industry occurred in the engineering industry in 1922, when the engineering employers locked out the members of the Amalgamated Engineering Union and forty-seven other unions over the refusal of the unions to permit unlimited overtime at the employers' discretion. A three-month dispute ended when the unions were forced to return to work following the exhaustion of their funds. In the coal industry a series of strikes and threats of strikes, demands for the nationalization of the coal industry from trade-unionists, and attempts to enforce wage cuts by employers led to the dispute which erupted into the General Strike of May 1926. Although the strike is more a matter of concern for a political history than a social one, it illustrated some important traits which are relevant to the place of organized labour within British social development. Notably, there was the remarkable ability of the trade-union movement to command the loyalty of working people. The call for a General Strike by the General Council of the TUC met with a virtually complete response by the workers called out, demonstrating convincingly that the trade unions could count upon the support of millions of workers if necessary. Amongst the coal-miners, the strike lasted eight months, until union funds ran out and the various districts were forced to settle on the basis of wage reductions and a lengthening of the working day.

Viewed as a contest between the TUC and the government, the General Strike was an almost complete victory for the government. Emergency powers were used to maintain essential supplies, essential information was distributed by the BBC and the government-controlled *British Gazette*, while the government proved capable of rallying influential sections of public opinion in what was represented as an unconstitutional attempt by the trade-union movement to use industrial action to decide the fate of the coal dispute. Most significant of all, however, was the reluctance shown by the TUC leaders to face the challenge of a General Strike with political overtones. It was the 'unconstitutional' nature of their proceedings which led the General Council to call off the strike within nine days, leaving the miners to carry on alone. Viewed and felt as a humiliating defeat by most trade-unionists, the General Strike was less a turning-point than a confirmation of trends already evident; notably an acceptance that reformist and constitutional methods were more likely to bring satisfactory results than head-on confrontation with the government. This was already apparent before 1926;

union membership had been falling since 1920, strike figures had fallen yearly since 1921 and funds were depleted by declining membership and the cost of the post-war strikes. Moreover, the strike itself had been conducted fairly peacefully. Although there were some violent clashes with the police and over 5,000 people were arrested during the strike, there was little evidence that the majority of trade-unionists saw it as anything other than a loyal response to the call of their leaders: a call on their solidarity rather than a call to revolutionary action.

The aftermath of the General Strike was marked by a more peaceful period of industrial relations in which the unions, further weakened in funds, membership and legal status, were forced to fight an often uphill battle to protect wages and conditions during the worst phase of the depression. Only with the economic revival of the middle and late thirties were unions strong enough to bargain more aggressively. In the engineering and motor vehicle industry, disputes broke out to secure union recognition, while in the mines a successful attempt was made to prevent the growth of company unionism. With the coming of the Second World War most unions were able to recover much of the ground lost in the depression years. As in the First World War, they became a vital part of the war effort, with concessions on wages, working conditions and industrial welfare. With important trade-union leaders like Ernest Bevin brought into government there was a powerful accession of influence and weight within government circles. Through the Labour Party, organized labour was able to make its claims for a post-war settlement, while in industry the demands of wartime transformed the bargaining position of workers, putting trade unions into a position which most had not experienced for almost a generation. In the conditions of almost full employment after 1945, unions were able to consolidate their wartime advances.

The trade unions in this period, however, never represented more than a minority of the working population. There were major variations in membership between different groups of workers. Union membership, expressed as a percentage of potential membership, was highest in the manual, male-

dominated sections of industry. Throughout the period there
remained a large disparity in the level of union membership
between male and female workers. Whereas in 1914 almost 30
per cent of male workers were unionized, amongst women the
figure fell below 10 per cent. Although there was an increase in
female union membership during and after the Great War,
rising as high as 24 per cent in 1919-20 compared with over 50
per cent for men, it fell below 15 per cent from 1923 until 1938,
falling to 12 per cent in 1933-4. With the Second World War
it again rose to levels comparable with that of the Great War,
though remaining at a level approximately half that of men. The
highest levels of unionization were found amongst industrial
groups such as the miners, railwaymen, shipbuilders, and iron
and steel workers. It was lower in white-collar occupations –
only 24 per cent in 1921, compared with 40 per cent amongst
manual workers. Moreover, in areas such as construction, agriculture, many of the new light industries and service and
distributive trades, union membership was low. In the furniture
trades, food and drink and tobacco, levels fell to 15 per cent
during the worst years of the depression, 1929-33. Amongst
trades dominated by women, juveniles, unskilled and casual
labour, union membership was usually low and often non-
existent. Even in industries where membership was relatively
high, the depression had the effect of reducing it quite significantly. In 1921 over three-quarters of coalminers belonged to
a trade union; in 1930 and 1931 the figure fell to just over a half,
though by the eve of the Second World War it had risen to new
levels, representing four out of five coal workers.

Clearly trade-union membership reflected the overall state of
the economy. In boom times, membership and militancy tended
to increase; but in depression membership fell and strike figures
declined. The severity of the depression from 1929 to 1933 even
led some of the strongest unions to shed members and made it
difficult to maintain organization in areas which had expanded
most rapidly in favourable conditions. None the less, trade
unions were already in the habit of claiming to speak for the
working class as a whole. Although representing a minority of

all workers, of whom, in turn, only a fraction were active members, they represented the most organized section of working people through the TUC, the Labour Party and local trades councils. Hence, however bitter some of the conflicts between management and unions or between the government and unions during this period, there was a growing acceptance of the place of the trade unions as a major power in the land. Trade-union organization increasingly came to reflect something of the structure of the industries with which it dealt. Amalgamations reduced the number of trade unions from 1,260 in 1914 to 781 in 1945, a trend which persisted whether union membership was rising or falling. Many of the unions to disappear were the smaller craft unions, while the largest unions increased in relative strength. The Amalgamated Engineering Union was formed out of nine smaller societies in 1920, the Transport and General Workers in 1922 and the National Union of General and Municipal Workers in 1924. A similar process in other areas of employment produced large organizations often involving hundreds of thousands of workers from many different industries. The largest union in 1938, the Transport and General Workers Union, was already a giant organization with over half a million members, including dockers, bus drivers, road hauliers, building workers, unskilled and semi-skilled operatives, chemical and power workers, and some clerical groups within its orbit. Even so, the division between skilled and unskilled workers was maintained by distinctive organizations in several industries; railway drivers, for example, were separate from other railway workers, and skilled workers separate from production-line workers. But the larger unions· were increasingly forced to maintain a full-time bureaucracy and a national headquarters. There was a growing tendency to conduct collective bargaining on a national level, the major responsibilities resting upon full-time officials. Hence centralization and bureaucratization formed two of the essential characteristics of union development.

After 1926, in particular, union leaders sought to exercise political influence through the Labour Party and the TUC rather than undertake clashes with government and employers. Moderate trade-union leaders like Ernest Bevin and Walter Citrine sought to run well-organized, disciplined unions which could exact the best agreements possible through negotiation while pursuing longer-term aims for social, economic and political change through the Labour Party. One result, already seen in the Great War, was that the national leadership could lose touch with the local membership. Unofficial and local strikes, often called against the wishes of the national leadership, were to become an important feature which affected the economy from the 1930s. In one of the most famous incidents, the London bus-men's strike of 1937 organized by a militant group of officials, it was the national leadership in the shape of Ernest Bevin who intervened to revoke the powers of the strikers' committee, declare their organization – the left-wing Rank and File movement – as subversive, and expel its leaders from the Transport and General Workers Union.

Bevin's style of autocratic, disciplined, moderate trade-unionism was, in fact, one of the features dominating union organization into the post-war era. Although condemned from the left as accommodation with capitalism, it reflected the acceptance by the trade unions of piecemeal and reformist tactics in the aftermath of the General Strike. These tendencies were, in fact, already present earlier. The trade unions and organized labour did not see themselves, by and large, as revolutionary bodies, but rather as a means of protecting and advancing the interests of workers within the existing economic and political structure. Reformism rather than revolution was to be the over-whelming emphasis of organized labour up to and beyond 1945.

7. *Health and Health Services*

Health

The period from 1914 to 1945 saw a general improvement in health standards in Britain, forming part of a process of falling death and sickness rates which began in the late nineteenth century. From the 1870s death rates fell almost continuously, with only a minor and temporary setback in the period 1916–1920 during the great influenza epidemic, which affected almost every country in the world. Thus the standardized death rate for England and Wales fell from 14.3 per thousand population in 1911–15, to 12.1 in 1926–30, and to 12.0 in 1936–8. As a result the average expectation of life rose from fifty-two years for men and fifty-five for women in 1910–12 to sixty-one for men and sixty-six for women by 1938. Though the death rates and life-expectancy figures contained many variations between classes and regions, the overall trend was improving. A breakdown of the mortality data reveals that while the decline in mortality in the age groups over five years had begun, in some cases, as early as the middle of the nineteenth century, the most important development in the first half of the twentieth century was the fall in death rates of children under one year (Table 15).

A major part of this decline in death rates came about through the reduction in the number of deaths through infectious diseases, such as tuberculosis, typhoid and pneumonia. The number of deaths from TB, the biggest killer in England and Wales in 1910, claiming 51,000 lives, was steadily reduced to only 27,000 in 1940. As Table 16 shows, some of the most dramatic improvements came in the diseases of infants and children.

Table 15: Infant mortality
(under one year) per 1,000 live
births

1900	142.0
1910	110.0
1920	82.0
1930	67.0
1940	61.0
1950	31.2

As well as a reduction in death rates, there were indications that general health standards were improving. One indication of this was in the classification of men called up for military service in the two world wars. When the Ministry of Labour and National Service reported on the results of their examinations of prospective servicemen in the Second World War, it was found that under a third were unfit for military service compared with almost two-thirds in the First World War, using the same system of classification. Also noticeable was a steady increase in the average height and weight of children and the earlier onset of puberty. For example, from the turn of the century, the increase in height amounted to an extra half an inch per decade in five- to seven-year-olds and about an inch per decade in ten- to fourteen-year-olds. The age of menarche (the first menstrual period) had also fallen from sixteen or seventeen years in the mid nineteenth century to around fifteen years by the 1930s. These improvements were noted by health officials and social investigators alike. Sir George Newman,

Table 16: Death rates per million population at ages under fifteen years

	Scarlet fever	Diphtheria	Whooping cough	Measles
1901–10	271	571	815	915
1911–20	123	437	554	838
1921–30	64	298	405	389
1931–9	46	290	197	217

Source: A. H. Halsey, *Trends in British Society since 1900*, Macmillan, 1972, p. 339.

the Chief Medical Officer of Health in the early 1930s, hailed the decline in infant mortality as 'one of the greatest single achievements in preventive medicine which have marked modern times'. Writing after the Second World War three distinguished social scientists noted: "The improvement in the state of the nation's health over the last few decades has been striking by any standard. In what measure it is due to greater knowledge, to better economic conditions, or to the extension of public health services may be open to argument; the fact and the magnitude of the advance are not.'

As this quotation suggests it was widely recognized that several factors had come together to reduce both mortality and ill-health. The 1937 *Survey of the Social Structure of England and Wales* attributed them to 'improvements in housing, sanitation, hygiene, and medical skill'. An exhaustive social study such as *The New Survey of London Life and Labour* attributed the progress found in standards of public health in London since the end of the nineteenth century to five main developments: the re-housing of the population in healthier conditions, better maternity care, the medical inspection of schoolchildren, the introduction of old-age pensions and steps to deal with venereal disease. It concluded that: 'there has been vast improvement in the health of the London population during the last thirty years. The gains accruing from advance in material prosperity, from greater cleanliness, from improved drainage, scavenging, and medical, surgical and nursing services, have far outweighed any added risks ...'

A crucial influence was the better diet made possible by higher average disposable incomes, whether through wages or social service payments, and cheaper food prices. The various 'poverty lines' constructed before and after 1914 were calibrated according to assessments of the minimum income required to maintain health. Poverty, it was clearly recognized, not only produced squalor, it also produced sickness and ill-health. Knowledge of nutritional science was improving and with it understanding of the importance of vitamins, proteins, amino acids and minerals. 'Nutrition' became a major aspect of research, carrying with it important implications. Many medical conditions were now recognized as 'deficiency diseases' and the importance of taking not only the right quantity but also the right types of food was recognized. One result was that there was great emphasis on diet as an agent of improving health, as one nutritionist argued in 1934:

Many of the commoner physical ailments and defects could be reduced or even eliminated by proper feeding. Indeed, it is probably no exaggeration to say that proper feeding of the population of this country would be as revolutionary in its effects on public health and physique as was the introduction of cleanliness and drainage in the last century.

While these advances in knowledge produced fresh areas of concern, provoking a major and often bitter debate about the existence of ill-health caused by malnutrition during the 1930s in particular, at least some of the growth in awareness of nutritional needs offered evidence of improvements in diet. Compared with the period before 1914, there was significantly higher average consumption of the more nutritious foods. Even those most critical of existing health and nutritional standards were forced to admit that conditions in the thirties were an improvement on what had gone before. John Boyd Orr, whose study *Food, Health, and Income*, published in 1936, was highly critical of the standard of nutrition which was still current, having drawn attention to the deficiencies which still existed in the dietary standards of many sections of the population, concluded his examination by saying that: 'Bad as the picture is, however, it is better than the picture of pre-war days. Since then, the national dietary has improved ... Accompanying that improvement in diet, there has been a corresponding improvement in national health.'

If higher standards of nutrition was one major factor in improving health, another was the progressive advance in housing and public health. The four million houses built in the inter-war years represented an improvement in living conditions for the individual families concerned as well as, in the case of the major slum clearance schemes, the removal of a significant source of infection and other health hazards. Even the hundreds of thousands of private houses built for the middle classes usually marked an improved environment as regards light, ventilation and modern drainage and toilet facilities. Indeed one of the principal attractions of 'suburbia' for those who could afford it was the chance to escape the dirt, noise and overcrowding of city and town centres. Disease was no respecter of status and the chance to escape to a cleaner, healthier environment was a major stimulus to the development of thousands of inter-war 'semis'. In the slums, the districts being cleared were the insanitary, overcrowded and verminous residue of the industrial revolution. The major thrust of public housing policy from before the First World War was towards the provision of a healthier environment. For example, the 'cardinal principles' of good design outlined by the Tudor Walters Report of 1918, which governed the houses built under the Addison Acts, included 'a sunny aspect for the living rooms and for as many bedrooms as possible, a cool position for the larder ... the avoidance of projections in the rear which cut off light and air' and toilets and bathrooms as a matter of course. For the one and a half million families who were rehoused by slum clearance in the inter-war years these represented important gains not just in quality of life and amenities, but also in health. The reduction of the incidence of diseases like typhoid, a product of poor sanitation, the lowering in the level of deaths caused by TB, partly caused by overcrowded conditions, and the curbing of epidemics of infectious disease through the provision of separate bedrooms and better-spaced housing can all in part be ascribed to improvements in housing standards.

At a local level, too, there was considerable activity in the field of public health. The opening of the twentieth century witnessed a widening of concern from sanitation and housing to embrace the detection and treatment of prevalent disease. For example the Interdepartmental Committee on the Health and Physique of the Population, appointed in 1903 in reaction to the poor quality of recruits coming forward for the Boer War, concluded with fifty-three recommendations affecting urbanization, overcrowding, atmospheric pollution, employment, alcoholism, the depletion of rural districts, food supply, 'the conditions attending the life of the juvenile population', venereal disease, insanity, vagrancy and many more. The influence of the report was seen in a series of Acts of Parliament which gave local authorities duties and powers relating to the physique, health, cleanliness, diseases and occupations of the population. Amongst the most important were the Open Spaces Act of 1906, the Education (Provision of Meals) Act, 1906, the Public Health (Regulations as to Food) Act, 1907, the Notification of Births Act, 1907, the Public Health Amendment Act of 1907, establishing the school medical service, the Maternity and Child Welfare Act of 1918, and Acts taking special measures against tuberculosis and venereal disease. Much of this effort was directed at the young, principally through the imposition of regular medical inspection of schoolchildren, vesting powers of treatment in the local authority, and providing school meals for 'necessitous children'. By the eve of the Second World War local education authorities were empowered by law to concern themselves with the following areas of health supervision amongst schoolchildren: medical inspection and treatment of children aged five to fourteen, including medical, dental and orthopaedic treatment, sanitation of school premises, control of infectious diseases in schools, systematic physical education and training, the provision of school meals, and special and open-air education for defective children. By 1935 there were 2,300 doctors and 5,300 school nurses engaged in the school medical service, and 1,650 school clinics providing treatment. In 1934 an act was passed empowering local authorities to make free or subsidized milk available to schoolchildren and by 1937 school milk was being provided for 3.2 million children either free or at a halfpenny for a third of a pint. There was also some extension of the provision of school meals, though this was determined by the financial and political situation of the local authority concerned. As a result only 4 per cent of children received free meals in 1939. The 1918 Maternity and Child Welfare Act empowered local authorities to extend their facilities in this field, including the provision of child welfare and ante-natal clinics, while under the Midwives Act of 1936 local authorities were obliged to provide trained midwives. By 1938 the number of infant welfare centres in England and Wales had risen to 3,580 and of ante-natal clinics to 1,795.

Infectious diseases remained a major responsibility of local authorities and most maintained isolation hospitals and tuberculosis sanatoria right up to the introduction of the National Health Service in 1946. The Venereal Diseases Act of 1917 and the Mental Treatment Act of 1930 gave local authorities further work in these fields. The Blind Persons Act of 1920 made Counties and County Boroughs responsible for the welfare of the blind. The Public Health Act of 1936, extended by the Food and Drugs Act, added control over areas such as slaughterhouses and food adulteration. Local authorities carried on the mundane but essential public health work of ensuring an adequate water supply and efficient sewerage and sanitation. The inter-war years witnessed the virtual completion of the process whereby municipal authorities took over control of the water supply, with all the extensive apparatus of reservoirs, pipelines and treatment plants that this involved. By 1935 80 per cent of the population of England and Wales was supplied with water by the local authorities, including most of the large conurbations. Much unspectacular activity between the wars went into the gradual improvement of both water supply and sewage disposal. It was an aspect of public health which rarely hit the headlines and was therefore easy to ignore, but to those with experience reaching back into the nineteenth century, the provision of a safe water supply and an efficient system of sewerage represented one of the major advances in the field of public health. As a writer in the mid-1930s put it, 'The development of a well-nigh universal system of piped house-to-house supplies is one of the great achievements of the century ... the difference which it has made to the health, cleanliness, and comfort of the people can scarcely be over-estimated.' Its importance was illustrated too by the reduction in the notification rate of deaths from diseases such as typhoid and paratyphoid – a continuing threat which was demonstrated by typhoid epidemics in Bournemouth, Poole and Christchurch in 1936 and at Croydon in 1937, the latter caused by a water supply contaminated by sewage.

Improvements in diet, housing and public health were of particular importance because the success of medical intervention varied very considerably from one area to another. For example, there was little that medical science could offer to combat the great influenza pandemic of 1918–19, described by one authority as 'one of the severest holocausts of disease ever encountered'. First arriving in Britain in the late spring of 1918, with fresh waves appearing in autumn 1918 and February 1919, it was responsible for 150,000 deaths in England and Wales, a small part of a total which world-wide came to over fifteen million. Many of the deaths occurred amongst young adults, ironically carrying away thousands of those who had hitherto escaped death in battle. Similarly, the great scourge of the first half of the twentieth century, T B, was conquered only through a complex mixture of preventive and curative measures, the former being by far the most important before 1945. At the beginning of this period T B was still a major problem, up to 1918 killing more people each year than smallpox, scarlet fever, measles, whooping cough and typhus fever put together, while as late as 1910 surgery for glands, bones and joints affected by T B accounted for a sixth of all operations. Although the tubercule bacillus was isolated in 1882, the principal cure until the Second World War remained good food, sunlight, fresh air and rest and the principal effort in treatment went into the provision of sanatoria where these could be obtained. In 1911 there were eighty-four sanatoria with 8,000 beds, by 1930 500 with 25,000 beds. An important preventive measure began in 1922 when the Ministry of Health ordered the pasteurization of milk, preventing the spread of infection from dairy cattle, but once the disease had been contracted no speedy cure existed until the development of antibiotics and chemotherapeutics in the 1940s. Although experiments with vaccine had begun before 1914, these did not become an effective force in combating the disease until after 1945, when BCG vaccine was made more effective. Otherwise, improvements in surgery, particularly lung surgery, showed some success in assisting recovery, and X-rays became an important diagnostic tool. As methods and experience grew, it became possible to carry out mass screenings; the first mobile mass radiography units were set up in Lancashire in 1943 and fifteen were at work by 1945.

Other diseases gradually yielded to improved medical treatment. Salvarsan, developed in 1910, provided a safer and more reliable treatment for syphilis than cures based on mercury. Treatment for all venereal diseases was assisted by legislation in the First World War, when local authorities were ordered to provide free diagnosis and treatment. The isolation of insulin in 1922 offered better prospects in the treatment of diabetics, and amongst the major infectious diseases pneumonia began to be treated with sulphonamides from 1935 and diphtheria and other childhood diseases by immunization from the 1930s. Radium therapy also proved a useful treatment for some types of cancer and there was a steady accumulation of technique in many areas of surgery. The First World War had produced widespread improvements in both brain and lung surgery and these proved of great value in peace-time. Following the first experiments in blood transfusion in the Great War, the practice was widely adopted during the Second World War, saving many lives both on the battlefield and in peace-time accidents. The world wars were also responsible for improvements in dealing with the consequences of major injury. Experience in orthopaedic centres of fixing and using artificial limbs was one of the products of the appalling carnage of the Great War. In the Second World War, a major advance lay in the development of plastic surgery under the remarkable team led by the New Zealander, Dr Archibald McIndoe. Badly burned airmen and tank crews were amongst the first to experience the delicate and lengthy processes of skin grafts and facial reconstruction which restored them to a semblance of normality.

The Great War had also highlighted an important new area in the treatment of mental illness and psychological disorders.

Initially, soldiers who became hysterical or catatonic, or simply ceased to obey orders, were not treated as casualties at all. But the growing scale of what became popularly and inaccurately described as 'shell-shock' led to a wider and more humane understanding of the whole spectrum of mental and psychological disorders. It was an experience which helped to inform a greater concern for such complaints throughout the inter-war years, although diagnosis remained uncertain and treatments often little more than rudimentary. Significantly, however, by the Second World War, psychological testing for officer recruits and a greater sensitivity towards the mental strains of war had become accepted.

Health Services

As well as developments in medical technique, there was also the question of access to medical treatment. The National Insurance Act, which came into full operation by the end of 1913, applied to approximately twelve million workers. By 1921 it had been extended to cover fifteen million and by 1938, almost twenty million, including youths of fourteen to sixteen. The scheme provided a free general practitioner service and sickness benefit paid through 'approved societies' such as trade unions and benefit clubs. Local insurance committees could also distribute benefit to the dependants of insured workers requiring sanatorium treatment, though, in general, only insured workers could obtain free advice and treatment. Hence workers' families had to be protected through private insurance schemes and sick clubs. Even under the health insurance scheme, the benefits paid varied considerably above a nationally agreed minimum and might include fringe benefits such as hospital treatment or dentistry, but might not. There were also complaints that 'panel patients' of doctors under the insurance Act were often treated less adequately than fee-paying patients. Although individual experiences varied greatly, there was some sense in which the Act had only gone half-way to creating a 'free' general practitioner service and some friction was bound to result. For the families of insured workers and most of the middle classes, reliance had to be placed on private insurance schemes and sickness clubs, which in 1937 covered an estimated ten million people. Those who were too poor or improvident to participate in the contributory schemes were forced either to pay for a doctor or to use the out-patients' department of a 'free' hospital. Other health services, such as ophthalmic, maternity and dental care, lay outside National Insurance provision and had to be covered privately. This resulted in a massive problem of decayed teeth, particularly amongst the poor, generally low standards of ante-natal and maternity services in poorer areas, and erratic provision of spectacles and eye-tests. Indeed one of the services offered by some of the larger department stores such as Woolworths were facilities for 'do-it-yourself' eye-tests where, for a few pence, people could test their own sight and purchase the pair of spectacles which seemed to effect the greatest improvement.

Hospital treatment was also unevenly provided. By 1939 Britain had about three thousand hospitals with approximately a quarter of a million beds. These were divided up into three main groups: the voluntary hospitals, the municipal hospitals and the Poor Law hospitals. The first of these, with the largest number of beds, were charitable institutions dependent for their existence on donations and patients' fees. They included some of the most famous of the London teaching hospitals as well as a large number of private foundations in the provinces. Already by the early 1920s many were finding it a hard struggle to maintain themselves in a more costly era of medical treatment but remained, until the National Health Service Act, completely independent. The municipal hospitals were run by local health departments and financed out of local rates, as were the hospitals which had grown up under the Public Assistance Committees to deal with sick and infirm paupers, usually the elderly.

Although there were proposals by the Dawson Committee in 1920 for a re-organization of the hospital service in which the government would finance a two-tier system of Primary Health Centres based on infirmaries and cottage hospitals, staffed by general practitioners, and Secondary Health Centres, based on the larger hospitals, these plans foundered on grounds of cost. Instead, a patchwork of hospital provision remained the norm. In 1928 local authorities were empowered, but not forced, to take over local Poor Law infirmaries, and several, including the London County Council, did so. While there was much co-operation between local authority and voluntary hospitals, the two systems remained separate. For example in 1922 a new scheme was introduced to enable people earning under £6 a week to pay 3d. a week for free treatment in a voluntary hospital; this became a popular form of medical insurance and many large firms made a bulk payment to cover their employees. By 1939, the majority of hospital patients paid for their treatment, either through insurance schemes or by arrangement with the hospital almoner. Only the very poor could be assured of free treatment, and even this was dependent upon the discretion of the hospital involved. While the number of hospital beds per head of population was growing and hospital treatment was slowly improving in effectiveness, the real area of concern lay in the organization of a hospital system which offered reasonable access to all and did not discourage those who required treatment from seeking it for fear of financial hardship.

Poverty and Health

There was also a considerable undercurrent of dissatisfaction with what had been achieved in terms of health and what remained to be done. Greater knowledge in such areas as nutrition and a more precise statistical delineation of the incidence of disease according to social class and region offered little scope for complacency. Above all, the growth of expectations about what could be done, building upon existing achievements, acted as a spur to the development of new areas of concern. A persistent refrain of the social investigators in the inter-war years was that the survival of poverty condemned a significant portion of the population to ill-health. Studies of the diet of the poor revealed only too clearly that 'in many cases income determined diet, which in turn affected standards of health. Thus, while the general health of the population was gradually improving, attention focused upon the areas of ill-health which remained and especially those which were associated with poverty. Undoubtedly, one of the most influential studies was John Boyd Orr's *Food, Health and Income*. Using an American standard of nutritional needs, he examined the diets of over a thousand families, divided into six income groups. He found that the lowest income group, composed of four and a half million people when translated onto the national scale, enjoyed a diet which was inadequate in all respects. The next group of about five million people had a diet which was inadequate in vitamins, calories and essential minerals. Only groups five and six, representing a third of the population, enjoyed a diet which met Orr's stringent requirements. His findings showed that a tenth of the population, including a fifth of all children, were chronically ill-nourished, while a half of the population suffered from some sort of deficiency.

Orr's findings were severely criticized on the grounds that he had applied too severe a standard and taken too small a sample; none the less his findings corroborated evidence gathered from other sources. An investigation in Newcastle-upon-Tyne, published in 1933, showed that at least a third of schoolchildren from the poorer districts of the city were unhealthy or phys-ically unfit. The results were matched with a sample of children from professional families. The comparison showed that poorer children suffered from eight times as much pneumonia, ten times as much bronchitis and five times as much rickets. A survey by Dr G. G. M'Gonigle in Stockton-on-Tees found that the death rate amongst the poorest section of the population, spending only 3s. a head on food, was twice that of the most affluent, who spent 6s. a head on food. He drew the conclusion that almost 37 per cent of all children examined showed some deviation from the 'normal' at the time of examination and these conditions were largely the result of poor diet and bad housing. Moreover, the situation was not confined to a few

black spots such as Tyneside; Dr M'Gonigle reported the results
of a survey carried out by the school medical staffs in a number
of education authorities in 1933, which found that 11.1 children
in every 1,000 were suffering from malnutrition of a sufficient
degree to require treatment, while a similar number required
observation.

The findings of John Boyd Orr and other investigators
suggested that a high degree of poor nutrition and ill-health was
built into the lives of the poor, especially poor children, irrespective of the effects of unemployment. The differences in dietary
standards uncovered by the investigators were reflected in the
mortality statistics for the different classes. Though there had
been considerable improvement in the general level of mortality, life expectancy was still determined by social class (see
Table 17).

Table 17: Mortality by social class: standardized mortality ratios,
1930–32

All occupied and retired	Married women 100	Single women 100	All men 100
Class I (Upper and middle)	81	60	90
Class II (Intermediate)	89	64	94
Class III (Skilled labour)	99	95	97
Class IV (Intermediate)	103	102	102
Class V (Unskilled labour)	113	112	111

Death rates were much higher in the poorer regions,
particularly those affected by high levels of unemployment.
Thus they were higher in Scotland, Wales and the North of
England than in the South of England. Standardized death rates
in England and Wales, which varied from Oxford (80) and
Cambridge (73) to the Rhondda (134) and Wigan (138),
averaged 113 per 1,000 in 1937. Within London, the more
prosperous suburbs, such as Harrow (73) and Ealing (78), had
low rates compared with the poor inner areas, such as Stepney
(115) or Finsbury (128).

There was also considerable concern about the infant

mortality rate in the thirties. The years since the turn of the century had shown major advances, mainly through the control of infectious diseases. None the less, epidemics of diphtheria and whooping cough still killed thousands of children each year. For Great Britain as a whole, however, the infant mortality rate had fallen from 142 per 1,000 live births in 1900–1902 to 68 in 1931. By 1938 it had fallen still further to 55 per thousand. Though official reports tended to regard this improvement as satisfactory, bringing the level of infant mortality near to the irreducible minimum, the social investigators found clear evidence that the infant mortality rate was still higher than in countries with a lower per capita income than Great Britain. Whereas the infant mortality rate for England and Wales averaged 57 per thousand live births in 1935 – the lowest figure for the thirties – the rate in New Zealand was 32, in Australia 40 and in Sweden 47. Even in comparable environmental conditions, international comparisons did not show Britain in a very favourable light. R. M. Titmuss quoted the example of Chicago, which had reduced its infant mortality rate from 74 to 38 between 1925 and 1937. In the same period, Liverpool's rate fell from 99 to 82. Within Great Britain, there were marked variations between town and country, and between different areas. Thus the South-East had an infant mortality rate of 47 in 1935, compared with 68 in the North, 63 in Wales and 76.8 in Scotland. The rate for Greater London was 51, while that for Jarrow was 114. Nor could the figures be simply dismissed as more special pleading, for the Registrar-General's *Statistical Review* confirmed the picture revealed by the social investigators (see Table 18).

The maternal mortality rate was also regarded with considerable concern – with some justice, for whereas there had at least been a fall in infant mortality, there was no comparable improvement in maternal mortality, which had showed little improvement since 1900. Indeed, after 1925 the maternal mortality rate began to rise, and it reached its worst point in 1934, with 4.6 deaths per 1,000 live births in England and Wales. By 1937, however, considerable improvement had taken place,

Table 18: Infant mortality rate by social class of father in England and Wales

		Rate per 1,000 legitimate live births 1930–32
Class I	(Upper and middle)	33
Class II	(Intermediate)	45
Class III	(Skilled labour)	58
Class IV	(Intermediate)	67
Class V	(Unskilled labour)	77

when the rate reached the lowest point ever recorded. There was much debate about the reasons for the obstinate refusal of the maternal mortality rate to yield the same dramatic improvements as the infant mortality rate. Great Britain seemed to be lagging far behind much of the continent and parts of the Empire in the quality of maternal care. A committee of the Ministry of Health which investigated the problem in 1929 concluded that half the deaths could be avoided by better ante-natal care, better training of midwives, and improved obstetrics and antiseptic methods. A dramatic improvement in the mid-thirties, however, came with economic revival. Moreover, in 1936, the Midwives' Act required local authorities to provide trained personnel, while the number of ante-natal clinics in England and Wales had risen to 1,795 by 1938. A limited start was also made to the provision of cheap or free milk to expectant mothers who attended Welfare Centres. Typically, it was not until the war that all expectant mothers were given free milk, orange juice, cod liver oil and vitamin tablets.

The Origins of the National Health Service

Hence, by the Second World War, health presented a mixed picture. On the one hand there had been obvious gains since the Edwardian era in mortality and morbidity rates and in such fields as public health. On the other there remained obvious deficiencies, particularly for the poor, as regards ill-health, access to hospital treatment and the absence of any comprehensive system of health insurance. Half the adult population remained outside the system of state insurance, including about fifteen million women and children under the age of five. Even those covered by National Health Insurance were not eligible for specialist treatment, and the inevitable result was that many failed to obtain the level of treatment or care that was required to ensure good health.

Criticism of the health services and plans for their rationalization had begun as early as 1918, when the Maclean Committee, part of the Ministry of Reconstruction, suggested the transfer of Poor Law hospitals to the county and county borough councils. The Dawson Committee had also offered a radical regrouping of hospital services in 1920, and in 1926 the Lawrence Commission attacked the hotch-potch of benefits and provision offered by the existing health insurance scheme, public authorities and insurance companies. It recommended that all insured persons should be offered complete dental treatment, an 'out-patient' service at hospitals, allowances for sick dependants and extended maternity benefits. A minority also wanted all dependants to qualify for treatment. These recommendations foundered in the face of government economy measures, but pressure for unifying the health service continued. In 1930 the British Medical Association issued *Proposals for a General Medical Service for the Nation* which suggested a system of health insurance for virtually all adults and their dependants. Benefits would include access to specialists and consultants, as well as ophthalmic, dental and maternity services. Health administration was to be concentrated on large local authorities, with hospitals operating on a regional basis. Similarly the Cathcart Committee on Scottish Health Services which reported in 1936 urged an extension of insurance benefits and a comprehensive national health policy.

A similar cast of thought was evident in the report by the Political and Economic Planning group on *The British Health Services* in 1937. This proposed an extension of National Health Insurance to the dependants of insured persons and to the self-employed earning less than £250 a year, as well as easier access to other services. Additional insurance contributions, bringing them up to 6d. a week for men and 5½d. for women, were to meet the cost of the extended scheme. Employers were to pay no more than they were paying at present, and a completely free service was rejected on grounds of cost. Hospital services were to be rationalized under regional boards and a determined effort made through the school medical service and a 'national nutrition policy' to eliminate deficiency diseases such as anaemia, rickets and dental caries. The report attracted considerable attention, being welcomed on publication day by leading articles in eleven national and provincial dailies. At least as important, it received a welcome from most of the specialist periodicals and journals. The *British Medical Journal* and the *Lancet* accepted its claim to be 'the first attempt to show how all the health services, preventive, curative, environmental and ancillary, work and fit together, what they have achieved, and where their defects and problems lie'. With such sentiments, the basis for a more comprehensive approach to health was already laid by the Second World War. The Beveridge Report of November 1942, with its recommendation for a comprehensive, free health service, expressed what was already a powerful current of opinion. This was shown in the Draft Interim Report of the Medical Planning Commission of the BMA and the Royal Colleges in 1942, which accepted the principle of a comprehensive health service. It was these increasingly common solutions which provided the basis for the acceptance by the wartime Coalition Government of the inevitability of a National Health Service, enacted by the post-war Labour government in 1946.

8. *Housing and Town Planning*

The improvement of housing conditions was one of the major social advances made between the wars. Although large areas of slums remained in the major conurbations, there were remarkable advances in the field of housing, in spite of an often unfavourable economic climate. The inter-war period saw the completion of over four million houses, two and a half million for private sale and the rest for rent by local authorities. The bulk of this housing boom came in the thirties, when nearly three million houses were built, mainly for private sale. Within twenty years, the housing situation was transformed: in 1918 there were 610,000 fewer houses than families while by 1938 there was a theoretical surplus of over 500,000 houses.

Housing

Slum clearance had been a preoccupation of enlightened local authorities and politicians for decades, but it was only after the Great War that it got underway to a significant extent. The war provided a major stimulus when Lloyd George inaugurated the scheme of 'homes fit for heroes' as a major part of the reconstruction campaign launched in the last years of the war. It was estimated that at least 800,000 houses were needed to replace the slums and make up arrears of house-building from the war years. The Housing and Town Planning Act of 1919, usually known as the Addison Act after its author, the Minister of Health, Dr Christopher Addison, required local authorities to survey their housing needs and offered government subsidies to cover the cost of building. In addition rents were controlled and subsidies were extended to private house-building.

Although 213,800 houses were built under the legislation, the subsidy arrangements proved too costly and were severely cut back in the aftermath of the economic depression in 1921, and in 1922 ended altogether. None the less, the Addison Act established housing as a national responsibility and proved the forerunner of later legislation. In 1924 the Wheatley Housing Act increased the state's subsidy for houses built for rent, and under its provisions more than half a million houses were constructed before its abolition in 1933. The Greenwood Housing Act of 1930, though suspended during the worst phase of the depression, provided subsidies for slum clearance. Under its provisions, more slums were cleared in the years before the war than in any previous period; between 1931 and 1939 local authorities built over 700,000 houses, rehousing four-fifths of existing slum dwellers.

Much of the new housing was built on extensive estates on the fringes of the main towns and cities. At Kirkby, near Liverpool, Solihull and Longbridge, outside Birmingham, and Becontree outside London, for example, large new council estates were created which were almost miniature towns in themselves. For many housing experts they represented the great hope for a better future through the provision of a physical environment which was a vast improvement upon conditions in the slums. In the most imaginative developments, in which the 'garden city' concept pioneered at Letchworth before 1914 was copied, the result was often attractive, with tree-lined avenues, extensive open spaces and adequate community facilities. Amongst the best examples were Welwyn Garden City, founded in 1920 and rapidly expanded in the thirties, and Wythenshawe, outside Manchester. The latter was founded by the efforts of one of the great housing pioneers of the inter-war period, Sir Ernest Simon, and planned as a garden suburb to house 100,000 people. By 1939, 7,000 houses had been built. Even the most utilitarian estates offered a far higher standard of comfort than had been possible for many families in the past. Basic amenities such as adequate space, light and ventilation, the provision of bathrooms and inside toilets, and well-built houses which avoided the depressing battle with damp and vermin so common in the slums were amongst the most tangible gains.

Elsewhere, local authorities were beginning to experiment with high-rise flats, often modelled upon similar developments in central Europe. At Leeds, the municipality pioneered the construction of large blocks of flats in the Quarry Hill scheme near the centre of the city, where 2,000 slum houses were demolished and 938 new flat dwellings built at a cost of £1½ million. There was a lively debate about the relative advantages of flats as opposed to houses, generally decided in favour of the latter. With these debates went the hope that a decent physical environment would abolish 'not only the slum house, but also the slum tenant'. Whatever the shortcomings of the new housing developments, there had been greater progress by the end of the thirties in providing an adequate solution to the housing conditions of the working class than in any previous decade.

But slum clearance was only the minor part of the housing picture, for the most dramatic developments took place in private house-building. Over two and a half million houses were built for private sale within twenty years. Houses were relatively cheap – a typical 'semi' could be bought for as little as £450, about twice the annual salary of an average professional man. Mortgages were available on very easy terms, with an average interest rate of around 4½ per cent and repayments which came well within the range of most of the middle classes and a significant portion of the better-off working classes. Deposits on new houses could be as low as £25, particularly towards the end of the thirties, when the number of house completions topped 350,000 and gave the market a more competitive edge. A typical example of the situation in the late thirties was a London company's offer of houses for £800 on a payment of £25 deposit, with all legal expenses paid by the builder. Speculative development could produce jerry-building and the uglier features of 'bungaloid growth', but nevertheless it was probably the most favourable period for house purchase in the twentieth century. Builders and estate agents wooed

potential customers with visits to new developments in the
suburbs and attractive rates of interest. The favoured style was
for smallish, uniform semi-detached houses, usually tiled rather
than covered with more expensive slate, lighter and airier than
Edwardian houses, with larger gardens, and more room for
garages, garden sheds and greenhouses. They were nearly all
wired up for electricity, but, except for a minority built with
some acknowledgement of changes in architectural style since
the nineteenth century, they were constructed on traditional
lines and decorated with pebbledash, leaded panes and mock-
Tudor timbering. While the growth of 'semi-detached' London
and the suburban estates around other towns and cities attracted
much adverse comment, there was little doubt that the new
housing offered much that people desired. Just enough in-
dividuality was built into each house to offer an illusion of
distinctiveness, but not so much that the houses were pro-
hibitively expensive. These middle-class suburbs lasted remarkably well, fulfilling the demands for modest domestic comfort,
away, but not too far away, from the crowded city centres.
'Ribbon development' and 'bungaloid growth' became terms
of abuse amongst rational planners and modern architects, but
they counted for little against the wishes of innumerable families
to obtain their own version of suburban contentment.

The net effect of the council and private house-building
schemes was a significant improvement in housing standards
since before 1914. In York in 1900 Seebohm Rowntree had
found nearly 6 per cent of the population living in overcrowded conditions, whereas by 1936 the figure was under 2
per cent. The number of slum houses had been reduced by
over half, from 26 per cent to under 12. Water supply and
adequate sanitation were available for almost every house and
the worst slums had been demolished and replaced by new
houses. The Housing Act of 1935 applied a fairly lenient standard of overcrowding; all living-rooms and bedrooms were
included and, allowing for segregation of the sexes, a house
was adjudged to be overcrowded if there were more than two
people per room. In the survey of housing conditions in the

country which followed it was found that only just under 4 per cent of nine million working-class houses could be regarded as overcrowded by this standard.

The corollary was an increase in average housing standards. The floor space of new working-class houses almost doubled between the mid nineteenth century and the inter-war period. The Tudor Walters Report was a landmark, laying down standards which erred on the side of quality rather than cheapness, so much so that the houses built under the Addison scheme represented some of the best twentieth-century council housing. A crucial feature of the recommended plans for house-building under the Addison Act, enshrined in the Tudor Walters Report, and one often ignored under later schemes, was that they had been altered according to the views expressed by the prospective tenants, through groups such as the Women's Labour League, resulting for example in the inclusion of parlours rather than 'through lounges' and the provision of separate bathrooms in all new houses. The basic trend in house design was towards separate rooms for cooking, eating, living and, of course, sleeping, itself a major advance on what most slum-dwellers had experienced. With improvements in layout went improvements in domestic comfort. By 1939 approximately a third of all families earning under £300 a year had a piped hot-water supply, usually from a back-boiler behind the fire. Two-thirds, however, were still forced to heat water on an open fire or possibly on the stove. Cooking was increasingly carried out on gas cookers, which were owned by two-thirds of all households, replacing open fires and kitchen ranges. In some middle-class homes, the new 'Aga' and electric cookers were also becoming more common. Open fires remained the main form of heating for more than 90 per cent of homes in 1939, but electric and gas fires for supplementary heating were owned by 60 per cent of households. With two-thirds of houses wired up for electricity by 1939, access was provided to amenities such as electric lighting and the increasingly wide range of electrically operated domestic appliances, such as radios, irons and vacuum cleaners.

But although the era witnessed significant advances in public and private housing, poor housing remained one of the most pressing social issues. The principal problem derived from a net shortage of houses at the beginning of the period which was being exacerbated by a trend towards a larger number of families. House-building had lagged behind demand for decades, in spite of local and central government attempts to remedy the situation. The main result was overcrowding, compounded by the poor condition of much of the older housing stock, producing problems of disease, damp and vermin. In 1935 it was estimated that approximately 12 per cent of the population lived at a density of more than two persons per room, in what was officially regarded as overcrowded conditions. London had one of the worst problems: a survey in 1933 revealed that almost half a million people in the capital were suffering from overcrowding. Almost half the families in Islington, Finsbury and Shoreditch were living at a level of three or more families per house, which usually consisted of four or five small rooms. In Finsbury 60 per cent of families were living in one or two rooms; Stepney had over 50,000 people living two or more to a room, while 16,000 lived three or more to a room. One four-roomed house in Shoreditch was found in a survey to contain thirteen occupants. Two of the rooms were taken by couples without children, while the other two were occupied by families. One consisted of a woman, a boy of sixteen and a girl of four who shared a small bed. The other family consisted of six people, including three small children. The room was described as 'terribly verminous, dilapidated, and damp; it is often smelly, and the roof leaks over the bed, though it has recently been mended'.

Outside London, almost every large town or city had its areas of old, overcrowded housing. The six most overcrowded boroughs in England and Wales were in the North-East. Of the population of County Durham, 20 per cent, a quarter of a million people, lived in overcrowded conditions. Liverpool had some of the worst slums in the country; 89,000 people lived at a density of two or more to a room, while 20,000 people

lived three or more to a room. The central wards of St Anne's
and Exchange had the worst housing. In St Anne's, 42 per cent
of families lived more than four families to a house. The *Social
Survey of Merseyside* commented:

Many of the larger houses in St Anne's Ward go back to the late
eighteenth century, when they were the dwellings of prosperous
merchants. Now they make slums even more deplorable than the
back-to-back cottage, each room sub-let to a separate family, dilapidated and comfortless, lacking sanitary conveniences and even taps
and sinks, nearly every family dependent for its cooking and heating
of water on an incredibly unsuitable bedroom fire-grate.

In 1932 there were still a hundred families in Liverpool living
in cellars of the type condemned by Engels in the middle of
the nineteenth century. Over a thousand houses remained in
eighteenth-century courts which, though structurally unsound
and in 'serious danger of collapse', could not be evacuated
because of a shortage of alternative accommodation for the
inhabitants. The other major conurbations had their share of
overcrowding: 68,000 people in Birmingham, 49,000 in Manchester, 41,000 in Sheffield and 38,000 in Leeds. Scotland
suffered from severe overcrowding more than England and
Wales. In Glasgow 200,000 people lived more than three to
a room, many of them in the tenement blocks of the dock-
side areas. Elsewhere the Royal Commission on Scottish
Housing in 1917 had described:

unspeakably filthy privy-middens in many of the mining areas, badly
constructed, incurably damp labourers' cottages on farms, whole
townships unfit for human occupation in the crofting counties and
islands ... gross overcrowding and huddling of the sexes together in
the congested industrial villages and towns, occupation of one-room
houses by large families, groups of lightless and unventilated houses
in the older burghs ...

Over half a million houses in the major conurbations were
condemned as unfit for human habitation. Many of these were
'back-to-backs' which had been due for clearance before the
Great War. Birmingham alone had 40,000 back-to-backs, built
at a very high density with outside toilets and water supply.

Areas of squalid housing, rotting with damp and infested with vermin, sprawled over the whole country. In South Wales, the Medical Officer of Health in Swansea condemned all the pre-1914 housing in the town as 'unsatisfactory in one respect or another ... the prevailing defects are decrepitude, dis-repair, lack of damp-proof courses, smallness of rooms, low bedrooms, small windows, narrow staircases, and lack of amenities'.

In Manchester, Sir Ernest Simon described conditions he had found in one house in the slum district of Angel Meadow:

> No. 4 F Street. The general appearance and condition of this house inside are very miserable. It is a dark house and the plaster on the passage walls, in particular, was in a bad condition. There is no sink or tap in the house; they are in the small yard, consequently in frosty weather the family is without water. In this house live a man and wife, and seven children, ranging from 15 to 1, and a large, if varying, number of rats.

Descriptions such as these were no exception in the social investigations of the inter-war years. Little special pleading was required to show that housing in many urban areas was grossly inadequate. The countryside fared little better. Over 4,000 parishes in England and Wales lacked a piped water supply and over 100,000 cottages were condemned as 'unfit' dwellings.

Emphasis on house-building both for private sale and for local authorities tends to obscure the fact that during the inter-war years almost two-thirds of all householders rented their house from a private landlord. Rented accommodation had been the norm in the nineteenth century and it continued to occupy the biggest sector of the housing market until after the Second World War. Housing of almost every description could be rented – single rooms in slum districts, nineteenth-century terraces or substantial suburban villas. While some rented accommodation was of good quality, much was indifferent, and some amongst the worst housing to be found in the country. Inevitably much of the most run-down rented housing served the poorest section of the community, though paradoxically rented accommodation in poor, overcrowded districts was often comparatively expensive. Fenner Brockway found people paying 11s. a week for a single room in some of the temporary lodgings in Birmingham known as 'whacks', and even more could be charged for some so-called 'furnished rooms'. When the homeless Forrester family arrived in Liverpool in 1931 with their seven children, they found themselves being charged 27s. a week for three dilapidated attic rooms without cooking facilities and with gaslight in only one room.

More typically, the average proportion of working-class income paid as rent was estimated by the *New Survey of London Life and Labour* at about 5 per cent, though inevitably there were wide variations, some paying as much as 38 per cent. Rent increases had provoked rent strikes in Glasgow during the Great War and a system of rent controls had been established in 1915 as one of the principal means of stabilizing living costs for workers. Rent controls remained after the war, but were gradually removed during the inter-war years. Rents could be altered on changes of tenancy from 1923, and during the 1930s more rented accommodation was decontrolled. The 1933 Housing Act removed controls from houses of a rateable value of £45 or over in London and Scotland and of £35 elsewhere in the country; and permitted alterations of rents on change of tenancy in medium-sized properties, while retaining controls on some four million lower-rated houses, about 40 per cent of the total. The Housing Act of 1938 maintained control of rents on properties rated below £35 in London and Scotland and £20 elsewhere in the country. But while in theory rent controls were maintained on cheaper housing, there was ample evidence that the relationship between tenant and landlord was far from satisfactory. The system of decontrolling rents on a change of tenancy could mean that identical houses were let at widely differing rents. In areas of housing shortage, landlords often failed to comply with the Acts and the poorest tenants frequently suffered from the most extortionate rents. Amongst left-wing writers there was a general consensus that the landlord was 'the spoilt child of the law', fuelling the desire amongst Labour councils and politicians to eliminate private landlordism and replace it with municipal housing. Some of these conflicts emerged in a series of rent strikes in East London in 1938 led by tenants' associations, aiming merely to secure reductions of rent in accordance with existing legislation and a proper level of repairs. In nine months in 1938 the Stepney Tenants' Defence League reduced rent rolls by £18,000 a year and secured £10,000 of repayments. In 1939 the Tenants' League, led by an Anglo-Catholic priest and a local communist, mounted a twenty-one-week rent strike which after battles with police and bailiffs and mediation by the Bishop of Stepney led to a widespread reduction in rents.

Such episodes, helped by the achievements of the municipal slum clearance schemes, set the stage in the late 1930s for the post-1945 eclipse of private landlords wherever possible. However, while Labour councillors and politicians looked forward to an era of mass public-authority housing, an equally spectacular development in private owner-occupation was taking place, which, after 1945, was to share with the local authorities in the virtual elimination of the private rented sector.

The Second World War was to have a profound effect upon housing in a number of ways. It brought both private and local authority building almost to a halt. Between 1935 and 1939 the average house completion rate was 330,000 per year; in 1944–5 it was just over 5,000 per year. Under 300,000 houses were built *in all* between 1939 and 1945. Meanwhile, the backlog of houses due for demolition increased. In 1939 there were still 550,000 dwellings waiting to be demolished under the slum clearance acts and another 350,000 'marginal dwellings' on the brink of classification as slums. To this backlog had to be added 475,000 houses destroyed or made permanently uninhabitable by enemy action, and a far greater number damaged. Even more pressing, two million wartime marriages added immensely to the housing shortage. As a result housing was to remain an urgent national priority in the years after 1945.

Town and Country Planning

By 1900 there already existed a handful of major 'planned' towns or estates, usually built by enlightened industrialists to house their workers, notably the Cadbury family's Bournville, near Birmingham, and the Lever brothers' Port Sunlight on the Wirral. These experiments in building better houses in a completely fresh, comprehensive development were taken further by Ebenezer Howard in the concept of the 'garden city', aimed at combining the advantages of both town and country, but no longer dependent on a single firm or benefactor. Howard's conception of self-financing medium-sized cities of 30,000 or so people, sited in open countryside and surrounded by a large 'green belt', would, it was hoped, attract people back from the overcrowded cities and stem the tide of rural de-population. Howard's influential ideas, announced in his book *Tomorrow*, published in 1898 and re-issued in 1902 as *Garden Cities of Tomorrow*, found expression in the formation of the Garden City Association in 1899. Four years later the first garden city was started at Letchworth and by 1914 housed 9,000 people. The town was financed out of privately raised loans and achieved its aims in the form of a mixed social community in which the standard of housing for the working classes was far superior to almost anything available elsewhere. 'Garden suburbs', such as those at Hampstead and Golders Green in North-West London, started between 1905 and 1909, were designed by Raymond Unwin, the architect of Letchworth. Built as dormitory suburbs to take advantage of the new under-ground line opened in 1907, they were not true garden cities, but represented the adoption of Howard's principles on a more limited scale, by the creation of a socially mixed community, with well-designed houses ranging from mansions to small cottages. By 1914 there were at least fifty housing schemes completed or being built on 'garden city' lines. But the major influence of Howard's concept lay, immediately, not in the building of complete towns or suburbs, but in growing concern about land use, urban layout and house design. For example the first Department of Town Planning was set up at Liverpool University by 1914 and in that year the Town Planning Institute was founded, to act as a professional organization for architects, engineers and town planners.

Although many of the early experiments in town development were carried out by private enterprise or through philanthropic organizations, the First World War led the government to build estates for munitions workers at Gretna in Scotland and Well Hall near Eltham to standards of layout and house design derived from the garden city concept. Indeed, Raymond Unwin and Frank Baines, the two principal architects involved, came from this background. Although the 'Homes for Heroes' movement did not explicitly lead to the construction of new towns, the standards set in layout and design were directly influenced by the new current of thought. Similarly, philanthropic efforts such as the Haig Memorial Homes and the British Legion Village near Maidstone continued to reflect the desire for a vastly improved model for housing developments. A few companies, such as the London Brick Company, Bowaters, Crittalls, and the Czech footwear firm Bata, continued to build high-standard company estates during the interwar years. Increasingly, however, the central area of debate was seen to be the influencing of government legislation on land use and the promotion of the planning ideal in new housing developments. Architects and planners, such as Raymond Unwin, Barry Parker, Patrick Abercrombie, Frederic Osborn and Patrick Geddes, developed the 'garden city' concept and combined it with foreign ideas to produce a distinctive British planning movement. Unwin, like Howard, looked towards low densities in housing developments, about fifty or sixty people per acre, the standard adopted by the Tudor Walters Report of 1918 and applied widely in municipal estates such as the Wythenshawe satellite town built in 1930 by Unwin's assistant, Parker. Both Unwin and Parker championed large green belts around urban developments, while from the United States came the idea of 'parkways' – scenic roads linking urban communities – and of neighbourhood units containing all major facilities and free of through traffic. Patrick Geddes, trained as a biologist, urged the need to study regional settlement and economic patterns with regard to the human geography of a wide area. His technique of the regional survey, analysis of results, followed by a plan, provided the working method of later planners. Only by a large-scale approach, Geddes believed, could the tendency for further concentration of urban development be overcome. Further influenced by the work of men like the American Lewis Mumford, whose *The Culture of Cities* was published in 1938, the regional planners were already before the Second World War looking towards schemes for decentralizing the giant conurbations. Patrick Abercrombie, Professor of Civic Design at Liverpool from 1915 to 1935, and subsequently Professor of Town Planning at University College, London, was to weld many of these ideas into a comprehensive survey of the London area. Some younger architects too, training in the 1930s but more influential after 1945 than before, were also beginning to take up the ideas of the Swiss architect Le Corbusier, with his characteristic style of large multi-storey blocks set in landscaped parkland.

Nevertheless, the town and country planning movement had only limited impact before 1939. Another private enterprise garden city was started by Howard at Welwyn in Hertfordshire in 1920, but like Letchworth it suffered from financial problems. Wythenshawe, outside Manchester, started in 1930 as a planned development for 100,000 under the initiative of E. D. Simon, and designed by Parker, contained many of the new ideas: a surrounding green belt, zoned industrial and residential areas, and well-designed low-density housing with ample gardens and avenues. No other large-scale plans, however, were realized between the wars, and planning legislation proved relatively ineffective. The Housing, Town Planning, etc., Act of 1909, reflecting Howard's ideas, was designed to secure 'the home healthy, the house beautiful, the town pleasant, the city dignified and the suburb salubrious', but only provided for local authorities to control the development of *new* housing areas, primarily with a view to public health. The Housing and Town

Planning Act of 1919 did little in practice to broaden the basis
of town planning: the preparation of schemes was made obliga-
tory on all boroughs and urban districts having a population of
20,000 or more, but the time limits were first extended (by
the Housing Act of 1923) and finally abolished by the Town
and Country Planning Act of 1932. The latter extended
planning powers to almost any type of land, but its operation,
like that of the Restriction of Ribbon Development Act, 1935,
was limited. While local authorities had the right to prevent
undesirable development, many were unable to afford the high
cost of compensating owners for the loss incurred when they
were forbidden to develop. At a time when some local
authorities were financially hard-pressed by the effects of the
slump on rate income, these regulations often remained a dead
letter. Similarly, while local authorities had the power to draw
up schemes for development, there was no compulsion on them
to do so. The administrative structure was also weak, and many
of the smaller district councils were unable to cope with the
financial and administrative burdens involved. The central
authority – the Ministry of Health – had no effective powers
of initiation or of granting financial assistance to local authorities. As a result, as late as 1942 only 3 per cent of Britain was
covered by operative planning schemes, many of which did
little more than accept and ratify existing schemes of development.

But the ideas of the garden city movement and of the town
planners were beginning to gain acceptance by the late 1930s,
stimulated by the vast expansion of suburban and industrial
development and the growing pressures of road traffic. The
New Towns Group formed in 1918 argued for a government
policy to build properly designed new towns in the regions.
Plans for the rationalization of land use and the restriction of
'urban sprawl' attracted increasing attention between the wars.
The rapid growth of London led to the setting-up of a number
of advisory committees which included the Greater London
Regional Planning Committee (1927) and the Standing Conference on London Regional Planning (1937). In 1933 the

former received a report from Raymond Unwin, urging the creation of a 'green girdle' around London to act as a barrier to urban development and provide recreational space. After Labour won control of the London County Council in 1934, Herbert Morrison, its Chairman, who had worked at Letchworth and was a strong proponent of town planning, inaugurated a pioneering scheme to secure the protection of 25,000 acres of 'green belt' from development, confirmed in the Green Belt Act of 1938.

Elsewhere some authorities were drawing up plans for comprehensive redevelopment, with new municipal housing estates forming part of ambitious schemes of town planning. In Liverpool, for example, new estates were grouped in a semi-circle round the outer limits of the city, on a system of arterial roads, radiating out from the city centre. In 1935 Sir Ernest Simon looked forward to a large-scale reconstruction of the southern half of the city of Manchester:

> In Manchester practically all the houses in the slum belt, numbering about 80,000, will have to be demolished and replaced by modern houses or flats, before the city's housing can be regarded as satisfactory. This means that there will be a splendid opportunity for replanning the central area on the best modern lines, and for making a comprehensive plan for Manchester's whole future development; it is most important that this opportunity should be utilized to the full, so that all the congestion and ill-health and waste caused by the lack of any planning when the slum belt was first built may be prevented in the future. The essential thing is that all the work which is done – clearance, rebuilding and new development – should be carried out as a part of a unified scheme; experts are unanimous in condemning a policy of piecemeal slum clearance without regard to their relationship to the requirements of a city as a whole.

This was the authentic voice of the inter-war planner and, already in the 1930s, the essential ingredients of post-war development were there: the appeal to 'experts' or to continental experience (Simon also looked to the 'better-planned German cities'), the comprehensive approach and the implied application of wider powers. Indeed, many of the plans which were only to be realized after 1945 were being formulated in

the pre-war years, often in conjunction with those who saw
town planning not just as a technique for controlling the layout
and design of residential areas, but as part of a policy of national
economic and social planning. Town and country planning,
like birth control, free secondary education and a comprehensive health service, had become part of a progressive consensus
which found its opportunity with the Second World War.

The primary concern of the planners with urban development almost inevitably had wider implications, not only in
terms of regional planning, but also in regard to the countryside
and the national problems of industrial location and distribution. Rural conservation became a movement of some significance after 1914, drawing on a disparate group of enthusiasts
who included not only town planners, but also figures from
other walks of life. The Council for the Preservation of Rural
England set up in 1925 included many people who were not
professional planners, but one, Patrick Abercrombie, who
spanned the world of rural conservation and town planning.
Increasingly, there was a realization that the fate of the countryside was inextricably bound up with that of the towns. By the
mid-1930s, some 60,000 acres each year were being taken from
agriculture by urban and road development. There was a
passionate outcry against the suburban spread of London, much
of it on prime agricultural land, ribbon development along the
new arterial roads and the gradual encroachment of traffic and
day-trippers upon rural areas. Although ribbon development
was partly brought under control by an Act in 1935, the
planning procedures were slow and cumbersome. With new
pressure groups, such as the Ramblers' Association and the
Youth Hostels Association, representing leisure interests, there
was growing concern in the need to protect particular parts of
the countryside from excessive development. In parallel with
the urge to conserve was the demand for right of access, frequently articulating a long-standing conflict between the rights
of the public to use the countryside and the rights of private
landlords to restrict access. Anti-landlordism had a particularly
powerful emotive appeal in some areas of Scotland and Wales

and was, in part, transferred into the cry of 'public access' championed by the Labour Party and left-wing groups between the wars. By the end of the 1920s the campaign focused upon the provision of 'national parks' such as had already been established in parts of Europe and North America. An official National Park Committee reported in 1931, but no government action was taken. None the less, incidents such as the mass trespass on Kinder Scout in the Peak District in 1932 and the Access to the Mountains Act of 1939 foreshadowed a major reappraisal of this area in the Second World War.

Moreover, on a national level, the problems of the depressed areas led to consideration of the need to control the expansion of industry in the South-East and secure more even distribution of development. The implications of such a policy were made the subject of the Barlow Commission, set up in 1937. The Commission was given wide terms of reference and its recommendations, published in January 1940, provided a blueprint for post-war planning policy. Although the Commission produced two minority reports, its members were unanimous in their condemnation of the existing situation and the inadequacy of both policy and machinery. Reviewing the history of town planning they noted that 'legislation has not yet proceeded so far as to deal with the problem of planning from a *national* standpoint; there is no duty imposed on any authority or Government Department to view the country as a whole and to consider the problems of industrial, commercial and urban growth in the light of the needs of the entire population'.

The Barlow Commission has been called 'the beginning of the planners' "breakthrough" ' after which the major disagreement was less about the direction of policy than on how it should be translated into practice. Abercrombie, a member of the Commission, was signatory to one of the minority reports, calling for a ministry with strong executive powers to carry out a national planning policy. The impact of the Second World War in this area was decisive. In the face of the threat and later the reality of bombing, a policy of industrial relocation was undertaken and controls over the siting of factories and the

utilization of land accepted as essential. Moreover the destruction wrought by bombing turned 'rebuilding Britain' from a
vaguely desirable objective into a necessity. Aided by the
powerful collectivist sentiments released by the war and the
widespread interest in reconstruction, the blitz precipitated an
avalanche of schemes for the new Britain in which town
planners and architects vied with each other in the ambition
and scale of their plans. Under the headline 'The New Britain
must be Planned', the modern architect Maxwell Fry outlined
in *Picture Post* in January 1941 a five-point agenda of 'what
we want':

everybody to live in cheerful, healthy conditions, which only proper
planning can ensure; an attack on the slums to begin immediately after
the war; a bold building plan to civilize our industrial towns in twenty
years – or less; plans for industry, housing, schools, hospitals and
transport; a plan to get the best out of town and country: to bring
green grass to the towns, and town amenities to the village.

Pictures of modern flats, factories, hospitals and road schemes
were contrasted with the haphazard and dilapidated condition
of existing towns. Fry was in no doubt about the agent of these
plans: 'It is for the Government to make up its mind what kind
of a country we are, and to plan the larger issues accordingly.'
   Hardly had the dust settled on the bomb damage of 1940
than plans for large-scale replanning were pouring off the
drawing boards. These were encouraged by the appointment
in October 1940 of Lord Reith as the head of the new Ministry
of Works, not only to supervise repairing bomb-damaged
buildings but also to consult other departments and organizations about the post-war rebuilding of cities. One of Reith's first
actions as Minister of Works was to appoint a panel of consultants to advise him on post-war planning. Ten were members
of the Town and Country Planning Association and its
secretary, Osborn, was appointed under-secretary in the department. A series of planning objectives were drawn up which
followed closely the views of progressive planners. These
included: controlled development of all areas and utilization of
land to the best advantage; limitation of urban expansion;

redevelopment of congested areas; correlation of transport and all amenities; improved architectural treatment; and preservation of places of historic interest, national parks and coastal areas. Although Reith was dismissed in February 1942, his initiative in these areas had set in train a series of plans for comprehensive redevelopment.

One such was Reith's appointment of Patrick Abercrombie and the LCC architect J. H. Forshaw to draw up a plan for the rebuilding of London. The result was *The County of London Plan*, published in 1943, and a further report, commissioned by Reith's successor, Wyndham Portal, the *Greater London Plan* of 1944. Others were the establishment of committees under Mr Justic Uthwatt to examine the crucial question of compensation for planning development and the Scott Committee on the future of the countryside. Plans were also inaugurated for the reconstruction of cities and towns such as Glasgow, Exeter, Hull and Coventry. The example of Coventry perhaps best exemplifies the dovetailing of pre-war concerns with the effects of the blitz. In 1938, it became one of the first cities to set up an Architectural Department. An exhibition in May–June 1939 illustrated plans for a redesigned civic centre, with lectures by such well-known authorities on town planning as Thomas Sharp, author of *Oxford Re-Planned*, and Clough Williams-Ellis, builder of the Italianate village of Portmeirion in Snowdonia. These plans remained in an abstract stage until the destruction of much of the centre of Coventry in November 1940. At their first meeting after the blitz, the General Purposes Committee recommended the setting-up of a City Redevelopment Committee to consider 'the steps which it will be desirable for the municipality to take to secure a worthy replanning and redevelopment of the city'. Coventry was chosen by Lord Reith as one of a handful of cities to be used as a prototype of large-scale urban planning. Although there were divisions in the local authority as to how radical the plan for the traditional city centre should be, it was entirely symptomatic of the mood of the times that both the City Redevelopment Committee and Lord Reith should accept the more radical scheme outlined by

Donald Gibson, the city architect. Within six months of the
blitz which had devastated the city centre, an exhibition of
sketches and plans outlined a redesigned centre, based on the
principle of pedestrian shopping precincts, zoned development
and an inner ring-road.

The creation of the Ministry of Town and Country Planning
in 1943, followed by the Town and Country Planning Act of
1944, provided both the machinery and the powers for comprehensive redevelopment on the lines envisaged by the more
ambitious advocates of planning. Subsequently the 1947 Town
and Country Planning Act brought almost all development
under control by making it subject to planning permission.
Development plans were to be prepared for every area of the
country, the powers being transferred away from the small
district councils to the county and borough councils. Coordination of local plans was to be carried out by the Ministry
of Town and Country Planning, while development rights in
land were nationalized. Similarly, the New Towns Act of 1946
provided for the setting-up of Development Corporations to
plan and create new towns where considered 'expedient in the
national interest'. The corporations had wide powers of acquisition and management of the requisite areas 'and generally to
do anything necessary or expedient for the purposes of the new
town or for the purposes incidental thereto'.

Similarly, the Second World War provided a receptive
atmosphere for a reappraisal of the economic and recreational
role of the countryside. By 1941 L. F. Easterbrook, the
agricultural expert and journalist, was urging the need for a
'Land Commission' which would operate a national strategy
to apportion land for agriculture, forestry, building, roads,
allotments, factories, playing fields and national parks, while
others supported the demand for public access to the countryside and the creation of specially designated areas as 'lungs' for
the urban areas. The Scott Report, published in 1942, urged
the establishment of a planning system embracing the countryside as well as the town, mainly with a view to preserving the
best agricultural land from urban development. It also recom-

mended the creation of National Parks, and following the appointment of the first Minister of Town and Country Planning in 1943, the government committed itself to this idea. The issue of control of land use remained more contentious; a White Paper on the control of land use was shelved by the Coalition Government and not dealt with until the Town and Country Planning Act of 1947 under the post-war Labour administration. The proposal for National Parks, however, received further support in the Dower Report, published in 1945, and that of the Hobhouse Committee, which proposed setting up a National Parks Commission paid for out of public funds. These were eventually embodied in the National Parks and Access to the Countryside Act of 1949.

Hence, by the late 1940s, the planning movement had acquired both the government support and the legislative machinery which were to form the basis for many of the town and country planning schemes after 1945. The experience of the inter-war years had in fact been dominated by unplanned development. Slough and Kidlington, the encroachment of 'metroland' into the home counties, and the using-up of the fertile Lea Valley for housing and industrial development were far more typical than Welwyn Garden City or Wythenshawe. The Second World War, however, put the planners firmly in the saddle. In part, at least, their work was beneficial. Low-rise, low-density housing estates dominated the council house building programme well into the post-war era. New towns, National Parks and a more coordinated approach to regional planning offered genuine advances for thousands of people and spared many parts of the country from the worst excesses of piecemeal and unplanned development. Nevertheless, there were already some signs of insensitivity to popular feeling and a lack of appreciation of what could happen to the most civilized schemes when translated into reality by private interests or local politicians. Peter Hall has remarked on the tendency of the early planners, with one or two exceptions, to see themselves as 'omniscient rulers', drawing up schemes on the basis of what they believed to be best for people, usually without consulting

them. By 1939 some council estates had already been constructed which dumped young married couples miles from
parents and immediate kin, often dependent on uncertain
transport to reach work and entertainment, and on estates whose
neat, geometric designs lacked many of the basic social
amenities, such as shops, pubs and meeting places, essential to
a satisfactory life. It took a certain insouciance, or plain
ignorance, to rehouse dockers at Hull on greenfield estates, miles
from the dock gates, where they had to turn up early each
morning simply to find out whether there was any work for
them to do. Undoubtedly, many of these errors sprang from a
perfectly well-intentioned desire to get people out of the slums
– almost at any price – and provide them with a better physical
environment.

In the generation or so after the Second World War, these
tendencies, formulated between the wars and given powers
of implementation during the 1940s, were to do more to change
the face of Britain's cities and towns than the effects either of
depression or of war. The dual legacy of the first half of the
twentieth century was a phase of almost chaotic unplanned
development, supplemented increasingly from the 1930s by a
planning movement amongst whose 'achievements' – for better
and worse – we still live.

9. Childhood, Youth and Education

Historians have noted changes in the attitudes to children as early as the eighteenth century, with the development of the romantic movement and greater concern for the children as individuals – potential adults who deserved proper nurture and education. A declining infant mortality rate from the late eighteenth century may also have encouraged more 'affectionate' attitudes. By the Edwardian era, a middle-class family with only one or two children could devote more time, energy and money to their offspring than their forbears had been able to. The 'needs' of children were not just endured by parents, but often given with interest and concern, as was shown in the continuing demand for private education and the widening range of consumer goods aimed at children. But these changes were not confined to the middle classes. During the first half of the twentieth century more and more children were being brought up in smaller and better-provided families. Children born in the decade 1911–21 grew up in households which averaged 3.4 children, only a fifth of which were owner-occupied; by the end of the Second World War the average child grew up in a household with only one other child, and a third of houses were owner-occupied.

A declining birth rate and higher living standards did not leave the working classes untouched. As Paul Thompson has written:

> With fewer children the home was less likely to be overcrowded, cleanliness was easier, there was more time for individual affection and less need for regimental discipline, and as spare resources increased it became possible for working-class parents to convey affection through giving birthday presents. The gentle, home-centred working-

class family of two or three children already existed in the early twentieth century, and it was to become increasingly common.

Although Richard Hoggart believed it to be 'a working-class tradition of long standing' to indulge not only children but young people all the way up to marriage, there was little doubt that fewer children and greater prosperity permitted even more attention than before. There was already an extensive literature on childcare dating from before the First World War, much of it strongly medical in tone, and appealing primarily to an educated, middle-class readership. Increasingly this literature, with its primary concern for physical survival, was being replaced by a literature for all classes which stressed the social and emotional needs of children, foreshadowing the 'progressive' theories of child-rearing popularized by Dr Spock in the 1940s. Some of these attitudes filtered through to a much wider audience via the popular women's magazines of the 1930s, which along with their romantic stories and articles on fashion and cooking also devoted space to features and correspondence concerning childcare. Concern for children, reflected both in personal behaviour and in social policy, was also to make education a central feature of social debate.

The enhanced status of children and young people was reflected in legislation. The Children's Act of 1908 consolidated the existing law and recognized the need for their legal protection. Imprisonment of children was abolished and special remand homes set up for those awaiting trial, which had to take place in special 'juvenile courts'. In 1933, the Children and Young Persons' Act extended responsibility for children to the age of seventeen and included a careful definition of 'care and protection'. It also established 'approved schools' and further regulated juvenile court procedure. The 1937 Factory Act gave more protection to young workers in the tradition of the nineteenth century; hours of work were restricted and better training enforced for young people working in dangerous industries.

There was a very significant growth in organized youth

movements, encouraged by government, philanthropic bodies and the churches. 'National efficiency' fears and humanitarian social concern found common expression in a network of clubs and organizations aimed at youth, in which religious and moral justifications blended with concern about national vigour and imperial decline. The years around 1900 have been identified by some as the period when the conception of 'youth' as adolescents, at a particular stage in biological, psychological and social development, became fixed. In this process the polarization of delinquent and disciplined youth became well established and with it the idea of youth organizations to channel young people into suitable recreations. The growth of these youth organizations was one of the major features of the first half of the twentieth century. Although affected by the anti-militarism and anti-imperialism which followed the Great War, they none the less frequently continued to inculcate conservative and conformist attitudes in matters of morals, religion and politics. Membership of the Boy Scouts and cubs rose from 152,000 in 1913 to 438,000 in 1938, and of the Boys' Brigade from 65,000 to 161,000, by which time there were 10,719 Scout groups and 2,756 Boys' Brigade companies in the United Kingdom. In contrast, membership of the Church Lads' Brigade fell from around 36,000 in 1911 to about 20,000 in 1931 while the number of units had fallen from 1,557 to 1,073 in 1939. A similar decline was registered by the Army Cadet Force – from 41,000 in 1913 to 20,000 in 1939. There was, however, much stronger growth in girls' organizations. The Girls Guildry, founded in 1900 and concentrated mainly in Scotland, had 24,000 members by 1939, with 475 companies. The Girl Guides, growing out of the Scout movement in 1910, started with an initial 8,000 members and rose, with the brownies, to become the most popular girls' organization by the Second World War.

The growth of these organizations, especially the Scouts and Guides, was an almost entirely spontaneous phenomenon, which clearly filled a need both of parents and children for recreational activity. Although widely spread throughout the

British Isles and over all classes, there was some tendency for
the Scouts and the Guides to appeal most strongly to middle-
class families and areas of the country. In 1921, the heaviest
concentration of Scouts per thousand boys aged ten to nineteen
was in London and the Home Counties. The recreational aspect
of scouting and other youth organizations was obviously
attractive to children and youths with spare leisure time. For
the pit boy and the mill girl, they were less likely to appeal,
though Boys' Brigades were quite strong in working-class
areas.

More generally, there was some evidence of a youth 'problem' even before 1914. Indeed Paul Thompson has remarked
that 'the continuity of twentieth-century youth culture is more
striking than new developments'. A lower school-leaving age
than after 1945, a lower age of puberty and a later age of
marriage meant that there were more working, unmarried
adolescents than in later periods. Between the wars police and
parents were less concerned with sexual promiscuity than with
the sheer uncontrolled indiscipline of youth. Fears of 'rowdy-
ism', amplified by the school strikes of 1911 and subsequent
years, the youth disorders of the summer of 1919, and the rise
in juvenile delinquency between the wars (see pp. 373–6)
focused upon adolescent 'ill-discipline'. Although a distinct
'teenage' culture was to await the affluence of the years after
the Second World War, there were manifestations of it before
1939. Young people could often find work more easily than
adults because they could be employed at cheaper rates. The
demand for labour in the Great War and the cost-cutting
encouraged by the depression meant that there was a large
group of relatively affluent young people, without family
responsibilities, who presented a market for clothes, mass entertainment and recreational opportunities of other kinds. In the
upper echelons of society, the 'gay young things' represented
a particularly affluent group who spear-headed, or were
thought to spear-head, progressive attitudes in morals and ideas
between the wars. More typical, however, were the young men
and women between fourteen and eighteen who were able to

obtain work at low rates, but whose lack of family commitments enabled them to have some margin of income available for personal consumption. On the other hand, the presence of mass unemployment also sparked off fears of ill-discipline and moral laxity which were reflected in concern about the rising juvenile crime rate and deliberate attempts to meet the problem of juvenile offences with special courts and penal procedures.

One manifestation of 'respectability' amongst aspirant members of all classes was the attempt to inculcate sober and disciplined habits amongst the young. As these ideals advanced with rising affluence, the pressure on the young to conform, at school, in youth organizations and in general behaviour, intensified. Badges of respectability and maturity such as school uniform, the first suit, the 'key to the door', examination results, medals and certificates of attainment seem to have had at least as much importance between the wars as they had before 1914. In some respects, it seems, the years between the end of the nineteenth century and the years after 1945 mark the heyday of the attempt to make youth respectable, model adults. To describe this as an imposition of middle-class mores upon working-class youth may be right to a certain extent, but it underestimates the powerful forces towards respectability at work in the early twentieth-century working classes themselves. Only a few small groups, such as the largely middle-class Kibbo Kift, founded in 1920, and the Woodcraft Folk of 1925, openly set out to challenge the political and cultural orthodoxies of the day. Although scarcely radical in themselves, with their interesting blend of naturalism and socialism, they suggested something of a less conformist approach to the role of youth in the twentieth century.

Only a minority of young people ever participated in youth organizations, though it was quite a large minority. All, however, were influenced by education, the labour market and the influence of the wider culture. In spite of the prevailing concerns about young people's indiscipline, there is little evidence apart from a few of the 'gilded young' that the young were generally doing anything other than following the moral standards of their elders between the wars. A minority might indulge in sexual promiscuity, but illegitimacy rates remained low and were not to rise significantly until after 1945. In working-class areas, 'going steady' was still accepted as the normal preliminary to engagement and marriage, a situation which appears to have altered little between the Edwardian era and the post-1945 period. A minority might also get into trouble with the police, but the great majority did not. For most young people, youth was a period of relative freedom before the assumption of parental responsibilities, rather than of licence or ill-discipline.

Education

Britain entered the Great War already possessing a system of free compulsory elementary education up to the age of twelve or fourteen. As we have seen, the war stimulated demands for social reforms, including an improvement of educational provision, particularly secondary education. This found expression in the Fisher Education Act of 1918, which encouraged the Board of Education and the local authorities to build up an all-embracing system of education from nursery schools to adult evening classes. Compulsory education was made universal until the age of fourteen, removing all the concessions previously offered to part-timers and 'early-leavers', which had allowed many working-class children to leave school at the age of twelve. Local authorities were permitted to raise the school-leaving age to fifteen or to provide day-continuation for youths of fourteen to sixteen for one day a week. The Act also expressed the hope that no children or young people would be debarred from receiving the benefits of any form of education through the inability to pay fees.

Many of these aspirations were frustrated by the 'Geddes Axe' and the economy measures forced on the government from 1921. Government expenditure on education had risen between 1913–14 and 1921–2 from £14.7 million to £51.0 million, but by 1923–4 had fallen to £41.9 million. Capital expenditure waso reduced, as was the planned increase in current expenditure. The reductions were felt most sharply in the virtual extinction of the continuation school programme and the perpetuation of serious overcrowding and staff shortages. The effect of government economy, which at one time had envisaged raising the school entry age to six (from five) years, and a cut of three times the figure eventually announced, emphasized the problem which dominated the education debate between the wars, the provision of adequate secondary education for all.

In 1923 almost three-quarters of children in England and Wales were being educated in the elementary schools they had entered at the age of five and in which the main emphasis was on rudimentary instruction in the three Rs. Only a small minority of children – some 7.5 per cent – were receiving 'advanced instruction' in grant-aided secondary schools or at junior technical schools. Most of these schools charged fees, although there were some 'free places' for which examinations took place at the age of eleven. The remaining children were those who had either managed to escape compulsory schooling altogether or the 6 per cent who received private education at the public schools. Many educationalists and others lamented the separation of elementary school education from secondary or public school education for a minority. It was this cutting-off of the great majority of the population from advanced education which led the Labour Party to adopt the principle of secondary education for all, as the next stage after elementary or 'primary' education. The policy statement 'Secondary Education for All' put the aim as being: 'that all normal children, irrespective of the income, class, or occupation of their parents, may be transferred at the age of 11 + from the primary or preparatory school to one type or another of secondary school, and remain in the latter till sixteen'.

These aspirations were reflected in the Hadow Report, the product of a Consultative Committee set up by the Labour government of 1923 under the chairmanship of Sir W. H. Hadow. Its findings greatly influenced the structure of the education system up to and beyond the 1944 Act. Appearing

in December 1926, the Report's major proposal was the
abolition of the old conception of 'elementary' education and
its replacement by two levels of education: 'primary' education
to the age of eleven, followed by 'secondary' education. Two
types of 'secondary' school were envisaged: existing 'secondary'
or 'higher' schools were to be renamed 'grammar schools',
providing a more academic education, while the others, including the senior departments of the old elementary schools,
were to become 'modern' schools, at which all children would
remain until the age of fifteen. The crucial ingredients were
therefore a raising of the school-leaving age, a distinct break
in education at the age of eleven, and the provision of secondary
education for all of a kind suited to their abilities.

The Hadow Report was accepted, but progress towards
implementation was delayed by the consequences of the economic crisis of 1929–31. None the less, by 1938 almost two-thirds
of all children over eleven were in the reorganized 'modern'
schools, while the grammar schools operated for a minority
of fee-paying and scholarship pupils. In 1926 the Conservative
government had also taken an important initiative when certain
fee-paying schools, then outside the public sector, were allowed
to qualify for 'direct grants', usually in return for taking a
number of scholarship boys. This decision merely ratified
arrangements which had been reached informally between particular schools and their local authorities. Dulwich College, for
example, undertook in 1920 to take a percentage of local
authority pupils in order to ease its financial problems. By 1928
the school was educating about 100 LCC scholars at any one
time. Meanwhile the extension of the school-leaving age to
fifteen, envisaged by the government to take place in 1931,
was delayed by the difficulties of accommodating the voluntary
and church-run schools and by the financial difficulties of the
early 1930s. Re-enacted by the Education Act of 1936 and
intended to be implemented from September 1939, it was again
prevented by the outbreak of the Second World War.

Scotland inherited an educational system which was separately organized and widely regarded as superior to the English,

particularly in regard to the higher percentage of pupils going on to secondary education and what was seen as a more accessible system for the clever child from a poor background. There was, if anything, some evidence of a relative decline between the wars in the performance of Scottish education when compared with the rest of Britain, primarily caused by the expansion of secondary education in the rest of the United Kingdom. As a result Scotland's share of all secondary pupils in the UK fell from 18.0 per cent in 1913 to 15.3 per cent in 1938. Moreover, local all-ability schools were supplanted after 1923 in Scotland by a division between 'junior' and 'senior' secondary schools which anticipated the Hadow Report south of the border in reserving only one category, in the Scottish case the 'senior secondaries', as places of academic education, creating in the larger towns and cities a similar social gulf to that found in the English system between 'grammar' and secondary 'modern' schools. Scottish education was also affected by successive administrative reorganizations which included a complete overhaul of the system of local government in 1929 and the sweeping away of its existing Local Education Authorities and school management committees, themselves only in existence since 1918. One effect was to force the professional organizations into a series of defensive battles over redundancies, wage cuts and loss of status which militated against major education initiatives.

Education represented a relatively minor area of government interest between the wars, with no major legislation between 1918 and 1944 and a distinct sense amongst many critics that the aspirations of the war years and the Fisher Act had been lost amidst the search for economy. None the less, there was an increase in the net public expenditure on education in the United Kingdom during these years, from £65.1 million in 1919–20, to £92.8 million in 1929–30, and to £107.5 million in 1939–40. But while education spending remained at about 6 per cent of government expenditure, local authority spending continued to rise. Education remained one of the largest items of local authority expenditure and rose during this period from £23.7 million in 1919–20 to £46.7 million in 1937–8, by which time the local authorities were carrying more than 50 per cent of the cost of education. Capital expenditure on new buildings, refurbishment and equipment witnessed an important growth by the end of the 1930s. In 1935–8 just under £50 million was spent in this way, approximately double that of ten years earlier. There was also an increase in the number of secondary schools and pupils, rising from 187,647 in 1914 to 470,003 in 1938, while the number and proportion of free places grew, rising from under a third in 1920 to almost a half in 1938. Moreover expenditure per child, 'capitation', and pupil–teacher ratios were also moving in a favourable direction by the end of the 1930s.

There were also expanding opportunities in higher education. The numbers of those receiving some form of higher education at universities, teacher training colleges and other forms of further education rose from 25,000 in 1900–1901, to 61,000 in 1924–5, and to 69,000 in 1938–9. The number of university students, 42,000 in 1924–5, was double the figure in 1900–1901 and had risen to 50,000 by 1938–9. Most of this expansion took place in England and Wales with the founding of new 'red-brick' university colleges, awarding London University degrees, at Nottingham, Southampton, Exeter, Hull and Leicester, and of the University of Reading in 1926. The founding of the University Grants Committee in 1919 provided a means of channelling state finance to the universities, and brought them into a more coherent relationship with central government. Total government expenditure on higher education rose from £3.9 million in 1920–21 to £9.8 million in 1937–8, while that from local sources, mainly rates, grew from £4.2 million to £10.3 million. English university expenditure rose by over 90 per cent between 1924 and 1937, though in Scotland by only a third of this, resulting in a decline of student numbers from 10,400 to 9,900. The higher education sector, however, remained small. Only 13,200 of those entering employment in 1934 were from universities out of a total of 554,500. The total higher education sector only accounted for 27,700. As late as 1938 only 2 per cent of nineteen-year-olds were receiving full-time education.

Adult and continuing education also saw some expansion, though less than that anticipated in the Fisher Act. The Workers' Educational Association, formed in 1903, called for a 'highway' to avoid the exclusion of millions of children from educational opportunity, and attracted a host of often very dedicated tutors and teachers from the universities and schools to give part-time adult education. A similar role was performed by the university extra-mural classes, which enrolled as many as 80,000 students before 1914. This type of education continued to flourish between the wars in spite of government economies and inevitable difficulties of staffing and finance. In 1934 over two million students were enrolled for part-time classes in England and Wales in Technical Colleges or Evening Institutes controlled by Local Education Authorities. In addition, more than 60,000 students were involved in adult classes organized by the WEA and the universities. The largest proportion of these students, about 700,000, were enrolled for technical and commercial subjects relating to particular professions, but music and art accounted for 107,000. As well as their 50,000 full-time students, the universities of England and Wales were also responsible for 6,500 part-time students as well as another 7,500 occasional students. For some at least, these classes provided a crucial lifeline to higher educational qualifications. Indeed, the large investment of time, money and concern in the whole issue of adult and further education was a reflection of the still powerful hold of voluntaristic and self-help principles. G. D. H. and M. I. Cole noted in 1937:

One of the most important and least noticed facts of the modern world is the great increase in the number of persons who possess minor technical qualifications which are enough to raise them, both in their estimation and in their earning power, above the ruck of the unqualified or of those whose sole qualification is based on manual apprenticeship. The 'black-coated' proletariat consists to an ever increasing extent of these qualified workers who have laboured away in the evenings to advance themselves, and by that means have in most cases raised themselves a step up the social ladder.

While not unaware of its limitations, the Coles felt that:

almost unobserved by the academic world the mass of minor technical qualifications grows; and perhaps some day this new system of education, working up from below, will become powerful enough to challenge the complacent egotism of the established monopolies in the higher professions and of the recognized 'seats of learning'.

But the Coles realized that this substantially 'makeshift' education, directed primarily towards filling the gaps in formal education and advancing qualifications in the sphere of existing vocations, was no substitute for advantages gained through private education. Indeed, from one point of view the private system enjoyed a 'golden age' in the inter-war years. Rising real incomes for the middle classes and growing competition from the state sector provided considerable stimulus for private education. The number of pupils in 'efficient' independent schools in England and Wales rose from 22,000 in 1914, to 82,000 in 1930, reaching 204,000 by 1950. The number of schools represented at the Headmasters' Conference rose by over a third, many other 'minor public schools' and preparatory schools opened, while existing schools expanded with new building and dormitory accommodation. Although the numbers attending the public schools were only a fraction of the total school population, they had a wholly disproportionate influence upon the English educational system.

This pre-eminence was demonstrated by the role of the public schools, particularly a handful of the major schools, in educating a high proportion of those in key positions in British society (see pp. 350–53). In addition, they provided approximately a quarter of all university students between the wars, with a marked domination of Oxford and Cambridge, where they supplied the overwhelming majority of undergraduates. That almost half the top jobs in the country were filled by people who had been to one of only five public schools was one aspect of public school influence, but on a more subtle level they also dominated the ethos of secondary education. For example, public school stories had a tremendous vogue in the years before and after the First World War, of which the work of Talbot Baines and Frank Richards were the archetypal examples. In spite of the publication of more critical accounts, such as Alec Waugh's *The Loom of Youth* (1917) and Robert Graves's *Goodbye to All That* (1929), the stereotype of the ancient and fashionable public school continued to dominate popular conceptions of what a 'good school' should be. Orwell was only one of many to recognize that the school stories published in popular children's magazines like the *Gem* and *Magnet* (written by Frank Richards) exercised a powerful influence by emphasizing the 'glamour' and snobbery of public school life and conjuring up an ambience of 'lock-up, roll-call, house matches, fagging, prefects, cosy teas round the study fire, etc., etc.'. Read not only by public schoolboys but also by many working-class children as well, the public schools in this stylized form were an accepted part of the social landscape. As important, they shaped the character of the state secondary and 'grammar' schools in features such as houses, prefects and corporal punishment. G. D. H. Cole (Cliftonville Preparatory School and St Paul's) complained of 'the almost irresistible tendency' for Local Education Authorities to set up 'colourable imitations' of the public schools, with many of their snobberies and rituals. Professor Robin Pedley, the educationalist, recalled the 'culture shock' of entering Richmond Grammar School between the wars:

When, by a curious stroke of fortune, at the age of fourteen I was translated from my village elementary school to the ancient grammar school ten miles away, I entered a different world. For the first time I wore a tailored grey suit, stiff collar, and school cap. I felt a guilty turncoat when the elementary-school children of the town chanted 'Grammar, grammar matchstalks' derisively at us as we walked long-trousered through the cobbled streets. Inside the school too, my life was turned upside down. It was not only that for the first time I encountered such subjects as Latin and French, physics and chemistry, algebra and geometry: I had expected that. What amazed me was the elaborate apparatus devised to get boys to do what the staff wanted. Essays and tests all reaped their quota of marks, religiously added up and announced at half-term and end of term. There were colours for doing well at rugger and cricket; points for one's house, prizes for this, lines or even the cane, for that ... The grammar school's strangely formal rituals were in fact copied from the 'public' school Olympians.

The reality was that the better public schools were very effective educational institutions and also worked as efficient 'governing-class seminaries'. With buildings and resources far superior to those of many state schools, the best were able to attract good staff, for which public school teaching provided a relatively secure, comfortable and prestigious career. Nor were the public schools mere passive recipients of a growing demand for private education, for the period saw the beginning of several important educational experiments which would have been impossible in the state system. A. S. Neill's school, Summerhill, started in 1924, based itself on the need to develop 'hearts not heads' under the influence of Freud and Neill's own views of the necessity for 'freedom' in all matters. Dartington Hall, founded in 1926 as an integral part of the Dartington Hall Trust Community, near Totnes in Devon, was also based on liberal progressive lines. Co-educational, with good food and single bed-sitting rooms instead of dormitories, the school allowed its pupils considerable freedom. Other independent developments in this period included Bembridge School on the Isle of Wight, founded in 1919, Rudolf Steiner's Wynstones and Michael Hall, while Bertrand Russell and his wife ran Frensham Heights, Beacon Hill, from 1927 to 1943. Together these progressive experiments were only a tiny portion of even the private educational sector, but nevertheless illustrated a tendency shared by an increasing number of educationalists to liberalize children from pointless discipline, encouraging rather than enforcing character development and, often, displaying a more open attitude to sexual matters.

These features, however, were overshadowed by a fierce debate about the availability of secondary education. A mere fraction of children from public elementary schools in England and Wales – the highest figure was 14.3 per cent in 1938 – were admitted to a secondary school, where they could continue their education at an advanced level and beyond the age of fourteen. Secondary education and the grammar schools tended to be dominated by the middle class, who could afford fees, while the completely separate public school sector was effectively closed to those on working-class incomes. Many working-class families could not afford the loss of earnings involved in children staying on at school beyond the statutory age, still less pay fees. Only a small minority of working-class children were able to jump the hurdle from the elementary schools to secondary education, aided by scholarships and free places. Although individual education authorities, such as County Durham, did as much as possible to help children to overcome financial handicaps by offering up to 100 per cent free places, access to secondary education and to the 'life chances' associated with better qualifications was essentially rationed by price. Countless children were undoubtedly denied an education commensurate with their abilities, with a consequent wastage of talent. The loss was greatest amongst working-class children, but affected others of modest means too. Perhaps the group most heavily discriminated against were working-class girls, whose education was often considered secondary to that of boys. By one estimate in 1935, less than half of the children of 'higher ability' in the population as a whole were receiving secondary education. Thus, in a not untypical year, 1934, of 555,000 new recruits to employment of all ages, 85 per cent came from elementary schools, 70 per cent leaving at the lowest permissible school-leaving age of fourteen. Only a tenth of those entering employment were over sixteen.

Inevitably, these inequalities were carried over into higher education, which was dominated by the middle and upper classes. In spite of a doubling in the number of English university students between the wars, only four or five out of every thousand products of the English elementary schools reached the universities. Without mandatory grants to cover fees and maintenance and with only a few scholarships, the financial obstacles to a university education for the children of all but the wealthy were very severe. While a few particularly bright pupils from state schools and working-class backgrounds were able to reach universities or teacher-training colleges, there were considerable disincentives to them. Women again, particularly working-class women, were the group least likely to receive higher education.

Less than a quarter of English university students in the mid-1920s were women, and in Scotland there was a decline of 26 per cent in women attending universities between the wars.

It was this sense of a wastage of talent which animated the demand for free secondary education for all, espoused by many educationalists and by many sections of the Labour movement before the Second World War. But while the desire for more equal access to secondary education and greater equality of educational opportunity was a major preoccupation, there was also considerable concern about the physical conditions in the existing state system. An indication of the general situation was that in 1932 the official standard of classroom size for elementary schools was fifty pupils. In 1934 there were still 6,000 elementary classes in England and Wales with over fifty pupils. In many of the older elementary schools, inherited from the nineteenth century, two, three or more classes were conducted in the same large space, sometimes with partitions in between, often not. In the case of secondary schools, where the official maximum classroom size was thirty, in 1934 there were no less than 60,000 classes in English and Welsh schools with over forty pupils and another 52,000 with over thirty. Among classes consisting wholly of 'senior' pupils, over eleven years of age, only 10,000 had less than thirty pupils. Similarly, in 1932, two-thirds of all schoolchildren attended schools built before 1900, while 1,500 schools remained on an official 'blacklist' which designated them as virtually unfit for their purpose. Many schools were grim Victorian fortresses, ill-lit, badly ventilated and with primitive sanitary arrangements, where facilities for physical education, practical work and scientific education were virtually non-existent. As late as the 1930s only one school in ten had a canteen or dining-room, while the availability of free school meals was determined by the financial position of individual authorities and, to some extent at least, by their political complexion. In many areas, virtually no provision was made to assist poorer children to make the best of education by ensuring that they were sufficiently well-fed and healthy to attend to their lessons.

Another cause of concern in the inter-war years was nursery education. It was increasingly recognized that some of the most crucial years for educational provision were those before the age of five. The Women's Group on Public Welfare in their survey of the conditions of evacuees commented: 'We cannot afford not to have the nursery school; it seems to be the only agency capable of cutting the slum mind off at the root and building the whole child while yet there is time.' Similarly, campaigners for women's rights saw the provision of nursery education as a crucial aspect of freeing women to take up opportunities outside the home. Some of the earliest nursery schools were set up in Lancashire, on a voluntary basis, in order to assist the large numbers of women working in textile factories. During the middle and late 1930s there was some development of this field by the local authorities, but at least half the nursery schools in the country were run by voluntary agencies and only one child in ten aged between two and four years was in a grant-aided nursery school in 1940.

The Road to 1944

The Spens Report of 30 December 1938 accepted the principle of free secondary education and a higher school leaving age, though within the context of a tripartite division of secondary education which was now to include the 'technical school' as well as 'grammar' and 'modern' schools. Acknowledgement was also given in the Report to the use of progressive methods of teaching: curiosity must be encouraged; schools brought into touch with 'life'; and examinations not allowed to dominate curricula unduly. The Spens Report was widely applauded by the teaching profession. The *Schoolmaster* called it 'momentous', 'an educational Magna Carta', while the national press, including the *Daily Herald*, the *Daily Telegraph* and *The Times*, also expressed support. The Spens Report, however, was overshadowed by the threat of war and by the relatively conservative interpretation put upon it by the Board of Education. The Report's acceptance of a refined version of multilateral education clearly rejected the 'multi-bias' or 'comprehensive' solution, while the Board of Education refused to accept the viability of free secondary education in 'present financial circumstances'.

As in other spheres, however, the Second World War produced at least a partial victory for progressive opinion. By 1941 it was recognized that the shift in attitudes encouraged by the war was likely to lead to the acceptance of the Spens Report, and in May of that year the Board of Education circulated some detailed proposals for reform of secondary education to local authorities and professional associations virtually identical to those implemented in 1944. A great stimulus was given by the appointment of R. A. Butler as president of the Board of Education, for Butler was a strong advocate of a system of free secondary education as outlined by the Spens Report. His determination was crucial in pushing the Board's officials into discussion of new plans, in circumventing Churchill's opposition to major domestic legislation during the war and in negotiating the difficult question of the role of religious schools in the reorganization of secondary education. By 1942 various schemes were being discussed both inside and outside the educational world. The Labour Party supported the idea of multibias or comprehensive schools at its 1942 conference and one of the memoranda discussed by the Board of Education from the director of education at the LCC, Graham Savage, advocated a scheme of seventy to eighty comprehensive schools for London, each of 2,500 pupils, containing within them grammar, technical and senior elementary pupils. For Savage, educational planning had a major role to play in 'social engineering': 'Whilst it is true in some degree that our system of education must be a reflection of the order of society in which it is set, it is wise in planning reforms to look ahead and to plan education a little in advance of the existing state of society, and our ideas on education should be informed by sociological ideals.' The 'sociological ideals' Savage had in mind were 'the evolution of a classless society'.

Hence some proposals for educational reform breathed the

same radical and Utopian air as the Beveridge Report. The result, however, was less radical than this. Both Board officials and more conservative politicians were prepared to go only as far as the provision of free secondary education under the tripartite scheme foreshadowed in the Hadow and Spens Reports. Indeed the conventional view of the Board that the tripartite system was the one best suited to the distribution of innate mental abilities in the school population received confirmation in the Norwood Report of 1943, *Curriculum and Examinations in Secondary Schools*, which rationalized the tripartite system by means of a threefold classification of types of 'child mind'. As a result, the White Paper on education prepared in 1942–3 was only a limited victory for progressives; while accepting the raising of all post-primary schools to secondary status and abolishing fees, the Butler Act was shaped by the continuing acceptance that only a minority of children were suited to an academic education, that an accurate selection of children could be made at the age of eleven and that the special position of the grammar schools must be preserved. Similarly, notions of a radical overhaul of the relationship of the public and state sectors were quickly shelved. The Fleming Report on the public schools in 1944 confined itself to recommending that they should accept a quarter of their pupils from the state sector, a proposal which was never implemented.

The Butler Education Act of 1944 proposed the fusing of elementary and secondary schools into one system, divided into two stages: primary for children up to twelve and secondary up to fifteen or beyond. Raising the school-leaving age to sixteen was also envisaged at some point in the future. Within the state system, schools were to be maintained by local authorities under the 'control and direction' of a Minister of Education. Local authorities were obliged to provide secondary education in schools 'sufficient in number, character, and equipment to afford all pupils ... such variety of instruction and training as may be desirable in view of their different ages, abilities, and aptitudes ...'. The interpretation of this principle by the officials of the Ministry of Education and many local authorities was generally for a system of the three types of school suggested by Hadow and Spens – grammar, technical and modern. As a result the system which emerged in the period after 1945 proceeded on the assumption that the tripartite division would be implemented. Even the first Labour Ministers of Education, Ellen Wilkinson and George Tomlinson, did not attempt to deflect their officials from their preference for separate types of secondary school. Only a minority of authorities, notably London, Middlesex, Coventry, Oldham and the West Riding, decided to pursue the comprehensive model of secondary education proposed before the Second World War. The private sector remained outside and separate from the state system, subject only to inspection and approval by the Ministry of Education.

Thus the Butler Education Act and the system of state education which emerged after 1945 was a compromise which accepted a generally hierarchic approach to education. Although this outcome can be presented as part of a large-scale conspiracy of backward officials and conservative politicians to frustrate enlightened, progressive opinion, it was also the case that for much of this period the conservative tone of the Board of Education tallied with a significant body of opinion within the country at large. It was relatively predictable that many Conservative MPs, according to one report, 'Applauded the White Paper on Educational Reconstruction and the Education Bill, since those measures incorporated many key Conservative beliefs, notably the belief in the relevance of traditional religious values, the belief in variety and quality rather than "gross volume", the belief in the desirability of preserving educational privileges and the belief in hierarchy'. Less obvious, perhaps, was that the tripartite system was also tenaciously supported for some years after 1945 by many Labour-controlled authorities which had painstakingly built up a meritocratic system of selective secondary schools. Robin Pedley has noted twenty-eight local authorities which were Labour-controlled for at least twenty years after 1945 which took no steps to implement comprehensivization.

In a sense then a certain conservatism in educational matters was common on both sides of the party divide. There was little doubt that for many the Butler Act went as far as they wished to go. Education, moreover, did not figure particularly high in most people's demands for post-war reconstruction – according to a survey of attitudes commissioned by R. A. Butler from the Ministry of Information, it ranked after employment, housing and health. Interest was expressed mainly in the plans to abolish fees and raise the school-leaving age. In that sense the 1944 Education Act represented a remarkably accurate barometer of the level of consensus on educational provision. Inevitably, however, the most progressive thinkers felt frustrated. Even before 1939 the research undertaken into mental testing using psychological and sociological techniques at the London School of Economics suggested that the relationship between ability and opportunity was low, particularly for working-class children. These findings, printed in the *Sociological Review* for 1935, subverted the interpretation of intelligence tests given by Dr Cyril Burt in the 1920s, which stressed the inherited character of abilities and formed the basis of the Board of Education's and later Ministry of Education's justification for a tripartite system. As late as 1947, a Ministry of Education pamphlet, *The New Secondary Education*, continued to follow the view articulated in the 1930s and early 1940s that different types of school had to be designed to match the definition of children's abilities obtained through a test at the age of eleven.

There is little doubt that education occupied an important place in the progressive consensus which emerged in Britain between the wars. In some respects at least, sections of the Labour movement, liberal educationalists and some local authorities were already moving on a quite different tack from that enshrined in the Butler Education Act. For those who saw the role of education as lying in the field of democratic social engineering – promoting a 'classless society' – it was inevitable that 1944 should only be the starting-point for a debate which was to reverberate through the post-war years. Equally, concern for education derived much of its impetus from a concern for the child as an individual. New thinking on the methods and purpose of education, seen in the experimental schools in the private sector and the growing interest in educational psychology and child development, was beginning to have an impact in the feeling that children should be more broadly educated, enjoy their schooling and learn through their own curiosity and interests. Concern with 'social engineering', seeing education as the crucible of a better society, also encapsulated many of the most fundamental philosophical and political debates of the period. For some, education was *the* social issue, investing it with a central importance in the political debates after 1945.

But if there was a reaction against the compromises contained in the 1944 Act and the failure to grapple with the divide between public and private sectors, it is important to recognize that it was a compromise that gave many people what they wanted. While the education of working-class children remained a cause of concern, there were real beneficiaries of the educational developments up to 1945. By the 1960s there was already talk, for example in Anthony Sampson's *Anatomy of Britain*, published in 1962, of a Britain governed by a 'meritocracy', drawn primarily from the better grammar schools and public schools. This was not a new phenomenon. From the First World War, an increasing number of grammar school pupils were able to go to university and enter some of the higher positions of British life. While the top public schools retained a strong grip on the higher levels of the British establishment, perhaps the most significant feature of the first half of the twentieth century was the ability of large numbers of not particularly prosperous middle- and lower-middle-class households to place their children in fee-paying grammar schools and minor public schools. Demonstrably, the clientele of the grammar schools, especially the direct-grant schools, was middle-class. From 1902 they provided an avenue of advancement for two crucial segments of the population, a minority, the very brightest of the working class – the 'scholarship' boys and girls – and, overwhelmingly, the middle class, to university

or further education of another kind, and on to some of the
top positions. Similarly, the expansion of the 'minor' public
school sector and growing middle-class affluence provided an
important dimension to the broadening of educational provision for the comfortable, but not necessarily rich, middle class.
In this respect, the history of educational development in this
period represented most significantly a widening of opportunity
for the middle classes, the group who were to provide the bulk
of the 'meritocracy' reflected in post-war social analyses.

10. Unemployment

If one social issue dominated this period, it was unemployment. Whatever the advances in economic growth, in overall living standards and in the developments of mass consumerism, leisure and social welfare, it was the problem of mass unemployment which did more than any other to give the inter-war years their image of the 'wasted years' and the 'long weekend'. The thirties in particular were to acquire an almost legendary reputation as the 'devil's decade', summed up in the images of the dole queues, the hunger marches and the means test. From 1921, when the post-war boom began to falter, until the first months of 1940, Great Britain suffered mass unemployment on an unprecedented scale, with never less than a million people – a tenth of the insured population – out of work. By the winter of 1921–2 more than two million were out of work in the United Kingdom, a figure which fell only slowly during the 1920s. A moderate recovery in the late 1920s was overtaken by a new and severe depression which followed the Wall Street Crash of 1929 and a world-wide decline in trade and industrial activity. Britain's worst years for unemployment were those after the financial and political crisis of 1931. From 1931 until 1935, the number of those officially classed as unemployed never fell below two million, while in the winter of 1932–3 unemployment reached its highest point when almost three million workers, a quarter of the insured working population, were out of work. Moreover, as official statistics excluded large groups of workers, such as agricultural labourers, the self-employed and married women, who were discouraged from signing on for the dole, the total number of unemployed was almost certainly higher than official figures revealed.

The Problem of Unemployment

The causes of unemployment between the wars were complex. As always there were those whose physical, mental or other qualities made them only marginally members of the labour force, employable in boom conditions, but always vulnerable to unemployment in less prosperous circumstances. As well as the normal casualties of genetics, obstetric mishap, accident and disease, Britain also carried between the wars the additional casualties of the Great War, as many as two and a half million sufficiently disabled to be in receipt of a government pension. Pension rates, however, were far from generous, forcing most partly disabled servicemen into the labour market at a most unpropitious time, and ill-designed to meet the realities of those seeking manual work. Limbs were 'costed' with clinical precision; a missing whole right arm (from the shoulder) provided a pension of 16s. weekly; 14s. if below the shoulder but above the elbow; 11. 6d. if below the elbow. Left arms were costed at 1s. less for each joint. A formerly skilled man could be effectively crippled by the loss of fingers or hands, but forced to seek employment to supplement his pension. Men gassed or psychologically disturbed fell into another category, usually receiving a small pension, but often effectively debarred from heavy manual labour or regular employment of any kind. Every town and city in the inter-war years had its partly disabled men, drifting in and out of employment according to the trade cycle, more often than not forced into marginal employment as newspaper sellers, bookie's runners or tea 'boys', or reduced to selling bootlaces and matches, or simply begging, to eke out a livelihood.

There was also a continuing problem of seasonal unemployment and casual work. In a fairly typical industrial town such as Middlesbrough in the 1920s, unemployment in the winter tended to rise to 10 or 15 per cent over that of the summer, mainly because building and construction workers were less likely to find work in winter weather and with shorter hours of daylight. The growing seaside towns like Blackpool,

Scarborough and Brighton were also vulnerable to 'slack time' in the winter months as catering staff, stall-holders and the myriad ancillary service staff needed for the leisure industry marked time, waiting for the summer boom. Even the new consumer industries suffered from this problem. The relatively prosperous car towns such as Oxford, Luton and Coventry were accustomed in the 1920s and 1930s to short-time working and lay-offs in the winter months because people tended to buy more cars in spring or summer. Hence, on average, even in the more prosperous years between the wars, the total of unemployed tended to be higher in December and January than in July and August.

The overall level of unemployment, however, also depended upon the cycle of boom and slump in world trade from which Britain as the major trading nation could not insulate herself. Minor troughs in world trade before 1914, such as those of 1903–5 and 1908–10, generally brought higher levels of unemployment as overall demand for British goods slackened and business activity declined. Britain's level of unemployment was already determined by what was happening overseas and in the markets of the world. From the First World War, however, these cycles took on a new and more severe character. The hectic post-war boom was followed by a more severe crash than encountered hitherto. A slow upswing during the middle and late 1920s was then halted by the Wall Street Crash of 1929, which shattered American business confidence and catastrophically reduced the level of world trade. As the ripples of financial disaster washed across Europe, the financial and political crisis of 1931 plunged Britain into a deeper slump than ever before. As the level of world trade fell sharply, hundreds of thousands were thrown out of work in Britain. The disruption of other major industrial economies, particularly Germany and the United States, seriously reduced the extent to which they could trade with Britain. Slack demand also forced down the price of many foodstuffs and raw materials. Although this had beneficial effects for consumers, particularly by reducing food prices, it also meant that primary producers such as Argentina, Canada, South Africa, India and Australia were less able to buy manufactured goods from Britain. The slump in trade reduced British exports in 1931–2 to a half what they had been in 1913, after they had climbed back by 1929 to over three-quarters the pre-war level. As well as the major export industries, the depression of 1929–38 reduced domestic investment and consumption, spreading unemployment through all sectors of the economy. Modest recovery began from 1933 as America began to pull out of depression and the level of world trade began slowly to pick up; even so, in 1937–8 unemployment rose again with another downturn in world trade, though by this time re-armament was beginning to act as an important additional stimulus to economic recovery.

This severe form of cyclical unemployment masked, however, an underlying problem of structural unemployment. Even in the peak years of economic activity between the wars, there remained high levels of unemployment in the staple export trades. Employment figures showed the crisis in the heavy industries during the 1920s. By 1929 the number of coalminers had fallen by a fifth from pre-war totals. The number employed in shipbuilding fell by a similar proportion and this pattern was repeated in textiles and the iron and steel industry. The traditional centres of heavy industry were already marked by large-scale unemployment even before the world crisis of 1929–1931. By 1929, a fifth of all coalminers were unemployed and a similar percentage of iron and steel workers. Almost one cotton worker in seven was out of a job and almost one in four in the shipbuilding industry. How concentrated the unemployment problem was in particular industries can be seen from the Pilgrim Trust's estimate that of a total of 53,000 men who had been out of work for more than a year in 1929, 38,000 were coalminers. They concluded that long-term unemployment was 'mainly a localized abnormality of coal-mining districts dependent on mines abandoned or permanently closed'. Thus a pattern was emerging clearly during the twenties of 'depressed areas' based upon the regions where heavy industry was situated. By 1929, the level of unemployment was two or three times higher in the old industrial areas than in London and the Midlands, where new industries had already begun to develop.

Although virtually no industry was left untouched by the depression of 1929–33, the worst effects were felt in the industries which had already been struggling during the twenties, and they retained a high level of unemployment when the economy as a whole entered a more prosperous phase after 1933. Thus the percentage of unemployed in the 'ailing giants' was consistently above the average level for industry as a whole (see Table 19).

Table 19: Percentage unemployment in staple trades compared to national average

	1929	1932	1936	1938
Coal	18.2	41.2	25.0	22.0
Cotton	14.5	31.1	15.1	27.7
Shipbuilding	23.2	59.5	30.6	21.4
Iron and steel	19.9	48.5	29.5	24.8
Average for all industries	9.9	22.9	12.5	13.3

Unemployment in the twenties was a regional problem, affecting most acutely the areas dependent upon the declining export industries. Although all regions were affected in the trough of the depression, by the middle and late thirties unemployment had reverted to the pattern of the previous decade. This was recognized in 1934 by the creation of the 'Special Areas' (South Wales, Tyneside, West Cumberland and industrial Scotland) which were to receive government assistance. These did not necessarily define the worst-affected areas of the country. Northern Ireland, for example, had the highest percentage of unemployment in the United Kingdom, but was considered to be beyond the scope of legislation at Westminster. Other areas had too varied a pattern of employment to give the whole region 'special' status and were left to fend for themselves. The striking disparity between the unemployment rates of the more prosperous southern half of England and the regions of the West and the North is shown in Table 20. Out of 1,717,000 registered unemployed in July 1936, over two-thirds were to be found in Scotland, Wales, Northern Ireland and northern England. The northern districts alone accounted for almost three-quarters of a million and Scotland over a quarter of a million, many of them long-term unemployed.

Table 20: Unemployed as a percentage of insured workers in regions of Great Britain

	1929	1932	1937
London and S.-E. England	5.6	13.7	6.4
S.-W. England	8.1	17.1	7.8
Midlands	9.3	20.1	7.2
Northern England	13.5	27.1	13.8
Wales	19.3	36.5	22.3
Scotland	12.1	27.7	15.9
Northern Ireland	15.1	27.2	23.6

Source: M. P. Fogarty, *Prospects of the Industrial Areas of Great Britain*, 1945, p. 5; *Ulster Year Book*, 1932, 1935, 1938.

It was structural unemployment which marked out the areas of persistent social distress between the wars, areas which even after the Second World War were still to require considerable government support and help in order to keep unemployment rates from rising too high. The problems of the depressed areas were indeed long-term ones, based essentially on the changing pattern of Britain's trade, new factors in the location of industry, especially the shift from steam to electricity, and the growth of consumer and service sector employment. Much of the 'new' industry of the inter-war years was sited in the South-East and Midlands, near to the consumers, by-passing the older industrial areas. Occasionally, a hard-hit region might be fortunately placed for the development of a new industry, such as the ICI chemical complexes developed on Teesside near to the run-down Durham pit villages and the idle shipyards of the Tyne and Wear, but until the government took a hand in encouraging industrial relocation, first through its Special

Areas policy and, later, to meet the demands of the strategic dispersal of industry to counter the threat of enemy bombing, many of the depressed areas found themselves with a size of labour force and types of industry for which full employment and recovery were virtually impossible.

Within the depressed areas there were wide variations of experience, depending upon the industrial complexion of the area and changing circumstances. In South Wales, for example, some areas had very much higher unemployment rates than others. In 1934, 74 per cent of male workers were unemployed in Brynmawr, 73 per cent in Dowlais and 66 per cent in Merthyr. Conditions, however, were less severe in the coastal towns of South Wales, and the eastern half of the coalfield suffered more than the anthracite and tinplate districts of the west. The coal industry accounted for 45.6 per cent of insured workers in 1929 and 37.1 per cent in 1935, when the worst of the depression was over. It also provided the highest percentage of unemployed. Unemployment amongst coalminers reached 42.4 per cent in 1932 and was still 34.4 per cent in 1935. In 1932, 85,600 miners were out of work in South Wales and in 1935 the figure still stood at 55,105. The western valleys of Neath, Swansea and Amman maintained a higher level of employment than the rest of the region, although even here the lowest level of unemployment was 22 per cent in 1931. The worst affected areas were the mining towns of the inland valleys, such as Merthyr, Rhondda and Aberdare. These three valleys accounted for over half the total of unemployed between 1931 and 1935 in South Wales. In the Merthyr and Rhondda valleys, unemployment was actually higher amongst coalminers in 1935 than in 1931. In 1935, 45.6 per cent of miners in Rhondda and 51.5 per cent in Merthyr were out of work.

While there were great variations even in the most depressed areas, the greatest disparity existed between the relatively prosperous towns of southern England and the depressed areas (Table 21). Thus whereas Glasgow had a total of 89,600 unemployed in 1936, Birmingham, a city of comparable size, had only 21,000. Similarly, Brighton had only 3,000 unemployed

Table 21: Percentage of insured workers unemployed in various towns
in 1934

Jarrow	67.8	Coventry	5.1
Maryport	57.0	Oxford	5.1
Merthyr	61.9	Luton	7.7
Motherwell	37.4	St Albans	3.9

compared with Oldham's 15,000. As the thirties wore on, the
contrast between the reviving industries of the southern half
of England and the depressed areas tended to grow. Though
the absolute level of unemployment fell in many of the depressed areas, the gap between them and the more prosperous
regions tended to widen. The Pilgrim Trust investigators
studied six communities: Rhondda Urban District, Crook in
County Durham, Blackburn, Leicester, Deptford and Liverpool. In Deptford they found only 7 per cent of the industrial
population unemployed, while in the Rhondda Urban District
the figure was 35 per cent. They concluded that there were
two major differences between the depressed areas and the more
prosperous regions: not only were the numbers of unemployed
greater, but there were more long-term unemployed (see
Table 22).

With this regional distribution of the long-term unemployed,
it was hardly surprising that they predominated in the depressed
export industries upon which these regions depended for their
livelihood. Their numbers were greatest in coalmining, ship-

Table 22: Unemployment in summer 1936

	Unemployment per 1,000 insured workers	Percentage of unemployed out of work for twelve months or more
South-East	62	6
London	76	7
South-West	89	12
Midlands	101	22
North-West	186	23
North-East	212	26
Wales	322	37

building, the iron and steel industry, and cotton textiles. Also high on the list of long-term unemployment were pottery workers and seamen. The Pilgrim Trust investigators found 52,000 men in 1936 who had been out of work for over five years and 205,000 who had been out of work for two or more. In Crook Town they found that nearly three-quarters of the unemployed had been out of work for over five years.

The 'Dole' and the 'Means Test'

By 1921 a majority of workers and their dependants were covered by the National Insurance scheme introduced in 1911 and greatly extended as a result of the Great War. When Britain first began to experience mass unemployment in 1921–2, unemployment benefit offered a sum equal to about a third of the average wage, with six weeks of contributions required for each week of benefit, up to a maximum of fifteen weeks. Workers had to prove themselves available for work by 'signing on' every day at the labour exchange during working hours. From the summer of 1921, an unemployed man over eighteen could receive 15s. for himself, plus 5s. for a wife and 1s. for each child. Several large groups of workers, however, lay outside the provisions of National Insurance, notably agricultural workers, domestic servants and the self-employed. If unemployed and without any other means of support these groups had to rely upon the Poor Law, usually in the form of 'outdoor relief', or upon private charity. But the insurance scheme soon ran into serious difficulties as the number of unemployed rose and the duration of spells of unemployment became so great that increasingly large numbers would have been thrown on to the Poor Law. As a major reason for the development of the National Insurance scheme had been to avoid people being forced on to the Poor Law by spells of unemployment, the government resorted to a series of expedients which allowed the unemployed to claim benefits to which they were not yet entitled by virtue of their contributions, but which it was hoped they would cover by future periods of employment.

An unemployed person might find themselves on any one of a number of relief scales: the standard insurance scheme; the new range of 'uncovenanted', 'extended' or 'transitional' benefits; or the Poor Law. According to their political persuasion, governments tinkered with the regulations, altering the duration for which benefits could be obtained, the 'gaps' between one form of benefit and another, and the rigour with which household circumstances were assessed. At the local level, much also depended upon the officials responsible for the administration of relief through the labour exchanges or the Poor Law. In Labour-inclined areas, the provisions of the Poor Law might be generously interpreted, leading to clashes with governments bent on economy in 1921–2 and in 1926. After 1929, the abolition of the Poor Law and the provision of relief for some of the unemployed through the Public Assistance Committee of the local authorities raised similar problems. The members of such committees were often a combination of experienced Poor Law officials and co-opted councillors and local figures who reflected predominant local interests. These were often sympathetic to the unemployed, but forced by pressure from central government to restrict benefit levels and apply rigorous criteria for those admitted to relief.

For the unemployed, the crucial questions about the administration of relief were whether benefit was allowed and at what level. For example, considerable disruption and ill-feeling was generated by the requirement introduced in 1927 that applicants for unemployment benefit had to show that they were 'genuinely seeking work'. This phrase had originally been introduced in 1921 as an additional test of eligibility for the benefits to be paid after entitlement to the standard forms of insurance had run out. It was now, however, applied to all unemployment benefit and placed the unemployed in a particularly vulnerable position in that the onus of proof that they were entitled to any benefit at all lay with them. For the man or woman unemployed through no fault of their own, often in areas where there was virtually no work to find, the regulations were often a humiliating farce. More important, they could, in the hands of less sympathetic officials, lead to many being refused benefit on flimsy pretexts. Just how many were deprived of benefit in the late 1920s in this way has been shown by what happened when the stipulation was removed by the Labour government in 1930. The number of claimants for benefit more than doubled within two months, including 60,000 who had never been registered at the labour exchanges before. While they may have included some of the natural rise in unemployed and a few who were taking improper advantage of the easier regulations, there seems little doubt that they included thousands who had been debarred from unemployment benefit who were, under somewhat less stringent rules, entitled to claim it. Even then, an applicant could be disqualified from benefit if he failed to accept a vacancy of which he had been notified and disqualified from benefit for six weeks if he disregarded written instructions from the employment exchange.

More notorious for its effects upon the entitlement and level of relief was the battery of economy measures brought in following the financial crisis of 1931. Under these, the level of unemployment benefits was reduced by approximately 10 per cent, the regulations governing entitlement to benefit were tightened, and many married women were cut off from benefit by the Anomalies Act. It has been estimated that this last measure disallowed 134,000 married women from benefit by the end of 1931. The most emotive part of this package, however, was the 'means test'. The period for which unemployment benefit could be drawn as of right was limited to twenty-six weeks. After this period those requiring relief had to apply for 'transitional payments'. Although they were to be paid through the employment exchange, the claimants had first to undergo a household means test carried out by the local Public Assistance Committee, the successors to the Poor Law Guardians. The Committee then notified the employment exchange of the circumstances of the claimant and assessed what rate of relief they should receive. The maximum payment for an adult male was 15s. 3d. and the aim of the PAC scrutiny was to economize on the level of relief by a strict assessment of available income.

The means test became one of the most despised aspects of the inter-war years and long after the Second World War a source of bitterness and ill-feeling. In part, this was because many of the people subjected to the test were coming under scrutiny for the first time. Many skilled and respectable workers now found themselves under the rules of bodies operating with many of the personnel and attitudes associated with the Poor Law. While relief had been obtained from the labour exchange, some vestige of self-respect was still possible but, for many, the transfer to a body tainted with the relief of 'pauperism' provided a lasting humiliation. Interestingly, it was often the skilled workers who wrote to the newspapers to complain about the nature and conduct of the investigation. Assessment of 'means' involved relieving officers visiting people's homes, prying into their circumstances, suggesting they sell items of furniture, or reducing relief because of savings, or income from sons, daughters or pensioners living within the household.

By January 1932, almost a million unemployed were coming within the scope of the means test. Resources had to be disclosed under threat of legal sanction. Large numbers of people were debarred from unemployment benefit and many others found their relief reduced. In Lancashire, it was claimed that only 16 per cent were awarded the full 'transitional benefit', while a third were disallowed altogether. The TUC compiled a dossier of cases of acute hardship caused by the operation of the means test, including cases of young people and pensioners forced to move out of their family home because their earnings or pensions had led to a reduction in the unemployment relief of the householder. Within a year, 180,000 people were removed from receipt of unemployment benefit, while over the country as a whole, half of those applying for 'transitional benefit' had received less than the maximum payments. £24 million were saved in the first year of operation, but at a cost in terms of petty humiliation and disruption of families which was to make the means test one of the most emotive symbols of administrative callousness.

The insecure grip which many of the unemployed felt they

had on benefits as a result of the means test was compounded by the government's attempts to rationalize the system of unemployment benefits under the Unemployment Insurance Acts of 1934–5. Initially it had been claimed that the changes would be entirely beneficial. Under Part I of the Act in 1934, the economy cuts in levels of benefit were restored and provisions made to bring agricultural and 'black-coated' workers within the scope of unemployment insurance. Part II of the Act set up the Unemployment Assistance Board, which was to take responsibility for all insured workers who had exhausted benefit by being out of work for more than 156 days. Thus the responsibility for 'transitional benefits' was to be taken out of the hands of the local authorities and the PACs. A national administration with its own scale of relief payments was to provide more settled and centrally funded benefits for the unemployed. In addition, the UAB was to take over the able-bodied unemployed at present supported by the Poor Law. The Poor Law authorities would then be left to cater for their original concern, the sick and the aged. The scheme also had the benefit of taking the unemployment issue out of politics by setting up the UAB as an independent body which could recommend alterations in the scale of relief or contributions without submitting them for parliamentary approval. When details of the scheme were published, however, there was an outcry because relief scales were often lower than those paid by the local authorities. In places such as South Wales, there were mass demonstrations, while MPs and local councillors were deluged with letters and petitions of complaint. The government was forced to introduce a Standstill Order, re-establishing the old level of payments and slowing down the implementation of the new legislation. Even with these concessions, the means test remained in force until the early years of the war, although its administration was relaxed.

Coping with the complexities of unemployment relief proved one of the most daunting and demoralizing tasks for the unemployed. Its rules and procedures were sufficient to tax the cleverest minds in the country and it left many of the unemployed with a lasting impression of bureaucratic harshness and petty-mindedness. Nevertheless, observers with memories of the years before the introduction of unemployed insurance were convinced that the dole marked at least some advance on the past, in most cases keeping the unemployed off the Poor Law, with its peculiar stigma and humiliations. The extension of unemployment insurance in the early 1920s undoubtedly reflected government fears of widespread unrest following the Russian Revolution and the strikes of the post-war years. Similarly the extension of the various *ad hoc* payments showed a desire to avoid forcing the mass of unemployed back on to the Poor Law as before 1911. One writer, in *The Third Winter of Unemployment* (1923), noted, reflecting this unease, 'the success of the relief measures in meeting essential needs for food, and in giving relatively most assistance to the irregularly employed and low-paid workers who can most easily be collected into a mob'. Moreover, in comparison with many other countries, Britain's provisions were relatively generous. America had no system of unemployment insurance until it was introduced by Roosevelt as part of the 'New Deal' in the 1930s. Indeed it was an American social investigator, E. W. Bakke, who, after studying the unemployed in London, suggested that the 'dole' had alleviated the worst physical effects of unemployment:

It has kept the diet from falling to unhealthy levels; it has kept the workers from falling in arrears on their rent; it has made it unnecessary to dispose of house furnishings to the extent which would have been necessary without it; it has to some extent made it possible for men and women to keep up their associations with their fellows longer; it has kept unrest at a minimum . . .

This was a rather over-sanguine view, based on experiences in a relatively prosperous part of London which suffered from little long-term unemployment. As the social investigators showed, unemployment was a major cause of poverty between the wars, a poverty defined as not having enough income to maintain health. In eastern London as a whole in 1928 it was found that, in any given week, a third of all poverty was the result of unemployment. However, it also reflected the typical pattern of short-term unemployment in London in that only a small percentage of households were in full-time poverty as a result of unemployment. In York in 1936 Rowntree found that 28.6 per cent of poverty was caused by unemployment, a much higher percentage than had been the case in 1899. Although the whole problem of poverty had diminished, the unemployed now made up one of its largest elements. Very similar results were found in Bristol in the late 1930s; of the remaining pool of poverty, almost a third was caused by unemployment. These investigators proved what was obvious to many, that a considerable proportion of the unemployed and their families did not have sufficient on which to live, Rowntree noting tersely that 'The relief at present is not sufficient to raise the recipients above the minimum.'

The percentage of the unemployed in poverty varied widely from one area to another and at different times. A study in Sheffield in the winter of 1931–2 found 42.8 per cent of the families of the unemployed in poverty; Rowntree's survey of York in 1936 found 72.6 per cent; while the Pilgrim Trust found that 30 per cent of the households in the six towns they studied were living below a strict 'poverty line' and 14 per cent were on it. Moreover long-term studies of the unemployed in particular communities reveal that a crucial element remained the level of prices of food, housing, heating and other essentials. Higher prices in the early 1920s, especially, have been shown in a study of Middlesbrough to have made the task of managing on unemployment relief much more difficult than in the early thirties, when prices, especially those of food, had fallen considerably. The situation was further complicated by the different relief scales applied locally. Once National Insurance had been exhausted, many of the unemployed became dependent on the levels of relief offered locally by the Board of Guardians or the local PAC. Some areas, as a matter of policy or because of economic circumstances, were able to offer more generous relief than others. Even after a degree of rationalization had been introduced in 1934–5, some types of relief were generally higher than others. In the late 1930s, it was found that almost four-fifths of those dependent upon the Unemployment Assistance Board were in poverty, compared with only two-fifths of those on local relief scales. While there is little doubt that many of the unemployed lived in poverty, no hard and fast generalization can be made about its exact dimensions because local and individual circumstances varied so much.

Life on the Dole

Unemployment started with loss of work or, for the young, a failure to find it. A trite point, but one which for some could be a shattering experience. A lifetime's work could be terminated at a few hours' notice, sometimes with consideration and tact, often not. One shoe-worker from Leicester who had worked thirty-seven years with the same firm described to the Pilgrim Trust how the new manager went through the workshops saying 'The whole of this side of this room, this room and this room is to be stopped.' For others there was the protracted business of gradually being squeezed out of work, first on short time, then perhaps with intermittent lay-offs, until the final shutdown. For those put out of work, like those seeking it for the first time, there was then the problem of finding a new job, the frustrating task of visiting crowded labour exchanges, scanning newspaper job pages, following up rumours and stories of vacancies at this factory or that or in neighbouring towns. For most, the chance of finding work often dominated the first weeks or months of unemployment. Men might walk or cycle miles in the search for work, queue for hours at factory gates, or turn up for casual work even when the outlook was almost hopeless. Examples were cited of old men with virtually no prospect of working again who 'yet make it a practice to stand every morning at six o'clock at the works gates in the hope that perhaps they may catch the foreman's eye'. The search for work undoubtedly dominated the minds and activities of many of the unemployed, but there came a point for others when a form of fatalism and depression set in: the gradual realization that work was going to be difficult, if not actually impossible, to find. For some, particularly the young or unattached, this was the point at which they might consider making a radical move, saving or borrowing to take a train or a coach out of the depressed areas, or migrating on cycle or on foot from one part of the country to another.

As well as loss of work, unemployment meant a serious loss of income. A survey of about 800 families in Stockton-on-Tees in the early 1930s revealed that the average income of families where the wage-earner was unemployed was 20s. 2½d. a week, compared with 51s. 6d. for families where there was no un-employment. The Pilgrim Trust assessed that the average drop in income was between 45 and 66 per cent, and this figure was confirmed in a Ministry of Labour study in 1937. The result, as we have seen, was that many of the unemployed were plunged into poverty. But not all were. For, although benefit levels were lower than the average industrial wage, they were also higher than earnings in a number of industries. By the late thirties one survey of South Wales revealed that a third of single men and almost a half of married men were receiving more in unemployment allowances than in their last job. More-over, by the early 1930s, newspapers were carrying discussions of how it was possible to achieve an adequate standard of living on the 'dole'. In *The Road to Wigan Pier* George Orwell quoted a newspaper which asserted that by purchasing the right items it was possible to ensure a balanced diet on as little as 3s. 11½d. per week. The reality was often different: income depended upon the relief scales in particular localities, the local cost of living and the ability of individual families to cope on a re-stricted budget. As with low-income families in general, it was found that, while some could manage adequately, others on the same income found it impossible. Large families usually meant a much harder struggle, with high proportions of those with two or more small children suffering from poverty as a result of unemployment.

In most areas the loss of work by the husband meant the

loss of the sole breadwinner. Although the number of women at work was increasing, the percentage remained low and married women were often the first to be laid off in times of depression. Behind the statistics for unemployed men stood a much larger number of people in their families affected by loss of income. It was inevitable that a large number of those thrust into poverty were the wives and children of the unemployed. This produced inescapable consequences of poor diet and ill-health. By the end of the thirties there was an impressive catalogue of evidence from the depressed areas that unemployment was producing poor nutrition and ill-health. Total accuracy was difficult because the clinical signs of malnutrition were disputed and there were variations between one part of the country and another as to what were regarded as 'normal' standards of health and nutrition. Thus in 1933 the Minister of Health felt able to claim that 'there is at present no available medical evidence of any increase in physical impairment, sickness or mortality as a result of the depression or unemployment'. Others disagreed. In Stockton-on-Tees Dr M'Gonigle compared the death rates for employed and unemployed living in the same area in 1931-4 and found a higher level amongst the unemployed. The sample was small, however, and not everyone was prepared to accept the validity of the evidence. Similar arguments were conducted about the levels of infant and maternal mortality and the incidence of poverty-related diseases such as anaemia and TB. Interpretation of the statistics proved, and has still proved, difficult, particularly in regard to the effects of unemployment as opposed to more generalized poverty. Death rates, sickness rates and diet were all worse in the depressed areas, but they had always been so, even in times of full employment.

The most that could be demonstrated was that unemployment was having adverse effects upon standards of diet and nutrition. These inevitably had some effect upon the health and well-being of individuals and families. Analysis of the food actually consumed by the unemployed illustrated that there was a marked tendency for changes in diet to occur: meat, eggs,

fresh vegetables and fresh dairy produce were cut down because
they were relatively expensive, while cheap 'fillers' – bread,
potatoes, margarine, jam, stew, tea and condensed milk – tended
to increase. While it was true that a clever housewife could
fashion perfectly nourishing and varied meals from cheap ingredients, the reality was that many of the unemployed, like
the poor in general, were reduced to a monotonous, stodgy,
ill-balanced diet often lacking in proteins, vitamins and other
essential items, wiping out the advantages of improved real
living standards which were becoming available in the inter-war
years for those in work. The evidence was obvious enough
to those who visited the depressed areas from the more prosperous areas of Britain; people actually looked thin and ill-
nourished. Even if clinical tests of malnutrition proved incon-
clusive, observers would record the white, gaunt faces of the
unemployed, their bad teeth, the way their clothes hung off
them from the loss of pounds in weight. Often it was the wives
and children of the unemployed who suffered most. The
Pilgrim Trust, not usually given to exaggeration, saw the rise
in maternal mortality as one of the most serious consequences
of unemployment because women were 'literally starving
themselves in order to feed and clothe the children reasonably
well'. They cited evidence which suggested that 3,000 women
a year were dying in childbirth because of the effects of poor
nutrition, strain and the reduction in local health services as
a result of 'economy'. In a third of the homes the Pilgrim Trust
visited, the wife was suffering from some form of ill-health.
Children, on the whole, were found to be the beneficiaries,
far more of them showing signs of better care and attention
than of gross neglect even amongst the long-term unemployed.
Where sacrifices had to be made, they ran along predictable
lines, with fathers and children gaining at the expense of wives
and mothers. Some children undoubtedly suffered. Although
there was a highly charged debate about the consequences of
unemployment upon the infant mortality rate in the 1930s,
many were convinced that deficiency diseases were commonest
amongst the families of the unemployed. Evidence piled up

in the pre-war years that the incidence of rickets, anaemia, TB and dental problems amongst children was one manifestation of the effect of unemployment.

Most tragic of all, and something which explains the reluctance of officials to accommodate the evidence of deterioration, was that these problems were occurring in a context of considerable improvements in health. One gets the impression that older Ministry of Health officials, by no means unconcerned with health problems, were mesmerized by what had been achieved rather than what remained to be done. Men who had seen large falls in mortality and morbidity rates, through their own energetic pursuit of such things as the School Medical Service, were frequently reluctant to admit to protagonists of the family poverty lobby, or avowedly left-wing critics like Dr M'Gonigle, Alan Hutt or Wal Hannington, that their house was in anything but good order. Hence the most that was conceded was that in the depressed areas unemployment was retarding the rate of improvement enjoyed by more prosperous parts of the country.

While the debate about the precise impact of unemployment raged at a high level amongst writers, politicians, doctors and civil servants, the unemployed had to get on with the business of coming to terms with being out of work. For many, indeed, the most difficult problems lay not in physical health and living standards, difficult as these could be, but in the psychological adjustment to unemployment. For most, work had meant more than a mere place to earn a living, but a whole social milieu around which the rest of their lives were constructed. Work organized the daily and the weekly routine – times of getting up, going to bed and meals, the friends one had and how free time was spent. The disruption of this pattern was often deeply felt. Cases were sometimes reported at coroners' courts or in the newspapers of men who had killed themselves within hours of hearing that they had been thrown out of work. For others, the break with normality was less dramatic in its consequences, but none the less difficult to accept.

Reactions to the early stages of unemployment varied

enormously from individual to individual, depending very much upon age, sex, level of skill and personality, as well as family and social environment. Some were numbed or shocked by losing work. There is ample evidence that many felt *ashamed* of being put out of work, particularly the more skilled workers and the middle classes, taking unemployment as an affront to their status and self-respect. Men who had taken pride in their work often showed the most severe reactions. Cases were reported of men who concealed the fact of their unemployment from their wives and families for days or even weeks. For others, initial reactions might be mitigated by the prospect of getting work again, so that the routine of looking for a job replaced one of going out to work. For yet others, there was often a short-lived 'holiday' period, as they enjoyed a few days' rest and did some odd jobs about the house. As unemployment lengthened, however, different reactions came to the surface. Amongst older men in the depressed areas, it was usually obvious that the chances of obtaining a job were extremely slim. The Pilgrim Trust noted:

Anyone who has visited a number of these older men, and knows the hopelessness of men faced with an empty future – whom neither education nor work has ever given an opportunity to learn how to spend leisure – knows the urgency of their case. Five years in a man's life is a long time; and if at the end of five years' uncertainty there is only (as there is now) the certainty of a pension at a yet smaller rate, it is a fate that can scarcely be tolerated. The ordinary working man is not very easily moved, and the sight of some of these older men, broken down and unable to speak for the moment as they looked ahead into the future, is not one that will be soon forgotten.

Early reactions were usually replaced by hopelessness, apathy, fatalism and depression. Ministry of Health investigators in South Wales in 1929 'were struck more by the aspect of depression among the unemployed men and their list-lessness than by any other sign of poverty'. One of the results of the Great War was a greater awareness of psychological and psychiatric illness, and an increasing realization that many of the unemployed were suffering from depression and nervous illnesses. Dr J. L. Halliday in Glasgow published a survey of a thousand sick unemployed men in the 1930s in the *British Medical Journal* which concluded that a third of them were suffering from 'psycho-neurotic' diseases, the percentage rising as unemployment lengthened. Doctors and local medical officers blamed boredom, poor diet and worry for the emergence of abnormal psychological conditions ranging from mild nervous or physical complaints to complete breakdown or suicide. Indeed, although precise correlation of suicide rates with unemployment is virtually impossible, there was evidence that unemployment led to suicide in some cases. Usually these were men who had been out of work for several months, such as the case recorded in the *Birkenhead News* for January 1932 of an unemployed mechanic found hanging from a tree in Tranmere Woods, who was reported to have been out of work for fifteen months and became depressed; or the following autumn of a man who committed suicide following six or seven months out of work because he believed himself incurably ill and on whom the coroner gave a verdict of suicide 'with evidence of depression from unemployment and illness'. Fenner Brockway compiled a dossier of these reports in his *Hungry England*, including one of a Birmingham man who, having been unemployed for years, drowned himself after going before the local means test committee, having his relief reduced to 10s. 9d. per week and being threatened with its removal altogether. The coroner described it as a 'very distressing case' in which the means test decision was 'the last push', making him 'temporarily insane'. The Home Office statistics in the early 1930s indicated that two unemployed men were committing suicide every day, though it remained difficult to prove unemployment as the sole cause of suicide.

There was also widespread concern that prolonged unemployment could bring a deterioration in the whole household – a fall in standards of cleanliness and self-respect as a result of worklessness. As early as 1923 one study noted the beginnings of deterioration:

Once out of work the man's reserves begin to go; for a time savings will supplement insurance allowance; or corporate savings in the form of trade union out-of-work benefit will supplement it. But many unions are no longer able to pay their accustomed benefits, and the pressure of exceptional need in the end may drive men to the Poor Law who two years ago would have found such a resort inconceivable ... The full effect of unemployment on standards of living is not yet apparent, since the acquisitions of the boom period in the way of clothing, furniture and the like, are not yet worn out. But the signs of wear are appearing; and there are no renewals.

By the late 1930s the signs of this deterioration were more and more evident. In South Wales the Carnegie Trust, like other investigators, found that in many cases there was an almost heroic attempt by both unemployed men and their wives to keep up a reasonable standard of cleanliness and respectability, but also discovered those where women 'had lost all pride in personal appearance and appearance of the home'. Unemployment was a great leveller, reducing to standards and habits of poverty those who had often only recently climbed out of them. Debt, frequent recourse to the pawnshop, less concern for the home and a gradual run-down of clothes, furniture and personal standards were commonplace.

One of the major concerns was the effect of unemployment upon young people. Commentators were already in the early 1930s talking about unemployment 'seriously sapping the physical and mental potentialities of those who would normally be the backbone of the community ten or fifteen years hence'. As for the older unemployed, unemployment might first bring little more than a sense of release, but when prolonged it led to a 'manifestation of irritability and aggressiveness'. Others were concerned about the loss of morale amongst the young unemployed. Always a useful vehicle for concerns about social well-being, the young were regarded by many social investigators as the real barometer of the evils of mass unemployment. The Carnegie Trust concluded that the central problem was loss of self-respect, leading many to refuse attempts to help them and resentment at being 'messed about'. They were 'touchy' and 'unpredictable', primarily because of their failure to find any place for themselves in society. It was a short step from such observations to worrying about the employability of the young unemployed in the future. The Pilgrim Trust was alarmed to find a third of young men in Liverpool allegedly 'work-shy', unwilling to consider work even if it was available. For those imbued with the work-ethic, here was a profound and troubling problem: that a whole generation had been blighted with an attitude which rendered 'normal' life impossible.

Inevitably such fears led on to wider social concerns, that the unemployed would turn to crime, riot in the streets or join extreme political groupings. Enforced idleness and the release of people from the normal disciplines of work seemed to many, not only those in positions of responsibility, to offer serious dangers to the social fabric. Journalists were only echoing the sentiments of teachers, magistrates and parents when they headlined the view that 'idleness' led directly to 'crime'. It was a view rooted firmly in popular conceptions of daily life and conventional morality, but the reality was somewhat different. In spite of widespread fears to the contrary, the unemployed do not seem to have turned to crime on a large scale. While criminal statistics are notoriously difficult to interpret, often reflecting changes in recording procedures or in the policing of certain types of crime rather than a rise in actual crime, as was shown in the 1940s, no significant link could be drawn between rates of unemployment and rates of crime amongst adults. People might well believe that unemployment turned people to crime, but this was more a reflection of their own anxieties than of the actual behaviour of the unemployed. There was, however, stronger evidence to show that high rates of unemployment helped to promote crime amongst the young. Chief Constables and prison governors were certainly of the opinion by the 1930s that increased juvenile crime was partly the result of unemployment. When the Home Office came to investigate the matter in the 1930s they found that the rise in juvenile crime 'appears to be part of a general problem', in which unemployment was only one of a number of factors.

Protest against unemployment, such as there was, did not on the whole seriously threaten the stability of British parliamentary democracy. The most militant protests were made by the National Unemployed Workers Movement (NUWM), founded in 1921. From the early 1920s they mounted a series of campaigns, including 'hunger marches', to persuade central government to alter its provisions for the unemployed. In the early 1920s, demonstrations took place in London and other cities which attracted a considerable amount of attention. One tactic which proved particularly effective was the disruption of 'Remembrance Day' services by bands of unemployed workers. For a time, at least, the Labour movement and the NUWM found it easy to make common cause as champions of the unemployed, but increasingly from the late 1920s the NUWM and its 'hunger marches' became identified with the Communist Party, which provided most of its leaders. As a result, its campaigns in the trough of the depression, which brought contingents of marchers from the depressed areas to London, as in 1932 and 1934, were branded with the taint of communist subversion by the government and viewed with suspicion by the leadership of the official Labour movement. None the less, the contingents of marchers from places such as Wales, Scotland and the North passing through the more prosperous parts of Britain attracted a great deal of sympathy and help from local Labour parties, trade unions and voluntary bodies. For many the sight of the drab ranks of marchers became the most potent image of mass unemployment.

But, while at its peak in 1931–2 the NUWM claimed a membership of between 50,000 and 100,000, it patently failed to mobilize more than a fraction of the unemployed even in the worst years of the depression. Its leader, Wal Hannington, admitted as much in 1936 when he blamed the opposition of the Labour Party and the TUC and the 'apathy' of many of the unemployed themselves. For a time, however, there did appear some threat of widespread disorder. In the autumn of 1931, there were clashes with police in Bristol when NUWM marchers lobbied the TUC conference. In September and October 1932 there were serious disturbances in Belfast, Birkenhead, Manchester and London during the NUWM campaigns against the means test. In 1935 there were widespread protests in South Wales against the UAB regulations, bringing an estimated 300,000 people onto the streets, as well as disturbances in Sheffield. In many of these incidents the police acted toughly against protestors, with baton charges and a constant toll of arrests and prosecutions for the leaders. By the middle 1930s the NUWM was in decline, though it continued to mount a number of campaigns for such things as 'winter relief' right up to the outbreak of the Second World War and much valuable work was done in fighting individual cases before benefit tribunals and means test committees. Whatever its tactics and political stance, the NUWM had been one of the few organizations to attempt to defend the unemployed as a group from government 'economy'.

Ironically, the most famous of all the 'hunger marches', the Jarrow Crusade, was one of the few not run by the NUWM and was also one of the smallest. Two hundred men were organized in 1936 on the initiative of the local town council and the help of their Labour MP Ellen Wilkinson to march on London and present a petition on behalf of the town. The tone of the march was impeccably apolitical, both Conservative and Labour party officials helping in its organization, and it dissociated itself completely from a much larger march of several contingents to London being organized at the same time by the NUWM. The 'respectability' of the march and its cooperation with the authorities earned it more sympathy and publicity than any other. Press comment was favourable, newsreel cameras were permitted to film it and the marches were given a sympathetic reception in the capital. They obtained little else, though the name Jarrow went into history as the symbol of mass unemployment.

On the whole there was little evidence that the unemployed were inclined to become politically militant on a large scale. The short-term unemployed looked still to getting a job, while

the long-term unemployed often lapsed into a fatalism and
depression in which politics did not rank very high in the list
of priorities. Left-wing activists, like Hannington or Allen Hutt,
commented on the demoralization and despair which affected
recruitment to either the Communist Party or the NUWM.
Likewise, the Carnegie Trust found from their study of unemployed young people in South Wales that only a fraction
were politically involved, noting:

It has, perhaps, been assumed too readily by some that because men
are unemployed, their natural state of want and discontent must express
itself in some revolutionary attitude. It cannot be reiterated too often
that unemployment is not an active state; its keynote is boredom –
a continuous sense of boredom.

Similar comments came from the Pilgrim Trust in County
Durham who, surprised by the absence of a sense of grievance
amongst the miners, noted their 'determination to make the
best of things'.

There were, of course, exceptions. At times and in some areas,
there was a more militant mood. The espousal of the cause
of the unemployed by the London Labour boroughs in the
early 1920s created a much more politicized atmosphere than
in other areas. Equally, South Wales in the 1930s emerges as
a kind of hot-bed of militancy where strikes, unemployment
demonstrations and political activity tapped broad support
among the unemployed, trade-unionists, Labour supporters and
communists. Analysis of particularly radical communities,
'Little Moscows' like Mardy, has suggested that their radical-
ism was less a question of conditions being worse than in other
depressed villages or towns, than the presence of particularly
effective local leaders. The evidence also suggests that these
conditions were not typical. The peculiarly politicized atmosphere of 'Red Clydeside', Poplar or South Wales did not add
up to a massive swing to the 'Left' by the unemployed. Even
at its peak in the inter-war years, the Communist Party had
less than 18,000 members and even this figure was achieved
in the late 1930s after the trough of the depression was past,

reflecting the entry into the party of middle-class people rather than workers. The N U W M was an impressive movement, but touched only a fraction of the unemployed. Meanwhile the extreme Right had little success either. Mosley's British Union of Fascists probably never had more than 40,000 members and, while some of these were out of work, they represented a tiny minority of the total unemployed. Neither electorally, nor through their allegiance to extremist groups, did the unemployed deliver a profound shock to the political system.

Rather, as unemployment became familiar to many of the depressed areas and the percentage of long-term unemployed grew, there was a tendency for people, in Orwell's phrase, to 'settle down' to unemployment. Unlike many other countries, Britain had become accustomed to depression during the 1920s, so that unemployment was familiar in the depressed areas. The descent into mass unemployment was no sudden thing in 1929–31 as it was in Germany and the United States, but an intensification of conditions already present. The effects were therefore partly to accustom people to settling down to life on a 'fish and chip' standard, 'making do' in all sorts of ways. Olga Cannon records in her life of Les Cannon, later President of the Electrical Trade Union, how they existed with £2 per week unemployment benefit to provide for a family of seven children and three adults. In good Lancashire 'self-help' traditions, the children were set to work to help to make ends meet with paper rounds, selling firewood and picking coal. Similar examples of 'good husbandry' were found in other areas too – families who lived on their wits and reserves of common sense to survive in bleak and often meagre circumstances. For some, there was a major falling-off of standards, a reduction in basics which affected them deeply: for the skilled or otherwise 're-spectable' workers a descent into poverty or near poverty which was shameful. For others, however, unemployment simply meant a fall into the standards and habits of poverty prevalent amongst the still considerable section of 'the poor'. In cities such as Liverpool and Glasgow, the unemployed slipped easily into a 'culture of poverty', familiar to many before 1914, and

escaped from only briefly in the years after the Great War.
The unemployed, particularly the long-term unemployed,
were reduced to the standards of living and quality of life common amongst the working classes before 1914, while those in
regular work were able to move far beyond them. Thus, in
Liverpool, the Pilgrim Trust found that:

> In spite of all attempts at 'decasualization', the labour required by
> the life of the Port is still largely intermittent, and this does not only
> apply to dockers. Down at the docks, there is no means of telling
> which of the men standing about are the 'employed', waiting for their
> turn to be taken on and confident that they will be; which of them
> are those for whom jobs are far between; and which are the 'long
> unemployed' who step forward, if a man is wanted, with the feeling
> that this is only another in an unbroken series of failures which they
> count by years. Often the appearance of their hands and faces is tell-tale,
> but the experience of being on the market to 'wait for a job to turn
> up' is common to all of them, employed, under-employed, and un-
> employed alike. There is none of the experience felt so keenly by the
> unemployed weaver of Blackburn, when his 'own' factory gates are
> closed and he must stand outside and watch the privileged go in. In
> Liverpool the queue is not a new or humiliating experience. The
> chances are that even during employment the worker has used the
> 'continuity rules' to supplement his income by signing on. To draw
> public money does not characterize a separate class of unemployed.
> The habit of lounging at street corners, or at a tearoom bar, or in
> front of the 'pub' is not a painful new experience that is part of his
> adjustment to unemployment, but is long familiar to him and does
> not mark him as unemployed. His wife, too, has always been used
> to him coming home at noon and spending the rest of the day idle
> at home or in the neighbourhood. Thus for the Liverpool unemployed
> man the unemployed are not beings of another world, struggling with
> problems alien to him, but they are in a state which he also knows
> to some degree.

Hence unemployment did not mean the same to everybody.
There was a sense in which unemployment depended upon the
perception of the unemployed themselves in relation to their
expectations and experiences. But it was a reflection, overall,
of rising living standards and higher social standards that the
levels to which the unemployed were often reduced marked

a cause of concern. The average unemployed man and his family lived at a level enjoyed by many of the poorer working classes prior to 1914, it was only in relation to a higher standard of living and a higher sense of social concern that the unemployment question should be assessed.

For many in the late 1930s, unemployment represented an affront to rising standards of living and a painful reminder of social inequality. It was often, to commentators, the comparison with more affluent standards present elsewhere that made unemployment and its attendant social evils appear so scandalous. Certainly, mass unemployment seemed to reflect a waste and degradation which shocked broadly 'liberal' opinion and more avowedly socialist writers alike. The experience of mass unemployment provided the launch-pad for the social reconstruction of the Second World War. It threw into relief what still remained to be done in the field of social improvement and formed part of a broad attack in the Second World War upon the policies of inter-war governments. It fuelled all the aspirations for social improvement and the desire to produce a better society.

11. *Social Policy*

Any view of the development of social policy in the first half of the twentieth century is inevitably coloured by the network of social legislation carried out between 1944 and 1948 in fulfilment of the Beveridge Report and the government White Papers of 1944 which created what has been called the 'Welfare State'. This legislation created a system of comprehensive National Insurance, Family Allowances, National Assistance and the National Health Service, and was backed up by the housing, education, health and other welfare services carried out by the local authorities at the behest of the government. The phrase 'Welfare State' was first used by Sir Alfred Zimmern in the late 1930s to distinguish between the policies of the democracies and the 'war state' of the dictators. Both the definition of what is meant by the term and the interpretation of social policy it suggests raise important questions, but Arthur Marwick has offered a working definition of 'Welfare State' which emerged in the 1940s as 'one in which full community responsibility is assumed for four major sectors of social well-being: social security, which means provision against interruption of earnings through sickness, injury, old age, or unemployment; health; housing; and education'.

Social Security

One of the principal components of what was, after 1945, to be called the 'Welfare State' lay in a commitment by the state to ensure a minimum standard of income for its citizens, particularly in regard to safeguarding them against a reduction of earnings through old age, sickness or unemployment. The

Liberal administrations before 1914 have generally been credited with laying the foundations of this system through their legislation which established old-age pensions, labour exchanges, and health and employment insurance based upon contributions from the state, employers and employees. There also remained in existence the Poor Law, charged, until 1929, when its functions were largely absorbed by local authorities and central bodies, with the relief of the destitute and the able-bodied poor not provided for by other means. National Insurance, the Poor Law, and its successors remained the principal forms of social security throughout this period.

By far the most difficult and controversial problem to emerge after the Great War was that of the relief of the unemployed. The 1911 unemployment Insurance Act covered only two and a quarter out of nineteen million workers, and only fifteen weeks' benefit could be drawn in each year. The essential premise of the fund was that it was intended to be self-supporting in normal years, even if there might be deficits in exceptional circumstances. The First World War, however, witnessed a major expansion of the system, so that by 1921 it covered twelve million workers and an increased range of benefits fixed at a level of about one third of the average wage. This extension of the unemployment insurance system has been described by Bentley B. Gilbert as primarily the result of expedients and concessions which derived from the experience of the Great War, part of a process of social reconstruction which was the product both of genuine idealism and the fear of social upheaval. The 1920 Act continued the principles of the pre-war scheme. Contributions and benefits were increased, but entitlement to benefit remained, as before, at fifteen weeks per year, subject to daily 'signing-on' at the labour exchange. In the following year the Unemployed Workers' Dependants Act provided additional benefits for an unemployed man's wife and children. These two Acts provided the basis for the system of unemployment insurance between the wars. Although most manual workers were included, important groups, such as agricultural workers, domestic servants and the self-employed, lay outside its provisions for most of the period.

As unemployment rose to unexpectedly high and persistent levels during the 1920s, a series of Acts was passed to provide levels of benefit outside those originally provided under the insurance scheme. Workers who had not paid enough contributions to qualify for 'standard benefit' or had exhausted their benefit allowance of fifteen weeks, extended to twenty-six in 1921, qualified for special payments, variously termed uncovenanted benefit (1921), extended benefits (1924), transitional benefits (1927) and transitional payments (1931) paid in anticipation of future contributions. These *ad hoc* solutions destroyed the actuarial basis of the unemployment insurance fund and demonstrated the failure of the original schemes of 1911 and 1921 to cope with the exceptional nature of unemployment between the wars. In most cases, however, they were hedged around with greater restrictions, involving checks upon household circumstances, and 'gaps' in the payment of benefit. As a result, instead of being covered by insurance, many of the unemployed were being forced to apply to the Poor Law and, after 1929, to the Public Assistance Committees of the local authorities.

The burden of financing unemployment benefit, which by 1931 was costing the government £120 million per year, only £44 million of which was met by contributions, played an important part in the political crisis which overthrew the Labour government of 1929–31. Cuts in unemployment benefit in the autumn of 1931 resulted, including the introduction of the means test on the transitional payments paid after insurance benefit had been exhausted. Recognition that the exceptional nature of unemployment had outstripped the original insurance scheme was contained in the next phase of legislation, the Unemployment Assistance Board Acts of 1934–5. Under these measures, the locally paid transitional payments were to be funded by the Treasury out of general taxation and responsibility for the payments taken over by a new body, the Unemployment Assistance Board. The Board applied uniform rates and applied a standardized means test, both to those who had exhausted 'standard benefit' as well as those who fell outside other provisions. The Unemployment Assistance Board represented an important attempt to rationalize provision for the unemployed. The introduction of the new regulations, however, provoked an outcry when it was found that the rates to be paid were sometimes lower than the locally administered transitional payments. A Standstill Act had to be introduced in February 1935, modifying the operation of the scheme so that the old rates were kept wherever they were more favourable and delaying the absorption of people relieved under the Public Assistance Committees into the U A B scheme. Not until 1937 were the majority of the unemployed relieved under the P A Cs transferred to the U A B.

The End of the Poor Law

Responsibility for the relief of the poor and destitute had rested since the 1830s upon the Poor Law Unions and the 'workhouse'. Although by 1914 many of the harshnesses of the nineteenth-century Poor Law had been mitigated by the more generous provision of 'outdoor relief', anywhere between a third and fifth of those dying in the larger cities and towns could expect to end their days in the workhouse. Institutionalization and – in some cases – the still humiliating conditions provided for those relieved, continued to lead many to fear old age, infirmity or destitution. The introduction of old-age pensions, unemployment insurance and sickness benefit had begun to relieve some of the greatest pressure before 1914, but the Poor Law, whether in the form of the workhouse or 'outdoor relief', remained the essential place of last resort in case of need for all those who had no other resources on which to call.

Hence the Poor Law Guardians remained until 1929 as the ultimate 'safety net' which dealt with those who slipped between other forms of provision. The chief institutions maintained by the Guardians were the general mixed workhouses and the Poor Law infirmaries. By 1914 there were also usually

homes for children, varying from intimidating blocks built in
the nineteenth century to pleasanter 'cottage' homes, as well
as a small number of old people's homes. Specialized buildings
for those with infectious diseases, vagrants and convalescents
were also to be found in some of the larger unions. The term
'workhouse' technically only applied to the mixed institutions
where work was imposed to deter able-bodied applicants, but
it was generally applied to the whole system, as most people
still had to enter the general workhouse for medical inspection
and classification. Although from 1913 the term 'workhouse'
was abolished in favour of 'Poor Law Institution', the traditional
stigma remained. In 1920 there were 270,569 inmates in various
Poor Law institutions, broken down by the Ministry of Health
in that year as shown in Table 23.

Table 23: Inmates of Poor Law institutions, 1 January 1920

	Percentage distribution of inmates in various institutions, 1 January 1920	Percentage of all expenditure on indoor relief
Lunatic asylums and homes for the feeble-minded	33.3	28.8
Children's homes	11.4	11.8
Infirmaries	8.6	13.9
Workhouses	41.7	42.5
Others	5.0	3.0

While institutional relief absorbed 77 per cent of all relief
expenditure in 1918-19, at a time of high employment, the
growth of heavy unemployment increased the demand for
outdoor relief. By the mid-1920s, a minimum of 350,000-
450,000 unemployed received relief under the Poor Law provisions and, in the worst years, such as the aftermath of the
General Strike, as many as 1½ million were making claims on
the Poor Law. While the institutional costs of 'indoor relief'
were the heaviest burden on poor rates, with the cost of unemployment amounting on average to only 18 per cent of total
cost even in 1928, for the hardest-hit localities the cost of pro-

viding for the unemployed was absorbing as much as a half of all Poor Law expenditure by the late 1920s, putting intense strains upon the local rating system.

Indeed, by the late 1920s, the unsatisfactory nature of the Poor Law was widely recognized. In addition, since the Great War there had been friction between the central government and local Boards of Guardians about levels of relief. The most celebrated case was at Poplar in the early 1920s (see p. 309), and in 1926 Neville Chamberlain, as Minister of Health, had taken powers to replace local Guardians in West Ham, Chester-le-Street and Bedwellty for paying out too much in relief (see p. 310). A reform of the Poor Law was seen as an essential component of a rationalization of unemployment insurance and this was made part of Chamberlain's Local Government Act of 1929. As a result, the Poor Law, as it had existed since the nineteenth century, was overhauled. The Local Government Act, with a related act for Scotland, followed by the Poor Law Act of 1930, dismantled the administrative structure of the old system. The Poor Law Unions and the Boards of Guardians were swept away and their powers vested in the local authorities. The Poor Law hospitals, mainly dealing with infirm old people, were transferred to the local authorities, who were instructed to form Public Assistance Committees (PACs) for the relief of destitution. Administratively, the end of the Poor Law was seen as a major advance, enshrining proposals outlined as early as the 1909 Report on the Poor Law, but in terms of buildings, treatment and the perception of the poor and unemployed themselves, the transformation was less obvious. The Poor Law hospitals and workhouse buildings remained in use to care for the aged and infirm who were incapable of looking after themselves and, while now administered by the local authority, often still retained the stigma and austerity of the Poor Law.

None the less, the Local Government Act and the later creation of the Unemployment Assistance Board profoundly altered the operation of the PACs. These were now able to develop more specialized services dealing with the different

categories of people who fell outside existing forms of insurance
or unemployment relief. The Unemployment Assistance Board
was scheduled from 1935 to take over responsibility for 800,000
able-bodied unemployed maintained by the PACs and 200,000
others in receipt of poor relief. But the delay in implementing
the UAB regulations meant that as late as March 1937 150,000
unemployed, plus 250,000 dependants, still came under the
PACs. Once in force, from 1 April 1937, the numbers relieved
by the PACs rapidly fell to a mere 70,000 in all. Without the
unemployed to support, the PACs were able to concentrate
primarily on children, the elderly and the sick. By the mid-
thirties only a fraction of these people, just over a tenth, were
receiving relief in institutions, the largest single group being
the sick. The rest were receiving 'outdoor relief' in their homes,
continuing the trend towards home-based services in cash and
kind which was already evident before 1914. With the coming
of war, it was the Unemployment Assistance Board rather than
the Public Assistance Committee whose role was expanded. As
unemployment fell, the UAB was made responsible for all
those 'distressed' by the war. In 1940 its name was changed
to the Assistance Board, whose role became that of providing
emergency aid to those in need and not catered for by the
expanded insurance services. Eventually renamed the National
Assistance Board under the National Assistance Act of 1948, it
assumed responsibility for all those who were still being relieved
locally by the PACs.

The other pillar of the Liberal welfare legislation before 1914,
non-contributory old-age pensions, was expanded and revised
during the inter-war years. In 1919 pensions were raised to 10s.
a week and in 1940 the Old Age and Widows' Pension Act
provided for supplementary pensions to be drawn from the
Assistance Board, subject to a means test. At the same time
the retirement age for women was reduced to sixty. Even before
the Great War the Labour movement had been demanding that
pensions should be paid from the age of sixty out of general
taxation. Financial constraints, an ageing population – increasing the number of those who could benefit from improved

pensions – and the conservative attitude of most inter-war governments frustrated this development. Instead, Neville Chamberlain, as Minister of Health in the 1920s, set out to superimpose upon the non-contributory pension scheme a new contributory system which would be paid as of right from the age of sixty-five, not seventy as in the 1908 Act. This was linked with other benefits in the comprehensive Widows', Orphans' and Old Age Contributory Pensions Act of 1925. The scheme followed the principles of the pre-war National Insurance Act in being financed by contributions from employers and employees and subsidized by the state. It provided an insured worker with a pension of 10s. a week between the age of sixty-five and seventy, with pensions for widows, children's allowances for widows and payments for orphans of insured persons. An Act of 1937 also opened the scheme to self-employed workers. The result was a limited but important extension of pension provision, partly financed by workers themselves. Its other consequence, entirely typical of the piecemeal extension of welfare provisions between the wars, was to create a highly complex multi-tiered system of pensions: the non-contributory scheme of 1908 for those over seventy, subject to a means test; the 1925 contributory scheme covering those between sixty-five and seventy who were entitled to non-means-tested benefits after the age of seventy; and those covered by a wide variety of company and private insurance schemes. As in other spheres it was the Second World War which led to the effective rationalization of the pension system. Old-age pensions were brought within the new social insurance system which was established by the National Insurance Act of August 1946. Although Beveridge had assumed a twenty-year transitional phase, the new Labour government decided to implement immediately an old-age pension of 16s. a week from October 1946.

The Second World War also saw the introduction of family allowances. As early as 1909 Lloyd George, as Chancellor of the Exchequer, introduced income tax allowances for children in his budget, though at this time these were irrelevant to the working classes, who usually paid no income tax. However, concern with family poverty, the birth rate and the place of women was leading some to consider that a system of child allowances was desirable. A small committee, first set up in 1917, became in 1924 the Family Endowment Society, the main pressure group for family allowances between the wars. Its three leaders, Eleanor Rathbone, Mary Stocks and Eva Hubback, were all middle-class women who had been involved in the women's suffrage movement. The main figure, Eleanor Rathbone, had studied at Oxford, where she was strongly influenced by the idealism and social reformism characteristic of progressive liberal circles before 1914. A woman of independent means, she had gained experience of child poverty before 1914 while doing charity work in the Liverpool slums and in helping to administer separation allowances during the First World War. In *The Disinherited Family*, published in 1924, she argued strongly for a wage system which would adapt itself to the needs of families. By the early 1920s the society was advocating a national family allowance system, providing 12s. 6d. per week for mothers, 5s. 0d. per week for the first child and 3s. 6d. per week for each subsequent child. Although never large, the society enlisted powerful support from men such as William Beveridge and Seebohm Rowntree. The latter, in particular, had demonstrated before 1914, and was to go on to demonstrate several times more between the wars, that the payment of child allowances would eliminate a major element in the 'poverty cycle'.

But a mixture of financial stringency, particularly bearing in mind the large estimated cost of an effective scheme, and the reluctance of governments and administrators to accept that family poverty was as severe as the social investigators suggested, prevented the implementation of a family allowance system before the Second World War. In particular, civil servants and more conservative politicians were concerned about the principle of 'less eligibility' – the presentation of a gap between levels of benefit and wages. Experience between the wars of the addition of dependants' allowances to unemployment benefit had aroused the spectre of raising levels of benefit higher than wages. The fear – a prevalent one throughout the inter-war period and beyond – was that over-generous state benefits would destroy work incentives and reduce the mobility of labour. These reservations began to be overcome in the winter of 1939/40, when interest in family allowances was expressed by the government as part of a temporary wartime scheme to contain wage increases and control inflation. When this danger passed, however, there was some predisposition to postpone the introduction of family allowances until after the war or of introducing them only on a contributory basis.

The social consensus achieved in the early years of the war, however, played an important part in altering the terms in which the debate was conducted, for the Beveridge Report of December 1942 made family allowances a cornerstone of the proposed system of comprehensive social insurance. Heavily influenced, as he acknowledged, by the social investigations of the 'impartial scientific authorities' of the inter-war years, Beveridge concluded that between a quarter and sixth of 'want' was caused by the failure to match income to family size. He, unlike many pre-war officials, did accept the arguments of the family poverty lobby led by bodies like the Family Endowment Society and the Child Minimum Council that a system of family allowances would help to eliminate a sizable area of poverty. With the backing of Beveridge and the widening support for social reconstruction, plans for implementing a family allowance scheme were developed. Significantly, they were accepted, at least in part, by the Treasury as a means of raising family income without tackling the even more expensive option of introducing a minimum wage. As a result the 1945 Family Allowance Act provided for an allowance of 5s. for the second and subsequent child. At this level, the allowance was set well below that suggested by Beveridge of 8s. or Boyd Orr's recommendation of 14s. and was, in fact, the figure suggested in 1942 by the committee of senior civil servants set up to evaluate the Beveridge Report. Two influences, the need to preserve wage incentives by not setting benefits too high and the necessity to accede to a powerful current of public opinion in the aftermath of Beveridge, accounted for the compromise scheme ultimately accepted. At a cost of £57 million in 1945, it was recognized as one of the cheaper alternatives available to counter family poverty, far less so than the introduction of a minimum wage.

The Role of the State: Central and Local Government

There were important connecting threads in many aspects of social policy during this period. If one stands out, it is the growing pressure upon the state to take on greater social responsibilities and to intervene to provide direct help to the most vulnerable sections of the community. Many of the social inquiries pointed squarely to the need for the state to extend its activities in almost every sphere of welfare. As a result spending on the social services continued to increase after 1914, carrying on a trend in rising social spending evident in the Edwardian era. In 1913–14 government expenditure on poor relief, health, insurance, old-age and other pensions, and unemployment insurance, net of contributions, amounted to £22½ million; by 1921–2 it had risen to £179½ million; and by 1933–4 to £204 million. The most significant increase occurred at the time of the Great War, but even during the inter-war years high unemployment and an ageing population pushed up expenditure to new levels on unemployment assistance, poor relief and non-contributory pensions. In addition, extra expenditure was devoted towards housing, education and a new contributory pension scheme for the elderly, widows and orphans. At the same time employment in government social service departments, especially those dealing with insurance and assistance, doubled between 1914 and 1928 and trebled by 1939 to 25,000. Local authority expenditure on housing, education and poor relief also increased. Local authority expenditure on health, housing and education alone rose from £45 million in 1913–14 to £271 million by 1938–9. Social welfare expenditure at both national and local level, as a proportion of national income, increased from 5.5 per cent in 1913, to 10.3 per cent in 1924, and to 13.0 per cent in 1938, rising as high as 15.8 per cent during the trough of the depression because of the cost of unemployment benefit. Social welfare spending formed, with defence and debt servicing, the main elements in government expenditure during the inter-war years, with spending on social welfare exceeding the other two in most peace-time years. Social services expenditure accounted for an average of 36 per cent of all government spending in the 1920s, rising to almost 50 per cent during the worst years of the depression. However, the proportion of government expenditure going to the social services remained at approximately the same level as before 1914, about a third, though as the share of national income spent by government had doubled, the volume of spending showed a significant increase.

The Second World War emphasized this trend both in the expanded range of services taken over by government and a further increase in spending. Total expenditure on the social services rose as a percentage of national income, though the exact amount is difficult to calculate because of transfers of items such as private insurance schemes and voluntary hospitals into the state sector. According to one estimate, expenditure on the social services as a percentage of gross national income rose from 9.8 per cent in 1937–8 to 14.8 per cent in 1947–8. Total spending on social security, education, health and housing had increased from £520.4 million in 1938–9 to £1,013.1 million in 1947–8. Much of this increase was accounted for by inflation and the creation of the National Health Service, but increased pensions, family allowances and other subsidies more than covered the reduction in the cost of unemployment benefit. The Second World War, like the Great War, had raised the level of social spending, though not quite as dramatically as is sometimes thought.

The local authorities also remained a crucial component in the administration and provision of services. Indeed the period from the late nineteenth century to the Second World War might well be called the heyday of local government. Within the administrative structure laid down by 1900, local authorities had both a democratic apparatus and an independent system of finance through rates, borrowing and the provision of municipally owned services such as gas, water, electricity and transport. As we have seen, one tendency was for central government to pass further responsibilities on to the local authorities. The abolition of School Boards and their replacement by Local Education Authorities (LEAs) in 1902 and the transfer of Poor Law functions, including hospitals, to the local authorities in 1929 illustrated this tendency. Moreover, many of the new responsibilities assumed by the state were placed in the hands of the local authorities. In crucial areas such as housing, education and the administration of poor relief, the initiatives of central government had to be carried out by the local authorities and it was local officials with whom most people had to deal. The net result was a greatly expanded field of activity, which was shown in increased expenditure. Total local authority expenditure in England and Wales rose from £140 million in 1913 to £533 million in 1939. Much of this increase was accounted for by welfare spending, which more than trebled during the period. Part of this increase was locally financed. Total rate receipts for local authorities rose from £68.2 million in 1913 to £177.3 million in 1938, while there was an even larger increase in local authority borrowing, rising from £17.5 million in 1913 to £122.7 in 1938. However, during this period, central government took an increasing share in paying for the more costly items of local authority spending. Central government grants provided an increasing percentage of total local authority expenditure, rising from 22 per cent in 1913–14 to 41 per cent in 1938–9. From being a minor component of local government revenue, 13.6 per cent in 1913, only a third of the income from rates, government grants rose to 20.6 per cent in 1938, equal to three-quarters of rate receipts.

Hence the expanded functions of local government in the social sphere went hand in hand with greater dependence upon government grants. At the time of the reorganization of the Poor Law in 1929 the President of the Salford Board of

Guardians complained: 'An uneasy feeling is growing in the mind of the nation that the constant drift towards centralization ... indicated the increasing power of bureaucracy with a corresponding loss of the rights of the people.' The tendency for central government to limit the autonomy of local authorities through control of its finances was emphasized by the most celebrated clash between central and local government in the inter-war years, when in 1921 some of the Labour councillors and Guardians in the London Borough of Poplar were sent to prison for refusing to contribute their quota of rates to the London County Council. Their protest formed part of a long-running battle by the borough, one amongst several in the London area to suffer from heavy unemployment, to pay higher rates of relief than those recommended by the Ministry of Health. Although the affair had direct political overtones, with the Labour councillors taking a stand on ideological grounds and the Mayor of Poplar, George Lansbury, later leader of the Labour Party, stating forthrightly his view that 'If people starve on wages, there is no reason why they should starve on relief,' it also raised the crucial question of who should govern the level of local expenditure on social welfare. Neville Chamberlain summed up his objections to 'Poplarism' as being the recognition by the Guardians of a fixed, usually high scale of relief, usually granted at the maximum level; refusal to apply household means tests; the granting – technically illegal – of relief to people engaged in industrial disputes; and the violation of the principle of 'less eligibility', by granting relief in excess of local minimum wages. As a result 'Poplarism' became a term to describe any 'lax' system of local authority spending.

As the depression lengthened, the potential for more Poplars was only too evident, particularly in Labour-controlled areas. Half a dozen London boroughs, and local authorities in places such as South Wales, Durham and parts of Yorkshire and Lancashire, were similarly disposed. The Ministry of Health already had powers to refuse to grant loans and to impose surcharges through the District Auditor, but backed down for fear of further confrontation. None the less, Bills were prepared

between 1922 and 1925 for the suspension of Boards of
Guardians who refused to comply with Ministry of Health
regulations. In 1926 the issue of central control of local authority
expenditure once again came to a head as a result of the General
Strike and the large numbers thrown on to poor relief by the
miners' stoppage. In pursuit of the desire to restrict poor relief
solely to the relief of destitution and to prevent Labour
Guardians from using it to support strikers, an Act was passed
giving the Minister power to suspend Boards which were
unable or unwilling to function according to prescribed rules.
As a result the West Ham, Chester-le-Street and Bedwellty
Boards of Guardians, all of whom had exhausted their borrowing powers and gone bankrupt, were suspended and replaced
by Commissioners appointed by the Ministry, who then administered the Poor Law according to Ministry requirements.

Central powers were reinforced by the Audit Act of 1927,
disqualifying Guardians surcharged for over £500 from serving
on local authorities for five years, and in 1928 by the placing of
the Metropolitan Common Poor Fund in the hands of eighteen
Ministry of Health nominees. These measures were backed up
by visits of Ministry of Health inspectors to all Poor Law unions
suspected of 'unorthodox tendencies' and the publication of
their usually highly critical reports in the press. Even after the
abolition of the Guardians in 1929 and the transfer of their
powers to the Public Assistance Committees of the local
authorities, there were similar disputes in 1931–2 arising from
the implementation of the means test as part of the National
Government's economy campaign. Several PACs, more than
twenty in number, by no means all of them Labour-controlled,
were 'warned' by the Ministry of Labour and threatened with
suspension if they refused to comply. This revolt, perhaps the
last and most widespread rebellion by local government in the
twentieth century, was crushed. Durham and Rotherham
PACs were suspended by the end of 1932, while the other
rebellious authorities, faced with the painful choice of making
the best of the situation by carrying on in the hope of mitigating
the operation of the means test or handing over powers to a

Commissioner, were forced to toe the line. It was the experience of provincial obtuseness in 1931–2 which finally convinced Chamberlain of the need to 'depoliticize' the issue of unemployment relief and take it out of the hands of the local authorities, resulting in the setting-up of the Unemployment Assistance Board in 1934.

Similar battles occurred in the field of education. Higher spending on education in the inter-war years was largely due to extra local authority spending, rising by 44 per cent between 1921 and 1940, compared with only a 13 per cent increase in exchequer grants. Conflict arose almost as soon as the 'Geddes Axe' eroded the basis of the Fisher Act, that central government would support educational development by the local authorities at a level of a minimum of 50 per cent of their expenditure. As a result part of the increased expense of education was transferred to the local authorities, so that the cost of education began to bear more heavily on rates than taxes. In 1925–6 the Board of Education attempted to remove the principle of support for local authority education expenditure as a fixed percentage of total costs and to cut expenditure overall. Its effect would have been to force up rate expenditure on education. Faced with massive protest from local authorities, teachers and MPs the Board of Education beat a retreat. In 1931, however, the Board secured a major victory over the local authorities under the stress of a national emergency. The principle of 50 per cent support for local education expenditure was abandoned and local authorities forced to default on the Burnham agreements concerning teachers' pay, in spite of almost 1,800 protests to the Board. In education, then, the local authorities got the worst of all possible worlds. Denied central government funding to the level anticipated in 1918, they were forced to support a higher proportion of education expenditure, but denied ultimate responsibility for the shape of education in their localities. The legislation of the 1940s still further eroded the autonomy of local government with the setting-up of nationally financed health, education and welfare services. These usually required local authorities to submit their proposed schemes for the administration and development of their services to the Minister, or else gave him wide discretionary powers over the local authorities undertaking those services. Combined with the nationalization of utilities, such as gas, electricity and water, between 1945 and 1948, and the transference of local government functions to *ad hoc* bodies, the ascendancy of local government in welfare as in so much else was clearly at an end. Ironically too by 1945, the Labour Party, once the champion of local autonomy over welfare provision, had itself, in the interest of centralized planning and nationalization, become one of the principal agents of the decline of local government. With the extension of welfare services there was an inevitable increase in cost, leading in turn to local authorities depending more and more heavily upon the national exchequer. Power inevitably followed the purse, so that by the early 1950s a serious diminution in the functions and powers of local government was widely accepted as having taken place.

The Nature of Social Policy

If the assumption of greater responsibility by central government was one of the most persistent features of social policy in this period, there was also considerable consistency in the spirit of its operation, at least until the 1940s. Liberal welfare legislation before 1914 was designed to humanize and extend social welfare provision, but it represented a transitional phase in which many traditional attitudes remained. National Insurance was a major innovation, but one which also enshrined belief in individual responsibility and orthodox financing. Moreover the concern not to offer relief on terms which were higher than the lowest wages represented a similar carry-over of nineteenth-century ideas. These were represented in the battery of 'tests' and distinctions between 'deserving' and 'undeserving' which were characteristic of so much of the administration of the benefits of various kinds between the wars. The extension of pensions on a contributory basis in 1925, the application of the 'not genuinely seeking work' clause in the late

1920s, the introduction of the means test in 1931 and the reluctance to adopt a comprehensive health service or a system of family allowances provide obvious examples of the persistence of these attitudes. The assumptions they contained, like most climates of opinion, had complex sources. There was, for example, considerable reluctance to interfere with the operation of a competitive economic system. The attachment to the principle of 'less eligibility' was an obvious example. Incentives for individuals to find work and provide for themselves were fundamental to a very broad spectrum of opinion. Similarly, the idea of a minimum wage was anathema to those concerned about the competitiveness of British industry and there was reluctance to advocate it even amongst some of those who knew its potential for eliminating poverty. These attitudes were reinforced by the economic policies pursued by most governments in this period. Economic orthodoxy, from which there were very few dissentients before the 1940s, advocated a balanced budget and a careful and prudent allocation of expenditure in order to maintain business confidence and preserve the value of the currency. Social welfare was a major item of expenditure and as such was a source of repeated concern to government. No sooner had ambitious proposals been adopted for an expansion of welfare services after the Great War than the 'Geddes Axe' fell upon expenditure of all kinds, including social welfare. Although the Labour governments of 1923–4 and 1929–31 attempted more generous provision and easier access to welfare, they too were trapped in the toils of financial orthodoxy and an adverse economic climate, leading ultimately to the political crisis of 1931 when the Labour government broke up under the strain of reconciling its social priorities – particularly maintaining unemployment benefits – with the need to cut government spending. After 1931 this economic orthodoxy permitted only limited extensions of welfare spending. Subsequently, in the light of the experience of other countries such as Sweden and the USA, and the spread of Keynesian ideas about the role of government spending in increasing economic activity in general, this approach could be criticized. However, Keynes's ideas were not fully articulated until 1936 in the *General Theory of Employment, Interest and Money* and were not accepted by the great majority of financiers, economists and administrators until the 1940s.

Similar attitudes were also found in local government and especially amongst the rate-payers – one of the strongest sources of opposition to increased local authority expenditure before and after 1914. Businesses who paid commercial rates could channel their views through Chambers of Commerce and also possessed an extra influence through the survival of the business vote, not abolished until 1946. As well as using the ballot box, middle-class householders formed rate-payers' associations and put up candidates in local elections, often to 'ginger up' local politicians on the rates issue. Moreover, in some areas, the rate-payers included a significant proportion of working-class house-owners. With rates levied on house value rather than income, this could make working-class owner-occupiers at least as sensitive to rate rises as the middle classes. Above all, however, local politics and council representation were dominated by shop-keepers and small businessmen, to the extent that the inter-war years have been called the 'golden age of the shopocracy' in local government. In a fairly typical industrial town such as Wolverhampton, for example, businessmen, shopkeepers and publicans accounted for over half the councillors in the decade 1930–40. For these people, concern about high spending on social welfare and caution about high borrowing were only to be expected. In addition, times of hardship tended to exacerbate the conflicting interests of rate-payers and the recipients of relief, as the need for greater relief expenditure would often coincide with difficulties for local firms and important groups such as local shopkeepers. As Norman McCord has written of the North-East:

A study of many Boards of Guardians during the 1920s will show them facing two conflicting pressures, both of them representing a genuine case. On the one hand the vociferous champions of the un-employed urged the expenditure of more generous sums in relief, on the other hand representatives of a variety of organizations which included ratepayers argued that any substantial increase in rate demands would break the precarious financial viability of many ratepayers, who were also hard hit by economic depression.

McCord has noted a number of other concerns which influenced rate-payers in their attitude to local expenditure on welfare. One was outrage at the abuse of public funds by the 'scrounger' and the 'parasite' – a complaint by no means confined to the middle classes. Although in terms of total expenditure and measured against need only small sums were involved, stories of fiddling, fecklessness and abuse had a disproportionate effect on public opinion. Local newspapers in the inter-war years (as after) were peppered with correspondence and editorials expressing resentment at the expenditure of rate-payers' money on the drunken, the vicious, the improvident and the feckless. While it would be easy to conclude that these were expressions of primarily middle-class attitudes, they could be found just as readily in newspapers serving primarily working-class communities. Hence in January 1931, a Wolverhampton local newspaper condemned 'the airy manner in which Midland spending authorities are breaking the back of prosperity by imposing on those who come after us appalling financial burdens to pay for present extravagance'. Blaming the dole and the 'grandmotherly state' for the increase in spending, it went on:

The dole system which makes it easy to exist when increased effort is required tends to encourage laziness in those of weak moral fibre, and increases the number of parasites at the bottom end of the scale. It depreciates character when character is already weak and already under temptation to give in to circumstances, and at the same time it diverts huge sums of money from productive industry, which provides the nation's sustenance and finds work for the people, to the maintenance of an army of unemployed who are required to render no service whatever in return for what is given them.

It is not difficult to find similar comments from other areas, even those hard-hit by the depression. The *Birkenhead News* in January 1932, under the headline 'Long Live the Means Test', claimed that it was a measure 'welcomed by every fair-

minded citizen' and looked forward to its massacre of the 'dole
brides'.

This type of *cri de cœur* of the anguished rate-payer, repeated on innumerable occasions, did not, however, prevent
the expansion of the activities of local authorities and an
almost inexorable rise of current and capital expenditure. If we
take one example, the borough of Wednesbury in the West
Midlands, the increase in expenditure is clearly shown (see
Table 24).

Table 24: Wednesbury Corporation Finance, 1913–47

	Rate (s.d.)	Revenue expenditure £	Capital expenditure £	Loan debt £
1913–14	8.0	24,000	—	125,000
1926–7	15.6	67,000	41,000	963,000
1936–7	14.4	113,000	183,000	2,385,000
1946–7	18.0	111,000	590,000	3,025,000

Source: J. F. Ede, *A History of Wednesbury*, Wednesbury, 1962, p. 387.

Rising rate revenue and access to funds through government
grants and local authority loans oiled the wheels of municipal
improvement and permitted the more ambitious authorities to
undertake projects unthinkable before 1914, such as the building
of satellite towns, as at Manchester-Wythenshawe, and the
comprehensive slum clearance and redevelopment carried out
by the LCC under Herbert Morrison. Elsewhere, it permitted
modest and piecemeal advances. In Wednesbury, for example,
in 1920 the local Medical Officer had specified two chief tasks
in public health: connection of all houses to the sewers in order
to eliminate the use of ash privies, and the reduction of overcrowding. By 1930 the first of these was virtually achieved,
with 2,000 ash privies removed and only 129 left, and a new
main sewer completed with the aid of a £35,000 loan. In
addition dry ashpits had been replaced with galvanized iron
dustbins for refuse. All houses by 1943 had a piped water supply,
though even by that date 200 houses were still supplied by stand-

pipes and outside taps. After a very slow start in eliminating overcrowding, little better in 1931 than in 1921, the council built 2,304 houses in the decade 1931–9, including several new estates, some provided with playing fields, allotments and health clinics. In three years 900 houses were erected, by the end of 1935 almost one council house a day was built, and in 1938 a total of 587 houses were completed in one year.

Although many problems remained, examples such as this help to explain the change in climate which even Conservative local authorities shared by the late 1930s. Central government grants and sanctioned loans permitted a much greater increase in local authority spending between the wars than could have been either financed from the rates alone or tolerated by the rate-payers. Aided by the economic recovery of the middle and late 1930s, even Conservative councillors were beginning to see an increase in the local authority debt as the best evidence of a progressive authority, particularly if most of the costs were financed by central government.

Philanthropy and Social Service

Private philanthropy had played a major part both in the provision and evolution of social policy in the nineteenth century. Even with the growth of centralized welfare and the expanding work of the local authorities, the activities of national and local philanthropic services remained immense. Well-established bodies like the Salvation Army, the Charity Organization Society and Dr Barnardo's Homes continued to flourish, and new ones appeared. The National Council of Social Service, founded in 1919, sponsored local councils in urban districts and worked with groups such as the Women's Institutes in rural areas. Supported by the Prince of Wales, the organization received government grants under the Special Areas Act of 1934 to set up training centres and recreational facilities in areas of heavy unemployment. As many as a thousand centres were operating by the end of the 1930s, with between 150,000 and 200,000 men involved at various times, in some areas such as South Wales, organizing re-settlement schemes and small-holdings on reclaimed land. Half of the 115 nursery schools by 1939 were provided by voluntary effort, as were a quarter of the maternity and Child Welfare Centres and all the Family Planning Clinics. Often in partnership with local or national government, private charitable organization provided between the wars, as C. L. Mowat noted, 'for the blind and the halt, the unmarried mother, the prisoner; it provided the lifeboat service, the missions to seamen, the funds for aged governesses'. Amongst the most important activities of private philanthropy, however, were the private hospitals. The 1,013 voluntary hospitals in 1935 provided about a third of the hospital beds in the country. Their support involved major fund-raising activities, including the soliciting of sub-scriptions, appeals, bazaars and flag days. In 1937 it was esti-mated that 900 charitable organizations raised over £4¾ million, half of it for hospitals and dispensaries.

There were also the great benefactors, such as the Carnegie United Kingdom Trust, founded by the Scottish-born Ameri-can multi-millionaire Andrew Carnegie in 1913. It funded public libraries, village halls, youth organizations, playing fields, adult education, music festivals and much else. The Ratan Tata foundation set up by an Indian steel millionaire was another which supported social activities, as did the Pilgrim Trust, founded in 1930 by the American E. S. Harkness, which sponsored the famous report into the effects of unemployment in the late 1930s, as well as encouraging medical research, music and the arts. Lord Nuffield, the motor millionaire, was perhaps the most spectacular benefactor of the inter-war years. He had donated more than £10½ million to charity by 1940, £4 million going to Oxford University alone, £2 million of it to endow medical research and £1 million to found a new post-graduate college, at Oxford, devoted to the study of the social sciences.

Beneath these large organizations and great benefactors lay the myriad local and small-scale charitable efforts which had done so much to distinguish British society before 1914. In an age when central government responsibility for welfare was growing, it is all too easy to overlook the still considerable part played in local communities by charitable organizations. By the 1930s almost every community of any size had its networks of Rotary Club, Inner Wheel, Women's Institute and Towns Women's Guild, many of which combined social with charitable functions, as well as church-based societies and branches of national charitable organizations. Moreover, the study of local newspapers between the wars, particularly of towns badly affected by unemployment, reveals a considerable amount of charitable effort, including soup kitchens, Christmas parcels for children and families, boot clubs, hobbies and recreation centres, and free access to allotments. While the overall impact of such efforts is difficult to assess, they showed the continued vitality of the philanthropic traditions of the past and ability to command a powerful community response.

Of more significance for the shaping of social policy as a whole was the tendency for philanthropic groups to act as the pace-setters for official action, as in the case of family planning, child allowances, nursery schools and the 'garden city' movement. Moreover, there was no necessary contradiction between philanthropic effort and government activity. The 1909 Report on the Poor Law had urged a re-ordering of relations and closer liaison between voluntary and official bodies. It was entirely characteristic of the still strongly voluntarist and *laissez faire* attitudes found up to and beyond 1945 that private groups and institutions were called upon to supplement official efforts and, sometimes, act as semi-official agencies, receiving support and funds from central and local government. Bodies such as the National Council of Social Service represented an essentially voluntary organization which received official backing and funds. It was a form of compromise between state provision and private initiative which was to continue even after the greatly expanded welfare role of the state during the Second World War. However, as with local government, there was a marked tendency for central government to play a larger share in the partnership, absorbing some of these groups into a semi-official role and often determining their effectiveness through the allocation of funds or the official recognition of their case. For many of these organizations, such as the Family Planning groups or Family Endowment Society, their ultimate aim was to have their views accepted in official circles and put into operation.

Equally important and underpinning many of the social policy initiatives in this period was the continuing development of a climate of social concern which expressed itself not only in philanthropy but in direct and indirect attempts to influence government policy and public opinion. A major part in this was played by the social inquiries which, beginning at the end of the nineteenth century, painstakingly investigated social conditions. Much of this social investigation was encouraged by an empirical and scientific approach to social questions which was itself the product of a spirit of rational optimism based upon the proved advances of science, belief in progress and, amongst some, deep Christian commitment. The young Lord Woolton, trained in science at Manchester University before 1914, recalled his motivation in undertaking a social survey in Edwardian Liverpool:

> I was twenty-four, and I decided to spend two years making what I optimistically believed would be a cold and dispassionate scientific investigation into the problems of poverty. I went to this slum district in the south end of Liverpool in the same spirit as the medical scientists who were at the time inquiring into the causes and cure of tuberculosis. I knew that the problem was one involving knowledge of facts and experience of people and that I could not get it from books. ... I hoped that a period of detailed study would enable me to answer – at any rate to my own satisfaction – the prevailing question of the time – 'Why are so many people poor?'

Malcolm Muggeridge saw these inquiries as emanating from a passion for facts and statistics: 'Facts were wanted about everyone and everything – cross-sections of society, symptomatic opinions and observations, detailed investigations and statistics.' The accuracy of this observation was demonstrated by the existence in the late thirties of a magazine called *Fact* devoted to a range of social, economic and political questions. Also symptomatic of this spirit of scientific inquiry was the formation of the social reporting organization Mass Observation by the anthropologist Tom Harrison and the journalist Charles Madge in 1936. It recruited observers to report on almost every aspect of daily life and social behaviour, outlining its concerns as: 'ascertaining the facts as accurately as possible; developing and improving the methods for ascertaining these facts; disseminating the ascertained facts as widely as possible'. Although a great deal of material was rather unsystematically collected, Mass Observation's studies of such things as drinking habits in *The Pub and the People*, published in 1943, added another dimension to social investigation, one which was co-opted by the government during the Second World War as a means of gauging civilian morale. It also had a parallel in the setting-up of the first branch of the Gallup polling organization as the British Institute of Public Opinion in 1938.

But beside the investigatory work of the social scientists and others, the inter-war period, and especially the thirties, was marked by an explosion of literature, journalism and comment on social questions. Again, much of this followed in a tradition established before 1914 in the exploration of 'darkest England', but there was also a stronger documentary quality seen in much of the writing, for example, in the travelogue-style literature which explored the character of Britain, such as J. B. Priestley's *English Journey*, published in 1934, and the *Walks and Talks* series produced by the Conservative MP Sir Arnold Wilson. By the end of the thirties, the illustrated magazine *Picture Post*, founded in 1938, was beginning to use photo-journalism to investigate both trivial and serious items, including social issues such as unemployment. It was, indeed, the issue of mass unemployment which stimulated much of the social discussion of the period. In a sense it was *the* problem – the one most frequently re-searched, discussed and investigated. To the academic inquiries has to be added a whole *genre* of 'dole literature', of which probably the best-known examples are Walter Greenwood's novel *Love on the Dole*, set in depression-scarred Salford, and George Orwell's *Road to Wigan Pier*.

An important new influence lay in the presentation of social issues through film. The documentary movement, pioneered by people such as John Grierson at the GPO film unit and directors like Alberto Cavalcanti and Robert Flaherty, had, by the outbreak of the Second World War, produced short films dealing with such issues as malnutrition, the depression in South Wales, housing problems and anticipations of future welfare provision. While the impact of such films is hard to estimate, there was an audience of millions for the film version of *Love on the Dole*, produced in 1941, and the propaganda films of the Second World War by people such as Humphrey Jennings and Paul Rotha which offered a vision of post-war society based upon some of the more progressive ideas circulating before 1939.

Middle Opinion

A crystallization of these views emerged in pressure groups such as Political and Economic Planning (PEP), established in 1931, and the Next Five Years Group, formed in 1934. Covering a broader range than the single-issue groups, they presented reports and analyses on a wider range of economic and social issues which, generally, looked forward to the legislation of the 1940s. Arthur Marwick has stressed the importance of such groups in fostering the development of 'middle opinion', a progressive consensus which embraced a broad spectrum of public opinion and pointed towards a managed economy and the expansion of the social services. Indeed, the list of those involved in PEP during the 1930s and early 1940s represents almost a gazetteer of progressive opinion: it included the banker Basil Blackett, businessmen such as Laurence Neal and Israel Sieff, the scientist Julian Huxley, the educational pioneer and National MP Kenneth Lindsay, architects and town-planning enthusiasts such as Maxwell Fry, Raymond Unwin and Ernest Simon, the anthropologist Tom Harrison, academics such as

Alexander Cairncross, John Maynard Keynes and William Beveridge, and sympathetic MPs such as Harold Macmillan and Sir Arnold Wilson. Major reports were produced on housing, social services, the health services, the press and the location of industry which foreshadowed many of the developments of the 1940s. Its shorter 'broadsheets', over 150 of which had been produced by 1940, provided discussion on a wide range of topics of economic and social concern. PEP had a strong technocratic outlook, drawing most of its support and research groups from managers, academics and other experts. Its General Secretary, Max Nicholson, has summed up the thrust of much of its work as being: to supersede piecemeal treatment of public policy by coordinated policies founded on 'fact-based' and 'research-based' programmes; reliable decision-making based upon accurate and comprehensive forecasting; and the implementation of policy through democratic principles, extended still further through participation and devolution. By collecting information, stimulating discussion and producing its reports, PEP hoped directly to influence government action.

The Next Five Years Group tended towards a less technocratic style. Its members again included many of those involved in progressive causes between the wars, especially in education and the social services, including Seebohm Rowntree, H. G. Wells, Siegfried Sassoon, R. C. K. Ensor, H. A. L. Fisher, G. P. Gooch, J. A. Hobson and William Temple. Again, the proposals of the Next Five Years Group anticipated many of the developments of the 1940s, such as a National Development Board, greater public investment in housing, the coordination of social services to achieve a 'national minimum', the expansion of secondary education, and town and country planning. The young Harold Macmillan was especially active in the group, eventually taking charge of it and its periodical *New Outlook*. The views he expressed in *The Middle Way*, published in 1938, pointing towards a managed economy and the expansion of welfare services, came close to expressing the essential ingredients of what both PEP and the Next Five Years Group wanted in the way of a change of direction by the National Government. Macmillan, with a few other radical Tories, such as Robert Boothby, Julian Amery and Duncan Sandys, represented a strand of Conservative thinking which already accepted much of the argument of 'middle opinion'.

Undoubtedly, too, the Labour movement was a major and growing force for social reform. Pre-1914 Labour Party conferences had urged the nationalization of hospitals under a National Health Service, while in Parliament most Labour MPs voted for Lloyd George's National Insurance legislation. The 1918 policy statement, *Labour and the New Order*, drafted by Sidney Webb, also contained the demand for a minimum wage, a minimum standard of working conditions, a maximum working week and the expansion of the social services, especially health, housing and education. Thus the 1918 Labour Party annual conference unanimously adopted a resolution calling for a 'unified Health Service for the whole community', followed up in 1922 with a joint Labour Party and TUC proposal for a free 'Public Medical Service' to be administered by the local authorities under the supervision of the Minister of Health. In housing, it adopted as its official policy the idea of low-interest loans from the central government to the local authorities. In spite of having had only a short period of minority government, the Labour Party in the 1920s had developed some ambitious long-term policies. Faced with the worsening of the depression and the break-up of the MacDonald Labour government in 1931, some of these ambitions were curtailed and effort concentrated upon evolving a new strategy. Following 1931 the trade unions came to play an increasingly important part in shaping Labour policy. Ernest Bevin, for example, in his pamphlet *My Plan for 200,000 Workers*, proposed raising the school-leaving age to sixteen, encouraging early retirement and the shortening of the working week. Meanwhile a number of prominent Labour figures, such as G. D. H. Cole, Hugh Dalton and Herbert Morrison, were beginning to reshape Labour policy towards an acceptance of planning and Keynesian economics. *Labour's Immediate Programme* of 1937 looked forward to an increase in old-age pensions, an extension of the health services and a reduction of child mortality. Thus by the outbreak of the Second World War, the Labour Party was once again moving strongly in favour of greatly expanded social services. These concerns were expressed by the 1942 Labour Party conference which called for a comprehensive scheme of social security; adequate cash payments to provide security whatever the contingency; a scheme of family allowances; and a National Health Service. Independently having generated some of the earliest and most ambitious proposals for social reform, the Labour Party now found itself swimming very much with the mainstream of 'middle opinion' after a period of confusion and defensiveness in the 1930s.

The Evolution of Social Policy

A number of major themes emerge from the evolution of social policy which were of importance for British society both before and after 1945. The first is the importance of what is sometimes called 'collectivism', the belief that the state had a primary responsibility for the welfare of its citizens and the improvement in the quality of their lives. At the end of the Great War Seebohm Rowntree wrote:

> I submit that the day is past in which we could afford to compromise between the desires of the few and the needs of the many, or to perpetuate conditions in which large masses of the people are unable to secure the bare necessities of mental and physical efficiency.

The extension of state control during the war had proved a decisive experience for him, as for others. Hence Rodney Barker has written that the dominating political arguments of the second quarter of the twentieth century were 'of how the state should use its powers, not about what powers it should have'. Although *laissez faire* ideas remained a powerful influence on social policy, experience of the inter-war years confirmed amongst a broad range of opinion the necessity for a commitment by the state to improve the social conditions of the people.

Liberal improvers, progressive Conservatives, and socialists found themselves sharing some common ground in the assumption that it was the duty of the state to provide a better life for its citizens, which found expression in support for comprehensive social welfare, a national health service and a more humane treatment of those in need. It was an assumption which was to continue to find acceptance in the burgeoning of state welfare and social services.

Increased state intervention and central direction went hand in hand with faith in a more rational and ordered treatment of social questions – an essentially technocratic approach – which found its most characteristic expression in the enthusiasm for 'planning' which emerged in the 1930s and was to play an important part in the shaping of British society after 1945. Planning, at least in the form of extensive control of the 'reins of economic power', had traditionally occupied a central place in socialist thought, and public control of economic resources, production and allocation were part of the essential features of left-wing thought between the wars. This was emphasized by admiration for the achievements of the Russian Revolution and the Five Year Plans, so that during the inter-war years socialist writers such as G. D. H. Cole supported planning in contradiction to the chaos, irrationality and waste of the capitalist system. Capitalism was indicted as a gigantic muddle, whereas socialism stood for rationality and a coordinated approach to economic and social questions, with planning as the practical expression of socialism. In similar vein in 1934 Barbara Wootton in *Plan or No Plan* advocated the advantages of economic planning and central management in promoting equality, fairness and a reduction in unemployment, while Douglas Jay in *The Socialist Case* in 1938 argued that collectivist planning was the only way to achieve a just and fair society.

But while the socialist concern for planning was important, not least in view of Labour's victory at the polls in 1945, perhaps the most significant feature of the inter-war years was the acceptance by 'middle opinion' of the need for planning without the destruction of the capitalist system. In part this flowed from the faith in scientific solutions expressed by the young Lord Woolton and 'new Liberals' such as Rowntree and Beveridge, as well as many social investigators in the years after 1914. Whatever the disillusionments caused by the war, it served to stimulate faith amongst some sections of opinion in empirically based and rationally organized policies. Elements of this thinking can be found in the plans for post-war reconstruction formulated from 1917 onwards. Although frustrated by government cuts and the onset of the depression, the technocratic approach to social and economic problems emerged with renewed vigour with the deepening of the slump after 1929 and the growing consciousness of the persistence of serious economic and social problems. Dissatisfaction with the post-war world provoked in many minds the idea of greater coordination and control of policy. Problems could be solved if only the situations were properly analysed, a strategy evolved and powers taken to implement it. Such views embraced everyone, from those seeking *ad hoc* solutions to particular problems to those of both Left and Right who had more thoroughgoing 'plans' for social transformation. In this respect, both the extreme Left and the extreme Right had much in common in wanting to take over control from the established authorities and inaugurate a complete reformation of economy and society. Sir Oswald Mosley – as much a product of this approach as anyone – shared with socialists like G. D. H. Cole a profound disillusionment with the 'old gang' of politicians and the 'muddle' of *laissez faire* capitalism. What was more important, however, was that these sentiments were not confined to the periphery of politics. Even ostensibly conservative figures such as Neville Chamberlain saw their task as to bring 'order and logic' to public affairs, seen primarily in his abolition of the Poor Law and the creation of the centralized system of unemployment benefit under the Unemployment Assistance Board.

Planning, then, was not a uniquely left- or right-wing cause between the wars. The crucial response came from progressive capitalists, professional people, academics and centrist politicians who found in it a means of advance over a wide range of social and economic problems. Up to the 1930s, the word 'planning' was still primarily associated with town planning and landscape gardening and the first official use of the term came in the Housing and Town and Country Planning Acts of 1909 and 1919. As late as 1933, however, the *Oxford English Dictionary* did not recognize the existence of the single word 'planning', though it was by then coming into use on the continent as an alternative to totalitarianism, particularly in the fields of economic management and social policy. The formation in 1931 of Political and Economic Planning and the publication as a 20,000 word supplement to the *Week-End Review* of 'A National Plan for Great Britain' inaugurated the use in Britain. The article criticized the 'hopeless confusion of the post-war years' which had created the risk 'that in incompetent hands this country may go drifting on either towards a sharp crisis which might have revolutionary consequences, or to dictatorship, or perhaps worse still to gradual decline ...' In its call for 'rigorous constructive argument' and a general reorganization of the political, social and economic structure of the country it articulated the frustrations of a broad spectrum of opinion with existing tendencies. In *Reconstruction* in 1933, Harold Macmillan wrote that: '"Planning" is forced upon us ... not for idealistic reasons but because the old mechanism which served us when markets were expanding naturally and spontaneously is no longer adequate when the tendency is in the opposite direction.' Although the totalitarian overtones of 'planning' attracted some criticism and many socialists remained cool about the concept of a basically capitalist planned economy, the idea of planning had entered the mainstream of 'middle opinion' by the Second World War.

Viewed in perspective, the planning enthusiasm of the 1930s and 1940s represented the fusion of the still vital forces of optimism and social concern with the scientific and technocratic spirit of the twentieth century. Characterized by its faith in 'experts', a certain high-mindedness, and impatience with what Max Nicholson called the 'chronic and unshakeable boneheadedness of major elements in British society', the planning movement was, for better or worse, to have an important influence in the Britain that emerged from the Second World War.

12. *Wealth, Class and Elites*

The Distribution of Wealth

In spite of the still wide differences between various groups, the inter-war years saw the beginning of progress towards a more equal distribution of incomes, a process which was to be accelerated by the Second World War and continued into the post-war years. The distribution of wealth, however, was much more unequal than incomes and was to prove far less amenable to redistribution. This is shown by the persistently high percentage of all personal wealth owned by the wealthiest 1 per cent of the population, whether in land, property, stocks and shares or other assets (see Table 24). Moreover, even the

Table 24: Percentage of all
wealth owned by top 1 per cent of
individuals

1911–13	69
1924–30	60
1936–8	55
1946–8	50
1951–5	42
1960–62	42

reduction in the percentage owned by the top 1 per cent was not redistributed over the population at large, but, primarily, to the wealthiest 5 per cent who, in 1937, owned 79 per cent of all wealth. The other side of this coin was that in 1937, as in 1911, the great majority of the population had very little personal property. Three-quarters of the population of Britain, some eight million families, would, in 1937, if they had sold everything they possessed, have realized less than £100 each – for all intents and purposes they were essentially propertyless. Even after the Second World War, when the pound had roughly halved in value, 62 per cent of the population possessed private capital of less than £100. Thus, whatever the movement of incomes, between 1914 and 1945 Britain saw relatively little redistribution of wealth in spite of many indications to the contrary.

However, as a growing capitalist economy between 1914 and 1945, Britain offered increased opportunities for the accumulation of wealth. In 1880–1909 only twenty-two people left fortunes of over £2 million, but between 1910 and 1939 no fewer than sixty-one, while the annual number of millionaire fortunes rose from an average of almost ten in 1910–14 to thirteen in 1925–9. Nor was wealth accumulated only by the very rich. The number of estates worth more than £100,000 increased at a much faster rate after 1918 than in the Edwardian era. Indeed, much of the growth appears to have taken place at the level between £100,000 and £500,000, reflecting the success of increasingly large numbers of smaller merchants, retailers and manufacturers both in the war and in the post-war boom. Hence in 1925–9 an average of almost five hundred fortunes of over £100,000 were declared compared with an average of under three hundred in 1910–14. Although there was some falling off from this figure in the worst years of the depression from 1930–34, in the years prior to the Second World War more fortunes of over £100,000 were left than in any previous period of British history.

It was part of the myth of the 'lost generation' that the Great War had not only wiped out a generation, but also impoverished a whole class – the old landed interest. Thus Charles Masterman, in his *England after the War*, published in 1922, wrote:

In the retreat from Mons and the first battle of Ypres perished the flower of the British aristocracy ... In the useless slaughter of the Guards on the Somme or of the Rifle Brigade in Hooge Wood, half the great families of England, heirs of large estates and wealth, perished without a cry ... I note that sales are being announced every day in the newspapers, of historical country houses and of estates running into many thousands of acres.

It was a theme taken up by popular authors like Dornford Yates, one of whose novels, set in 1919, centred on the fortunes of an old estate, Merry Down, inhabited by the Bagots:

> One of the old school, Sir Anthony had stood his ground up to the last. The War had cost him dear. His only son was killed in the first months. His only grandson fell in the battles of the Somme. His substance, never fat, had shrunk to a mere shadow of its former self. The stout old heart fought the unequal fight month after month. Stables were emptied, rooms were shut up, thing after thing was sold. It remained for a defaulting solicitor to administer the *coup de grâce* ... On the twelfth day of August ... Merry Down was to be sold by auction ...

Being fiction, the prospective purchaser, Dunkelsbaum – 'origin doubtful' – was thwarted and the house passed into the 'good clean hands of an ex-Etonian'.

Undoubtedly, there was a grain of truth reflected in this fiction. Since the agricultural depression at the end of the nineteenth century there had been financial pressure on many smaller landed families whose resources were solely bound up with land. Higher taxation and the raising of death duties in the Great War pushed some of them over the edge altogether, either immediately after the war or during the agricultural depression of the 1920s. Land sales boomed in the immediate post-war years – half a million acres were on sale by the summer of 1919. The 1919 budget, raising death duties to 40 per cent on estates over £2 million, contributed to a fresh avalanche of sales, about a million acres being sold during the year. Amongst the sellers were many of the wealthiest families. The biggest sale of 1920 was the Duke of Rutland's disposal of half his Belvoir estate (28,000 acres) for £1½ million and other large disposals included the sale by the Duke of Sutherland of over quarter of a million acres in Scotland.

Such sales excited great gloom: 'The old order is doomed,'

wrote the Duke of Marlborough, while, in scarcely less sepul-
chral tones, *The Times* claimed in 1920:

> England is changing hands ... Will a profiteer buy it? Will it be
> turned into a school or an institution ... For the most part the sacrifices
> are made in silence ... The sons are perhaps lying in far away graves;
> the daughters secretly mourning someone dearer than a brother, have
> taken up some definite work away from home, seeking thus to still
> their aching hearts, and the old people, knowing there is no son or
> near relative left to keep up the old traditions, or so crippled by
> necessary taxation that they know the boy will never be able to carry
> on when they are gone, take the irrevocable step.

By the end of 1921 the *Estates Gazette* concluded that a quarter
of England had changed hands, a figure confirmed by F. M.
Thompson, who has noted that whereas in 1914 only 11 per
cent of agricultural land in England and Wales was occupied
by its owners, by 1927 owner-farmers occupied 36 per cent;
almost a quarter of agricultural land had passed from being
tenanted into the possession of owner-farmers. In the most
intense period of activity, between 1918 and 1921, between six
and eight million acres changed hands, the largest and most
rapid transfer of land at least since the dissolution of the
monasteries, and possibly since the Norman Conquest.

Land sales fell away after 1921, but there continued to be
a trickle of major disposals of land throughout the inter-war
years. Returns from agriculture remained low as rents fell to
pre-war levels in spite of a virtual doubling in prices and the
cost of labour, by 1936 reaching the lowest point since 1870.
The repeal of the Corn Production Act of 1921, offering
guaranteed prices, began a disastrous period of falling agricultural prices as cheap foreign food flooded the home market.
Prices of wheat fell through the floor, dropping to a sixth of
pre-war levels and showing a general decline of 50 per cent
between 1929 and 1931. Although the introduction of agricultural protection after 1932 and the setting-up of marketing
boards improved the situation, the pressure throughout was on
reducing costs and, if necessary, selling land. The Duke of Portland, surveying the situation in 1937, opined that

large estates ... have been and still are being broken up, and the houses attached to them sold to individuals most of whom have had little or no connexion with the land ... Many of the great country houses, when not in the occupation of strangers, or used for other purposes, quickly become derelict ... when I first lived at Welbeck the great neighbouring houses, such as Clumber, Thoresby and Rufford, were all inhabited by their owners ... Now not one ... is so occupied, except for a few days in the year ...

The real losers in this process were the landed gentry, a group whose fortunes had been in decline since the agricultural depression of the late nineteenth century. Without the spread of resources and means to diversify of the larger landowners, the inter-war years took a heavy toll of smaller, long-established families. It has been estimated that of the gentry families existing in Essex, Oxfordshire and Shropshire in the 1870s only a third retained their country seat by 1952. In that period, a third of the country houses in Shropshire had simply disappeared. Similarly, many of the new owner-farmers created in the re-distribution of land in the post-war years found the combination of the fall in prices and fixed mortgage payments ruinous. By the 1930s *The Times* claimed that half of Norfolk was virtually owned by the banks. In spite of a measure of revival in the late thirties, a struggling agriculture and half-derelict farms and houses formed a drab complement to the problems of the depressed areas. A government inquiry, the Scott Report, published in 1942, described the situation:

Less arable land was to be seen in the landscape, the number of derelict fields, rank with coarse matted grass, thistle, weeds and brambles, multiplied; ditches became choked and no longer served as effective drains; hedges became overgrown and straggled over the edges of other fields; gates and fences fell into disrepair; farm roads were left unmade. Signs of decay were to be seen also in many of the buildings ... the landscape of 1938 had, in many districts, assumed a neglected and unkempt appearance.

The number of owner-farmers remained at its 1927 figure up to the Second World War. Although a major redistribution of landed wealth had occurred in 1918–21, it had been virtually stopped in its tracks by the depression. Nor had the redistribution been a radical one. The bulk of land had gone to former tenants, 'new men' of business or finance, or to banks and syndicates. In spite of considerable encouragement in the form of the Smallholding Acts of 1919, 1926 and 1931, easier loan facilities through the Agriculture Credit Act of 1928, and a considerable amount of philanthropic interest in 'back to the land', there was no peasant take-over of the great estates. Farms remained large by continental standards and in spite of the long-drawn-out decline of the old gentry, continued after 1945 with still higher taxation and estate duties, landed wealth remained concentrated in relatively few hands.

Paradoxically, however, the sale of land and the rationalization of households helped to perpetuate a wealthy landed class in the inter-war years. F. M. Thompson has suggested that while a number of great landowners may have been forced to sell property in settlement of death duties or other debts, only a minority of the wealthiest did so. Of the forty noblemen who sold part of their estates in the first half of 1919 in only six cases had death duties become payable since 1914. Sale of land often meant shedding an asset with a poor return compared with mortgage payments from former tenants or with other forms of investment. Many of the wealthiest landed families emerged into the inter-war years still in possession of their country seats, frequently with smaller acreages, but often with healthier incomes and a more viable basis for maintaining their position than before 1914. Indeed, even in the decade before the Second World War, more than thirty landowners had gross annual rents of more than £25,000 and four of more than £100,000, while the deaths of some of the great landed magnates revealed still substantial fortunes. The 11th Duke of Bedford left £4.7 million on his death in 1940, Wentworth, 1st Viscount Allendale, left £3.2 million in 1923, and Alan, 8th Duke of Northumberland, £2.5 million in 1930. In inter-war Britain there were still approximately thirty landed millionaires and over seventy half-millionaires.

However, the contribution of the landed proprietors to the

wealthy elite was declining. It has been estimated that as late as the 1880s half of the men leaving estates valued at over £500,000 were landowners, but that by the outbreak of the Great War their place was increasingly being overtaken by those who had made their money elsewhere. Hence between 1920 and 1939 landed proprietors accounted for approximately a sixth of all estates left worth over £500,000. An indication of this change in the distribution of wealth was that of the three largest fortunes left between 1910 and 1939 none came from a landowner: the largest, in 1933, was the £36.7 million left by Sir John Ellerman, the shipowner and financier; next was the £13.5 million left in 1927 by the brewer, Edward Guinness, the 1st Earl of Iveagh; and the third was the £10.5 million left in 1930 by James Williamson, 1st Baron Ashton, a linoleum manufacturer.

Although traditional sources of manufacturing wealth were well represented in the ranks of those who were millionaires or half-millionaires from 1914 to 1945, including coalmining, engineering and textiles, one of the most striking features of the distribution of wealth during these years lay in the growth of fortunes earned through the consumption industries, especially food, drink and tobacco, accounting for a quarter of all millionaires between 1920 and 1939. These included famous brewing dynasties, such as the Guinnesses, Whitbreads, Charringtons and Worthingtons, so that by 1920–39 the number of millionaire brewers alone was equal to the number of cotton and chemical millionaires. Amongst the food manufacturers, families such as the Frys, Cadburys, Leas and Blackwells were represented, and amongst the tobacco giants, the relations of the Bristol-based Wills family. Another important consumer-orientated group were the newspaper barons like Alfred Harmsworth, 1st Viscount Northcliffe, who left a £5.2 million estate in 1922. But in spite of the growing representation of these new sources of profitable business, greater than in any earlier period, the most significant feature of the wealth-owners of the first part of the twentieth century was that they earned their wealth not in manufacturing, whether in 'old' or 'new' industries, but disproportionately from commerce and finance, as merchants, bankers, shipowners, merchant bankers, stock-brokers and insurers. In the inter-war years this group accounted for almost 40 per cent of all millionaires and almost 50 per cent of half-millionaires.

In a sense, these men and the larger financial and commercial group were typical of a development of some importance for the nature of wealth creation in twentieth-century Britain. They were men who made their fortunes by the processing of wealth rather than by creating it. Few of the merchant bankers were self-made men, but heirs to family businesses which reached back to before the turn of the nineteenth century. There were, undoubtedly, cases between the wars of thrusting businessmen who accumulated great wealth. Many of them, such as William Morris, Viscount Nuffield, the motor manufacturer, were already millionaires by the outbreak of the Second World War, but did not reveal the full extent of their wealth until their deaths after 1945. In a similar category were active business men such as Alfred Herbert, the machine tool manufacturer, who died aged ninety-one in 1957 worth £5.3 million, William Stephenson, the chairman of Woolworths, who died aged eighty-three in 1963 leaving £3.5 million, or Joseph Rank, who left £5.9 million in 1972 from his cinema and foodstuffs business, all of whom built up part of their fortunes between the wars. They also included men such as Horace Moore of British Home Stores, Simon Marks of Marks and Spencer, and Sir Montague Burton of Burton's, all of whom left fortunes of over half a million after 1945. However, the main feature of the 'very wealthy' in Britain even after 1945, when it includes those who were making money between the wars, was that they were drawn very heavily from the commercial and financial sectors, who accounted for over 40 per cent of all millionaires and almost the same percentage of half-millionaires in the years 1940–69. This was also reflected in the geographical distribution of the wealthy in Britain between the wars. By far the largest percentage, almost a third, were based on London, the centre of finance and investment, with fewer based on the provincial cities and towns than had been the case before 1914. While powerful and wealthy provincial families continued to exist, notably among both the territorial magnates, like the Earl of Derby in Lancashire, and the regionally based commercial families, like the Wills in Bristol and the Rootes in the West Midlands, one of the distinctive features of the wealthy in the inter-war years was that they were increasingly a metropolitan rather than a provincial class.

The important researches of W. D. Rubinstein have indicated some of the principal features of the wealthy in Britain compared with other countries. They demonstrate that the most typical sources of wealth in the inter-war years were not the spectacular fortunes of men like William Morris or the Wills family, but the financial and mercantile fortunes of families like the Rothschilds and the Sterns. In that sense, the City of London was more typical of wealth creation in the inter-war years than Lancashire or Cowley. Even the great landowners, the Bedfords, Derbys and Sutherlands, retained a much greater predominance in the wealth-owning structure than the representatives of the second industrial revolution. Those who argue, therefore, that the entrepreneurial spirit was not as strong in Britain as in other countries during the nineteenth and twentieth centuries have a point, but not the one often made: entrepreneurial initiative could undoubtedly reap rich rewards in Britain during the first half of the twentieth century, but the examples of spectacular fortunes made through innovative initiative and enterprise were set amongst an even larger number who made their money by the servicing of wealth rather than by its creation. In so far as the property developer, stockbroker, banker and landowner continued to be amongst the most wealthy men of Britain after 1940, accounting for almost half of the greatest estates, it was a trend which was simply a continuation of something which was already evident before 1914. In Britain between 1914 and 1945, the self-made entrepreneurial millionaire was the exception rather than the rule.

Second, however, it has to be noted that the wealthiest men

in Britain did not compare either in scale of wealth or social power with those on the continent or in America. It has been estimated that the wealthiest American multi-millionaires of the late nineteenth and early twentieth centuries were usually ten or twenty times richer than the richest British millionaires. In spite of the fabulous wealth of men like the Duke of West-minster, Sir John Ellerman or William Morris, they were dwarfed by the vast conglomerate fortunes built up by John Pierpont Morgan or Henry Rockefeller. In large part this reflected the relatively conservative nature of British wealth creation in the twentieth century as well as the more limited opportunities for massive accumulation presented by the British economy, for, however promising the opportunities offered to wealth creation in Britain, they failed to match those which later industrialization and still unexploited resources gave to the businessmen of Europe and the United States.

Third, the road to riches was very diverse. People could make their wealth in widely different ways in spite of the dominance of finance and commerce, and there were still a minority of 'self-made' men who were in the process of making their fortunes in inter-war Britain. However, the conservatism of wealth in Britain was already showing up in the fact that only a small minority of millionaires or half-millionaires were self-made men. Location, particularly in the financial heart of Britain, the City of London, was often more important than entrepreneurial effort. Even the archetypal penniless Jewish immigrant was far less likely to make a fortune than the relatives of an established Jewish banking house in the capital. Making wealth was less often a matter of race or exceptional entre-preneurship than of being located in the kind of trade which made wealth creation relatively straightforward. The typical plutocrat in the Britain of 1914–45 was more likely to have inherited a substantial sum to start off with and to be situated in a sector of finance and commerce where further accumulation was easier than in other areas.

In spite of the still heavy concentration of wealth at the upper end of the property-owning spectrum, there was evidence of some shift of property from the higher to the middle and lower levels. In 1900–1901 only 17 per cent of the population left enough property for it to be recorded in the probate records. Between then and the outbreak of the Second World War there is evidence of a greater spreading of wealth without necessarily eroding the main inequalities between richest and poorest. Hence in 1938–9, while the estates of just four millionaires accounted for more than the estates of over 85,000 of the poorest of those who died, the most striking feature was that the percentage of all adults leaving *some* property was almost double the figure in 1900–1901, some 33 per cent. While two-thirds of the population still died with nothing, the bulk of this gain came at the lower end of the spectrum – in small estates worth up to £500. In large part this reflected the growing importance of house-ownership for a section of the middle classes. It also reflected the growth of small savings between the wars, especially through building societies, insurance policies, and post office and savings banks. Hence while a substantial portion of the population remained propertyless and, as late as 1953, a third had no liquid assets at all and only a fifth of the population owned its own home, there was already evidence by the Second World War that the ownership of some wealth was gradually filtering through to a larger sector of the population, even if the percentage owned by the wealthiest section remained very high.

Class

Class is an elusive concept, yet it is one which clearly formed an integral feature of British society. However arbitrarily it is defined, the terminology of class formed a part of common speech from the early nineteenth century and found acceptance as part of the normal vocabulary in the twentieth. The relationship of this terminology with actual and operative conditions of everyday life raises immense difficulties, above all because, while some analyses of class start from fixed assumptions about how classes can be defined, the boundaries of class are at best blurred and usually quite difficult to establish definitively. None the less, broad notions of what constitutes class form part of both popular and academic discussions of society in the twentieth century: they accord primarily with occupational and cultural divisions within the population as a whole. The former derives essentially from a view of the kind of work which people do and the cultural attributes which were attached to it. The difficulties of these divisions are easily illustrated: a clergyman living in a poor country parish might well have had an annual income less than that of a skilled printer working in Fleet Street; culturally, however, most would have little difficulty in assigning the former to the middle class or the latter to the working class. Habits of work, dress and speech, inherited notions of status attached to particular careers and life-styles, and, in Britain as a whole, regional differences all con-tribute to the complexity of the concept of class. Difficulties in defining the boundaries of class are compounded by the presence of evident and commonly perceived stratifications within classes. The preference for the euphemism 'classes' in-stead of 'class' represents an awareness that differences between, say, 'rough' and 'respectable' in the working class, or between 'lower' and 'upper' middle class, may be at least as important to the people and society concerned than differences between broader categories. Again, the point has often been made that the similarities in values and life-style of, say, a skilled artisan and a small shopkeeper may well give them more in common than either had with a casually employed unskilled labourer or a peer of the realm.

Nevertheless, it has generally been accepted that broad occupational categories provide a basis for distinguishing between the social classes in Britain, providing that their in-evitable limitations are borne in mind. Because they only refer to the 'economically active' population, they omit important groups at both ends of the social spectrum. Some of the very wealthy throughout this period were effectively 'unoccupied', forming a category of men, and some women, who were of 'independent means'. At the other end of the scale, in 1911, were two and a half million men who were 'unoccupied' whether because of sickness, incapacity or unemployment. Moreover, not the least of the injustices from which women have suffered is the automatic ascription to them of the social class of their husbands. Of the eleven and a half million women in 1911 who were classed as 'unoccupied', it might well be the case that a majority can be safely ascribed to a class based upon their husband's occupation, but when one comes to consider the cultural and social ramifications of class, it takes only a brief acquaintance to recognize that the tone and style of a household could as well be determined by the background and aspirations of women as much as the occupations of men. By and large, however, as the Oxford sociologist A. H. Halsey has argued, in any industrial society, the occupational structure provides the starting-point for the 'anatomy of class': 'Groups and individuals differ first according to the terms on which they can sell their skills and their labour on the market, and second according to the actual conditions of their work – its autonomy, or lack of it, its intrinsic satisfactions, and its attendant amenities.'

The extent to which occupational changes modified conceptions of class is one of the most difficult features of inter-war social history to chart with any accuracy. Class was so inextricably bound up with notions of status that it is almost impossible to delineate the infinite gradations which might be applied. Occupation, background, education, habits of speech, dress and recreation could combine in kaleidoscopic fashion to produce an impossibly complex set of steps in the social structure, but an observer with a fine 'nose' for class, such as George Orwell, had little difficulty in assigning class by accent or dress. Amongst the denizens of a London doss-house he found a drunken ex-Etonian, immediately recognizable by accent and shoes from its more typical clientele. Similarly, most contemporaries would have had little difficulty in assigning themselves and others to one of the broad categories of social class. The working classes were those in manual occupations, employed by others, essentially propertyless and living by hiring their labour to others;

they possessed a basic literacy and numeracy, sufficient to fill in a 'perm' on the football pools, work out the odds on a race-horse, pen a basic letter or postcard, and understand a payslip. Physically they were, on average, shorter, more lightly built and less healthy. Life expectancy was significantly shorter for them, as the working classes had a higher attrition rate from infant and maternal mortality, as well as from every other disease. They were less well fed and their children left school earlier with fewer prospects of advancement than the children in other classes. But these features were less obvious than clothing or accent. Cheap mass-produced clothing combined with rising affluence made it possible for the better-off sections of the working class to dress somewhere near the standard of the upper classes, at least on some occasions, but the differences in day-to-day wear between working-class men and women and the members of other classes were still obvious. Flat-cap and muffler were still almost standard uniform in working-class districts, while many older women still tended to dress in black. Working clothes and overalls marked out the manual worker from the man who went to work in collar and tie and usually did not expect to get his clothes or hands dirty at work. These were still crucial factors in the nuances of class, enshrined in injunctions from ambitious working-class parents that their children should obtain a 'collar and tie' job and not work 'with their hands'. Speech offered a complex gazetteer of class dif-ferences. Dialect was gradually losing its hold in places like the North of England, while Welsh suffered considerable erosion through a deliberate policy of Anglicization in schools and the decline of Welsh nonconformity: by 1914, for example, the language of trade-union business and of political meetings in an area like South Wales tended to be English, not Welsh. Regional accents remained strong, but there was little difficulty in picking out the 'educated' language of the middle and upper classes. The growth of private and state secondary education provided largely better-off children with a style of speech and vocabulary different from that of the bulk of the working class. The growth of radio and, later, of talking pictures tended to reinforce snobberies about language and accent. The so-called 'Oxford accent', employed by B B C announcers, was a curious, clipped speech officially described as 'received standard Southern English'. It was far removed from any common speech in use in working-class areas – some thought by any class, anywhere – and was essentially based on a rather artificial conception of the English of the upper classes.

Clothes and speech were the obvious badges of class, difficult to gauge accurately at the margins, but clear enough for the great majority of people to be able to assign themselves to 'upper', 'middle' or 'working' class. Material collected by Mass Observation from 1936 and from Margaret Stacey's survey of the Oxfordshire town of Banbury carried out after the Second World War confirmed that approximately half the population described itself as 'working class', a little less than half as 'upper-middle, middle, and lower-middle' class, and only a small number, about two in every hundred, as the 'upper' class. Within these broad categories, however, it was clear that people made subtle distinctions about their status and relationship to others. As has already been suggested, differences within classes were often at least as important in people's minds as the differences perceived between classes. Stacey found it possible to distinguish three categories within the 'working class', widely recognized by people themselves, between 'rough', 'ordinary' and 'respectable'. 'Rough' might include those frequently in debt, drunken, feckless, living at a standard which fell short of standards of 'respectability', which might include staying out of debt and away from the pawnshop, keeping up the rent, a tidy home, paid-up funeral insurance and regular employment. Robert Roberts described how, when neighbours quarrelled in his Salford slum, the symbols of status formed part of a formidable calculus controlled by the local matriarchs:

One waved, for instance, a 'clean' rent book (that great status symbol of the times) in the air, knowing the indicted had fallen in arrears. Now manners and morals were arraigned before a mass public tribunal ... Purse-lipped and censorious, the matriarchs surveyed the scene soaking it all in, shocked by the vulgarity of it all, unless, of course, their own family was engaged. Then later, heads together, and from evidence submitted, they made grim readjustments on the social ladder.

For the middle classes, salaried status, a widening range of consumer goods such as motor cars and domestic appliances, better housing — increasingly house ownership — and the possession of domestic servants were important clues to a family's status. For example, considerable significance might be attached to having a uniformed maid. One middle-class woman remarked of the early 1930s: 'I remember girls at school judging each other's wealth by the number of maids each had. And sometimes, I suspect, inventing an extra one to impress their friends. We had two.'

Were class barriers crumbling in Britain between the wars? Many felt not: to some, indeed, the polarizations between classes seemed as acute as ever. In their social survey *The Condition of Britain*, published in 1937, G. D. H. and M. I. Cole concluded that Britain was still essentially 'two nations', or taking account of the growing numbers of 'middle groups' lying between rich and poor, 'three nations', with a still high degree of social rigidity. John Hilton, in 1938, in *Rich Man, Poor Man*, also argued that the distribution of wealth was still too grossly unequal for there to be anything other than a highly stratified society. George Orwell's explorations of 'low-life' and the depressed areas led him to describe England as 'the most class-ridden country under the sun'. Such views have to be treated with caution: the Coles were avowedly socialist writers and Orwell an ex-Etonian with a peculiar sensitivity to nuances of status and class. None the less, class distinctions were obvious enough for more than a few writers to remark on them. For example, during the Second World War Mass Observation found that the political change people most commonly desired to see after the war was a reduction in class distinctions. Moreover, there is a case for arguing that these years saw the development of a much more pervasive sense of class, particularly through the growth of the trade-union movement and the rise of Labour as the main opposition to the Conservatives. Mass union membership and the declining influence of some bodies, such as the churches, which transcended class boundaries, left the way open for attachment to much broader, class-based associations. Although, for many, union membership and a vote for a Labour candidate might count for little, both were becoming part of the way in which working people might identify themselves. The early part of this period, particularly between 1910 and 1926, had been times of great political excitement and industrial militancy. There does not have to be too indiscriminate an acceptance of the notion of 'class-consciousness' to recognize that the effects of events such as the 'Red Clydeside' or the miners' strike of 1926, not to mention the depression, the hunger marches and the means test, could sharpen class divisions, at least for some. Moreover, in some areas at least, such as South Wales, parts of Lancashire and Yorkshire, and Clydeside, the rise of the labour movement was as much a social as a political phenomenon, in which whole communities were inextricably bound up with the rise of a form of 'labour culture', revolving around union branches, trades councils, miners' welfare institutions, the Co-op, women's sections and local working men's clubs. In turn, there was also increasing consolidation of the middle classes around the Conservative Party, as the Liberal Party went into decline and the Labour Party emerged as the main challenger. Stacey found in Banbury that 'The disparity of attitude and interest, for example, between the small scale traditional proprietor and the large scale non-traditional manager ... is obscured by a common opposition to the Labour Party and its policies ...' Indeed, if the psephologists have anything to tell the social historians about the inter-war years, it is that this period saw the consolidation in national and local elections of a two-party system, Conservatives representing largely middle-class voters and Labour representing the working class. This was not a universal picture and areas of particular political complexity stand out, but if more stable political allegiances were hallmarks of a strengthening of class feeling, then there is some evidence to suggest that this was happening between the wars.

This should not, however, be confused with arguing that

class conflict was necessarily sharp or open. Political allegianc
was worn fairly lightly by the great majority of electors and
only a small minority were activists in political parties or trade
unions. Nor can the class structure be regarded as static. The
growth of the 'salariat', of people such as managers, civil
servants, schoolteachers and technicians, and the upward movement of women workers to clerical and administrative jobs,
represented a degree of social mobility to which both increased
educational opportunities and an expanding economy contributed. Although the majority of people continued to die in the
social class in which they were born, there was a significant
degree of movement from one class to another. Individual
examples abound of men and women who moved up or down
the social scale. One of the writers mentioned above, John
Hilton (1880–1943), had a career almost straight out of Samuel
Smiles. Starting life as an apprentice to a mill mechanic in
Bolton, he attended evening classes at Bolton Technical School;
later he became foreman and manager of an engineering works;
then a lecturer and technical journalist; he moved on to become
a civil servant, and by the 1930s was not only Professor of
Industrial Relations at Cambridge, but a regular weekly broad-
caster for the BBC and a writer in the *News Chronicle*. There
were also examples of self-made men of business, such as John
Sainsbury (1844–1928), founder of the supermarket chain,
whose father was a worker in the frame and ornament trade
in Lambeth; Robert Fleming (1845–1933), 'the pioneer of the
investment trust', son of a Dundee shopkeeper; Ernest Gates
(1873–1925), son of a bricklayer who acquired the Saltaire
Worsted Mills and left £938,000 on his death; and most
dramatic of all, William Morris, Lord Nuffield (1877–1963),
who, starting work in a bicycle shop at the age of sixteen,
amassed one of the largest fortunes ever seen in Britain. Politics
too, particularly Labour politics, had its share of upward social
mobility: Ernest Bevin, who after an elementary school education and working as a farm labourer and carter became a
trade-union secretary, and ultimately Minister of Labour in
Churchill's wartime coalition and Foreign Secretary under

..tlee from 1945 to 1951; or Labour's first Prime Minister, Ramsay MacDonald, who was the illegitimate son of a Scottish servant girl and a ploughman and rose through journalism and politics.

There was also movement the other way. Amongst the down-and-outs encountered by George Orwell was 'Bozo', son of a bankrupt bookseller, who after work as a house-painter, a spell in the army and work in Paris, following a serious accident and a crushed foot, had settled down to a makeshift life as a pavement artist or 'screever' in London, usually sleeping in cheap lodging houses, the casual wards of the workhouse or on the Embankment. At a higher social level, the tendency for even the very wealthy to share their property equally or nearly equally amongst their heirs frequently led to younger sons and daughters adopting a rather lower social status than their parents – what one historian has noted as the translation 'from stately home to villa', living on unimaginative investments at a comfortable but not particularly lavish scale, perhaps a generation or more later to be absorbed into the ranks of 'distressed gentlefolk' through the effects of inflation and successive subdivision of capital. Ex-officers begging in the street were a common sight for some years after the Great War and the impoverished 'gentleman' was almost a stereotype in several works of fiction. For example a highly successful novel of 1932, *Sorrell and Son*, told the story of a bankrupted gentleman, scrimping and saving to maintain the vestiges of respectability and send his son to public school. No less important, and much more common, were the often small but decisive movements within the social structure – skilled men and clerks driven into unemployment, for instance, often desperate to retain self-respect through pathetic marks of self-esteem, a worn-out collar or a battered suit, quite literally starving in some cases, rather than sell their tools, the crucial symbol of their former status.

Such examples illustrate that Britain was far from being a completely static or closed society and that both upward and downward social mobility were possible. There was also some fudging of the sharper distinctions of class with the growth of affluence and mass consumerism, particularly in the more prosperous parts of Britain and amongst the 'new middle class'. The new super cinemas might have different prices for circle and stalls, but they offered the same comfort and quality of entertainment to everybody, whether shopgirl or local bank manager. The new chain stores also catered for a wider social spectrum than the traditional corner shop or the exclusive department store. Neither social mobility nor mass consumerism had abolished class differences between the wars, but they increasingly blurred some of its sharper edges.

A Governing Class?

Up to 1914 one of the most striking features of British society was the continued importance of the landed aristocracy in politics and government. The landed aristocracy of the late Victorian and Edwardian period was relatively small in numbers, but both wealthy and influential. Between 1886 and 1916 almost half the members of the Cabinet were aristocrats, with only a slightly smaller proportion coming from a land-owning background. But the changes in the social, economic and political structure of the country were gradually undermining their position. The creation of new peerages, 420 between 1911 and 1950, increasingly brought into the aristocracy men of business, public service and political background. Considerable numbers were drawn from industry, the law, and the armed forces, but, numerically, the largest single group of men elevated to the peerage between the wars were former members of the House of Commons, including middle-class and professional men put forward by the Labour Party to increase its representation in the Upper Chamber.

Between 1916 and 1935 almost a quarter of all Cabinet personnel were drawn from the aristocracy, while less than a quarter came from the working class, almost all of them during Labour's short periods of office. Conservative administrations were composed, by and large, from men of aristocratic or upper-middle-class origin, including amongst the former some of the largest landed magnates in the country. In 1886–1916, half of the Conservatives entering the Cabinet had been aristocrats; between 1916 and 1935 they still formed a third; and a quarter as late as 1935–55. In contrast the Labour Party's elite was composed almost equally of members of the middle and working classes. While Cabinet Ministers were generally of a rather higher social status than their followers, the House of Commons represented a predominantly middle- and upper-class complexion. No less than 68 per cent of Conservative MPs of the period 1920–40 had been educated at public schools, over a quarter, 27.5 per cent, at Eton. The number of MPs of working-class background never rose above a third between 1916 and 1955, and these sat almost exclusively on the Labour benches. At the other end of the social spectrum was a strong upper-class element, representatives of the landed aristocracy and big business, sitting predominantly on the Conservative benches. In 1928, the House of Commons still contained fifty-eight sons of peers or baronets. In between, men of middle-class background were distributed between the parties.

If the political rulers of Britain were drawn predominantly from the upper and middle classes, the senior elements in the Civil Service were even more socially exclusive. According to a survey carried out by the WEA at the beginning of the Second World War, of 271 Home Civil Servants earning £1,000 a year or over whose educational background was known, more than two-thirds, 190, came from public schools, forty-three of them from Eton, Winchester, Rugby, Harrow and Marlborough. A similar percentage of the Indian Civil Service and Dominion Governors were from a public school background. Although these figures related to those educated in the Edwardian era, Civil Service recruitment only slowly widened. In 1929 over a quarter of those entering the higher Civil Service by open competition came from twelve major public schools. Ten years later, the figure was a fifth, with about a third of all entrants coming from one type of public school or other. Even with a system of competitive examination, the educational advantage of the best public schools, combined with the interview tests, which probably favoured public school and Oxbridge products, meant that the higher reaches of British administration were heavily dominated by men of a similar background. Even by 1950 its composition had changed relatively little and was to be a cause of concern well into the post-war era.

The traditional 'top' professions were also dominated by men of a similar background. In 1942, fifty-six out of sixty-two Bishops of whom we have information were public school men and twenty-one out of twenty-four Deans; for the Appeal and High Court Judges the number was thirty-three out of thirty-seven, while two-thirds of all County Court Judges, Recorders, Metropolitan Magistrates, and Stipendiary Magistrates were public school men. A particularly interesting case was represented by the army, which had traditionally drawn heavily upon the aristocracy and landed gentry to staff its officer corps. These two groups together provided 33 per cent of all Colonels and 42 per cent of Generals in the army in 1914. The army remained a narrow world, cultivating the tribal loyalties of its regimental system, and an ethos of sport, hunting and social exclusiveness. Although the flow of recruits from the landed gentry was reduced in the 1920s as a result of the depression in agriculture, there was little evidence of an extensive broadening of social recruitment to the officer corps.

The business elite was a more differentiated body, but in several sectors public school influence was strong. Eighty-six out of 103 directors of the three major banks in 1940 were public school men, no less than sixty-five from the five major schools; similarly, of fifty-two directors of the four main railway companies, forty-three were public school products and thirty-four from the five top schools. According to a survey of 1,000 leading manufacturers in the steel industry, 87 per cent of those entering in 1905–25 came from the highest social class, and even in 1935–47 the figure was 80 per cent. In an industry with smaller units of production, the hosiery industry, the number of leading manufacturers from an upper-class background was just under a half. One marked tendency, however,

with the growth of larger firms and combines was the success
of managers and accountants, unrelated to the founders, in
climbing to the top of industry. A prime example was Sir Francis
D'Arcy Cooper, a member of a firm of accountants, who
assisted in the reorganization of Unilever and in 1925 succeeded
its founder William Lever, Lord Leverhulme, as chairman.
There were the self-made men, Lever himself, William Morris
and Lord Woolton, director of Lewis's, the Liverpool-based
department store chain. Another feature was the entry into
politics and government by businessmen, particularly during
the First World War under Lloyd George's premiership. Several
were rewarded with peerages, and some continued to play a
significant part in the politics of the inter-war years, though
the number of Cabinet Ministers from an entrepreneurial or
managerial background between 1916 and 1955 was pro-
portionately quite small – only a third that of the professions
and little greater than that of the landowners. None the less,
a business background accounted for several of the most prominent political figures in this period, Bonar Law, the
Chamberlains and Stanley Baldwin, for instance.

In general, the most remarkable feature of the main elite
groups in this period – in politics, administration, the professions
and business – was their similarity of educational background,
particularly in the importance of a public school education and
the influence of the two ancient English universities, Oxford
and Cambridge. According to figures worked out by R. H.
Tawney in *Equality* in 1931, of 691 holders of 'high office' in
the church, state and industry for whom information is available, 524 or 76 per cent were educated at public schools. Eleven
years later, the investigation by the WEA suggested that of
830 office holders, 636 had attended public schools, a percentage
virtually identical with the earlier figure, at 77 per cent. Of
these, 40 per cent had attended one of five schools, Eton,
Winchester, Rugby, Harrow and Marlborough. Such a
similarity of background gave the leaders of the major elite
groups in British society considerable homogeneity, particularly
facilitating a degree of common outlook and shared assump-

tions. Although the trade-union leadership stood apart from this establishment, the Labour Party itself contained a significant portion of men of similar background.

Some changes were taking place in the elite. The emergence of the Labour Party and the growing influence of trade-unionists within it brought some men of quite different and often humble backgrounds to the forefront of the political stage. The Great War was to bring Labour politicians and trade-unionists into positions of government and high administration, as again in the 1940s, ultimately to form a government with a clear majority in Parliament for the first time in 1945. There was also some evidence of the broadening of the basis of recruitment to the higher posts in the Civil Service. In the business world, there was evidence of the supplanting of entrepreneurs by the growth of large-scale combines headed by managers. In another way, the old nineteenth-century elites based on commerce, land and manufacturing were increasingly conflated into one, based primarily on London and the South-East and increasingly dominated by financial wealth.

Even so, the dominant groups at the centre of British life were still a remarkably homogeneous group at the outbreak of the Second World War. They also derived greater importance from the growing role of central government and changes in the character of local elites. The latter showed distinct changes by the first half of the twentieth century. Even by 1914, in most areas the local landowners had already given way to the salaried officials of local government or come to share local prestige with new men of business and finance. While vestiges of an almost feudal influence remained, particularly in parts of Scotland and the more thoroughly rural areas of Britain, increasingly the substance of power had passed into other hands and a figure such as Lord Derby was recognized as something of an anachronism by the 1920s. The number of 'county men' with strong local ties represented in Parliament was falling. In the general election of January 1910, 65 per cent of Conservative MPs elected for the first time for 'county' seats were local men, while by the 1918 election the number had fallen to 46

per cent. Similarly the number of local men re-elected for
county seats showed a fall, though rather smaller than of those
elected for the first time. Even so, old-established county names
like the Talbots from Sussex, Herberts from Somerset and
Carews from Devon were amongst those still being elected to
seats for rural areas in the 1920s. A seat such as the Ludlow
division of Shropshire was still represented in the 1920s by the
descendants of two families, the Clives and the Herberts, who
had held the seat since the eighteenth century. But the numbers
of such men were on the decline. In part this was a result of
the heavy casualties of younger sons from titled and landed
families in the First World War. But it was not merely a matter
of the war. Not only were fewer of the landed class going into
Parliament in the 1920s and 1930s, but fewer of those that were
were being elected to represent their localities. The 'knight of
the shire', a local landed man representing his area in Parliament,
was now becoming a thing of the past.

By 1900 a substantial portion of the House of Commons
was made up of businessmen representing the constituencies
from which they derived their livelihoods. Like the landed
gentry before them, these representatives of local commercial
or manufacturing wealth often saw political representation as
a natural by-product of local status. It has been estimated that
the strength of local business interests represented in the House
of Commons increased considerably after the 1918 general
election. Over three-quarters of the newly elected Conservative
borough members were local men, compared with only a third
in 1910. Many of these were businessmen, such as Sir Herbert
Austin, C. E. L. Lyle and Douglas Vickers. But these figures
do not necessarily represent a predominant trend. It has been
noted that even before 1914 many wealthy businessmen tended
to move away from direct involvement in their local communities. Many moved into country estates outside their local
town, to local seaside resorts, spa towns, or the upper-class areas
of London and the larger provincial cities. In many cases such
movements signalled a break with their local communities –
an 'abdication of the governors' – which left the field open

for local professional men, small businessmen, the 'shopocracy', trade-unionists and political nominees. While the typical MP of the inter-war years was still likely to be a local businessman, the very wealthy had often already moved beyond involvement in local matters.

By the 1930s it was not uncommon for a local aristocrat to sit on the board of a London-based company, something quite rare fifty years earlier, but have only marginal involve- ment in the affairs of his locality. It was increasingly common for managers to be put into local firms as the second and third generation of entrepreneurs moved into a more cosmopolitan or less closely involved relationship with their localities. Local landowners and manufacturers were more and more drawn into a wider world of business, partly through the effects of the depression on local industries, but also through the inevitable need to diversify to protect capital. Thus amalgamations, diversification and the entry of nationally based concerns in- evitably undermined purely local sources of wealth. Manu- facturing, like landowning, families were moving into finance, banking, insurance, investment, holding companies and property where local interests were not crucial. They were also under challenge from the growth of the Labour Party and the trade-union movement. Hence the kind of political and social domination exercised by many men of wealth before 1914 was being undermined, though not entirely eliminated. In so far as there were exceptions, they tended to be self-made men or those who, for one reason or another, still felt the desire to play a local role. Examples of both types can be found both before and after the Second World War. First-generation busi- nessmen such as William Morris were prepared to act as local benefactors or even participate in local politics, but, by and large, the very wealthy saw their role in a national context. Local government was increasingly dominated by the lower- middle classes, the 'shopocracy' rather than the 'plutocracy'.

13. *Religion, Crime and Punishment*

Religion and Belief

One of the most significant features in twentieth-century Britain has been the decline of organized religion, judged both in terms of the allegiance and membership of the Christian churches and their role as arbiters of public conventions and private morality. From what, with hindsight, appears a peak of membership and influence in the late-Victorian and Edwardian era, the Christian churches began a period of relative decline which became precipitate after 1945. Increasingly, Christianity and formal religious adherence of other kinds was becoming a marginal feature of British society, in which secular conventions increasingly dominated public and private life.

In institutional terms, organized religion remained numerically significant throughout this period. Combined church membership for the Protestant denominations and the Catholic Church in Britain totalled almost eight million people in 1914 and remained at or near this figure in 1945. This apparent strength, however, reflected serious signs of decline. By 1914, although the Christian churches reached a higher total of active members than ever before and wielded a still important influence, their membership comprised only a fraction of the total population. While in the generation before 1914, church membership showed both an absolute rise and a rise relative to the total population, it was followed by a sharp decline during the Great War. In spite of fresh growth during the 1920s, in which the churches virtually held their own as a proportion of a still-growing British population, by the early 1930s membership as a percentage of the adult population went into decline. The Second World War emphasized this trend, as total church membership fell further by 1945 and declined even more as a percentage of the total population:

Table 25: British church membership, 1910–50 (thousands)

	Episcopalian	Scottish Presbyterian	Nonconformists	Catholics
1910	2,418	1,232	2,020	2,216
1920	2,410	1,281	1,963	2,502
1930	2,529	1,299	2,001	2,781
1940	2,255	1,311	1,874	3,023
1950	2,077	1,304	1,696	3,499

Source: R. Currie, A. Gilbert and Lee Horsley, *Churches and Church-goers: Patterns of Church Growth in the British Isles since 1700*, Clarendon Press, Oxford, 1977, p. 25.

All the churches lost ground substantially during the Great War. Conventionally this has been seen as a direct result of the effects of the horror and carnage of the war, the association of many churchmen with bellicose patriotism, and the disruption of traditional communities and values by the experience of mass soldiering. Stephen Koss, in *Nonconformity in British Politics*, has echoed many other commentators:

However much a commonplace, it is no exaggeration to say that war, when it came unexpectedly in August 1914, dealt a shattering blow to organized religion. The churches never recovered from the ordeal, either in terms of communicants or self-possession. Thereafter, men looked elsewhere, if anywhere, for their moral certainties. Yet we must remember that here, as in other situations, wartime experiences only hastened and intensified trends that were already under way.

Indeed there is much truth in this, but as the last sentence indicates the most pertinent features of the falling away of religious adherence lay in a longer-term process which can be identified from the late nineteenth century. For the Protestant churches in particular, the critical feature, apparent by 1914, was the diminishing ability of the churches to recruit large numbers

of new members from outside their existing circle of adherents
or their families. Alan Gilbert has pointed out that the Methodist
and nonconformist churches in the early twentieth century
retained their·relative numerical position only because they
relaxed membership standards to accommodate declining levels
of commitment, improved recruitment of members' children
through institutions such as Sunday schools and denominational
education, and continued to benefit from the formal and informal social pressures favouring public religiosity amongst
sections of the middle classes. Increasingly, however, the
churches were faced by the decline of three of the main features
which had helped to sustain high levels of church membership
in the nineteenth century. In the traditional rural parish, the
Church of England, and in some of the new industrial towns
and villages of the industrial areas the nonconformist chapels,
had been centres of communal life. It was already apparent by
the mid nineteenth century that large-scale urbanization tended
to dissolve the communal role of the churches and that, broadly
speaking, the larger the aggregation of population, the fewer
people went to church. This was not only because the churches
had initially failed in their provision of new churches and
organizations to meet the needs of urban society, but because
the varied and complex nature of mass urban society militated
against the churches playing the dominant communal role they
had performed in the rural parish or the small pit village. In
the urban environment, the churches had to compete much
more fiercely for adherents against the rival attractions and
focuses of loyalty and commitment, such as the local pub, football team or place of work. Hence church membership and
attendance tended to hold up most strongly in rural areas and
in the smaller communities, while in the larger towns and cities
and the growing suburbs it reached its lowest point.

The churches too played an important political role in the
years up to 1914. The rivalry of Church and Chapel, between
Conservative and Liberal, played a big part in maintaining and
shaping the allegiance of a broad swathe of the community. The
bitter battles over the Education Act of 1902, over issues

such as the drink question, and the disestablishment of the Anglican Church helped to keep religious concerns near the heart of political debate. Even before 1914, however, the advent of a more class-based politics, witnessed in the rise of the trade unions and the Labour Party, was tending to dissolve the traditional Church–Chapel rivalry. The *Methodist Times* after the First World War summarized working-class attitudes in the Rhondda valley as 'we don't want your gospel, we want a new social order'. Certainly by the 1920s, many of the concerns which had mobilized Liberal or Chapel feeling were clearly seen as outmoded by the great majority of the religiously uncommitted population. The political disintegration of the Liberal Party and the inability of the nonconformist churches to redefine a political role for themselves went hand in hand. By the Second World War, church membership was no longer a major determinant of political affiliation, except in one or two areas of the British Isles. When Margaret Stacey carried out her study of Banbury in the 1940s, she found that while religious allegiance continued to exercise some influence upon the social networks of organization and affiliation within the community, it was class and social status which dominated.

In addition, the churches were faced with increasing competition as providers of recreational and leisure outlets. The dense network of church-based societies, boys' clubs, outings and meeting places which had proved so prominent a feature of Victorian and Edwardian society found increasing competition from the more varied opportunities offered to what was at once an increasingly urban, affluent and privatized society. Kenneth Richardson has described what might pass for a microcosm of these organizations in Edwardian Coventry:

At the beginning of this century the young men of the Holy Trinity Bible Class used to engage in an interesting piece of social rescue every Sunday morning. Starting from their headquarters at the old Grammar School, they worked through long-vanished slum streets such as the Rope Walk and the Chauntries, looking for drunks who were still stupefied from the previous night in those days of the unrestricted licensing hours. They found them lying in the gutters or on the stone floors of their lodgings and took them back to their headquarters to give them cocoa, a little food and some warmth. Then they exhorted them, probably without success, wrote letters for them, since these were illiterate and lonely men, and sent them on their way ... In these days before 1914 a young man found it easier and more pleasant to build a purposeful life if he belonged to a Bible class or had some other religious connection.

It was not that such organizations ceased to exist, but that they were central to fewer people's lives after the Great War. The war itself, by drawing so heavily upon the group loyalties of such bodies for recruits, cut a swathe, either directly or in-directly, through the young activists and members of church organizations. Stephen Koss cites the evidence of Charles Royle, Liberal MP for Stockport during the 1920s, about the fate of the local chapters of the National Brotherhood movement: more than six hundred of its members volunteered in the Great War, and 'although the big majority came back to the town only a small number resumed their membership of the Brother-hood'. As well as the often shattering experience of the war on individual religious allegiance, the war was part of a general widening of horizons and opportunities, exposing the 'churched' to the influences of the majority of religiously in-different and to a wider range of experience. Between the wars, the churches were forced to compete more and more with the rival attractions of professional sport, mass entertainment and home-based leisure pursuits. The three-services-a-Sunday family, still to be found in some staunch religious households, was an increasing rarity. Moreover, by associating themselves with the strict Sunday of the Victorian middle classes and with condemnation of many of the new leisure pursuits, the churches often distanced themselves still further from the mass culture. As Alan Gilbert has remarked: 'By forcing potential clients to choose between themselves and the "new paganism" of worldly recreations they courted rejection.' With half-day holidays on Saturday and reduced working hours, the tradi-tional 'Sabbath' was inevitably subsumed by the modern, secular 'weekend'. While, compared with that of most continental countries, the British 'Sunday' retained a rather dour quality, assisted by bodies such as the Lord's Day Observance Society as well as by Reith's conservative views on Sunday broadcasting, something of the earlier strictness had gone by the inter-war years. Although many shops were closed, pubs (at least in England) were open, as were cinemas and seaside resorts. Even more significant was the growing mobility and privatization of Sunday. The Sunday afternoon drive was already well established by the late 1930s and few thought it odd that the Bank Holiday weekend should mean as busy a time for the holiday resorts on a Sunday as on any other day. For others, Sunday was already the day for domestic activities, gardening, home improvement or hobbies. A home-based recreational pattern, by no means confined only to the suburbs, seems to have been one of the major factors undermining regular church attendance.

Indeed the figures for church attendance reflected an even more stark picture of decline than those for church membership. For example, Seebohm Rowntree was in a position to evaluate three censuses of attendance at churches on a specimen Sunday in York which span this period (see Table 26). The obvious feature was the absolute decline in church attendance in spite of an increase in population from 48,000 in 1901 to 72,248 in 1935, and to 78,500 in 1948. In other words attendance had fallen from 35.5 per cent of the population in 1901, to

Table 26: Church attendance by adults in York, 1901, 1935 and 1948

	1901	1935	1948
Anglican	7,453	5,395	3,384
Nonconformist	6,447	3,883	3,514
Roman Catholic	2,360	2,989	3,073
Salvation Army	800	503	249
Totals	17,060	12,770	10,220

17.7 per cent in 1935, and to 13.0 per cent in 1948. Not only were attendances lower but by 1948 they were disproportionately composed of women and the elderly. For the great majority of British people by the late 1940s, churches were places to be entered only for the major ceremonies of life – birth, marriage and death. Even here, however, there was evidence of a falling-off; the number of civil marriages rising steadily from a mere 16 per cent in 1901 to 30 per cent by 1945.

But within the context of a loss of church membership and a decline in church attendance there were important signs of readjustment and revival in some aspects of the Christian churches. Although the impact of the Great War upon both Christian faith and practice was substantial, there were some positive results. This was due less to a 'flight to the churches' – which some thought they perceived in the first years of the war – than to a reassessment of the role and purposes of religion in the modern world. For the 1,985 Anglican clergy who served as army chaplains, as well as for those at home, the war had often proved a profound spiritual ordeal. Apart from their direct experience of war, thousands of clergymen's sons had died in the fighting. The awful catalogue of death and destruction led some to question the fundamentals of their faith and ministry, while others were exposed more fully than ever before to the failure of the church to play a major part in the lives of most ordinary soldiers. The war positively forced many of the clergy into a position where they had to confront the dechristianization and secularization of the mass of the people. Desire for reform found expression in the Life and Liberty Movement founded in 1917, whose objective of increased self-government for the church drew upon the general desire for a renewed church representing all classes to serve the post-war world. Particularly strong amongst the army chaplains, including men like Dick Sheppard, later Vicar of St Martin-in-the-Fields, it proposed a democratically elected Church Assembly, an equalization of clerical stipends, abolition of the parochial system and a volunteer army of mission priests to re-evangelize the country. In

1917 its Council reported that many of the army chaplains were 'almost in despair' at the failure of the church to readjust to its responsibilities in the modern world, in support of which there was even talk of a 'general strike' against coming home, which was defused only by the personal intervention of the Archbishop of Canterbury.

By 1920 the more radical movement had been snuffed out, but it left a legacy of concern about the place of the church in society which was to surface repeatedly in the years between the wars. Nor had direct experience of war universally destroyed religious faith. An acute shortage of ordinands was relieved by a special call to the ministry addressed to those in the forces. By November 1918, over 2,700 names of service candidates had been submitted. A School of Instruction was set up in France shortly after the armistice and with a school at Knutsford in Cheshire produced sufficient clergy by 1921 to prevent a breakdown in the parochial system. Also to emerge from the war was the Toc H movement, formed by Neville Talbot and Philip 'Tubby' Clayton in a rented house in Poperinge near Ypres in 1915 as a club for troops. Called Talbot House after Neville's younger brother who had just been killed (Toc H was signaller's shorthand for Talbot House), Clayton described it as 'a home from home where friendships could be consecrated, and sad hearts renewed and cheered, a place of light and joy and brotherhood and peace'. With recreational rooms and an upstairs chapel, the house developed into a combination of YMCA and mission chapel which offered both an easy-going approach – on the chaplain's door there were the words 'Abandon Rank All Ye That Enter Here' – with an often intense religious life. On Easter Day 1916 there were ten celebrations of the Eucharist from 5.30 a.m. onwards. The scene in May 1916 when Archbishop Davidson confirmed thirty-seven men in the Upper Room captures something of the atmosphere: '... the old Archbishop sitting in his chair, with the lighted candles behind him as the darkness came on, and the candidates kneeling before him, while outside in the street there was the ceaseless rumble of troops moving up to the Salient and the intermittent sound of firing.' Candidates for confirmation signed a pledge that 'If God decides to bring me through this war, I vow to take it as a hint from Him that I shall help and serve the Church in future through the life that he gives back to me'. Toc H's pledge roll provided many of the candidates for service ordinands and Clayton supervised the Knutsford centre. In 1919 the Toc H fellowship was founded, opening houses as meeting places for ex-servicemen dedicated to 'Fellowship, Service, Fairmindedness and the Kingdom of God'. Sponsored by the Prince of Wales, it received a Royal Charter in 1922 and fresh branches were set up throughout the inter-war years. As well as promoting 'the traditional Christian fellowship and service manifested by all ranks of the British Army on Active Service during the war', it aimed at promoting social service, fostering a sense of mutual responsibility and mitigating 'the evils of class-consciousness'.

Another important result was the 'National Mission of Repentance and Hope' launched by the Archbishops in the autumn of 1916 as a deliberate attempt to respond to the spiritual needs of the nation in wartime. Although its precise impact was hard to determine, it was followed up by five committees charged with producing reports on various aspects of the life of the church and the nation. Published in 1919, they provided a major stimulus to post-war change. Their report 'The Worship of the Church' promoted the cause of Prayer Book revision which culminated in 1927 and 1928. Another, on church government, foreshadowed the Enabling Act of 1919 which produced some self-government in the church. The fifth report, 'Christianity and Industrial Problems', aroused controversy for its radical, Christian socialist tone. None the less, it became the Charter for the Industrial Christian Fellowship created in 1919. Although none of these results was in any way particularly radical, they expressed both a strong desire for a degree of readjustment and a strong emphasis on social concern. As with so many areas affected by the war, this strand merely emphasized pre-war thinking. Social concern had been one of the major stimuli to the demand for church renewal before

1914 and foreshadowed the Life and Liberty movement, notably in the Church Reform League of 1895 and the Representative Church Council of 1903. William Temple, son of Archbishop Frederick Temple, was a leading light in the Life and Liberty movement and in 1909 had chaired the Student Christian Movement conference at Matlock which stressed social concern as one of the major issues. The Collegium group of the SCM produced a book, *Competition*, in 1917 which was a plea for a more collectivist society. During the war, members of the SCM deepened their commitment to the social gospel, a new awareness of the role of women and a concern for education and the arts. Charles Gore, Bishop of Oxford from 1911 to 1919, regarded the war as indicating the collapse of a competitive society and played an influential part in emphasizing the primacy of corporate over individual interest. A notable product of this line of thought was R. H. Tawney's *The Acquisitive Society* of 1921, which argued for the organization of industry as a service to the community. His *Religion and the Rise of Capitalism* (1926) was also dedicated to Gore. Tawney's Christian socialism had a wide influence, emphasized with the publication of *Equality* in 1930. Social concern was also shown in the creation in 1923 of a permanent Social and Industrial Committee of the Church Assembly and the ecumenical conference COPEC (Conference on Christian Politics, Economics and Citizenship). Progressive churchmen such as Temple, Gore, Raven and Tawney played a leading part in its preparation, which resulted in 1921 in the appointment of twelve commissions on a wide variety of social questions and a conference in 1924 under Temple's chairmanship. Similarly, some churchmen saw it as their duty to speak out on individual matters and on conflicts between capital and labour, including attempting to intervene in industrial disputes. In 1919 and 1921, Archbishop Davidson offered to mediate in the railway and coal strike. During the General Strike of 1926 Archbishop Davidson addressed an appeal for conciliation from the churches to the government, TUC, and employers which both the BBC and the official *British Gazette* refused to publish.

Other churchmen became heavily involved in support for the League of Nations as an expression of Christian witness in the political sphere. There was some disquiet at the terms of the Versailles Treaty and considerable support in the 1920s and 1930s for disarmament and pacifist movements. Steadily emerging as the leader of the progressive wing of the Church of England in 1932, William Temple, as Archbishop of York, preached before the International Disarmament Conference in Geneva. His sermon, widely broadcast, towards its end de-nounced the War Guilt clause, for which he was severely criti-cized. On a more practical level, Archbishop Davidson tried to help German prisoners held captive in France long after the Armistice and promoted the Save the Children Fund to relieve the sufferings of German children affected by the continued British blockade of German ports.

The 'social gospel' inevitably meant a fresh approach to liturgy and theology. *Songs of Praise*, first published in 1925, has been noted for its liberal, optimistic tone. Alan Wilkinson has referred to its 'non-sectarian type of Christianity', expressed in 'its modernist approach to sacramentalism, its liberal attitudes to other religions, and its benignly immanentist theology which made it attractive to those in the post-war period who were impatient of creeds, dogmas, religions and social divisions, and traditional language about "sin" '. There was a section on 'Social Service', while a group of 'National' hymns was followed by an 'International' group. Pastoral needs and a broader theology also led to the attempts at Prayer Book revision in 1927 and 1928. These failed because of parliamentary opposition, though the revised forms were brought into use by some of the clergy.

Another important strand was the increasing stress on ecumenism. Again there was evidence of this before 1914. In 1910 Archbishop Davidson had agreed to address the World Missionary Conference at Edinburgh, the assembly which is usually regarded as the beginning of the modern ecumenical movement. The war further stimulated ecumenical thinking. At home, in many parishes, united services were held and it became more common to invite Free Church ministers to take part in national occasions in parish churches. United appeals from church leaders in support of the League of Nations in 1918, for a settlement of the railway strike in 1919 and over the General Strike in 1926 foreshadowed similar appeals in the Second World War in support of social welfare legislation. The Lambeth Conference in 1920 produced an appeal for a 'united Church', though little practical progress had been achieved by 1939 in spite of discussions and contacts with other churches. At the very least, it inspired some hope for better relations in the future, a cause to be taken up after 1945.

For the Free Churches, the period was also one of difficulty, with some encouraging signs. Falling membership rolls and church attendance affected them as much as the Church of England. Although the experience of denominations differed somewhat, all shared in the fall in membership brought about by the Great War, a measure of revival in the 1920s, and then further decline in the 1930s and 1940s. In autumn 1933 J. B. Priestley visited a Birmingham nonconformist chapel for Sunday morning service during his 'English Journey':

It did not belong to the particular denomination that had claimed me, willy-nilly, when I was a boy, but nevertheless my first discovery was that this service was almost exactly like the ones I remember from thirty years ago, and that the people taking part in it had not changed a great deal. The chief difference in the congregation was there were fewer young people in it, and especially young men. I doubt if there were half-a-dozen men under thirty-five in the chapel. If there were any boys present, they escaped my eye. There were a few little girls, a sprinkling of older girls and young women, and all the rest of the congregation and the choir were middle-aged. But I suppose that in my chapel-going days, there would actually have been twice the number of people at this service.

The decline of the Liberal Party also brought about a diminution of the social and political influence of the nonconformist groups. Once a vital electoral force in places like Wales, Cornwall and the West Midlands, they were hard pressed to muster prominent churchmen as active local politicians. According to Stephen Koss, the 1929 election returns 'left no doubt that

political Nonconformity continued to exist chiefly as a figment
of men's imaginations'. In places such as Cornwall, where
Methodism virtually functioned as an unofficial Established
Church, there was a distinct decline both in attendance and
the vitality of individual congregations. The Fore Street
Methodist church in Redruth saw a decline in its Sunday school
rolls from a peak of 756 in 1909 to 209 by 1945; its Burial
Club had gone by 1930; and its Provident Club was wound
up in 1941 when its membership (seventy-four) had fallen to
a quarter the 1908 figure. Membership in 1947 was, at 122,
less than half the 1900 total. Even in Wales, where the chapels
were still important, living on the legacy of the bitter Church–
Chapel rivalries and occupying a central place in the rural communities of the centre and north, there were signs of decay.
The great Welsh nonconformist cause of the disestablishment
of the Anglican Church in Wales, achieved in 1920, proved
something of a false dawn, as the burden of debt, the decline
in Welsh-speaking and the persistent forces of Anglicization
and mass consumerism undermined the position and influence
of the chapels. Increasingly, secular activities and attitudes were
eroding the hold of the chapels upon Welsh life, even in rural
areas. While chapel membership and attendance remained high
in absolute terms up to the Second World War, Wales was
reflecting the secular tendencies seen elsewhere in the British
Isles.

   None the less, elements of adaptation and vigour remained
in nonconformity. New facilities to provide for women and
children were widely adopted, with youth clubs and Young
Women's Fellowships, aimed at retaining and strengthening
recruitment amongst existing members and their families.
Ecumenical discussions brought some important marks of
recognition from the Anglican and secular establishment. In
November 1918 the King and Queen attended a Solemn Service
of Thanksgiving arranged by the Free Church Council at the
Albert Hall – the first time a reigning monarch had attended
a Free Church occasion. Although ecumenical discussions proceeded little further between the wars, there were important

moves to reunion within the Free Churches, especially the separate Methodist denominations. One reunion in 1907 was followed in 1932 by the coming together of the Wesleyan, United and Primitive Methodists as the Methodist Church. In Scotland, the United Free Church, the main dissenting group, joined the established presbyterian Church of Scotland in 1928, producing a more united presbyterian church than for more than a century, which in 1930 could still claim the allegiance of 26.2 per cent of the population. The Iona Community, founded in 1930 by the socialist and pacifist George MacLeod, sought a stronger ritualistic and socially committed Scottish church, working both in the Clydeside slums and in rebuilding the medieval abbey of Iona. Groups like the Scottish Protestant League also kept up a level of political involvement, spurred by anti-Catholic feelings rarely found south of the border.

The Catholic Church both increased in number of members and improved its position in relation to the other churches during this period. Continued Irish immigration and a substantial number of conversions, whether through inter-marriage or amongst laymen of other denominations, marked this period of growth. Both in its Irishness and in its indigenous guise as an embattled sub-culture, Roman Catholicism proved far more resistant to the pressures of cultural secularization. Crucially, too, the Catholic Church won the battle lost by the nonconformists in 1902 in securing on favourable tems, though also at considerable financial cost to their adherents, separate denominational education through the 1918 and 1944 Education Acts. Rowntree found in York in 1947 that the Catholic congregations retained a higher proportion of both males and young people than the Anglican or nonconformist churches. Although in the longer term Catholicism was to suffer from some of the inroads into adherence and commitment common to other churches, this process was much slower, leaving the Catholic Church with almost as many nominal adherents in 1970 as all the Protestant churches combined.

In spite of an overall decline of adherents and attendance in relation to the total population, Christianity continued to influence many aspects of civil society and social behaviour. Christian opposition to divorce, artificial birth control, obscenity, drink, homosexuality and the 'continental Sunday' helped to shape the character of Britain between the wars. A slow, piecemeal change in public attitudes to these questions was taking place, but resistance by the churches could often prove decisive. Sunday opening of public houses was still prohibited in parts of Wales and Scotland, while the Bishop of London was instrumental in defeating an extension of opening hours throughout London. The opposition of churchmen to divorce, in spite of an increasing divorce rate, also played a crucial part in the abdication of Edward VIII in 1936 because of his attempt to make a twice-divorced woman his Queen. The work of Marie Stopes to popularize artificial contraception was also dogged by the opposition of churchmen, especially Roman Catholics, while in Wales in 1927, attempts to play Sunday golf on the Aberdyfi links led to players being physically threatened. Gradual conciliation of the secular world was an underlying trend, but there was little doubt that up to the Second World War and beyond many churchmen saw their role as that of custodians of traditional morality for the whole community. Britain was to emerge into the post-1945 world with legislation in areas such as drink, sex and Sunday observance which reflected a Christian outlook no longer shared by the majority of the population. In other respects too Britain remained an ostensibly Christian society. Parliament was opened by prayers, the annual Remembrance Day service was a major national event couched in religious terms, and even a sporting event, the Cup Final, was introduced by the mass singing of the hymn *Abide with Me*, with little obvious sign of incongruity. An increasingly secular society, and one aware of its religious or areligious diversity, still found it necessary to turn to Christian ritual and imagery for expression. Especially in the organs of the state, the armed forces, prisons and the courts, as in other organized activities, from schools to the Boy Scouts, an at least formal Christianity remained a significant part of the culture.

Nor did overall decline in membership and adherence to the Christian churches necessarily imply any diminution of the search for stable and absolute systems of belief and practice. Some of the smaller sects, Jehovah's Witnesses, the Society of Friends, Christian Science, the Salvation Army and Seventh Day Adventists, continued to show growth, partly because they were able to demand a higher level of commitment from their followers and therefore reduce 'leakage'. Among important ethnic minorities, particularly the Jews, religion continued to provide a central source of communal expression. By 1950 there were approximately 240 synagogues in Britain compared with only eighty in 1900, serving a Jewish community which had risen from 160,000 to over 400,000. Others sought belief and commitment in new areas. There was interest in Chinese and Indian philosophy and in Celtic and primitive beliefs. To the young J. R. Tolkein, the folkloristic world of *The Hobbit* and *The Lord of the Rings* was a deliberate attempt conceived in the midst of the First World War to find 'something noble' for people to believe in. Yoga was introduced into Britain by a few civil servants and soldiers who had served in India, including Major-General Fuller, one of the pioneers of tank warfare, who wrote extensively on the subject. For some, Marxism undoubtedly offered a system of belief and an interpretation of the world about them which came close to a quasi-religious certainty. Influencing a significant group of intellectuals and writers in the late 1930s and 1940s as Communist Party membership rose to a peak of almost 50,000 during the Second World War, Marxism has a right to be placed in the same league as some of the dynamic elements in organized religion as a focus of belief and activity. Jason Gurney foune the intellectual luggage of part of his generation deposited – quite literally – on a hillside at Jarama in Spain as the British section of the International Brigade went into action in February 1937:

There was an extraordinary variety of objects among the debris – hand grenades, ammunition, machine-gun spare parts, and clothing and equipment of all kinds. But the personal items which had been jettisoned provided the strangest part of the collection. Books of all kinds – though the Marxist textbooks, which were large and heavy, lay fairly near the bottom of the hill. The rest were of an amazing variety, ranging from third-rate pornography to the sort of books which normally fill the shelves of the more serious type of under-graduate. There were copies of the works of Nietzsche, and Spinoza, Spanish language textbooks, Rhys David's *Early Buddhism* and every kind of taste in poetry.

Here perhaps was the real hallmark of the religious and intellectual currents which moved men and women in the first half of the twentieth century and were to influence post-war attitudes – plurality and uncertainty. Organized Christianity was to play a diminishing role in influencing public and private morality. None the less the traditional Christian values continued to influence much of the legislation and culture of post-war Britain. Neither diminished the continued search for new sources of belief and value which represent a significant strand of twentieth-century thought and culture.

Crime

The years between 1914 and 1945 witnessed nothing comparable to the rise in crime which had alarmed early Victorians or was to propagate fears of a 'crime wave' after 1945. Up to 1941 criminal statistics suggest a relatively stable crime rate, continuing a pattern which extended from the 1870s to the 1900s. From 1915 to 1930 there was an increase in recorded crime of modest proportions, approximately running at a level of 5 per cent a year, rising in the years between 1930 and 1948 at a somewhat higher rate of 7 per cent a year. Analyses of these figures have suggested the importance of long-term trends, slow growth in the 1920s, somewhat faster growth in the years from 1930 to 1950, but totally overshadowed by a more rapid growth thereafter, when recorded crime rose by over 10 per cent per year. The striking feature of these statistics is that, on the face of it, the major political, social and economic crises of the period had surprisingly little effect. The First and

Second World Wars both show a continuation of pre-war trends, and there is no clear-cut parallel between unemployment and crime; the worst years of the inter-war depression, 1921–2 and 1929–33, appear not to have had a decisive impact on total criminal activity.

Table 27: Crimes per 100,000 of the population

	Total rate	Index: 1901 = 100
1901	249	100
1911	269	108
1921	273	110
1931	399	162
1951	1,299	482

Source: F. H. McClintock and N. Howard Avison,
Crime in England and Wales, Heinemann, 1968,
p. 23.

But the figures in Table 27 demonstrate that the level of crime recorded by the police was growing, even if only at a moderate rate compared with the post-war explosion. There is little evidence that this increase was either the result of major changes in age or population structure. For example, it cannot be accounted for by an increase in the proportion of the population most likely to commit crimes, males between the ages of ten and twenty-nine. As in the past, the largest proportion of offences were larcenies, making up three-quarters of the total. Murders, apart from a rise in individual years after the First and Second World Wars, showed a fluctuating trend. Between 1923 and 1938 the annual average of persons committed to trial for murder was actually lower than at any period since the 1830s: 56.5 per year in 1931–8 compared with 70.7 in 1908–1913 and 72.4 in 1946–56. The major increases in crime lay with robbery, both simple thefts and breaking and entering. Two other major categories to increase, however, were juvenile and traffic offences. In England and Wales, juvenile offences grew from 12,200 in 1910 to 29,400 in 1938, though most of this increase was related to the 1930s. Motoring offences rose too from 55,500 in 1910 to 475,000 in 1938; they were mainly, however, minor offences. The analysis of these figures suggests that the main cause of the increase in crime was increased opportunity as growing affluence made larceny much easier. On the other hand there was a significant decline in drunkenness offences, reflecting changing leisure habits. In York, for example, Seebohm Rowntree found that the number of prosecutions for drink-related offences had fallen from 52.6 per 10,000 inhabitants in 1900–1909 to 12.3 in 1930–37. These findings were also borne out in national statistics, which in Scotland, as in England and Wales, showed a major fall in drink offences.

But figures for criminal offences recorded by the police are somewhat deceptive. In fact, the number of persons found guilty of offences was falling as a percentage of crimes known to the police, so that the number of 'proved' criminals was lagging somewhat behind the rise in crime. Whereas the number of offences known to the police rose almost 300 per cent between 1913 and 1938, the number of persons found guilty rose by only 50 per cent, from an average of 55,874 in 1910–14 to 75,337 in 1935–9. As the great majority of criminal offences were minor thefts, so the largest proportion were committed by petty criminals involved in small-scale crime. Although there was a significant portion of recidivism, the great majority of people tried in courts for indictable offences were first-time offenders, usually young males. While there was a degree of truth in the idea of a criminal class, in the sense that some people in some areas were more likely to be involved in crime than others, the majority of crime was a 'one-off' affair by casual criminals. Only in the big cities did the police face any significant degree of organized crime, though even in London this had barely developed to the degree it was to after 1945. Gang warfare in Glasgow during the 1930s, revolving around gangs involved in petty theft and local protection rackets, attracted considerable attention. Indeed, not least of the transatlantic influences on British culture was the adoption during and after the Second World War of a watered-down version of American gangsterism amongst some sections of the 'underworld', including fast cars, a network of protection, clientage, and some infiltration of the middle-class world through corruption at local government level. What was missing was the weaponry of the American gangster. Although the number of malicious woundings increased some seven times between 1921 and 1948, violence against the person in 1948 still made up less than 1 per cent of all crime, while the number of murders was lower in the 1920s and 1930s than before 1914. Strict firearms controls and a criminal culture which saw little need to kill rather than deter meant that the razor, cosh and knife remained the probable armoury of even the most ruthless criminals. The people most likely to resort to firearms were the desperate and the amateur, usually to kill themselves or their next of kin. It was a significant feature of British society that it retained even amongst its criminal fraternity a relatively 'low threshold of violence', in which resort to firearms on a large scale was neither expected nor considered. Most theft and non-lethal violence was urban, male and working-class, and murder usually occurred within the family or close circle of acquaintances. Middle-class crime was usually associated with fraud, embezzlement and corruption, growing opportunities for which developed with the greater range and volume of business carried out by local government, business and the professions. They remained, however, a relatively small proportion of offences. There was also a high increase in homosexual offences between 1921 and 1948, rising threefold between 1921 and 1938, then by about the same again to 1948. Even so, *all* sexual offences made up only a small fraction of total crime, a mere 8,161 of indictable offences in 1946 out of a total of 472,489.

Criminal and Penal Policy

In criminal legislation and penal policy, the inter-war years saw a continuation of trends evident as early as the 1890s, notably a re-emphasis on reformative rather than punitive aspects. The

Gladstone Report of 1895 has been credited with giving as much weight to reformation as to mere deterrence, condemning non-productive labour, such as the crank and the treadmill, and recommending greater attention to the individual needs of prisoners and the provision of libraries and communal workshops. In 1898 the number of offences punishable by flogging was reduced, a system of classification of prisoners developed and provisions for remission introduced. The probation system was started in 1907, and in 1908 the borstal system and juvenile courts were introduced. The inter-war years saw further concentration on young and juvenile offenders, reflecting both a wider concern with the young in general and concern with an increasing rate of juvenile crime. There was a growing emphasis on training and education for offenders up to the age of seventeen, the use of special courts, social and medical reports, and greater recourse to probation and other non-custodial sentences. Many of these initiatives were enshrined in the Children and Young Persons Act of 1933. The number of young offenders between seventeen and twenty-one years of age sentenced to prison was also reduced and probation and borstal training put forward as a major alternative. Proposals on these lines were incorporated in the Criminal Justice Bill of 1938, which recommended the wider use of hostels, remand homes, attendance centres and borstal training for young offenders. These were eventually implemented after the Second World War in the Criminal Justice Act of 1948.

Some liberalization of the treatment of adult offenders continued after 1914 with increasing use of probation, fines and other alternative forms of punishment. Between 1901 and 1931 the proportion of persons found guilty of indictable offences given custodial sentences fell from 53.1 per cent to 45.5 per cent, falling even more dramatically by 1951 to 16.8 per cent. The pace of change varied, however, from one part of the country to another. In 1922 it was estimated that a fifth of courts had not appointed a probation officer and in 1936 the percentage of persons found guilty of indictable offences and placed on probation varied from 43.8 per cent to 5.0 per cent in different courts. Scotland had a much more determined onslaught on custodial sentences, leading to a large fall in the prison population from 50,000 in 1901 to a mere 9,000 in 1951. In England and Wales, in spite of a rising crime rate, the prison population remained fairly stable, partly as a result of shorter sentences and the use of non-custodial sentences. Something of the harshness of the nineteenth-century prison regime was mitigated, with less recourse to purely punitive task work, the humiliations inflicted upon prisoners by the prison 'crop' and the use of 'silent' and 'separate' systems. Some experiments were attempted, with the first 'open prison' set up at Wakefield in the 1930s and facilities to improve industrial training in prisons.

Progress was relatively slow, however. The sentence of 'hard labour' remained on the statute book until 1948 and there was often little more reformative effect in the 'useful' work given to prisoners, sewing mailbags for example, than in the punitive tasks they were intended to replace. Prison governors retained a considerable degree of discretion and, according to the evidence of some conscientious objectors imprisoned during the Great War, the prison regime was frequently grim in the extreme, over-rigid in discipline and providing little reformative effect. One of the most serious prison disturbances in Britain in recent history, the Dartmoor 'mutiny' of January 1932, seems to have been caused by the combination of poor living conditions in the prison and the strains imposed by the transition from a popular governor to a new one, Colonel Turner. It was sparked off by the quality of food and fed by rumours of assaults on prisoners. The convicts imprisoned the Governor and Chaplain in their offices, seized the main buildings and set fire to some of them. After pitched battles with warders, extra police and soldiers had to be called in to quell the disturbance, in which one prisoner was shot while allegedly trying to escape. In the subsequent report on the 'mutiny' blame was laid on outside agitators and some prisoners were tried for sedition. None the less, the Governor was relieved of his duties and some further attention given to prison conditions.

A significant aspect of the growth of a more humane attitude to sentencing was shown by the decline in corporal punishment. In 1900, 7 per cent of all persons found guilty of indictable offences in England and Wales, some 3,260 persons, were flogged or birched. By 1946, however, corporal punishment was described as 'practically disused', and it was finally abolished for adult offenders in 1948. Pre-war figures showed its decreasing use: in 1938 only seventeen adults were flogged (for robbery with violence) and another forty-three juveniles birched for a variety of offences. In the case of juveniles the position remained that a boy under fourteen could be ordered to receive not more than six strokes with a birch if found guilty of an indictable offence. It was reported, however, that in the London juvenile courts 'there have been no birchings for many years, and although in some parts of England this form of punishment is still used, it appears that the majority of courts can have little faith in this, judging by the small number of birchings now ordered'. Corporal punishment was opposed by pressure groups such as the Humanitarian League and the Howard League for Penal Reform and there was considerable support for its abolition for all categories of prisoner in progressive circles. However, an attempt by the government to abolish birching in the Children and Young Persons' Bill in 1932 was defeated. Further pressure led in 1937 to the appointment of a Departmental Committee on Corporal Punishment. Its conclusion that corporal punishment had little deterrent effect, in spite of the disagreement of much of the police and the judiciary, led to a unanimous recommendation that the courts should no longer be allowed to order the corporal punishment of offenders, the position finally accepted by statute in 1948.

There were similar moves in favour of a reduction of the incidence of capital punishment. Here a major influence was the propensity of the judiciary and jurors to acquiesce in the idea of 'insanity' and 'unfitness to plead' in cases of murder. In the period 1908–13, 34.2 per cent of all murderers tried were dealt with under these headings; by 1931–8 the figure had risen to 47.4 per cent. An interesting barometer was the attitude towards infanticide, an issue which involved a complex set of changes in social perception both of criminality and of individual responsibility. The Infanticide Act of 1922 was so designed that a woman who killed a child which could be regarded as 'newly born' would certainly be acquitted of murder and the offence reduced to manslaughter or infanticide, thereby escaping capital punishment. In spite of this there was a case in 1927 of a woman who was sentenced to death for killing a seven-week-old infant on the grounds that the child could not be said to be 'newly born'. Though the woman was eventually reprieved, there was increased pressure for a more humane approach to the question. Eventually, in 1938, a new Infanticide Act provided that pleas could be entertained for children under twelve months of age and where the woman's mental imbalance could be attributed either to the birth of the child or to the 'consequent lactation'. The net result was that after 1938 it was much rarer for a woman even to be indicted for murder in this area.

More generally, both humanitarian and pragmatic arguments were adduced in favour of the abolition of the death penalty. The case of Robert True in 1922, when a plea of 'insanity' in a murder trial supported by psychiatric evidence was ultimately rejected by the jury and the Criminal Court of Appeal, marked an important watershed. True's reprieve by the Home Secretary has been identified as one of the last occasions in England which was to lead to protest about *not* hanging someone for murder; thereafter the weight of popular opinion tended to be against the imposition of capital punishment in less than the clearest-cut cases. A reflection of this mood was the setting-up of a Select Committee of the House of Commons in 1930 to discuss capital punishment in areas where insanity and diminished responsibility were at that time ill-defined. However, it was not until the post-1945 Royal Commission on Capital Punishment that a more decisive step was taken towards the curtailment or abolition of capital punishment.

As in penal policy as a whole, the issue of capital punishment reflected both a move towards a more humane and rehabilitative conception of penal and judicial policy, one which had its origins in the years before 1914, and the slow movement of opinion in crucial sectors to accept these ideas. Ideas of re-habilitating the young offender co-existed in the 1938 Criminal Justice Bill with a deterrent and retributive approach to the older recidivist. Growing concern for juveniles, fuelled by the rise of psychology, modern criminological studies and the social conception of adolescence, and reforms in particular areas such as infanticide, still left a criminal code and penal policy uneasily balanced between different philosophies, creating problems which were to become more acute when the post-war crime rate began to move far beyond that experienced before 1945.

14. *Leisure and the Media*

Leisure and Recreation

One of the most important developments in twentieth-century society has been the growth of leisure and recreation. Already by the Edwardian era, many pastimes and pursuits had been fashioned or transformed to meet the needs of a primarily urban and industrial society. In sport, entertainment and private recreations, one of the major driving forces was commercialization, drawing upon the increased spending power of a mass consumer market. Another was the increased leisure time available as a result of shorter working hours, paid holidays, longer life expectancy after retirement, smaller families and, for some, enforced idleness through unemployment. But the growth of leisure illustrates more than commercialism and more free time from work. With the growth of the media, it was part of the development of a more uniform and homogeneous society, partaking of an increasingly common culture. Notwithstanding regional and class differences, by 1945 only the remotest parts of Britain were insulated against the pervasive influences of the latest popular tune or major sporting event. In contrast, some aspects of leisure, particularly those centred around hobbies and domestic life, reflected an increasing home-centredness. The two themes of an increasingly common culture, balanced by the cult of domesticity and individual choice, dominated the development of leisure in this period.

The Great War proved only a limited disruption to the leisure pursuits developed in the Edwardian era. Professional sport gradually closed down in 1915, though seaside resorts continued to attract visitors throughout the war, as well as providing accommodation for recruits and convalescents. Cinema gained heavily in popularity. It was estimated in 1917 that approximately half the population went to the cinema once every week; with drink more expensive and opening hours restricted, the cinema offered a cheap alternative to the pub for a 'night out'. Significantly films were shown to troops in rest camps in France and elsewhere, some divisions having their own screens. Charlie Chaplin's role as the first great cinema star was already enshrined in the popular army song 'The moon shines bright on Charlie Chaplin', but newsreels and propaganda films were also common by 1918. The cinema still had a formidable rival in the music hall, with concert parties and visits from famous music hall artists to the base camps and rest areas. Harry Lauder, employed actively in recruiting at home in 1914 and 1915, was one who tirelessly toured France, getting as close to the front line as possible after his only son was killed there in December 1916. Quieter pleasures, too, seem to have flourished in wartime. Galleries and concert halls were crowded at home, while even at the front line books and newspapers were easily available by post. Harold Macmillan recalled lying reading Aeschylus in a shell-hole for several hours after being wounded at the battle of Loos, while copies of the *Oxford Book of English Verse* appear to have been almost as common in France as in any school back home. An astonishing amount of writing was done. Herbert Read wrote essays for the quarterly *Arts and Letters*, saw a volume of poetry through to publication and conducted a wide literary correspondence, all while commanding an infantry company in France and carrying out his normal soldiering duties.

The return to peace permitted a resumption of many of the patterns of leisure evident before 1914. Between the wars, consumption of alcohol never recovered from the effects of higher taxation and shorter opening hours, while reductions in the strength of beer and a steep relative rise in the price of spirits combined with changing social habits to reduce the number of convictions for drunkenness. These trends had been already evident immediately prior to 1914. In absolute terms expenditure on drink showed a fall of between a half and a third during the inter-war years. These changes reflected a fall in the consumption of beer as well as spirits. Production of beer for sale in the United Kingdom in 1910–13 had averaged thirty-four million barrels, but between 1920 and 1938 never rose above twenty-eight million, falling as low as thirteen million in 1933 and during the thirties generally running at about half the pre-war level. Seebohm Rowntree, like other writers, noted the change over pre-war habits, writing in 1936: 'One may pass through working-class streets every evening for weeks and not see a drunken person.' While the pub remained a central social institution in many areas, its grip was weakening. By the time Mass Observation came to study drinking habits in Bolton in the late 1930s, they found that the number of regular pub-goers was quite small: no more than a third of the electorate (men and women over twenty-one) were weekly visitors to the pub. Even on a typical Saturday evening, the most popular drinking time, the total clientele represented only about 15 per cent of the adult population. In 1948 a national survey suggested roughly comparable figures. Within these totals, men, predictably, drank more than women, and drinking tended to be concentrated in the age group twenty-four to thirty-four rather than amongst the young or the elderly. But there were signs of other changes. More women were using public houses, usually accompanied by husbands and boyfriends, especially the town and city-centre pubs. New, large public houses were built to serve the motorist on the suburban fringes of London, Birmingham and other big cities, offering a much higher standard of comfort and amenity. Dining-rooms, 'Art Deco' fittings and 'lounge' bars supplanted the elaborate glass and brass of the older 'gin palaces' and the basic features of the traditional 'local'. The 'cocktail', an American import, was the great vogue in fashionable circles with the opening of the first nightclubs in the early 1920s in London and the 'cocktail cabinet' becoming a status symbol amongst the affluent.

Smoking showed a remarkable increase. Expenditure on

tobacco rose from £42 million in 1914, to £204 million in 1939, and to £564 million by 1945. Some of this extra expenditure reflected increased taxation, but annual tobacco consumption per head grew from 2.19 lb. in 1914 to 4.0 lb. in 1938. Ten years later consumption had risen another 17 per cent, in spite of wartime restrictions. One estimate in 1948 suggested that more than twice as much was spent on tobacco as on fuel and light and four times as much as on other forms of entertainment. By that time 80 per cent of men and 41 per cent of women smoked, consuming an average of about half an ounce of tobacco per day, enough for twelve or thirteen cigarettes. Although the avuncular pipe remained common amongst older men, Stanley Baldwin even giving his name to a brand of pipe tobacco, it was the inexorable rise of the cigarette-smoking habit which dominated the scene. Popular brands were boosted by gimmicks like the series of cigarette cards, avidly collected by young and old alike. Between the wars, cigarettes retained a still relatively clean image. Little was known about the links between cigarette smoking and the various lung and heart diseases. Films and advertisements did much to popularize smoking, especially amongst women, as a fashionable symbol of emancipation, while for men, lighting a girl's cigarette became a romantic cliché of countless films.

There was also an increased amount of gambling. Horse-racing was avidly followed even before 1914, but the inter-war years saw the organization of nationally run football pools and the introduction of greyhound-racing. Figures for the total turnover from gambling varied considerably, but sums in the region of £300–500 million were being suggested by the 1930s. Although off-course betting was technically illegal from 1906, horse-racing remained an important component of working-class gambling and the law more remarkable for its breach than its observance. Greyhound-racing claimed as many as eighteen million attendances by 1931. As with horses, off-course betting was illegal, but the provision of greyhound tracks in most towns of any size made on-course betting much easier. Less space was required for dog-tracks than for race courses and more frequent meetings were possible. London had seventeen tracks by 1931, gambling on the 'dogs' taking perhaps a tenth of all betting turnover. The football pools, however, took an even larger share. By 1938 an estimated ten million people were sending in coupons with stakes totalling over £40 million.

This betting was small in scale, a few pence a week being sufficient for a 'perm' on the pools and a few shillings a week the most that many could afford on horse- or dog-racing. None the less, the amounts changing hands and the number involved were considerable. By the 1930s, the dog tracks were paying out over £400,000 in prize money, and had on the registers 60,000 greyhounds and 30,000 owners. In two seasons, £500,000 was spent erecting new totalizator machinery at Super Stadiums for greyhound-racing. In one stadium it was recorded that £100,000 went through totalizator machines in four hours, and operators were capable of dealing with 27,000 bets a minute. Gambling was big business; the vast new premises built by Vernons and Littlewoods to check football coupons employed hundreds of staff, providing £20,000 a week to newspapers in the form of pools advertisements, as well as huge business to the GPO in the form of ten to fifteen million letters and £3 million worth of postal orders. Bets were also made on games such as whippet-racing, pitch and toss, and Crown and Anchor. In spite of the widespread concern that gambling brought people to ruin, there is little to suggest that this was frequently the case; increasing numbers of people earned the extra margin of income to enable them to indulge in some form of gambling. For a minority of those on or near the poverty line, however, there was a sense in which gambling, even on a small scale, was a social problem in that it inevitably meant shortages of necessary food or clothing for themselves or their families. The New London Survey concluded that no more than a fifth of people at most bet 'to the point of ruin', most gambling well within their resources. Clearly, for many, gambling provided a relatively cheap form of diversion and excitement, with the prospect of a useful win. The attitude to gambling appears to have been less that of a frenzied 'rake's progress' than a fairly rational activity often carried on with a considerable degree of skill through form books, tipsters, perms and devoted attention to the sporting press. For some, betting could become almost a full-time hobby, earning local status and even bringing a regular income. Most factories and pubs had someone allegedly 'good with the horses', though for most it was a more casual pastime.

Gambling had some obvious attractions to the unemployed, filling time and giving some hope of better fortune, but observers noted that while the unemployed often continued to gamble they placed smaller bets. There were, however, some regional differences, notably in the peculiar 'atmosphere' the Pilgrim Trust found amongst the Liverpool unemployed, remarkable especially because it was not mirrored in other depressed communitie5. They commented on:

the all-pervading atmosphere of football pools, greyhounds and horses. This has become such an important environmental factor that, for the individual unemployed, it is an effort to develop interests un- connected with them. The extent to which the interests and indeed the whole lives of so many of the Liverpool unemployed centre round the pools must be seen to be believed. The queues at Post Offices filling in coupons, the number of 'guaranteed systems' for correct forecast on sale in Liverpool's poorest districts, the periodicals contain- ing nothing but pool analyses, the dirty and torn sports columns of the papers in Public Libraries, with the rest of the paper untouched (apart from advertisements of vacant jobs), are some measure of the strength of this interest.

These comments suggest that generalizations about the place of gambling in working-class life between the wars must be treated with some caution; regional differences, attitudes within different strata of the working classes, and personality and temperament all played a part. To an extent, however, interest in sport and inevitably in gambling did cross class frontiers. A big race winner or the result of a major football match was national news which was made increasingly part of a common, national culture through newspapers, newsreel and radio.

Although much interest in sport came from gambling, the British were also a nation of confirmed sports' spectators by 1914. Football, rugby and cricket were already established by the Great War, with the organizations, codes and much of the character they had after 1918. Football attendances continued to grow between the wars and in the major industrial cities and towns provided easily the most popular sport. The game obtained a national showcase for the FA Cup Final with the opening of the Wembley Stadium in 1923, at which an estimated crowd of 150,000 turned up for admission. Although it became customary for royalty to attend Cup Finals at Wembley in order to present the trophy to the winners and the match was fixed firmly as part of the national sporting calendar by the BBC, professional football retained a largely proletarian image. One or two famous players, such as Alex James and 'Dixie' Dean, did become almost household names, but football was gradually being displaced by rugby at 'good' schools and the old public school ethos of the game was offended by the rise of professionalism, its increasingly 'cloth-cap' image and the development of the football pools. Professional players were paid little more than the skilled artisan and the typical board of directors of a professional club tended to be drawn heavily from the ranks of the local business community, retailers and a scattering of professional men. Rugby Union retained a much higher social cachet, untainted by professionalism. Apart from South Wales, Cornwall and the Scottish borders, it was primarily a middle-class game, the proletarian element in the North playing the professional Rugby League, which, except for the annual cup final at Wembley, was largely ignored in the rest of Britain.

Cricket enjoyed a 'golden age' in the years between the wars, and was widely played at the universities, public schools and as a summer game in most parts of England, the more Anglicized parts of Wales, such as Glamorgan, and the eastern part of Scotland. Popular interest boomed in the twenties and thirties; cricket personalities and test matches were national news to an extent which eclipsed even football, a process much aided by press coverage and the advent of the radio broadcasting of test matches. Names like Hobbs, Sutcliffe, Hammond, Hutton and the Australian Don Bradman were far more widely known than the football celebrities of the day. Hence, in the 1930s, a purely cricketing matter, such as the 'bodyline' bowling controversy on the MCC tour of Australia in 1932, was capable of attracting comment on the BBC and questions in the House of Commons. Cricket between the wars retained its distinction between 'gentlemen', the amateurs, and 'players', the professionals. County sides were usually captained by amateurs, separate dressing-rooms for the different members of the same side were common, and the convention of referring to professionals solely by their surnames was retained in scorecards. Cricket was accorded a status in this period later to be accorded to football, attracting writers, journalists and even poets, which would never have happened with the more proletarian game.

Cricket, like association football and rugby, was underpinned at the local level by a host of clubs, teams and minor leagues. In places like the North-East and Scotland, football was organized on a massive scale, with school sides, factory teams, Sunday leagues and innumerable informal games. For many of the younger unemployed, it provided a major recreation, even for some the chance of finding a career when nothing else was available. Assessing the provision of space for playing games in 1929, the London County Council estimated that it had 350 cricket pitches, but more than 1,000 clubs applying to use them. Athletics were a less popular spectator sport between the wars, but the cult of 'healthy athleticism' for both men and women found some expression in the formation of the National Playing Fields Association in 1929 under the sponsorship of the Prince of Wales.

In working-class communities, boxing commanded a major following. For some it offered a chance of escaping from poverty in an era when there was no shortage of 'hungry fighters' and the poorest parts of Britain provided the ring with some of its most famous names. Tommy Farr, an ex-miner from South Wales, captured national attention when he was narrowly outpointed by the famous American heavyweight Joe Louis in America in August 1937. One of only three men ever to go the distance with Louis, Farr, with his modest manner, skill rather than big punch and poor background, struck a chord with the public which went beyond the confines of his sport. Attendances were large at big fights; for example 82,000 people watched the Cornishman Len Harvey fight Jock McAvoy at the White City, London, in July 1939. But behind the glamour of the big title fights, professional boxing had a squalid and often brutal aspect for much of the inter-war years. Poor medical supervision, the scandal of the fairground boxing booths where broken-down fighters eked out a living, and an absence of regulation led in 1929 to the formation of the British Boxing Board of Control, which brought professional boxing into a more civilized era. A voluntary body, it controlled through a system of licences everyone connected with professional boxing in Great Britain, whether boxer, manager, promoter, referee or time-keeper, provided medical attention and strictly controlled entry to professional status and the frequency of fights.

Far removed from boxing was the growing world of middle-class sport and recreation. Tennis, already noted as a feature of suburban life before 1914 and organized through the 'All England Croquet and Lawn Tennis Club' based on Wimbledon, was increasingly popularized through the Wimbledon championships and the glamour of stars such as Bill Tilden, Fred Perry, Betty Nuttall and 'Bunny' Austin. Moreover, tennis was one game, unlike football, rugby, cricket or boxing, in which women were able to participate freely, and, through the increasingly functional nature of tennis attire – one-piece 'short frocks', bandeaus, open-necked blouses, shorts and bare legs – provided a potent symbol of the discarding of earlier conventions. For middle-class men, golf provided an increasingly popular recreation, as new courses opened up on the fringes of the suburbs. Although more popular in Scotland than England, golf was on its way to becoming a badge of middle-class status, so much so that a particular style of golfing dress, 'plus-fours', became fashionable amongst suburban men who never went near a golf course.

Motoring also provided an important aspect of growing leisure opportunities for the middle classes. Although the phrase 'motoring for the million' was coined in 1919 when there were only about 100,000 cars on the roads, the inter-war years witnessed a huge expansion of private car ownership, reaching two million by 1939. Small 'family' cars like the Austin Seven were coming within the reach of some middle-class families. Capable of 50 m.p.h., it sold for £225 when it appeared at the end of 1922. By the early thirties an Austin Seven could be purchased for as little as £118 and a small Morris or other make for between £100 and £200. Cars brought in their wake a host of administrative regulations as well as changes in leisure habits for car owners. The speed limit was raised from 20 m.p.h. in 1930 to accommodate a new generation of motor vehicles. Car and petrol taxation was levied from 1909 and a system of driving tests introduced in 1935, but covering only those who did not already hold licences. Roads were first classified into 'A' and 'B' after the Great War and a programme of arterial routes and by-passes inaugurated. The Great West Road and the Kingston by-pass were opened in the mid-1920s, while the 'East Lancs' route between Liverpool and Manchester was officially opened in 1934 by King George V, who included in the same visit to the North the opening of the Mersey road tunnel, linking Liverpool and the commuter suburbs of the Wirral. Garages and filling stations mushroomed in the 1920s, as did transport cafés and new or refurbished public houses to serve the motoring trade. Traffic lights, road signs, roundabouts and pedestrian crossings, marked by 'Belisha beacons' (after Leslie Hore-Belisha, Minister of Transport, 1934–40), had all appeared by the Second World War. So also had the 'motoring offence' and the 'traffic accident'. Road deaths reached over 7,300 in 1934 and were to soar as high as 9,200 during the 'blackout' of the early years of the Second World War. These were amongst the highest figures ever recorded. In spite of a vast increase in road traffic after 1945, the peak figure in the post-war era was only 7,779 in 1972, when there were sixteen million motor vehicles on the roads instead of two million.

Although the internal combustion engine permitted important changes in retailing services, agriculture and goods traffic, the main impact of private motoring was on leisure, most cars being used for drives, excursions and holidays. By the 1930s, the Sunday afternoon drive and the Bank Holiday traffic jam were familiar features. Small towns and villages in southern England were opened up to day trippers, while relatively unspoiled parts of the country such as South Coast beauty spots, Cornwall and North Wales were exposed to the influx of motor cars. The trailer-caravan also appeared in the years between the wars and soon began to fill the roads and line available areas of beach and coastline. The long-distance coach or 'charabanc' ('chara' for short) was the nearest most came to the leisure opportunities offered by motor vehicles. Coaches offered a cheaper and in many respects more convenient form of travel than trains, particularly for excursions and day trips. No changes at stations were required, for example, and sports supporters, and factory and street outings, soon adopted them as the natural form of travel. Some regular long-distance 'express' coach services were opened in the 1920s and 1930s, but by 1939 these had not yet seriously eroded the railway's grip on passenger traffic. In an era when speed was often a great fascination, motor-racing proved popular to some. The Brooklands motor circuit, however, remained the only place where motor-racing was legal until the opening of the circuit at Donington Park in 1933. For better-off young men, a fast sports car was already one of the most desirable items.

Reaching further down the social scale, motor-cycles offered a cheaper alternative, both for travel to and from work and for leisure. The Great War had expanded production of motor-cycles and greatly increased knowledge of them, particularly amongst servicemen. In 1920 there were more motor-cycles than cars, and numbers reached a peak in 1930. During the 1930s, however, numbers declined by about a third, reflecting perhaps the effects of the depression on the humbler motorcyclist and the purchase of motor cars by the more affluent. Cycling, however, remained immensely popular, carrying on from its place in Edwardian Britain as a cheap form of transport and recreation. A new bicycle could be purchased for as little as £5 in 1932, or, more usually, for weekly instalments of a few shillings. National organizations such as the Cyclists' Touring Club and the National Cyclists' Union provided the organizational focus for one of the most popular mass recreations of the inter-war years.

More than 28,000 cyclists joined the CTC between the wars, sharing in a general move towards the pleasures and enjoyments of the countryside. Hiking and rambling boomed, particularly in the 1930s, when they combined a cult of healthy athleticism with the deep-seated fondness for the countryside which operated powerfully in British culture. The 'rediscovery of the countryside' was already well under way before 1914, but between the wars it rose into a passion, aided no doubt by the increasing availability of cars, motor-cycles and bicycles, and the readiness of large numbers of people of all classes to don strong shoes, shorts and ruck-sack in the quest for rural peace and tranquillity. For many, the countryside was the obvious place to escape to from the grimmer aspects of the industrial scene, still often grossly polluted and bearing the visible scars of industrial development. In many parts of Britain, a cheap bus or tram ride, or a railway ticket, could still bring people into virtually unspoilt countryside. In the *BBC Scrapbook for 1930* an unemployed man, John Nimlin, recorded how he and his unemployed mates started walking out from the City of Glasgow:

We explored Loch Lomond and the Campsie Hills, and we started camping out. One night round the camp fire we decided to start a mountaineering club: the Ptarmigan Club we called it, after the ptarmigan, a little bird that loves the mountains. Since then I've spent most of my spare time climbing ... I believe that during the slump there were many of the despairing and disillusioned who found a new meaning to life in the countryside.

One of the most pressing needs was for clean, cheap accommodation in rural areas. The answer came from Germany, which by 1914 had 200 *Jugendherbergen* (youth hostels). British visitors to Germany brought the idea back to Britain and by the late 1920s a number of organizations, such as the Northumbrian Trampers' Guild and the Holiday Fellowship, were providing basic accommodation in huts and shelters in places like the Pennines, the Cheviots and the Lake District; a Merseyside group was also examining suitable sites in North Wales. These efforts were brought together in 1930 with the founding of the Youth Hostels Association led by two men, Jack Catchpool and the historian G. M. Trevelyan, the latter becoming its first President. The YHA opened its first permanent hostel at Winchester and there were 297 hostels and a membership of 83,418 by 1939, when over half a million 'nights' were booked at the hostels by members. Separate associations were shortly formed in Ulster, Scotland and Eire, giving the whole of the British Isles 397 hostels and 106,524 members by the outbreak of the war. The Ramblers' Association also sprang up to cater for the new enthusiasm for hiking and walking.

For many, however, the chief focus of recreation was still the annual holiday and the regular bank holidays established before 1914. The growth of paid holidays provided an enormous stimulus to the holiday industry. In the early 1920s only one and a half million people had paid holidays, by 1939 over eleven million. The major holiday resorts, already well tuned to a mass market, boomed as never before after the Great War, so that over twenty million visitors went to the English seaside resorts by the late thirties. Blackpool, by far the most successful, had over seven million overnight visitors a year by the late 1930s. On the Bank Holiday Monday in August 1937 it had over half a million visitors, arriving in 50,000 motor vehicles and 700 trains (425 of them 'specials'). This popularity fuelled the growth of the resorts and an ever-wider range of facilities. These included open-air swimming pools, new fairgrounds, 'pleasure beaches', hotels, ballrooms and cinemas. From 1925 the Blackpool 'illuminations' became a permanent feature, after being stopped by the Great War, extending the summer season into the autumn and providing the resort with a new influx visitors, mainly for one-night excursions by coach and motor car.

A new development was the holiday camp, offering 'all-in' holidays based on chalets and providing modern catering and leisure facilities. The first holiday camps were set up by individual firms, trade unions and philanthropic bodies, but in 1937 Billy Butlin set up the first commercial holiday camp at Skegness. Two years later holiday camps had accommodation for more than half a million. Most people, however, who went on holiday for overnight or weekly stays at the seaside still relied upon hotels and 'digs'. The latter were by far the most common. The seaside 'landlady' was a figure of popular comment and repute, usually providing bed and breakfast, perhaps even cooking the food holiday-makers brought with them or bought themselves from local shops. Holidays of this type were becoming more and more common for ordinary people and for a majority provided the most obvious opportunity for a stay away from home.

Holidays abroad were also becoming more popular. The Great War produced a flood of British visitors to the battlefields and cemeteries of the Western Front, but in the 1920s an increasing number visited Europe for sheer enjoyment. Over a million Britons, mainly drawn from the wealthier sections of society, took their holidays in Europe in 1930. Fast express trains and steamer services offered a quick 'escape' to the continent and a number of new travel firms sprang into existence providing coach tours. France was still the most popular destination, with the South of France attracting the well-to-do, while it was still common for wealthy young Englishmen to spend some time on the continent in a kind of cheap version of the Grand Tour; France, Italy and, in the 1930s, Germany and Austria were common destinations. Monte Carlo with its casinos was the by-word for expensive pleasure; 'cruises' were popular amongst the more staid, and lengthy sea-journeys an inevitable part of going abroad if the destination was not Europe. Although air travel was becoming more common, it took only a fraction of the passenger traffic – still only a quarter of the North Atlantic route as late as 1948. The great passenge[r] ports, Southampton and Liverpool, catered for a large and almost inevitably wealthy clientele.

Even more influential than the spread of holidays was the widening range of entertainments offered by even the most modest towns. Music hall never really recovered from the effects of the rise of the cinema and the First World War. It survived, however, in an attenuated form in 'variety theatre'. *The Stage Year Book* in 1949 estimated that there were something under 400 theatres and music halls in England and Wales, eighty-nine of them in London. This was a large enough number to give most medium-sized towns a 'Hippodrome' or 'Alhambra' devoted to variety theatre and Xmas pantomime. In addition, several seaside resorts maintained pavilions at piers for summer shows. For most of the inter-war years, the variety theatre circuit provided the bread and butter for a host of musicians, artists and performers, only a few of whom could expect to find work in radio or cinema. Many of the most famous cinema 'stars' of the inter-war years, in Britain as in America, were in fact music hall or 'variety' performers who broke through from the stage. The serious theatre, primarily confined to London and the larger provincial cities, rallied to an extent from the effects of the Great War by branching out into light musical reviews and comedies. Noel Coward was, perhaps, the most talented exponent of a range which extended from light comedy to musical review. Musical shows such as *The Maid of the Mountains*, *Rose Marie*, *The Desert Song* and *The Vagabond King* also proved immensely popular. They were, on the whole, confined to a metropolitan audience, unless taken up by the host of amateur or repertory companies.

But these years were most important for the development of the cinema as an all-pervasive form of entertainment. By 1914 there were already 3,000 cinemas in Britain, many of them converted or part-time music halls. By 1939 the number had risen to almost 5,000, and, with the growth of the new purpose-built 'super-cinemas' of the 1930s, often with greatly enlarged seating capacity of up to 4,000. Mass Observation's

vork town' (Bolton) had fourteen cinemas by 1937 to serve
a population of 180,000 and with the pub and the dance hall
offered the most popular forms of mass entertainment. The
development of 'talkies' from 1927, and colour, greatly increased the attractions of cinema. The result was a surge in
cinema attendances, met by the large cinema chains which
adopted the principle of spending their way out of the recession
with a programme of cinema building. By 1939 something in
the order of twenty million cinema tickets were being sold
each week. Regular visits to the cinema were the norm: a
survey of Liverpool in 1937 found that 40 per cent of the entire
population went to the cinema at least once a week and 25 per
cent twice a week. In York in 1936 Seebohm Rowntree noted
that the seven cinemas attracted an audience of about 45,000
per week, almost half the population, while by 1939 ten cinemas
were patronized by about 50,000 people per week. The most
important feature of the cinema was its cheapness and the
quality of the entertainment it offered. A cinema ticket could
cost as little as 6d. – the price of a pint of beer by the mid-1930s
– or even less at the 'Penny Pictures' or Saturday morning
matinees, for which you were likely to get two or three hours'
entertainment, including two films, a newsreel, possibly a
cartoon or 'short', and 'trailers' for coming attractions.

The cinema had obvious attractions even for the poor. The
Carnegie Trust found that cinema attendance was the most
important single activity of the young unemployed in the late
1930s; they estimated that about 80 per cent attended a cinema
more than once a week and 25 per cent less than once a week.
For many it was clearly a matter of getting out of the house,
at relatively cheap cost. Without the stigma of the pub, it
offered a family entertainment. Women who would never dare
to enter a pub without a male companion could go to the
cinema with friends; for the young it offered a place for courting
couples to meet in privacy (and darkness); while children could
be safely packed off to the cinema on a Saturday morning for
a matinee. Moreover, as well as being a new source of entertainment, it offered a far higher standard of comfort than available

hitherto. Plush seats, wall-to-wall carpeting, exotic decor, lavish
auditoria and inviting entrance halls sold a 'luxury' feel which
was completely beyond the reach of the majority of their
audience.

The only serious rival to the cinema or the pub for a night
out between the wars was the dance hall. Dance music, much
of it American, was already becoming popular before 1914,
spread by sales of sheet music and gramophone records. The
foxtrot, for example, was introduced into London in July 1914
and received further impetus from its inclusion in musical
reviews in the capital. The coming of American troops to
Europe from 1917 and tours by American bands confirmed a
craze for American music and dance. The Hammersmith Palais
de Danse, opened in 1919, was one of the first to provide a
forum for the growing number of American-style 'jazz' and
'dance' bands. The sedate circle dances and waltzes were set
aside amongst the young for a whole new range of music and
dance. The most famous, the Charleston, arrived in England
in 1925. It was described by one newspaper as 'freakish, de-
generate, negroid'. Dance bands and records which had already
featured 'ragtime' music gradually adopted a form of 'commercialized jazz' with new instrumental line-up. Like the
cinema, the dance hall reflected greater opportunities for
women to go out and enjoy themselves. By the 1930s dancing
had become a national pastime, busily promoted by the building
of new dance halls and the popularity of the most famous big
bands, such as those of Roy Fox, Ray Noble and Lew Stone.
The first outside broadcast by the BBC of a dance band took
place in 1923, and in 1926 the BBC house band, the London
Radio Dance Band, made its first broadcast. Radio immensely
popularized particular performers like Jack Payne and Henry
Hall, who became household names. By the 1930s the BBC
had a regular nightly feature from 10.30 to 12.00 devoted to
one of the big dance bands. The most famous were able to
command large salaries at the top hotels and clubs; Bert
Ambrose was paid £10,000 a year as musical director at the
Mayfair Hotel in 1927 and in fashionable settings like the

Embassy Club mixed with high society, including the royal set. The wider audience, however, was reached through radio, gramophone records, tours and the countless, but far less famous, bands who sustained the local 'palais' or seaside ballroom. Again, like the cinema, dance halls were a relatively cheap way of spending a night out. Once a small admission fee was paid, several hours' entertainment was provided. 'Tea dances' in the mid-afternoon also proved popular with women and the unemployed. In the provinces, a typical medium-sized town like Rochdale had a number of occasional venues for commercially organized dances by the mid-1920s. By 1930 a town of this size, with a population of about 100,000, could offer half a dozen dance venues on a Saturday night in the summer, admission prices ranging from one to two shillings, although the first purpose-built dance hall was constructed only in 1934. By the 1930s the more frenetic and jazz-influenced dance crazes were being supplanted by the more melodic 'big band' sounds. However, by the late 1930s 'swing' music was beginning to be imported from America. Much popularized by American servicemen stationed in Britain during the Second World War, 'swing', 'jitterbug' and 'jive' were to form a new generation of dance and musical styles in the 1940s.

But if the cinema and the dance hall provided the major new opportunities for an evening out, there was also a continuation of earlier patterns. Reading and books proved immensely popular between the wars. The number of books published in the United Kingdom rose from 8,666 in 1914 to 14,904 in 1939, while sales went up, even during the worst phase of the depression from 7.2 million in 1928 to 26.8 million in 1939. Judging too from the number of books issued by public libraries, reading proved one of the most significant growth areas in leisure habits after 1914. In 1911 public libraries issued 54.3 million books; by 1924 85.7 million; by 1935 208.0 million; and by 1939 247.3 million. As well as the existing public libraries, mainly built before the Great War, the first mobile libraries were introduced in the 1920s to serve rural and suburban areas. One of the earliest, built in 1921 to serve the villages of Perth and Kinross, carried 900 books. As well as public libraries there were 'twopenny libraries' attached to tobacconists, sub-post offices and branches of chain stores like Boots. A new form of reading public was reached through cheap editions. Pocket libraries and complete works had already made an appearance by 1914. Woolworths offered a 6d. Readers' Library series by the 1920s, while in 1935 Allen Lane published the first 6d. paperbacks, the first two being a biography of Shelley, *Ariel*, by André Maurois and Ernest Hemingway's *A Farewell to Arms*. Pelicans, with a more deliberately educational character, such as G. D. H. Cole's *Practical Economics* and *Essays in Popular Science* by Julian Huxley, appeared shortly afterwards. A Penguin Shakespeare appeared in 1937 and was followed by a series of Penguin specials, dealing with important political and social issues. A wide public response was also attracted by the new book clubs. The most famous, the Left Book Club, founded in May 1936 by Victor Gollancz, had 60,000 members by the late 1930s, subscribing to books on a wide range of serious topics. Thousands of editions of seminal works, such as George Orwell's *The Road to Wigan Pier* and Ellen Wilkinson's *The Town That Was Murdered*, brought contemporary domestic and foreign issues to a wide audience. But the popular authors, in terms of sales, were usually less serious. For example a ballot taken at the Schoolboy's Exhibition in 1926 showed that the favourite books amongst the young were still the adventure tales of R. M. Ballantyne, G. A. Henty, Conan Doyle, Rider Haggard, Jules Verne, Captain Marryat and Rudyard Kipling. The school stories of Talbot Baines Rice and Frank Richards also commanded a major following, while younger children were already reading books such as *The Wind in the Willows* and *Winnie the Pooh*. Amongst an older public, detective stories by the likes of Agatha Christie and Edgar Wallace enjoyed a great vogue, while P. G. Wodehouse's creation of Jeeves and Bertie Wooster captured a large readership.

Reading was essentially a home-based leisure activity. The rise of house-ownership and council tenancies in the inter-war years encouraged the development of other domestic pleasures. Card games and commercial games like 'Monopoly' became more popular. Gardening, even at the basic level of merely clipping the hedges and roses or mowing the lawn, was already popular. Gardening clubs, horticultural societies, and a network of proudly kept gardens and allotments were on the increase, responding both to the practical need for many to supplement the family budget and the increasing home-centredness of people's lives which came with better standards of housing and higher personal incomes. Countless houses had their pets, while pigeons, whippets and greyhounds had their special devotees. Very little is known about the growth of minority pursuits such as dog breeding, 'serious' gardening, angling, scouting, keep-fit classes, table tennis, snooker and billiards, amateur dramatics, dressmaking and the thousand and one other ways in which people occupied their leisure time. By and large, the growth of mass entertainments, particularly the cinema, sport, dance halls and radio, does not seem to have destroyed the vitality or variety of hobbies and specialized recreations. If anything, they provided a range of activities to add to the pub and the music hall, while still leaving free time for the pursuit of individual pastimes.

For women, too, new interests were coming within reach. Although more women worked, the development of smaller families and higher living standards offered fresh, if often still largely home-centred, hobbies and recreations. For the more affluent the continuing availability of domestic service, boarding school education for the children, and servants or local delivery vans to look after the drudgery of day-to-day shopping often left plenty of free time. The city-centre department stores, hairdressers, cafés and coffee shops thrived on a custom made up of women 'going to town' for a day's shopping. For the less affluent, home-making was itself becoming a conscious leisure activity. The new illustrated women's magazines of the 1930s enjoined women to devote more of their spare time to cooking, house-furnishing, dressmaking and similar activities, now increasingly elevated to the status of hobbies, with special equipment, gadgets and literature. For some women, the pastimes became a principal means of developing a more fulfilling life around the basis of inevitable domestic chores; for others, however, it was a conscious deployment of leisure into spheres of activity which could in theory have been left to servants.

The most obvious feature of leisure activity between the wars was its growth. Higher standards of living and shorter hours of work, plus the extension of paid holidays to wider groups of workers, provided the impetus to an increase in almost every type of leisure activity, whether cigarette smoking, cinema, popular music, seaside holidays or reading. The beginnings of most of these developments were already apparent in the Edwardian era and their growth prefigured an even wider and more extensive growth of leisure in the affluence of the years after 1945. Many of these activities were now developed on a commercial basis in which the major brewing chains (themselves increasingly amalgamated and merged between the wars) were followed by the cinema and dance hall chains, record companies, sports equipment manufacturers, and press and publishing. Many of the new forms of entertainment were essentially more structured, occurring at set venues and at fixed times, fitting in with a fully industrialized work pattern. The more anarchic rural fair or traditional holiday, lasting for days, was already very much a thing of the past, only surviving in well-regulated and sanitized forms. One of the most persistent trends was for leisure activities to become less differentiated by region or class. The same films were as likely to be shown near Land's End as near John O'Groats, while the national administration of spectator sports and the increasing pervasiveness of national press and broadcasting made leisure habits more uniform. At the same time, however, there was more individual choice available. One of the reactions towards the commercialization and popularization of leisure activities was the growth of specialized groups within particular areas. Dancing might have been a mass activity for millions on a casual basis, but a few thousand might take it seriously enough to develop ball-

...om dancing competitions, run dance schools and make it their principal leisure activity. Similarly, as jazz music became an increasingly commercialized and popular form, its real devotees formed themselves into jazz clubs and patronized more specialized outlets. The same thing happened in the cinema, where those impatient with an endless diet of Shirley Temple, George Formby or Clark Gable formed their own clubs or private cinemas to watch foreign-language films. Increasing numbers of people had the time to devote themselves to their fads and fancies – everything from model railways to mountaineering – each with its own specialized literature and retail outlets. But even individual leisure choices tended to operate within an increasingly organized and centralized framework. The mass culture was hard to escape, even for the most determinedly individualistic.

The Press

By the 1930s the newspapers were easily the most important form of mass communication in Britain. According to a newspaper readership survey carried out in 1939, 69 per cent of the population over sixteen years of age read a national newspaper and 82 per cent one of the national Sunday papers. Given that an estimate of illiteracy and semi-illiteracy in 1945 concluded that between $16\frac{1}{2}$ and 22 per cent of the population were probably unable to read a simple newspaper paragraph, virtually the whole effectively literate population read at least a Sunday newspaper. In the years before 1914 there had been both an expansion of readership and a concentration of ownership, both of which continued after the Great War. Sales of the major national dailies rose markedly from four and a half million in 1910 to ten and a half million in 1939. Amongst the most successful was the *Daily Express*, whose circulation of under half a million in 1910 rose to almost two and a half million in 1939. The Labour-inclined *Daily Herald* also had a circulation of two million, followed by the *Daily Mail* and *Daily Mirror* with circulations around one and a half million by the Second World War. In 1920 there had been only two papers with million-plus circulations; in 1930 there were five; and in 1939 two at or above two million and three above a million.

Already by 1914 something of a distinction had grown up between the huge-circulation 'popular' newspapers and the smaller 'quality' press. This was reflected in the much smaller, but still rising, sales of *The Times*, from 45,000 in 1910 to 213,000 in 1939, and the *Daily Telegraph*, from 230,000 in 1910 to 640,000 in 1939. The success of the 'popular' newspapers was also seen in the rising circulation of the national Sunday newspapers. In 1937 the *News of the World's* circulation reached 3,850,000, compared with 1,500,000 in 1910; its major rival, *The People*, had a circulation of 3,406,000 in 1937 compared with 2,535,000 in 1930.

Overall the 'Sundays' remained the most popular newspapers, a position established before 1914. It was, however, amongst the mass national dailies that the greatest expansion was taking place, with an 80 per cent increase in daily sales between 1920 and 1937 compared with only 20 per cent for the Sunday journals. Although, by the mid-1930s, expansion of newspaper readership affected all social classes, frequency of newspaper buying increased markedly with income: those earning over £500 a year were the heaviest buyers of newspapers; those earning less than £125 were the least likely to buy. None the less, even amongst some of the poorest groups, such as the young unemployed in the late 1930s, newspaper readership was fairly widespread, even if it was often a question of scanning only the job adverts and the sports' pages. From the late 1930s, newspaper expansion continued at an even greater rate. Between 1937 and 1947, total daily sales rose from 9,903,227 to 15,449,410, while Sunday sales almost doubled from 15,700,000 to 29,300,000. The main thrust of this expansion was the growth of giant newspaper circulations, the *Express* and the *Mirror* both nearing circulations of 4,000,000. One Sunday newspaper, the *News of the World*, rose from under 4,000,000 to nearly 8,000,000.

One of the most important characteristics of the press between the wars was the growing distinction between 'popular' and 'quality' press foreshadowed by the *Daily Mail*. Even this had still been relatively conservative in layout and design, but once cheap newspapers became possible they soon adopted a style and presentation which, like the cinema and the chain store, appealed to a mass market. Influenced by American newspaper practice and by the tradition of the illustrated papers, newspapers moved increasingly towards the familiar style and layout of the post-1945 era. Advertisements were increasingly banished from the front page; headlines became larger; there was more illustration in the form of photographs and cartoons; while layout was re-organized in the 'staggered jigsaw', re-placing the ordered columns of the pre-1914 press. Raymond Williams has noted the change in style of the daily national newspapers between 1914 and 1937:

The *Express* of August 5, 1914, has a streamer headline in quite small type, and then a front page with ordinary straight-column setting, and small headlines which are little more than cross-heads except that two or three of them may appear above each item. By 1937 (the radical change having come in the late 1920s) the headlines are much larger, there is much more illustration, and the page is made up in the now familiar staggered jigsaw. The 1914 *Express* has $5\frac{3}{8}$ columns of ordinary printed news out of 7 columns; the 1937 *Express* $3\frac{1}{2}$ columns. By 1937 the other papers of this type are a virtual imitation of the developed *Express*, except that the *Mail* still has advertisements on its front page. Meanwhile, by the same date, the illustrated papers, *Mirror* and *Sketch*, gave only about a third of their front pages to ordinary printed news.

While circulation of newspapers rose, the number of national newspapers declined, from twelve national morning news-papers in 1921 to nine in 1947, and from twenty-one national Sunday papers to seventeen. The biggest contraction, however, occurred in the provincial press. The number of provincial morning papers fell from forty-one in 1921, to twenty-eight in 1937, and to twenty-five by 1947; and provincial evening papers from eighty-nine in 1921, to seventy-nine in 1937, and to seventy-five in 1947. A similar pattern is observable in the weekly press, mainly serving the provinces – the total in 19 of 1,485 had fallen to 1,162 in 1947. These trends toward smaller numbers of papers, though with rising total circulation, were continued after 1945. However, the press displayed characteristics similar to those of other mass-consumption industries in the growing concentration of ownership and a tendency for the large and successful to expand at the expense of the smaller-scale enterprise. Just as the big chain-store groups and the cinema chains increasingly came to dominate the scene in retailing and films, so the large newspaper groups were expanding and absorbing more readership. The process, mirrored in the commercial sphere in general, was twofold: the large newspaper groups became more successful in their own right, the 'popular' dailies and Sundays taking an ever larger share of the market, but also taking over larger numbers of provincial and weekly publications. Broadly speaking, the era between 1920 and 1947 was a halcyon time for the press. Intense competition became the norm: circulation wars were fuelled by more eye-catching layout, photographs, strip cartoons, crosswords, competitions and special offers for regular subscriptions. Newspapers set out to entertain in order to capture the largest market, crucial for the lucrative advertising revenue on which newspapers depended. In the absence of commercial radio or television, and with roadside hoardings as the only main competition, it was newspapers which provided the main channel for the new age of mass consumerism.

But the rise of the mass press in the context of growing readership and widening market did not preclude the expression of a range and diversity of news. Although the tendency of the mass press was towards a generally 'conservative' position, dictated by the pressures of circulation and advertising, there was room for the minority circulation Communist *Daily Worker*, founded in 1930, and the Labour-inclined *Daily Herald*, which received financial backing from the TUC from 1929 and achieved a mass circulation by the end of the 1930s. While the concerns and eccentricities of the great newspaper barons, such as Beaverbrook and Rothermere, were undoubtedly in-

ntial, the dependence of the press upon advertising and
rculation made it less a slave to political causes than to the
mass market. Apart from the *Daily Worker*, and a brief flirtation
of Rothermere's *Daily Mail* with the fascist movement in the
early 1930s, newspapers were, in the main, less radical com-
mentaries on society than reflections of it. There were, however,
journals and outlets where serious discussion could find expression. Newspapers such as *The Times* and *Daily Telegraph*
could take quite different stances on political issues such as
foreign policy. The *News Chronicle*, the *Daily Herald* and the
Manchester Guardian could usually be relied upon to provide
a more sympathetic response to left-wing causes. Political
weeklies, such as *Time and Tide*, the *Spectator* and the *New
Statesman*, also flourished. The last, edited by Kingsley Martin
from 1931, provided the intellectual focus for much of the
Left. The more highly politicized thirties also spawned a mass
of small magazines and journals, such as *Tribune*, founded in
1937. Amongst the most important of the new journals, however, were those appealing to the mass audience. The *Radio
Times*, launched in 1923, soon reached a very large circulation,
reflecting the new interest in broadcasting and the demand for
programme information. Especially significant was *Picture Post*,
launched in the autumn of 1938, the idea of a Hungarian
expatriate, Stefan Lorant, and backed by Edward Hulton of
the newspaper family. Its adventurous photo-journalism and
documentary style combined titillation and serious comment,
producing a circulation of over two million by the eve of the
Second World War and reaching nine million by 1949, eclipsing
the older, staider and more expensive *Illustrated London News*.

Moreover, the pattern set before the Great War of weekly
magazines concentrating on particular sectors of the market
rapidly developed during this period. Women's magazines
boomed as never before. At one end of the spectrum were the
expensive high-quality magazines, such as *Vogue*, founded in
1916, and *Harper's Bazaar* (1929). There were also lavish and
relatively expensive magazines concerned with the home, such
as *Homes and Gardens* (1919), followed by *Woman and Home*

(1926) and the *Woman's Journal* (1927). Less expensive and more widely read were *Women's Weekly* (1911), followed by the more colourful *Women's Own* (1932). By 1939 the most success-ful was *Woman*, launched in 1937 and priced at 2d., carrying romantic stories, hints on fashion and cosmetics, features on home management and recipes. As with the press in general, advertisements for the wide range of clothes, cosmetics and household goods aimed at women provided the financial under-pinning of the whole enterprise.

Children and young people also provided a mass market. The older *Gem* and *Magnet* were already rivalled by the *Boy's Own Paper*, and in the 1930s by *Hotspur* and *Wizard*. In upper-class families, *The Children's Newspaper* (1919) provided a digest of the weekly news, though it was relatively expensive. Much more widely read by younger children were *Rainbow* and *Chips*, both started before the Great War. One of the important innovations by the 1930s was the development of coloured 'comics'. The *Dandy* was launched in 1937 and the *Beano* in 1938. New tastes in popular entertainment were also reflected in the rise of *Film Fun* and the *Mickey Mouse Weekly*.

Broadcasting

Regular radio broadcasting began in Britain in 1922, the result of the great strides made in the science of radio telegraphy before 1914 and its adoption during the First World War for military purposes. Initially control of the new medium was vested in the British Broadcasting Company, but this was trans-ferred in 1926 to the first major public corporation in twentieth-century Britain, the British Broadcasting Corporation or BBC, independent of government but ultimately responsible to a Minister of the Crown, the Paymaster-General. At first radio listening was essentially an enthusiast's pastime, dependent upon the use of crystal sets, cat's whiskers, complex aerials and head-phones. But the introduction of the 'valve set' with attached loudspeaker soon replaced the more cumbersome apparatus, and by the 1930s 'mains' radio sets with built-in speakers were becoming a familiar part of the furniture in many homes. The radio revolution was illustrated by the number of licences issued, starting from a mere 36,000 in 1922, rising to two million in 1926, and to over eight million in the late 1930s. By 1939 a point had been reached where almost thirty-four million people were able to receive radio broadcasts, representing almost three-quarters of all households. Even so approximately three and a half million households, representing thirteen and a half million people, mainly the poorer sections of the population, had no access to radio. Licences, at 10s. for the period 1922–39, were not cheap, and this almost certainly acted as a disincentive to the poorer sections of the community. While crystal sets were relatively inexpensive at as little as £1, if rather inconvenient, the first 'cabinet' sets were firmly in the luxury bracket. Like motor cars and other consumer durables, however, the price of radio sets tumbled. By the early 1930s Currys were selling the new two- or three-valve sets at £1–£3 or on hire-purchase at one or two shillings per week. Smaller, more manageable sets were introduced using new materials, such as Bakelite, famous designers such as Serge Chermayeff and Misha Black producing 'modern' designs. Sales were also stimulated by the widely reported 'Radiolympia' exhibitions from 1926, by insistent press advertising and, above all, by great national events like the 1937 Coronation.

Hence the inter-war years saw the birth of mass broadcasting as a home-based entertainment. Apart from commercial stations such as Radios Luxembourg and Normandie broadcasting from the continent, bringing programmes like the 'Ovaltineys' and 'Horlicks Tea Hour' to those who could receive them, the tone of early radio was dominated by the conception of 'public service' broadcasting. The road towards competitive commercial radio, enjoying a tremendous boom in the USA, was spurned in favour of a monopoly service paid for out of licence fees, in which the emphasis was as much on instruction as entertainment. Many saw radio as the means of bringing culture to the people, and for a time at least it was almost unbearably serious in style. Until the 1930s, classical music and drama remained in the forefront of BBC programmes, but there soon developed a wider choice of programmes aimed at a mass market. The BBC's light music programmes popularized new dances and bands and generated their own entertainment industry with orchestras, bands, singers and comedians. Through its Regional Service, the BBC was able to cast its net widely to tap regional talent. Wilfred Pickles obtained his first work on radio (in Children's Hour) after auditioning at the Manchester studios, while the famous singer Kathleen Ferrier was 'discovered' by a regional radio producer, Cecil McGivern, at a charity concert in Workington, and made her first radio broadcast in February 1939 from Newcastle.

Radio, like other leisure pursuits, had a twofold appeal: to the serious wireless enthusiast and to the mass audience. During its pioneering days in the early 1920s, magazines such as *Wireless World*, *Popular Wireless*, *Amateur Wireless* and *Wireless Constructor* were selling hundreds of thousands of copies each week and wireless clubs such as the London Wireless Club, the Radio Association and, later, the Listeners' League provided an outlet for the devotees. The development of the mass audience, however, soon relegated the technical and scientific interest in radio to a minority hobby. For the general listener, the radio was a convenient source of entertainment and no more, increasingly part of the furniture of the average home. By the late 1930s, listener research was beginning to feed back to the BBC the nature of its audience and its listening preferences and habits. Variety, light orchestral music, dance bands and sport were amongst the most popular types of programme; chamber music the least. More women listened than men, more old than young; and the peak listening times were at mid-day and in the early evening, when audiences of between eight and ten million were recorded.

What changes did radio produce? Many felt it was a potentially revolutionary medium. Unregulated radio was feared because, characteristically, it was felt that it would soon pander to the lowest taste. Others, however, saw it as an 'improving' medium. In his *Broadcast over Britain*, John Reith, the first

Director-General of the BBC, nailed his colours firmly to the moral purpose of radio: 'I think it will be admitted by all, that to have exploited so great a scientific invention for the purpose and pursuit of "entertainment" alone would have been a prostitution of its powers and an insult to the character and intelligence of the people.' Confronted with the criticism that radio was giving people what the BBC thought they wanted, not what they needed, Reith was clear that 'few know what they want and very few what they need . . . In any case it is better to over-estimate the mentality of the public than to underestimate.' In effect this meant that the style of radio broadcasting remained somewhat conservative: religious programmes every day of the week, regular doses of culture and a strictly rationed portion of entertainment.

Radio reinforced much of the home-centred emphasis of other pastimes like reading, card games and domestic hobbies. It provided entertainment in the home, another alternative to the pub, and a cheaper rival to theatre and cinema. For women and children in particular it offered a widening variety of entertainment. In part at least the monopoly of broadcasting enabled the BBC to bring people into contact with new ideas, music and a wider world of news. It was, in this, only following in the footsteps of the press, but in a more immediate and accessible way. Similarly, the radio could also be seen as a homogenizing force both culturally and nationally. It soon defined a calendar of annual sporting events familiar to most people between the wars: the annual boat race between Oxford and Cambridge, the Wembley Cup Final, the Grand National, test matches, the Wimbledon tennis championships, as well as more occasional sporting contests, such as big boxing promotions. It institutionalized such occasions as the Remembrance Day service, the Monarch's Christmas message, started in 1932, and the Christmas service of lessons and carols from King's College, Cambridge, first broadcast in 1928.

In many ways radio merely made more effective the national cohesion already established by the press, the railways and mass education before 1914. Although there was an increasing awareness of national events, radio provided the means by which the latest news, sporting events and celebrities could be brought quickly to an audience of millions. In 1926 it had provided one of the crucial mediums of government control. Although Lord Reith resisted direct government interference, the continuation of radio broadcasts offered a vital alternative to the largely strike-bound press. Ten years later the sonorous refrain, spoken by Reith himself, that 'The King's life is moving peacefully to its close' tolled across the nation the news of George V's last illness. Edward VIII's abdication message was carried by wireless to the whole country, while in September 1939 the news of Britain's declaration of war against Germany was brought first, not by newspapers, but by radio broadcast in the words of the Prime Minister himself, speaking directly to the people.

The Arts

The twentieth century has self-consciously appropriated to itself the title of 'the age of modernism'. In cultural terms, modernism has been identified by Alan Bullock with 'new ways of looking at the universe both artistically and scientifically, new ways of understanding man and society, new forms of expression for what they saw and felt, which were different from any that had gone before'. As Bullock and others have argued, the origins of modernism lie in the years before 1914, in the astonishingly creative period which began in the last years of the nineteenth century and in which Britain shared, somewhat belatedly and haphazardly. Gathering pace after the Great War, several of its features were absorbed into the British cultural scene, frequently grafted on to more traditional concerns. Equally significant socially was the continued growth of many different kinds of cultural activity, developing their own outlets, practitioners, organizations and audience and providing Britain, by the Second World War, with the basis for a strongly based cultural revival, seen most strikingly in such fields as drama, music and sculpture. However, there persisted a separation between 'high' and 'popular' cultures, in spite of attempts to bridge it through broadcasting and education.

Undoubtedly the most pervasive form of artistic expression both before and after the Great War was literature. It has been said that the 'serious attack' on Victorianism began in the late Victorian and Edwardian periods, developing under the leadership of Bernard Shaw, H. G. Wells, Roger Fry, Joseph Conrad and E. M. Forster. This questioning of earlier moral and aesthetic values was shared by Irish and Anglo-American writers such as W. B. Yeats, James Joyce, T. S. Eliot and Ezra Pound. By the Edwardian period, the sense of a 'new' and 'modern' literature was already strongly established. It was to the year of the death of King Edward VII and the first Post-Impressionist Exhibition that Virginia Woolf pointed when she wrote: 'On or about December 1910 human nature changed ... All human relations shifted – those between masters and servants, husbands and wives, parents and children. And when human relations change there is at the same time a change in religion, conduct, politics and literature.'

This sense of a rapidly changing society promoted amongst many the search for new forms and conventions within which to express the social, moral and intellectual conflicts they experienced. In literature the degree of experimentation came up against the barrier of intelligibility, but it was significant that it was in 1914 that James Joyce began his seven years' work on *Ulysses*, a novel whose strange language, introspection and sexual frankness were to make it a major landmark in the history of modern literature. As in many other areas of modernism, the rejection of what were perceived as Victorian values could as easily proceed through the development of a new intensity and commitment as through radical experimentation in form. Even Rupert Brooke, whose famous war sonnets seemed to breathe the certainties of an era wiped away for ever in the Great War, had already used a more realistic language in some of his pre-war poems. The Great War also had its effect in heightening the realism, spareness, even brutality, with which the likes of Siegfried Sassoon, Wilfred Owen and others began to write in order to express the horror and reality of war. In the case of both Sassoon and Owen, a lyrical somewhat high-flown style was increasingly substituted by forceful language, jagged rhythms, soldiers' colloquialisms and direct speech. The range of techniques with which the 'war poets' – a not entirely satisfactory category for a group of writers whose individual experience and imagination defies simple classification – expressed themselves none the less reflected the characteristic of modernism, the

search for forms of expression capable of conveying a new
range of experience and consciousness.

In literature, as elsewhere, the Great War emphasized rather
than originated these new modes. It added, also, a note of anger
and contempt towards pre-war society. In the world of the
1920s and 1930s many writers would pour scorn on the ideas
and institutions of pre-war Britain. But while the war added a
new bitterness to those who were writing after 1918, this development was in the context of a broader-based re-evaluation
of the cultural inheritance of the nineteenth century. Strikingly,
one of the most famous assaults on Victorianism, Lytton
Strachey's *Eminent Victorians*, published in 1918, was a product
of the war years, but also drew upon the growing disillusion
with the mores of the pre-1914 era. Post-war literature broke
new ground either by breaching established conventions or by
setting a new tone and style. D. H. Lawrence's *The Rainbow*,
published in 1915, had already been condemned for indecency,
while *Lady Chatterley's Lover* remained banned in Britain from
its first private publication in Italy in 1928 until 1960 because of
its use of four-letter words. Similarly Joyce's *Ulysses*, published
in Paris in 1922, was banned in Britain because of its sexual
explicitness. The strong sexual theme in Lawrence's writings
reflected one of the conventionally perceived changes in inter-
war literature, a greater concern with what some writers saw as
a fundamental aspect of values and behaviour. Other kinds of
exploration were undertaken in T. S. Eliot's *The Waste Land* of
1922, depicting the bleakness of a materialistic, Godless age, and
in the instrospective novels of Virginia Woolf. But the currents
at work in literature were extremely diverse. Malcolm Bradbury
has spoken of the whole era in English literature from the 1890s
to the 1920s as 'a complex mixture of ongoing native preoccupations and a hospitable assimilation of foreign tendencies'.
Pre-1914 London had had an unusually rich concentration of
eminent writers in English, drawn not only from Britain, but
also from the United States, the Commonwealth and Ireland.
To an extent, the focus shifted after 1925 to the continent:
Joyce and Lawrence became expatriates and something of the

vitality of the literary scene ebbed. Nor must it be assumed that all writers were necessarily working with new concerns. John Galsworthy completed *The Forsyte Saga* only in 1922 and Arnold Bennett the *Clayhanger* trilogy in the midst of the Great War. In somewhat similar vein the Yorkshire writer J. B. Priestley enjoyed considerable success with his optimistic, cheerful novel about a group of touring players, *The Good Companions*, published in 1929. Two of the finest writers of the English language were beginning to make a mark in 1920s with their comic visions. P. G. Wodehouse's Bertie Wooster made his first appearance in *My Man Jeeves* in 1919, beginning a run of comic success which was to outlast the Second World War. In 1928 Evelyn Waugh published *Decline and Fall*, followed by *Vile Bodies* (1930), *Black Mischief* (1932) and *Scoop* (1938).

In so far as general trends were obvious in the literature of the period, there was some evidence of a growing seriousness and commitment in the late 1920s and 1930s. Part at least was shown in the great burst of anti-war writing which emerged after 1929. It had, in fact, already been foreshadowed in aptly titled books such as Philip Gibbs's *Realities of War*, published as early as 1920, but the years around 1929 witnessed a remarkable outpouring of comment and memoir, much of which was bitingly critical of the war and of the society which had given rise to it. That it was not a purely indigenous phenomenon was shown by the appearance in 1929 of Remarque's *All Quiet on the Western Front* and Hemingway's *A Farewell to Arms*. It was matched in Britain that year by Robert Graves's *Goodbye to All That*, Richard Aldington's *Death of a Hero*, Sassoon's *Memoirs of a Foxhunting Man* and *Memoirs of an Infantry Officer* (1928–30), Edmund Blunden's *Undertones of War*, and the staging of R. C. Sherriff's *Journey's End* in the West End.

But while, at the turn of the decade, literature appeared to be concentrated upon damning indictments of all that pre-war society had stood for, there was also something of a re-engagement with politics and values which formed a contrast with the self-absorbed and 'frivolous' twenties. In part the effects of the depression registered in books such as Walter Greenwood's *Love*

on the Dole, one of the few genuinely proletarian novels to
appear between the wars, and in the growing volume of semi-
documentary writing such as J. B. Priestley's *English Journey* of
1934 and George Orwell's *Road to Wigan Pier*, published in
1937. Amongst the younger writers, such as Priestley and
Orwell, W. H. Auden, Stephen Spender, Christopher Isher-
wood and C. Day Lewis, socialist and communist ideals, to a
greater or lesser degree, shaped something of the tone and style
of writing. Amongst older writers, too, there was a concern
with larger events. H. G. Wells, an early Fabian and by the 1920s
a strong supporter of the League of Nations as a prelude to an
ideal 'World State', produced in 1933 in *The Shape of Things to
Come* a prophecy of aerial warfare and mass bombing in the
event of a future war. International events such as the
depression, the rise of fascism, and the Spanish Civil War gave
much of the writing of the thirties a political feel rather lacking
in the twenties. The outbreak of the Spanish Civil War in July
1936 provided a focus for a large group of writers and artists of
broadly left-wing persuasion. But few writers fitted neatly into
any broad categories. Graham Greene had something of the
documentary approach and the realism found in films and
literature of the 1930s, but his sharp observations of the contemporary environment, including some of its political moods,
were informed more by the spiritual struggles which he
perceived through his Roman Catholic faith. T. S. Eliot's later
work was also less affected by politics than by the religious
and meditative concerns of a devout Anglo-Catholic.

The theatre provided few major masterpieces in this era,
though it remained a prestigious and popular medium. Shaw,
Galsworthy, Maugham, Barrie and Priestley were amongst the
most accomplished of the serious dramatists, but faced with the
growing competition of the cinema there was a tendency for the
theatre to concentrate upon musical revue and light comedy.
Noel Coward, Terence Rattigan and Ivor Novello maintained
an output which in style and content reflected a popular taste
directed away from 'serious' drama. Often brilliantly clever and
vastly enjoyable, the musical 'show' was the real crowd-puller

for the theatre after 1918. Moreover, in spite of the continued importance of the traditional repertoire, symbolized by the building of the new Shakespeare Memorial Theatre at Stratford-upon-Avon in 1932, the conventional assessment of the theatre between the wars has been coloured by what has been seen as the rather dated and sentimental character of many of the plays being written and produced. Others, however, have made a different and less severe judgement, seeing, as Jon Clark has, a period 'rich in variety, experimentation and creativity' between 1900 and 1939. The formation of the first repertory company at the Manchester Gaiety Theatre in 1908 by Miss Annie Horniman began an expansion of repertory theatre which by the late 1940s sustained approximately 200 'little theatres'. Amateur dramatic societies also flourished; as Seebohm Rowntree noted in 1951: 'To a steadily increasing extent over the last 20 or 30 years, groups of people who have come together primarily for other purposes have formed the habit of regularly putting on plays of various kinds. Thus community centres, youth clubs, women's institutes, social and sporting clubs, and many other diverse groups have made amateur theatricals a regular part of their activities.' By the late 1930s there were also an estimated 300 'Left' theatre groups performing plays and sketches, of which the best known was the Socialist Unity Theatre founded in London in 1936. Importantly, the popularity of theatre of whatever kind continued to provide a major recruiting ground for acting talent. Aided by the growing opportunities of radio and film, Britain continued to produce a stream of stage and film performers of world stature, bringing to British acting a prestige it was to continue to enjoy well into the post-1945 era. Judged as a performing art rather than on its literary merits, the British theatre was very lively indeed and remained capable of attracting large audiences.

In spite of its popularity, the cinema was less highly regarded between the wars than theatre – 'neither art nor smart' as one writer put it. It did, however, play a significant part in two particular directions, in the developing of British acting and directing talent, and the fostering of the documentary movement which did much to influence British cinema in the 1940s and 1950s. Taken as a whole in the 1920s, the British cinema industry was a fairly sickly growth. By 1926 the proportion of British films shown in British cinemas had fallen below 5 per cent, the overwhelming majority of films shown being made in America. Already many of the most talented actors and performers, notably Chaplin, had crossed the Atlantic, while American companies dominated the distribution network in Britain, making it difficult for British films to reach a mass audience. Of the 749 films shown to the film trade in 1926 only thirty-four were British and only two of them taken up by the American distribution companies. The Cinematograph Films Act of 1927, however, obliged renters and exhibitors to show a minimum quota of native films, set at 7½ per cent in 1928–9, but to rise to 20 per cent by 1935. As a result, some stimulus was given to British film production. Alfred Hitchcock was beginning to make a name with his carefully crafted suspense thrillers such as *Blackmail* (1929) and *The Thirty-Nine Steps* (1935). The influx of refugees from Europe, notably the Hungarian Korda brothers, injected some much needed life into the industry. Sir Alexander Korda's London Films produced a series of spectacular and successful costume dramas, such as *The Private Life of Henry VIII* (1933), *The Scarlet Pimpernel* (1934), *Sanders of the River* (1935) and *The Four Feathers* (1939), which nourished native acting and technical skills. A gallery of famous actors and actresses, Charles Laughton, Leslie Howard, Laurence Olivier and Vivien Leigh amongst others, were able to begin to develop their talents, although the tendency still was for most of them to look to the larger American industry for their careers. In general terms, the British cinema was able by the 1930s to produce and show films of wide appeal and high technical merit. There was little, however, in the British cinema to equate with the best foreign-language films shown in a scattering of 'art' cinema houses in some of the major cities, where the French cinema and the work of directors such as Sergei Eisenstein or Fritz Lang appealed to a small intellectual audience. Indeed, as others have noted, foreign 'serious' films,

such as Lewis Milestone's *All Quiet on the Western Front* (1930)
and Jean Renoir's *La Grande Illusion* (1937), had considerable
influence on attitudes amongst those who sought them out.
Perhaps the most important British contribution lay in the rise
of the documentary film movement pioneered by the Scot, John
Grierson. Here non-commercial films, sponsored first by the
Empire Marketing Board and then by the GPO film unit,
developed a more realistic approach, portraying something of
the lives of ordinary people and their problems. Films such as
Grierson's *Drifters* (1929), Anstey and Elton's *Housing Problems*
(1935) and Harry Watt's *Night Mail* (1936) prefigured the tech-
niques of wartime films such as Watt's *Target for Tonight* (1940),
Humphrey Jennings's *Listen to Britain* (1942) and *Fires Were
Started* (1943), and Roy Boulting's *Desert Victory* (1943).

   In contrast, Britain enjoyed a great expansion in the
performance and appreciation of serious music. A strong, if
somewhat eclectic, musical tradition built up before the Great
War undoubtedly played a large part. Venues for musical
performance had grown rapidly and with them an expansion of
performers and audience. The 'Proms', started in 1895 under Sir
Henry Wood, and a network of festivals and competitions
provided opportunities for composition, performance and
appreciation, while the strongly established choral traditions of
the North of England, Wales and the cathedral cities also played
a major part in the development of English music. Resort bands
and orchestras also provided a crucial opening for musicians. For
example, in 1925 the young Malcolm Sargent began his career
as a conductor on Llandudno pier. Amongst the most striking
features of the musical scene in Britain up to the 1920s was its
varied nature, in which classical music, operatic themes, British
songs and religious hymns formed part of a catholic blend of
'high-brow' and 'low-brow' elements. Sheet music and pianos
enabled a wide range of music to be brought into the home and
popular pieces such as 'The Lost Chord' or 'Rimington' sold in
their hundreds of thousands. The gramophone also brought a
wider range of music to a much bigger audience. Nothing,
however, could compare with the radio for expanding the

audience for serious music. The strong emphasis upon classical music in Reith's BBC, while not always popular, brought it into millions of homes. The 1920s have been identified by Philip Hope-Wallace as a period when there was 'a huge "growing up" of musical taste'; as well as an important group of indigenous composers, such as Elgar, Vaughan Williams, Walton, Bax, Holst, Bliss and Lambert, there was a slow digestion of contemporary and near-contemporary music from abroad. Conductors such as Henry Wood, Thomas Beecham, Malcolm Sargent and John Barbirolli brought to a wider audience some of the main currents of European music. For example, foreign composers and conductors such as Stravinsky, Prokofiev and Toscanini worked with the new BBC Orchestra, formed in 1930, conducted by Adrian Boult. As with the theatre, the strength of British music lay less in its indigenous creative talents, though these were not inconsiderable, than in the all-round strength of its performers and the growth of an audience. By 1911 the number of music teachers was almost double what it had been thirty years earlier, and by 1932 Sir Henry Hadow could claim that:

> The spread of musical education, and the interest which it encourages, is wider and deeper at the present day than it has ever been. Our schools of music, in London, in Birmingham and Manchester, in Scotland and Wales and Ireland, are at a high level of efficiency, and though they are sharing with the rest of the country in the economic stress are maintaining their quality and their influence unimpaired.

In the midst of the depression, Hadow could talk of a wave of music-making and appreciation 'flowing to flood tide'. New orchestras and venues, the BBC and film also provided often vital ingredients of patronage for composers and performers; for example, William Walton and Vaughan Williams were two major British composers who wrote film scores. Opera too was developing a wider audience. The British National Opera Company was formed in 1922, while the founding of the Glyndebourne opera house in 1934 provided a medium for the performance of many operas up till then relatively rarely performed.

One of the striking features of the period too was the development of ballet as a part of the high culture. The Russian ballet of Diaghilev had already established new canons of dance taste by the early 1920s. Important as a vehicle for interest in *avant-garde* music, decor and stage sets, the *ballet russe* provided the stimulus for the development of a British school of dancers, choreographers and composers for ballet, with Ninette de Valois and Frederick Ashton two of the most important pioneers. New ballets were produced by composers such as Arthur Bliss and Constant Lambert, while Mme Rambert's ballet club, later the Ballet Rambert, the Camargo Society, and the creation of the Sadler's Wells company provided fresh stimulus. An interesting facet of the career of J. M. Keynes, the economist, was his marriage to the ballet dancer Lydia Lopokova and his sponsorship of the Cambridge Arts Theatre, opened in 1936 with a performance of the Vic-Wells ballet *The Rake's Progress*, conducted by Constant Lambert. By 1939 Britain had a group of promising dancers, including Robert Helpmann and Margot Fonteyn. Most important of all, ballet had permeated the public consciousness as a legitimate art form and a focus for a distinct following.

In the visual arts, Britain had already by 1914 witnessed something of the 'shock of the new' in Roger Fry's Post-Impressionist exhibition and the dabbling in futurist and vorticist techniques by artists such as Wyndham Lewis and C. R. W. Nevinson. The Great War produced no great new movement in British art, rather it emphasized existing trends and, through the organization of Official War Artists from 1916, gave much encouragement to artistic activity. Artists such as John and Paul Nash, Henry Lamb, D. P. Roberts and Stanley Spencer were commissioned to produce work which frequently reflected new styles and approaches in the attempt to portray the realities of war. For some artists, such as Ben Nicholson, these experiences were to assist the development of an abstract style already filtering into Britain from the continent before 1914. But in many aspects English art tended to lag behind continental trends, remaining a provincial offshoot

of the mainstream of European development. Even so,
Britain retained a group of accomplished artists, usually working within well-established traditions, flourishing art schools
and an impressive amount of smaller-scale design and craft
work. Fashionable painters such as Augustus John or William
Orpen were matched by the highly individualistic talents of
artists such as Stanley Spencer, L. S. Lowry, and the typo-
grapher, engraver and stone-carver Eric Gill. Indeed sculpture
provided an interesting example of an area where almost out of
nowhere Britain was to achieve international recognition in the
mid twentieth century. The American-born Jacob Epstein, who
settled in London from 1905, achieved notoriety for his stone
carvings rooted in early or primitive sculpture which, frequently derided as indecent or blasphemous, bore the authentic
experimental stamp of 'modern' art. By the 1930s, Britain
possessed through Epstein, Gill and the younger sculptors Henry
Moore and Barbara Hepworth a clutch of outstanding modern
artists.

Modern currents in art also found expression in the world of
design. 'Art Deco', a design movement largely springing from
the Parisian fashion salons of the 1920s, was to become the hallmark of the inter-war years. A hotch-potch of ideas and motifs
rather than a coherent movement, its most striking characteristic
was the use of more formalized and geometric designs to replace
the curves and flourishes of the *art nouveau* popular up to the
Great War. The aesthetics of machinery and a fashion for
geometric forms, some of them influenced by the Egyptian
motifs popularized after the opening of Tutankhamen's tomb
in 1923, created a style which remained essentially eclectic,
borrowing from the 'modern' movement, primitive art and
exotic parts of the world with almost equal frequency. Something of a continuation of earlier preoccupations was shown in
the insistence on good craftsmanship and high standards of
workmanship on even the smallest objects, derived from the
nineteenth-century 'arts and crafts' movement. But the
'modern' component lay in the use of new materials such as
chrome, glass and plastics. Small-scale Art Deco work such as

the tableware designed by Clarice Cliff in the 'Bizarre' and 'Fantasque' series was also immensely popular. It was sold through department stores, illustrated in fashion and furnishing magazines and exported in large quantities. More generally, the passion for speed and 'streamlined' designs was reflected in the furniture, interior decor and vehicles of the period.

In the most social of the arts, architecture, Britain remained a curious blend of old and new. Most British domestic dwellings were built on traditional lines, though some 'modern' houses and blocks of flats were constructed embodying the functional and utilitarian aspects favoured by the pioneers of modern architecture. Similarly, many, if not most, of the great public buildings erected up to 1945 still derived their inspiration from neo-classical, Gothic or English domestic styles. The majority of new commercial buildings – dance halls, offices and shops – did not obey the demand of the moderns that buildings should be 'machines for living in' or that the sole criterion of design and ornamentation was 'fitness for purpose'. English architecture was, then, a somewhat confused picture. Amongst its most characteristic results were buildings as diverse as the monumental Battersea Power Station (1928), the extravagant Art Deco Hoover Factory at Perivale (1932) and the massive neo-classical rotunda of the Manchester Reference Library (1934). None the less, there was growing evidence that it was the 'international style' of modern architecture which was slowly becoming more influential. What were considered modern attributes, white painting of exteriors, utilitarian design, the 'jazzy' motifs of Art Deco and the use of modern materials such as steel, concrete and glass were increasingly common by the 1930s. However lavish and exotic the interiors of the new 'super-cinemas' built in the 1930s, their exteriors increasingly displayed characteristically plain façades and the functional construction of the modern style. Britain was exposed to these influences through the important international exhibitions, such as that at Stockholm in 1930, which set out the new canons of architecture in their specially constructed buildings. Refugee architects from Europe, such as Gropius, Mendelsohn and Breuer, also brought new ideas, as did the Russian émigré Lubetkin. His Tecton partnership was responsible for some of the most modernistic constructions in Britain between the wars, notably the High-point flats at Highgate, built between 1933 and 1938, and the famous abstract, concrete Penguin Pool at London Zoo. Also notable were the efforts of some local authorities to sponsor more adventurous designs, seen in the Health Centre built by Tecton in 1938 for the London Borough of Finsbury. One of the most important sponsoring agencies for new work was the London Transport Board. Under its Vice-Chairman from 1933 to 1940, Frank Pick, the Board encouraged modern art in advertising, posters, lettering and station design. Tube stations such as that at Arnos Grove (1932) illustrated the new trends.

Hence on the eve of the Second World War there was little doubt that the 'international style' was coming to some sort of fruition in Britain. Young architects like those who organized the Modern Architectural Research (MARS) Group in 1931 were increasingly influencing official and unofficial taste. Even so, the process of conversion to modern architecture remained patchy. The most prestigious architect working in Britain in this period, Sir Edwin Lutyens, was a typically transitional figure whose career had been made in the pre-1914 era designing a series of romantic country houses. Although some of his creations such as the Cenotaph, completed in 1919, had some-thing of the austere and abstract quality of modern architecture, many of his larger designs, such as those for New Delhi and the unbuilt Roman Catholic Cathedral in Liverpool, retained many of the traditional qualities increasingly rejected by the new generation. Many older and more conservative architects refused to follow the claims of the modern pioneers that ornament was a crime and that architecture was synonymous with engineering or building. As a result, although Britain increasingly came under the influence of the modern 'inter-national style' from the 1930s, the modern movement was only gradually absorbed.

Science

The social history of twentieth-century Britain has been shaped, like that of other developed countries, by the products of science and technology. Arguably, electricity and the internal combustion engine have proved the two most influential developments in social terms, but they form only the practical demonstration of a ferment of scientific discovery and inquiry which by the Second World War had split the atom, developed the first reliable antibiotics, produced radar, television and jet propulsion, and given British science a high international prestige which it was to carry into the post-war world. Domestically, however, science, particularly applied science, was not to conquer the heartland of British culture; science remained something of a world apart, in spite of the determined efforts of popularizers to bring it to a wider audience. In terms of educational provision and social prestige, science and technology continued to lag some way behind the arts, leading by the 1950s to real concern about a divide between two cultures, arts and sciences, with, holding an uneasy position between them, the new 'social sciences'.

In the natural sciences some of the most revolutionary work was being performed in physics. Einstein's 'theory of relativity' was beginning to be recognized as a major modification of the Newtonian idea of a mechanistic universe which had held sway for almost two hundred years. Verification of Einstein's theory of relativity during the total eclipse of the sun in May 1919 brought the idea of 'relativity' to the wider public, even if only partly understood. No less important was the work of Sir Ernest Rutherford, first at Manchester and later at the Cavendish Laboratory in Cambridge, on the nuclear theory of the atom. His team, including John Cockcroft, E. T. S. Walton, Sir James Chadwick and P. M. S. Blackett, succeeded in 1932 in splitting the atom, laying the basis both for the building of the atom bomb and for the development of nuclear power. Important work was also being performed in the biological sciences, especially in fields such as nutrition and genetics, both of which had direct bearing upon medical research. Research into radio, given a great boost by the First World War, was also developing rapidly between the wars. As well as its obvious commercial potential in broadcasting it was also reaching new frontiers in electrical science. As early as 1911 a Scottish scientist, A. A. Campbell Seinton, had proposed the use of cathode-ray tubes for electronic scanning, at transmitter and receiver. In 1925 the inventor John Logie Baird, following up his own line of research using mechanical scanning, eventually produced the first TV picture. However, Baird's system was to be by-passed by the use of cathode-ray tubes and electronic cameras, pioneered in Britain by the Russian-born Isaac Shoenberg, Director of Research at EMI from 1931. His team in association with Marconi provided the equipment for the world's first regular TV service, opened by the BBC at Alexandra Palace in 1936. Another off-shoot of radio research was the development of radar, led by the head of the Radio Department of the National Physical Laboratory, Sir Robert Watson-Watt. By 1936 the first radiolocation (radar) masts were being erected along the Kent and Essex coasts for the detection of enemy aircraft.

Amongst the variety of stimuli to scientific and technical advance in these years, one of the most important was war. Prior to 1914 there was evidence of a decline in the vitality of the established scientific bodies such as the Royal Society, the Royal Institution and the British Association, and little government backing for science. The Great War brought a major stimulus both in the form of a revitalization of interest in hitherto largely neglected aspects of science and government assistance in research. In 1915 a Committee of the Privy Council for Scientific and Industrial Research, assisted by an Advisory Council, was set up and by 1916 organized into a separate government department with ample funds. Another result was the boost given to the Medical Research Committee, first established in 1913, through which work on psychology and clinical medicine developed rapidly under the pressure of wartime needs. From April 1920 the committee was given permanent status as the Medical Research Council.

This 'institutionalization of science', as Arthur Marwick has called it, was to remain a feature after 1918. Although government funds for scientific work were severely restricted between the wars, in some areas they provided a crucial impetus, as in the £10,000 allotted for research into radio location techniques in 1935. Similarly the state-sponsored BBC provided the main driving force behind the development of radio and television. Generally speaking, however, government 'economy' meant that, apart from a few permanent organizations run on a shoe-string, the bulk of scientific and technical work was left to the private sector, with electronic firms like EMI and Marconi, the engineering and aircraft manufacturers, and chemical companies carrying on the bulk of research and development for their own commercial purposes. During the 1930s the amount spent by British firms in these areas multiplied sharply, by over three times between 1930 and 1938 alone, and the number of scientifically qualified personnel and technicians employed by them rose to over 4,300 in the same period.

With the coming of the Second World War, government spending once again began to play a major part in scientific development, enormously stimulated by the dire necessities of national survival. Funds were channelled through the Department of Scientific and Industrial Research and the Medical Research Council, and a number of advisory committees, principally from 1942 the Scientific Advisory Committee, were responsible for the selective encouragement of research and development of scientific work. By something of a hit-and-miss process, in which *ad hoc* solutions to urgent problems often took precedence, Anglo-American efforts in the Second World War were to produce atomic weapons, pave the way for atomic power and lead to the production of penicillin, radar and jet propulsion. In many cases these were American developments of processes started in Britain before the war. Professor Howard Florey's development of Sir Alexander Fleming's discovery of penicillin took place in America after 1941 because Britain did not have the resources to exploit the work fully herself. Similarly, the pioneer efforts of the Rutherford team in nuclear physics were concentrated in America under the Manhattan project and the production of the first atomic bombs. But in radar and jet propulsion Britain was able to develop the advances made in the inter-war years. The work of Watson-Watt had already borne fruit in the radar defences of the south and east coasts which played such an important part in the Battle of Britain. Production of centimetric radar permitted the development of nautical and airborne radar systems, as well as more sophisticated navigational aids. The jet engine, patented by Sir Frank Whittle in 1930, became part of an operational fighter plane, the Gloster Meteor, by the summer of 1944. Advances in wartime science also prefigured post-war development, not necessarily utilized while war was being waged. The atomic bomb foreshadowed the peaceful use of nuclear power, only inaugurated after 1945 as a by-product of the British decision to pursue an independent atomic weapons programme, while many advances in medicine, electronics and jet propulsion were to be fully utilized for civilian purposes only after 1945.

To the scientific developments of the era must be added the growing importance of the human and social sciences. Increasingly, the first half of the twentieth century saw a growing awareness of the potential influence of science upon society at large. In areas such as biology, nutrition and genetics, scientists were already raising some profound ethical and political questions. J. B. S. Haldane in *Daedalus, or Science and the Future* (1924) and in *Possible Worlds* (1928) and Julian Huxley in *Essays of a Biologist* (1923) and *Essays in Popular Science* (1926) brought some of these advances in the biological sciences to the notice of a wider public, while in his novel of 1932, *Brave New World*, Aldous Huxley foresaw a society peopled entirely by the products of the test tube.

Practical interest in psychology was greatly stimulated by the experience of 'shell-shock' in the Great War, while the work of people such as Havelock Ellis and Marie Stopes helped to popularize fresh insights into sexual psychology. Freud became a well-known name amongst the educated public between the wars and some of his techniques were being applied as early as 1917 to the treatment of shell-shocked patients in special hospitals at Maghull near Liverpool and Craiglockhart near Edinburgh. A few fashionable private practices were set up to provide 'psycho-analysis', while some of the language of psychology, 'nervous breakdown' – or more popularly 'nerves' – 'inferiority complex', 'repression', 'ego', 'sadism' and 'masochism', were passing into common speech. Psycho-analysis and intelligence testing also were becoming increasingly influential in child development and education, while in 1923 the British Medical Association suggested that in criminal trials there should be an impartial panel of psychiatric experts to which the accused could be referred in cases where mental disorder was suspected. Although this proposal was rejected, medical evidence of this type was increasingly made available in courts of law. A significant feature too of recruitment to the armed forces in the Second World War was the use of psychological tests for officers and a much more sophisticated awareness of the psychological stresses of warfare by the army medical service.

Amongst the academic pioneers of sociology in Britain was L. T. Hobhouse (1864–1929), a philosopher and political scientist who held the chair of sociology at London up to 1929. His work *Social Development* (1924) was very much a product of the interest in social evolution fashionable before 1914. The most striking feature of British sociology, however, was its empirical flavour, built substantially upon the work of Victorian and Edwardian social investigators such as Charles Booth, Seebohm Rowntree and Sidney and Beatrice Webb. British social investigation flourished as never before after 1914. Seebohm Rowntree's career spanned the whole epoch with a series of major social inquiries: *Poverty, a Study of Town Life* (1901), *The Human Needs of Labour* (1918), *Poverty and Progress* (1941) and (with G. R. Lavers) *English Life and Labour* (1951). Others, such as A. L. Bowley, the pioneer of the sample survey technique, H. Llewellyn Smith, Herbert Tout, John Boyd Orr and many more produced a series of 'scientific' studies into various aspects of British society. At no earlier time had British society been subject to such systematic and comprehensive investigation, with studies of social structure, living standards, poverty, employment, unemployment, health, housing, communal life, crime and so on. In 1927 A. M. Carr-Saunders and D. Caradog Jones produced *A Survey of the Social Structure of England and Wales*, with a new edition in 1937, and a companion volume (with C. A. Moser) *Social Conditions in England and Wales* spanning the period from the 1930s to the 1950s, produced in 1958. Interest too was being aroused by the work in anthropology carried on at London University by Bronislaw Malinowski and C. G. Seligman. The behaviourist approach to morality, especially sexual, was strongly influenced by books such as Malinowski's *Sexual Life of Savages in North Western Melanesia* (1929). Anthropology's wider influence was also seen in bodies such as Mass Observation, founded by the amateur anthropologist Tom Harrison in the 1930s. Anthropology, like psychology, appeared to offer a perspective upon the day-to-day world. There was related development in fields such as economics and political science. At Oxford a new Honours School, combining politics, philosophy and economics (PPE or 'Modern Greats'), was established in 1921. Elsewhere, the London School of Economics under the directorship of William Beveridge from 1919 to 1937 was transformed by the 1930s into what has been called 'the largest centre for the study of social sciences in Britain', attracting teachers and students from all over the world, while in 1937 the industrialist Lord Nuffield provided money for the setting-up of a post-graduate college at Oxford, Nuffield College, for the study of the social sciences.

Knowledge of the achievements of science were increasingly brought to a wider public. Writers such as H. G. Wells, with his pre-war scientific 'romances' such as *The Stolen Bacillus* (1895) and *The Time Machine* (1895), did much to stimulate an awareness of the more fanciful consequences of scientific discovery, though increasingly with books such as *The Science of Life* (1931) and *The Shape of Things to Come* (1933) he was taking on the role of popular educator. Indeed, one of the most striking features of the period was the ready market for books of scientific exposition for the layman. Professor Lancelot Hogben enjoyed great success with his best-seller *Mathematics for the Million*, followed shortly by *Science for the Citizen*. The astronomer and mathematician Sir Arthur Eddington achieved a similar aim with *Stars and Atoms* (1927) and *The Expanding Universe* (1933), emulated by Sir James Jeans in *The Universe Around Us* (1929) and *The Mysterious Universe* (1930). Wider awareness of science amongst the young was also brought by Arthur Mee's *The Children's Encyclopaedia*, *The Children's Newspaper* and the illustrated *My Magazine*, which included articles on a wide range of scientific matters tailored for a young audience. *Discovery*, a monthly magazine devoted to recent advances in the natural sciences as well as archaeology, history, and economics, was founded in 1920, while amongst the first Pelican paperbacks were books such as Julian Huxley's *Essays in Popular Science* and Jeans's *The Mysterious Universe*.

Scientific and technical advance was also its own most effective publicist. It was impossible for any curious or moderately intelligent person to ignore the changes occurring around them. Tinkering with cars, motor-cycles and electrical equipment offered many an introduction to science and technology. R. V. Jones, engaged in the field of scientific intelligence and 'beam' warfare, during the Second World War remembered the impact of radio on himself and others between the wars:

My main hobby in my schooldays was, as with many other boys of my generation, the making of radio receiving sets. There has never been anything comparable in any other period of history to the impact of radio on the ordinary individual in the 1920s. It was the product of some of the most imaginative developments that have ever occurred in physics, and it was as near magic as anyone could conceive, in that with a few mainly home-made components simply connected together one could conjure speech and music out of the air. The construction of radio receivers was just within the competence of the average man, who could thus write himself a passport to countries he could never hope to visit. And he could always make modifications that might improve his aerial or his receiver and give him something to boast about to his friends. I acquired much of my manipulative skill through building and handling receivers. when at last I could afford a thermionic valve in 1928, I built a receiver that picked up transmissions from Melbourne, which that station acknowledged by sending me a postcard carrying the signatures of the English Test Team.

Moreover, with the coming of the Second World War, scientists, engineers and 'boffins' in general were frequently portrayed as a crucial element in the fight for national survival and achieved a new level of prestige and public awareness. In post-war books and films, men like Reginald Mitchell, designer of the Spitfire, and Barnes Wallis, inventor of the 'bouncing bomb' used in the Dambusters' raid, were to become regarded as national heroes. Certainly, the work of scientists between the wars provided a strong contrast to the disillusion and fragment-ation of much of the artistic and literary world. The note of self-confidence was struck by Hogben in *Science for the Citizen* when he wrote: 'This is not the age of pamphleteers. It is the age of the engineers. The spark-gap is mightier than the pen. Democracy will not be salvaged by men who talk fluently, debate forcefully and quote aptly.' Similarly, C. P. Snow noted the characteristic optimism of the Cambridge scientists of the inter-war years; where other intellectuals shrank from the changes they saw about them: 'It was difficult to find a scientist who did not believe that the scientific–technical–industrial revolution, accelerating under his eyes, was not doing incomparably more good than harm.'

But it would be a mistake to take this too far. The curriculum of the great majority of public and grammar schools continued to emphasize a literary and humane education in which the classics maintained precedence. In many areas of British life, science retained less prestige than the arts. In 1928, for example, in his *The English Tradition in Education*, Dr Norwood devoted three chapters to religious teaching and only ten pages to techno-logical and managerial training. More than one innovator lauded after the Second World War was to feel that it was only the necessities of war which had forced a recognition of the real strengths and achievements of British science. Even after 1945, the extent to which science and technology had been accepted into the mainstream of British culture and education were to remain a cause for debate and concern.

Culture and Society

As already suggested, there is no obvious point in attempting to dragoon the highest forms of artistic, scientific and other intellectual activities into spurious trends and patterns. There are, however, some features of British cultural life in this period which raise important social questions. The first lies in the transitional character of artistic expression. There were few informed commentators who could be unaware that there was a high degree of experimentation and ferment taking place in the arts. Even more traditional and conservative figures writing in the fields of music and the visual arts found it necessary to mention, even if only to criticize, some of the new tendencies. A not untypical older figure, Sir Henry Hadow (1859–1937), educationalist, music scholar and historian, editor of the *Oxford History of Music* and a pioneer of establishing music as part of a liberal education, could in 1932 describe Schoenberg as an 'eager experimenter, so intent on his problem that he loses sight of his audience' and Hindemith as a 'virtuoso ... (who) has declared that he is not interested in the emotions'. To him, there was 'a real danger' that from these musical experiments 'the art may evaporate'. Similarly the painter and art teacher Professor Henry Tonks, Slade professor of art from 1917 to 1930, could, in the same year, write that 'A visit to almost any modern exhibition will reveal to the visitor how far deformation has gone and how little respect there is for the proportion and construction of the human body.' 'Who knows,' he lamented, 'perhaps in a hundred years a child who tries with his pencil to draw something he sees will be hurried off to a psychoanalyst.' Similarly, an established figure on the architectural scene such as H. S. Goodhart-Rendel, who had a string of influential architectural positions between the wars including President of the Architectural Association (1924–5), President of the Royal Institute of British Architects (1937–9), Slade professor of fine arts at Oxford (1933–6) and Director of the Architectural Association school of architecture (1936–8), could in 1934 firmly dismiss the 'sick scruples of utilitarianism', and insist that pure 'functionalism' in architecture 'meant death'.

These were not unintelligent or insensitive men. What they reflected were more traditional canons of taste in the arts and something of the inevitable clash of opinions between old and new, between younger and older generations. What it also illustrates is the danger of writing the cultural history of the first half of the twentieth century solely from the point of view of the rise of the modern movement. As in other spheres, men of an older generation generally held the most important positions in the institutions, schools and associations, and in cultural terms Britain often lagged some years behind the continent in the absorption of new ideas. When in 1905 the young Jacob Epstein showed his drawings to Sir William Rothenstein, later Principal of the Royal College of Art, and a relatively liberal figure in artistic terms, he advised him that he would find more sympathy in Paris than in London. The same could still be said for many of the modern architects fleeing from central Europe in the early thirties, who often found America a more congenial and forward-looking environment in which to work. Even in the 1920s, the critical battles being fought in the art world were over the reputation and worth of Cézanne and other post-impressionists at a time when Picasso and others on the continent had already passed beyond cubism.

That being said, it was the shock of the *avant-garde* and the restless experiments they brought with them which caused the greatest stir and which set trends for the future. Epstein's sculptures regularly roused fury from the popular press, while in 1931 the *Morning Post* apologized 'for publishing even a photograph of the least objectionable of Mr Henry Moore's statuary on view at the Leicester Galleries'. At any rate, on the popular or academic level it was impossible to escape the sense that something of a sharp break was taking place with accepted taste. The gap between, say, Stravinsky's *Rite of Spring*, first performed in London in 1913, and anything which had gone before was obvious to listeners and critics alike, as was the remarkable 'entertainment for reciting voice and instruments', *Façade*, first publicly performed in 1923, with music by William Walton, in which twenty-one poems by Edith Sitwell were read through a megaphone to the accompaniment of flute, clarinet, trumpet, saxophone, cello and percussion. In music as elsewhere in the arts, the driving force behind restless experiment was the rejection to a greater or lesser degree of what were perceived as the conventions and values of the nineteenth century. Amidst a diversity of new styles and moods was a common thread rejecting earlier canons of taste. If the moderns were not entirely sure what they were for, at least they knew what they were against: what were seen as the dead conventions of formal representation in art, the Victorian novel and nineteenth-century romantic music. In order to express new ideas, new forms were required, new styles of painting, of musical and literary expression and sculpture and architecture. Artists were now customarily seeing their role as expressing their own emotions and feelings rather than merely representing what they saw outside them. If traditional liberal and religious values were false and rationality a sham, artists were set free to draw their inspiration either wholly from inside themselves or to seek a new framework of values in the aesthetics of the machine, in function and utility, or from the primitive or natural world, from Asia or Africa, or from the virtues of good craftsmanship and sensitivity to materials foreshadowed by the arts and crafts movement.

To a degree, then, British art shared something of the restless search for values and forms characteristic of the modern move-ment as a whole. It also shared the development of a self-conscious *avant-garde*, committed to experiment and ploughing its own furrow irrespective of popular taste or that of the generally educated public. The romantic notion of the solitary artist starving in a garret and producing a great masterpiece was already well established by the end of the nineteenth century; what the modern movement further cultivated was the notion of 'art for art's sake', detached from any kind of outside appreciation. The importance of this was the increasing diffi-culty of the active *avant-garde* in securing general appreciation. Unlike the earlier purveyors of conventional wisdom and

absolute truth within a commonly accepted framework of
values and beliefs, the *avant-garde* pursued their personal visions
often incomprehensible to all but a few. None the less, the
most approachable of the moderns retained a sufficient degree of
patronage to prosper. Galleries like those in Leicester Square
and Burlington Gardens provided an outlet for contemporary
work, while fashionable Mayfair provided a source of rich
patrons, the 'best market' for new work, where according to
one contemporary 'people of uncertain standards of value
bought the paintings of impressive young men whom they had
met at parties'. More importantly London provided a concentration of at least curious exhibition-goers. More than 20,000
people visited the New Burlington Galleries during a four-week
International Surrealist Exhibition in the summer of 1936, at
which were shown works by European and English surrealists.
On the opening day it was reported that traffic in Bond Street
and Piccadilly was held up by 'the rush of young society' to the
exhibition. This was the exhibition at which Salvador Dali
appeared wearing a diving suit with a motor-car radiator cap at
the top and plasticine hands stuck on the body to deliver a
lecture in French, relayed through loudspeakers; 'props'
included a billiard cue and two Irish Wolfhounds.

Pre-1914 London already had its coteries and groupings of
artists and writers operating at or near the frontier of conventional taste, with their own patrons, magazines, presses and
meeting places. In spite of the removal of some of the bigger
names in the 1920s, they continued to flourish in the inter-war
years. Amongst the most famous was the Bloomsbury group,
centred around Leonard and Virginia Woolf, Roger Fry, Clive
Bell and Lytton Strachey. There was also the 'Seven and Five'
Society (seven painters and five sculptors) which included Ben
Nicholson, or the MARS Group of modern architects.
Chelsea, Bloomsbury and Soho became the centres of a
'Bohemian' world of artists and writers, clustering around the
music and art schools, galleries, theatres and book and magazine
offices. The sculptor Jason Gurney, soon to go to Spain to
fight for the Republic, described Chelsea in 1936 as:

still a largely slum area, in which most of the rooms were let off as squalid bed-sitters at ten bob a week ... The whole area around Sloane and Draycott Avenues was a dismal slum of back-to-back houses ... But there were several hundred studios, most of them occupied by working artists as they were so cold and derelict that nobody else would have tolerated them. The Chelsea Polytechnic had a flourishing art school and so, with one thing and another, there was a fairly active colony of painters and sculptors, and many young writers were also attracted to the area by its cheapness and general atmosphere.

But beyond the development of an English 'Bohemia' lay a broadening of artistic appreciation. More people attended concerts, plays, galleries and museums, received some education in the liberal arts at school, and increasingly sought to participate in them at an amateur or professional level. The gramophone and the radio assisted in music what the piano and sheet music had begun. In art, as Henry Tonks noted in 1932: 'Museums and galleries have been much improved during the last fifty years, and thus we are able to see magnificent collections of pictures, and are kept in close touch with the latest discoveries of ancient civilization in all parts of the world.'

Culture in the sense of an appreciation of the arts was a growing aspect of leisure in the years after 1914, one which was becoming an increasingly characteristic aspect of upper-middle-class life. There was, significantly, some evidence of the softening of the hard lines between the 'hearty' and the 'aesthete' at the public schools, and somewhat less insistence on the absolute primacy of games. For women and girls in particular, art, literature and music were acceptable aspects of 'womanliness' to be built into the curriculum of the girls' public and grammar schools. A few progressive schools, Dartington in particular, positively emphasized a broader, liberal curriculum, in which the arts played a prominent part.

How pervasive this broadening of the appreciation of the arts went is impossible to gauge with any accuracy. A strong streak of philistinism continued to pervade much of the style of upper-class life and some of the public schools. Even in many of the most affluent circles, the arts were not considered an essential

attribute of life-style or status. Some members of the Royal
Family, for example, were conspicuously uninterested in the
arts. Similarly, there were many of the aristocracy, old and new,
whose interests lay in the more traditional country pursuits. At
the other end of the social scale, generalization is difficult. The
strong choral and musical traditions of places like the North of
England or Wales, the self-improvement ethos of some sections
of the working class, and a meritocratic system of education
could bring some working-class people into the world of the
arts. One only has to consider the careers of people like D. H.
Lawrence, Walter Greenwood, L. S. Lowry, Henry Moore and
Kathleen Ferrier to recognize that it was possible for people
from relatively modest backgrounds to be exposed to and enter
the cultural milieu of Britain in this period. Yet for most the arts
remained a closed book. Growing appreciation of the arts frequently completely by-passed the bulk of the working classes and
much of the lower-middle class. Whatever the optimistic aspirations of the early BBC to bring Bach to the backstreets, there
was no denying that by the Second World War popular culture
and 'high' culture were still almost completely divorced. If anything, the divorce was made all the more complete by the development of a mass culture based on the cheap press and the cinema.
Apart from what Richard Hoggart described as the 'earnest
minority', the largest proportion of the working classes inhabited
a different cultural world, in which 'working-class people are
on the whole just not interested in artists or intellectuals; they
know of their existence, but regard them as oddities rarely seen
within their orbit, like snail-eating Frenchmen'. Increasingly, as
men like Hoggart and Raymond Williams described, there was
developing a more uniform mass culture, based on the products
of mass consumerism and leisure, reflected in the popular light
music of the BBC, sport, the mass circulation national daily and
Sunday papers, the women's magazines, and the consumer
durables and products offered by industry. This was a world
whose cultural galaxy was more likely to be peopled by Charlie
Chaplin, Tom Mix, Shirley Temple, George Formby, Gracie
Fields and Vera Lynn than by Dali in his diving suit.

If there was a common feature which linked both 'high' and mass culture it was its increasing metropolitanization. If the nineteenth century had been the great age of the provincial cities, the twentieth century belonged to London. By 1914, as we have seen, London already possessed a strong and vital cultural life, which drew upon not only the British Isles, but also the wider world for its talent. Although there was some diaspora of major literary figures in the 1920s, London continued to play the dominant role in setting the pace for both 'high' and mass culture. The capital provided the major concentration of music and art schools, galleries, orchestras, publishing houses, music publishers, literary and theatrical agents, theatres, museums and concert houses. It had the only full-time internationally recognized opera house and was the only place where ballet was regularly performed. The BBC was firmly based in London, with its headquarters at Broadcasting House, while the British rivals to the Hollywood studios, Denham, opened in 1936, and Pinewood, of the same year, were both conveniently placed near to London. In almost every field, London absorbed talent from the provinces; it was Wilfred Pickles, having put his feet on the first rungs of a radio career based in Manchester, who noted in the late 1930s, 'All the good men go to London. I wonder why?' A few years later he was to join the move south himself to take up a post as announcer. A similar trail was followed by journalists, artists and performers as diverse as Francis Williams, Godfrey Talbot, Henry Moore, Dylan Thomas and Kathleen Ferrier. For the last, a talk with Malcolm Sargent after he had heard her sing at a Manchester hotel in May 1942 led to the inevitable advice, 'He told her that he thought she had a great future but that she would find it difficult to get on unless she lived in London.' Within two months she had obtained a London agent (Ibbs and Tillett), and by the end of the year had taken a flat in Hampstead to begin a brilliant career, tragically cut short by cancer eleven years later.

London's cultural dominance was cumulative. As it grew, it generated more and more opportunities and patronage for up and coming talent. The answer to Pickles's question was usually the prospects of a better job and more money. For a provincial journalist like Francis Williams, who had developed his skills on a Liverpool newspaper, editorship of the *Daily Herald* represented a huge step up in the world as, of course, did living near London. For young writers like Vera Brittain or Winifred Holtby, or the young sculptor Jason Gurney, London continued to offer meagre but crucial spiritual and physical nourishment largely unobtainable in the provinces. Already, there was some consciousness that the provinces were in need of fresh stimulus if their cultural identity was to survive the pull of London. In spite of the promise of the repertory theatre movement, Miss Horniman was forced to give up the Gaiety Theatre in 1921 and her encouragement of a 'Manchester School' of dramatists. Manchester theatres, like those elsewhere in the provinces, were used primarily for trial runs of hopeful West End productions or to stage established successes. Even in the field of song-writing and show business, London tended to dominate; its tastes, new tunes, and dance crazes were what were soon presented to a national audience as the latest thing. In the arts, as in culture generally, London set the tone. As well as premiering the latest film, fashion or fad, it was plugged into the international world of literature, music and the arts. Hence, by the 1940s, there was a strong move for setting up a body which would help to stimulate provincial cultural life, a cultural equivalent of the Special Areas Act and the Barlow Report for industry. This came in 1945 with the founding of the Arts Council.

Broadcasting also played a large part in the standardizing process of British culture. Although from the 1920s the BBC developed a network of regional stations and provided some stimulus to local culture, especially in Wales, there was little evidence by the 1940s that regional broadcasting had produced anything other than a minor variant upon the national network. When in the late 1940s the Beveridge Committee on broadcasting investigated the situation, they found that control from London, shortage of funds and lack of initiative by regional directors had inhibited the development of a strong distinctive regional broadcasting. Indeed, the regions themselves did not in any significant sense reflect real communities. They were large, nebulous areas derived from a London-based view of the country, designed less to reflect genuine community needs than the facilities of national broadcasting. Instead, as a national service, emphasized in times of crisis such as the General Strike, the royal events of the 1930s, and above all by the Second World War, the BBC tended to impose a uniform stamp upon the cultural life of the nation. Its most pervasive effect lay in the BBC accent, a southern upper-class speech which, although caricatured mercilessly, reflected a powerful standardizing influence. It was sufficiently entrenched to make difficulties for a man with a regional accent like Wilfred Pickles becoming a national announcer in the early years of the Second World War. More subtly, for all its refusal to become a mere medium of entertainment, the BBC provided through its programmes and personalities a common culture embracing everything from the Weather Forecast to 'Uncle Mac' of Children's Hour. The press too was noted for its increasingly uniform quality. Writing in 1957 of the tendencies evident in the popular press over the past forty years, Richard Hoggart spoke of 'a more narrow but also more genuine' working-class culture 'being eroded in favour of the mass opinion, the mass recreational product, and the generalized emotional response'.

An important aspect of the growing mass culture was its Americanization. In books, films and popular music this tendency was already evident by the early 1920s. American film personalities regularly figured amongst the most popular box-office stars and it was inevitable with the decline of music hall and variety that indigenous live performers were forced to share or yield ground to the Hollywood idols, though some of these were themselves British — the cast of probably the most famous film of the thirties, *Gone with the Wind* (1939), had two British-born actors and actresses out of the four lead parts. The transatlantic success of a number of British artists, however did not alter the fact that the product was American:

an American film, of an American novel, about American history, and financed, produced and directed by Americans. Even the revival of the British cinema in the 1930s and 1940s did not seriously undermine the dominance of Hollywood. Similarly, popular music was heavily influenced by American rag-time, jazz and, later, 'swing' music. As in the cinema, Britain produced its own successful performers, but the style and format was essentially American. These trends were emphasized in the Second World War. The presence of hundreds of thousands of American servicemen, living, often for months on end, in Britain diffused an Americanization already heavily purveyed by books, film and music. In mass production, advertising and marketing techniques, American initiatives were already being copied even before 1914. American-style comics and cheap magazines were also beginning to become popular. Aided by the success of the Hollywood animation industry, by the 1940s cartoon characters – Mickey Mouse, Donald Duck, Popeye, Tom and Jerry – were household names with British cinema audiences and as comic-book characters for children.

In the arts, internationalization was already a common feature in the nineteenth century. Except perhaps in literature, Britain was part of a largely European culture whose most powerful influences were continental rather than indigenous. The revival of 'British music' and the dominance of English language literature undoubtedly maintained a powerful native element in British culture, but there were also the influences in literature of the Anglo-Irish authors, Shaw, Joyce, Yeats, O'Casey, and Americans, such as Henry James, Ernest Hemingway, Scott Fitzgerald and John Steinbeck. In music, art and architecture, however, Britain increasingly derived its influences from the continent. France was the dominant force in the years up to the 1920s, but increasingly central Europe, assisted by an influx of European refugees from the Nazis, became at least as important. The Bauhaus and Le Corbusier were to become the arbiters of one aspect of taste by the 1930s, with Scandinavia beginning to offer another fashionable element by the 1940s.

Although native appreciation and performance flourished, the pace was set in most spheres by what was happening on the continent.

By the 1940s, obscured by the tumult of war, there were clear signs of the post-war development of British culture. Perhaps one of its most striking features was the build-up of a large and appreciative audience for the arts in general. The British were, most probably, a more cultured people in 1945 than they had been in 1914. They read more books, listened to more music and probably had a higher regard for the performing arts than at any earlier time. Side by side was the growth of a mass culture, which was now more pervasive, active and uniform than ever before. While people had money to spend and free time to occupy – and after the rigours of war-time more of them would have more of both – the mass culture depicted by Hoggart and others would grow apace. Increasingly, it was a metropolitan or transatlantic culture, based on mass consumerism, uniform products and increasingly pervasive forms of communication, principally, the press, radio and cinema – with TV waiting in the wings. The paradox of post-1945 Britain would be in the expansion and divergence of its 'highbrow' and its mass cultures.

16. *Into Battle*

The Second World War had at least as profound an effect upon British society as that waged a generation earlier. Once again, however, the experience of war served as much to intensify existing social developments as to stimulate new ones. Most of the features emphasized by the war, such as greater state control of the economy, increased intervention to provide social welfare, the development of a more collectivist and egalitarian style of government, the stimulus to science and the arts, and the opening of British society to wider cultural influences, notably from the United States, had already been foreshadowed in the years before 1939. In a sense, the war marked a deceptive discontinuity in the social history of Britain.

The War Effort

The basic problem for the government was very similar to that of the previous war – how to utilize resources to the maximum and allocate them in the most effective way. The experience of the Great War was followed and the government acquired powers to control almost every aspect of life. The Minister of Labour was empowered to direct 'any person in the United Kingdom to perform any service required in any place'. Non-essential industries were cut back, a pool of essential labour created and complete direction of labour introduced. Conscription was introduced without delay, with categories of 'reserved occupations'. In 1941 women were effectively conscripted for war-work or for service in the women's branches of the armed forces, at first between the ages of twenty and thirty, but after 1943 from eighteen and a half to fifty. By the end of the war, Britain had the most comprehensive direction of its manpower resources of any combatant nation, with the possible exception of the Soviet Union. Almost eight million people were in uniform by 1945 and still the government was critically short of essential workers and basic manpower for its armies.

Control of labour was only one part of a vast armoury of bureaucratic control with which the British government fought the Second World War. Rationing was imposed on a 'points' system, but leaving certain basic commodities, such as potatoes and bread, uncontrolled. In order to ensure that standards of health were maintained, vulnerable sections of the population, such as expectant mothers and young children, were given essential foods free. One of the striking effects of the war was that, amidst a system of austerity, the general health of the population actually improved through the distribution of certain foods to priority groups. To finance the war, indirect taxes were raised to high levels and income tax put at 10s. in the pound. New ministries were created which regulated wartime society to an unprecedented degree. Government campaigns to encourage war production, to avoid the dissemination of useful information to the enemy, to instil sound practices in household management under rationing and to influence morale brought the average citizen much more closely into contact with the state than ever before.

The war, according to Henry Pelling, 'witnessed a formidable concentration of power in the hands of government, especially in the hands of the Prime Minister himself'. The number of non-industrial civil servants expanded from 387,700 in April 1939 to 704,700 in October 1945, including in its higher echelons many university dons and professional people co-opted for wartime duties. Regional Commissioners were appointed to coordinate local government services to deal with the consequences of air raids and, if necessary, to take over the functions of central government in the event of an enemy invasion. Although the BBC was never actually controlled by the government, it was nevertheless largely dependent on government departments for most of its information. The radio, moreover, became a major instrument of national opinion through its broadcasting of speeches by the Prime Minister, listened to by seven out of every ten of the home population in 1940, and its broadly supportive attitude towards the war effort. The newspapers were not directly censored, though incoming news was, and Defence Regulations empowered the government to suppress any newspaper or journal 'calculated to foment opposition to the war'. Although restraint was shown in the use of these powers, the Communist *Daily Worker* was suppressed from January 1941 to September 1942, while the *Daily Mirror* was warned that it might be suppressed for criticisms of the army in March 1942. Action was taken against groups considered dangerous. Members of the British Fascist groups were detained without trial in May and June 1940, including the leader of the BUF, Sir Oswald Mosley. In December 1940, some 1,250 British subjects were in detention, while a larger number of enemy aliens, many of them in fact refugees from dictatorship, were interned. By and large, these were not overly dictatorial controls, though they emphasized the tendency towards bureaucratic centralism already apparent before 1939 and displayed the readiness to resort to arbitrary power in an emergency which had been shown during the Great War and some of the civil unrest which had followed. In a sense, though, the government was able, as in earlier crises, to count upon overwhelming support from the great majority of the public in these actions. Although occasional criticism was voiced, especially during the low point of popularity of the Churchill coalition following the fall of Singapore and Tobruk in the summer of 1942, there was little need directly to coerce a population which largely supported the war effort. Freedom of debate in Parliament and a still relatively vigorous press continued to provide essential outlets for public opinion. Throughout the war, the Churchill government remained, in spite of the vast panoply of its powers, ultimately dependent on securing a majority in the House of Commons.

The most direct impact of the war was felt, not unnaturally, in the expansion of defence spending. Initially it was believed that the war would permit a degree of 'business as usual', with part of the cost of the war met by an export drive (actually mounted in the winter of 1939–40) and assisted by the fiscal restraints which had dominated pre-war economic policy. By 1940 it was apparent that these policies were no longer adequate; government expenditure was moving well beyond the framework of orthodox finance. In a series of newspaper articles and a book published in 1940, *How to Pay for the War*, J. M. Keynes pointed the way towards seeing the problem of war finance not merely in budgetary terms but as a question of the deployment of the total economic resources of the country.

Table 28: Government expenditure 1937/8–1944/5

| | Years ending 31 March (£ million) | | |
	Total	Defence	%
1937/8	919.9	197.3	21.45
1938/9	1,018.9	254.4	24.97
1939/40	1,408.2	626.4	44.48
1940/41	3,970.7	3,220.0	81.09
1941/2	4,876.3	4,085.0	83.77
1942/3	5,739.9	4,840.0	84.32
1943/4	5,909.3	4,950.0	83.76
1944/5	6,179.5	5,125.0	82.94

Source: *Statistical Digest of the War*, HMSO, 1951, p. 195.

The adoption of Keynes's policies in the War Budget of 1941 and the abandonment of pre-war economic constraints was one of the most important economic aspects of the war. Where people such as Keynes had failed in the thirties to convert the government to a policy of high spending to cure the chronic undercapacity in the economy and resolve the question of unemployment, the war transformed the whole nature of the debate. With the survival of the country at stake in 1940, radical steps had to be taken. 'Forced Keynesianism' permitted a great increase in government expenditure and involved the extension of state control to encompass almost every aspect of the economy and social life. The repercussions were soon apparent both in terms of employment and output. Britain still had over a million unemployed in April 1940, but between 1939 and 1943 the employed population rose by 2.9 million, mopping up existing unemployment and forcing the recruitment of large numbers of extra workers, many of them women. National income almost doubled from £4,671 million in 1938 to £8,340 in 1945 and, in spite of the mobilization of so much of the population into the armed forces, industrial production showed an overall increase. At its height the war was absorbing almost a half of the gross national product, representing a higher level of mobilization than in any other combatant nation. The results were seen in a large increase in the production of armaments. Although Britain re-armed late, she re-armed relatively quickly. Indeed, by the outbreak of the war Britain was actually producing more aircraft and tanks per month than Germany, though she had a tremendous backlog to make up to achieve parity in total numbers. Britain also mobilized more of her resources earlier than Germany, faced with the emergency of 1940–41. As a result output of small-arms and shells increased tenfold between the end of 1939 and the beginning of 1943; of guns seven and a half times; and of wheeled vehicles three and a half times. Between 1939 and 1944 over six million tons of merchant shipping were built, plus over a million tons of major naval vessels. The number of aircraft, in which Britain concentrated much of her resources, increased threefold between 1939 and 1944, including a tenfold increase in the number of bombers.

Inevitably there were heavy costs both in manpower and economic terms. The United Kingdom lost 270,000 men in the armed forces, to which had to be added the loss of 35,000 merchant seamen and approximately 60,000 civilians killed by bombing, although these figures represented only a half the number killed in the Great War. In contrast to the Great War, however, Britain suffered heavy material losses through enemy bombing. During the war as many as four million houses, almost a third of the total stock, were damaged by enemy action, including 475,000 totally destroyed, to which had to be added blitzed factories, schools, hospitals and other buildings.

Shipping losses were also heavy – more than thirteen and a half million tons were lost, which was almost two-thirds of the total British merchant fleet in September 1939. In actuarial terms the war cost £28,000 million, over two and a half times more than the First World War, and was largely financed out of increased taxation and government borrowing from its domestic population through compulsory saving schemes, such as 'war credits', only redeemed at a fraction of their true cost many years after the war. A large cut in the consumption of luxuries and the introduction of rationing to provide necessities at reasonable cost allowed a major shift of resources from consumption to production. Even so there was once again a forced sale of foreign investments before 'lend-lease' arrangements with America became effective. Even undamaged capital equipment was rapidly run down, particularly in transport, housing and machinery, leaving a large backlog of investment to be made up in the post-war years. As before, the specific requirements of the war involved a distortion of the economy's pattern of development. Shipbuilding, iron and steel, and coal-mining became crucial sectors for the war effort and were extensively developed against all the trends of the pre-war economy. Just as Britain was learning the painful lessons of re-adjustment from dependence upon its 'old staples', the war, with its specialized and, in an economic sense, haphazard requirements, reinforced the deployment of labour and resources into sectors which might otherwise have been obliged to decline, a factor which was to leave Britain with many of the same problems in the post-war years as had faced her throughout the inter-war period, with an over-concentration of labour in declining sectors and areas of industry.

On this plane, the economic effects of the war intersected with its political and social repercussions. Commitments to a high level of employment in the post-war years, enshrined in the Beveridge Report of 1942 and the government White Paper of 1944, ensured that the consequences of long-term economic readjustment were postponed in the interests of war production and social consensus. Moreover, however impressive the war effort in terms of production, the financial repercussions were potentially ruinous. Britain's financial resources were almost exhausted as early as 1941, but this was masked by the ability to obtain goods and raw materials from America under the system of lend-lease. The abrupt termination of lend-lease in 1945 left Britain in dire financial straits. Her debts in 1945 stood at £3,500 million compared with only £496 million in 1939, and her substantial pre-war reserves of gold, dollars and overseas investments had virtually all been dissipated by 1945. Only loans of $5,000 million from the United States and Canada, granted on terms which included the dismantlement of the system of imperial preferences and other unfavourable 'strings', saved Britain from bankruptcy. Even with this aid, the legacy of wartime exertion remained in the austerity of the post-war years and in the massive devaluation of sterling in 1949 from $4.03 to $2.80.

On the credit side, war again acted as a stimulus to several industries which were of importance for the future, such as motor vehicles, aircraft, electronics and chemicals. Technological development in jet propulsion, radar, atomic power, antibiotics and other fields also sprang from the war, contributing to a much greater role for science in post-war industry. Agriculture too had been greatly encouraged by the war, continuing and emphasizing a revival which had begun in the 1930s with the introduction of protection. The total area of tilled land increased by 66 per cent between 1939 and 1944, while the total net output of calories from British agriculture doubled. These increases were obtained not only by ploughing up grasslands but by the increased use of fertilizer to raise yields, extensive mechanization – quadrupling the number of tractors employed on farms between 1939 and 1946 – and an extensive system of loans and subsidies.

As a result the British economy emerged into the post-war world with both strengths and weaknesses. On balance, the challenges faced were overcome relatively successfully. Britain struggled through the difficulties of the post-war years to re-establish a high rate of economic growth and a viable international trade. A remarkably successful export drive, aided by the devastation wrought on pre-war competitors like Germany and Japan, provided the basis for a rise in industrial output. Industrial production exceeded its highest pre-war level by 1946 and thereafter continued to rise even faster than before the war. By 1949 industrial production was 80 per cent higher than in 1913 and, in spite of austerity and rationing at home, a basis was laid for the 'affluence' of the 1950s and 1960s. That this battle for economic survival was won only at the cost of post-poning an attempt to solve many long-term structural problems, such as the modernization of the transport network, the restructuring of the economic base of some of the old industrial regions, and the fundamental reappraisal of work and management practices, was to be one of the factors which conditioned Britain's economic performance and difficulties long after the post-war period.

The Making of the Welfare State: Beveridge and After

By the outbreak of the Second World War there existed a substantial body of opinion which looked forward to an expansion of the social services and an end to the mass unemployment of the inter-war years. This increasingly influential consensus found its moment in the Second World War, in particular in the atmosphere of national emergency produced after the evacuation of Dunkirk and the fall of France in 1940, and the mood of collectivism and common endeavour which – for a time at least – transformed the context of the debate about social policy. Paul Addison – with only pardonable exaggeration – has conjured up the climate of these years as consisting of 'Colonel Blimp being pursued through a land of Penguin Specials by an abrasive meritocrat, a progressive churchman, and J. B. Priestley'. In a similar way, the planning movement of the 1930s was to find its apotheosis in the conduct of the war and the plans for post-war reconstruction in almost every field from social security to new town development. PEP had set up a Post-War Aims Group even before the war began and within a week of the outbreak had circulated a draft on war aims. As well as devoting attention to the management of the war economy, it had by July 1942 produced a broadsheet, *Planning for Social Security*, which substantially anticipated the Beveridge Report in calling for a national minimum income, universal family allowances, a National Health Service and a Ministry of Social Security.

A similar barometer of opinion was the 'volunteer army' of post-war planners who launched a series of reconstruction projects in 1940–41. Amongst the most ambitious was the Nuffield College Reconstruction Survey, proposed by G. D. H. Cole, supported by influential backers such as Arthur Greenwood and John Reith, and financed from a Treasury grant. All three main parties had reconstruction committees working on post-war plans by 1941, while professional groups such as the BMA and the Town and Country Planning Association provided their own schemes. Entirely characteristic of these years was *Picture Post*'s special edition, 'A Plan for Britain', published in January 1941. Almost a catalogue of current progressive ideas, it contained proposals for a planned approach to unemployment, social security, town planning, house design, the countryside, education, health, the medical service and leisure. Contributors included Thomas Balogh, Maxwell Fry, A. D. Lindsay, Julian Huxley and J. B. Priestley. The proprietor of *Picture Post*, Edward Hulton, also formed the 1941 Committee under the chairmanship of J. B. Priestley to act as a ginger group on reconstruction policy.

Moreover, while individual churchmen, such as the famous 'Red dean of Canterbury', Dr Hewlett Johnson, had contributed to 'middle opinion' and supported left-wing causes before 1939, the war years brought to the fore a much more powerful mood of Christian social concern. On 20 December 1940 *The Times* carried a joint letter from the Archbishops of York and Canterbury, the Roman Catholic Archbishop of Westminster and the Moderator of the Free Church Council setting out five minimum social standards for a Christian community, including the abolition of extremes of inequality in wealth and possessions and provision of equal opportunities. Pamphlets expressing similar views, following the resolutions of an Industrial Christian Fellowship Conference at Malvern College in early 1941, sold over a million copies. In February 1942 the influential Christian socialist William Temple, Archbishop of York, became Archbishop of Canterbury. His book *Christianity and the Social Order*, published as a Penguin Special, sold 139,000 copies in 1942.

This growth of interest in social questions clearly drew upon pre-war experiences, but the war itself also created a special environment which helps to explain the enthusiastic reception of plans for social reform and provided the setting for the Beveridge Report. José Harris, the biographer of Beveridge, has listed a number of factors which were operating by 1942. First, social reform had an important part to play in fostering wartime morale, a role not lost on Harold Laski, who wrote in 1940: 'The way to victory lies in producing the conviction now among the masses that there are to be no more distressed areas, no more vast armies of unemployed, no more slums, no vast denial of genuine equality of opportunity.' Beveridge himself took up this theme in a radio broadcast in the same year, calling for a 'war of faith'. Second, the upheaval of the war itself, through greater mobility, evacuation and bombing, had also shown up many of the defects of the existing social services, particularly to those sections of the comfortable middle class who had little direct knowledge of the conditions to be found in the poorer areas of the great cities. Third, the war also increased the sense of social solidarity – a climate of common endeavour – which blunted some of the pre-war objections to increased social spending and encouraged more generous provision of social welfare. Tests on household income for those in need – the means test – was finally abolished by the Determination of Need Act of 1941, while the bringing of pensions and allowances for service families, and the relief of those in need as a result of the war and the other paupers under an all-embracing 'Assistance Board', helped to humanize treatment of the destitute. Fourth, the war again brought about

greater state intervention and control, creating fresh precedents
for peace-time. To protect children from the ill-effects of
rationing the state inaugurated a programme of free school milk
in 1940, followed later by orange juice, cod liver oil and vitamin
tablets. Free school meals and nurseries were introduced to assist
working wives, while factory canteens and medical and welfare
services were organized to assist war production. Richard
Titmuss remarked that:

by the end of the Second World War the Government had, through
the agency of newly established or existing services, assumed and
developed a measure of direct concern for the health and well-being
of the population which, by contrast with the role of the Government
in the nineteen-thirties, was little short of remarkable.

Fifth, the war acted to redefine the nature of social distress.
Unemployment virtually came to an end by 1941 and social
concern refocused upon the problems of low wages, large
families, housing and the elderly. As Harris puts it: 'For the first
time for twenty years the relief of poverty from whatever
cause rather than relief of unemployment became the major
problem and first priority of social administration.'

   The Beveridge Report arose from his Chairmanship of the
Committee on Social Insurance set up in June 1941 to inquire
into the anomalies that had arisen as a result of the haphazard
growth of social security in the previous half century and which
had left seven government departments directly or indirectly
involved in the provision of cash benefits. Beveridge took a
deliberately wide interpretation of his terms of reference which,
formally, were merely to survey 'existing schemes of social
insurance and allied services, including workmen's compensation, and to make recommendations'. Beveridge himself was the
crucial architect of the outcome. Most of his ideas were formulated and much of his Report drafted before he had heard
very much evidence. But the evidence when it came tended to
emphasize the drift of Beveridge's thought, already outlined in
several broadcasts and articles. Many of the witnesses looked to
some radical, even 'Utopian', social change as a result of the war,

while they usually expressed support for the kind of reforms that Beveridge had in mind. In this sense, the Report articulated much of the conventional wisdom of 'middle opinion', amplified by the aspirations released by the first years of the war.

In the final Report, which appeared on 1 December 1942, Beveridge underlined three guiding principles: the first was a blending of the 'experience of the past' with a radical approach towards existing vested interests; the second was that of comprehensive social planning to conquer the five giants standing in the way of reconstruction – Want, Ignorance, Squalor, Idleness and Disease; and the third principle was of 'cooperation' between voluntary and public action and between the individual and the state. Guided by these principles, the Beveridge plan assumed that the government would provide family allowances, create a comprehensive health service and maintain high employment. His plan for social insurance envisaged a single weekly flat-rate contribution which would provide a comprehensive system of social insurance 'from the cradle to the grave', including unemployment benefit, sickness benefit, disability benefit, workmen's compensation, old-age, widows' and orphans' pensions and benefits, funeral grants and maternity benefit. A system of 'National Assistance' was to be maintained for all those who fell outside the other benefits, to be paid for by the national exchequer. The rate of contribution was to be fixed at a level within reach of every employed person, with benefits paid at a 'national minimum income for subsistence', and the whole system coordinated by a new Ministry of Social Security.

Beveridge's scheme was not, as has been stressed many times, revolutionary. Through a 'deal' with Keynes at the Treasury, the financial implications of the Report involved only an extra £100 million per annum from central government, far less than Beveridge himself had initially estimated. Essentially, his proposals were a rationalization of existing insurance schemes, based on the time-honoured principle of contributions from employee, employer and the state. The preservation of the

principle of 'insurance' was a clear throwback to the days of
Lloyd George (and of the young Beveridge) and, as he explained
in a radio broadcast, his 'Plan for. Britain' was 'based on the
contributory principle of giving not free allowances to all from
the State, but giving benefits as of right of virtue of contributions made by the insured persons themselves'. It provided a
national minimum, not an allocation of relief on the basis of
need. None the less, the tone of the Report was radical,
particularly in Beveridge's expressed desire to abolish the 'five
giants', to give a new sense of purpose to democracy, to
promote national solidarity and define the goals of the war.
As he put it in the Report, if the Allies could 'plan for a better
peace even while waging war, they will win together two
victories which in truth are indivisible'.

With such sentiments, the Report was an immediate success and an astonishing best-seller for an official document.
A hundred thousand copies were sold within a month and
the Ministry of Information quickly seized upon it as a
morale-booster, ordering a special cheap edition for circulation amongst the armed forces (though this was later cancelled
on orders from the War Office). Total sales came to over
630,000, including an American edition of 50,000 and an
abbreviated edition distributed amongst underground and
resistance groups in occupied Europe. Discussed widely by
politicians, academics, journalists, welfare organizations and,
through the Army Bureau of Current Affairs, amongst the
armed forces, the Report quickly became regarded as a blueprint for post-war reconstruction, reflected in popular reference
to the Beveridge 'Plan'. Coming a few days after the victory of
El Alamein, the Report captured a mood of optimism and
articulated ideas which already commanded considerable
support.

But the Beveridge Report was just that, a Report, not
legislation. There was a much more cautious response to the
Beveridge proposals among politicians and administrators.
Above all, Churchill was opposed to passing major legislation
before the war was won. Parliament merely welcomed the

proposals and Churchill warned of 'a dangerous optimism' and the raising of 'false hopes'.

None the less, the enthusiasm aroused by the Beveridge Report and the wide support it achieved amongst Labour politicians, sections of the Conservative Party and a broad spectrum of opinion led to a series of government White Papers in 1944 organized by the Minister for Reconstruction, Lord Woolton. In February *A National Health Service* proposed a free, comprehensive health service covering every branch of medical and allied activity. In May, a paper *Employment Policy* accepted the Keynesian economic argument of using public expenditure to avoid cyclical unemployment. Decaying regions were to be given aid to create new industries along the lines of the Barlow Report of 1940. In September 1944, a third White Paper, *Social Insurance*, accepted most of the proposals of the Beveridge Report, especially the principle of comprehensive coverage for all persons and types of risk, and formed the basis for Labour's Insurance Act of 1946. With the Butler Education Act of 1944 and the introduction of the Family Allowances in 1945, the chief elements of the Welfare State were created in the last years of the war.

People's War, People's Peace?

Hence although the effects of the Second World War on British society were in large part a continuation of developments already evident before 1939, the war was responsible for some decisive changes. To a degree this reflected the great sacrifices demanded by the war effort from a very early stage through the introduction of conscription, the imposition of rationing and the exposure of the civilian population to air raids. The war forced the government to make some concessions to retain the allegiance of soldiers, war workers and their families. But there was also what has been called 'a change in the climate of social consciousness', in which the experience of the war, particularly in the period after the fall of France, provoked an intense and genuine sense of national unity.

Although not quite as uniform as was sometimes portrayed at the time, the period after Dunkirk, during the Battle of Britain and the Blitz did, for a time at least, forge a strong collectivist sentiment. For some, certainly, the presence of evacuated children from the slum districts brought home the still glaring inequalities of life in pre-war Britain. More generally, however, the mood of national solidarity and endeavour encouraged the concept of a fairer and more just society after the war. As Alan Milward has noted:

Lest the reality of this changed climate be doubted it needs only to be considered that in Britain at the height of the war Parliament began a reform of the education system and passed the Town and Country Planning Act. The administration of welfare provision lost some of the petty cruelty which had been its hallmark and was interpreted in a rather more generous spirit. A government which began by planning to fight the anticipated fearful reactions of its own subjects under bombing and combat was brought to realize that the enterprise of war demanded a greater amount of trust and cooperation between government and all its subjects. However vaguely conceived, the aims of reconstruction had to take the form of a job, an income and basic social security for everyone.

There was also a measurable element of redistribution of income as a result of the war. Wages were generally high through the willingness of government to concede to reasonable demands in return for uninterrupted production. Overtime and piece-work payments also swelled wage-packets, so that by 1944 average wage rates had risen 11 per cent above the cost of living index. Progressive income tax on higher incomes and an improvement in the position of the lowest-paid sections of the workforce meant that the share of national income taken by wage-earners increased by about £900 million between 1938 and 1947. According to one estimate, working-class incomes after tax during this period rose by more than 9 per cent, while middle-class incomes fell by more than 7 per cent. Although wealth and pre-tax incomes remained virtually as unevenly distributed as before the war, the combination of progressive taxation and price controls led to an increase in purchasing power for the poorer section of the community by as much as a quarter between 1938 and 1948.

Organized labour also emerged more powerfully from the war. One of the most forceful trade-unionists of the generation, Ernest Bevin, was co-opted into the War Cabinet and acted as Churchill's right-hand man in the government's dealings with organized labour. As in the previous conflict, trade-union members increased, from six and a quarter million in 1939 to just over eight million in 1944. Agreements were reached with the unions about the conduct of wartime industry and, although disputes arose towards the end of the war, the early years were largely free of disruption and trade-union officials were much more directly involved in the war effort than during the Great War. The propaganda of the 'People's War' put enormous emphasis on the essential role of factory workers in the war effort. Newspapers, newsreels and feature films gave the 'battle for production' almost as much prominence as the military struggle. The increased prestige and numbers of the trade-union movement confirmed the resurgence of the trade-union movement from the setbacks of the General Strike and the slump, consolidating the political and industrial influence of the trade unions in the post-war world.

The war too had important cultural effects. One often neglected feature was the impact upon Britain of thousands of foreign refugees and servicemen. The Americans were the most significant group, bringing with them their own styles of language, music and attitudes. The rather insular character of British society was exposed to a host of foreign influences in the tumult of war. The war years also provided a stimulus to the arts, assisting the artistic renaissance which was one of the most unexpected features of British society after 1945. Artists, writers and film makers found opportunities in wartime Britain to exercise their talents in a more popular direction, bringing them into contact with a wider public than ever before. The scientific and technological advances of wartime, most notably radar, the jet engine and atomic power gave science a prestige which it had never held before.

Thus in a number of respects, the Second World War left a more permanent mark upon British society than the First. Debate continues, however, amongst historians as to how profound the changes were and how far the war was responsible for them. Angus Calder in his social history of life on the home front from 1939 to 1945, *The People's War*, has argued that the effect of the war was not to sweep society on to a new course, 'but to hasten its progress along the old grooves'. Similarly Henry Pelling in *Britain and the Second World War* has questioned the extent to which the war did alter British society: there was less psychological shock than in 1914–18 and the major institutions of society – Parliament, political parties, the Civil Service, local government, the press, the law and the trade unions – 'all emerged from the war with slightly different surface features, but basically unaltered'. In contrast historians such as Paul Addison and Arthur Marwick have argued that a degree of change must be ascribed to the war, even if it was not as great as might have been envisaged or desired either by contemporaries or subsequent commentators. Both Marwick and Addison have drawn attention to the convergence of opinion towards the reformed capitalism and extended welfare provisions which formed the basis of the post-war consensus. Addison has written:

> In general, the reform programme originated in the thought of an upper middle class of socially concerned professional people, of whom Beveridge and Keynes were the patron saints. To render capitalism more humane and efficient was the principal aim of the professional expert. In World War II the humane technocrat provided a patriotic compromise between Socialism and Conservatism which virtually satisfied the desire of the Labour Party for social amelioration, without in any way attacking the roots of exploitation and injustice.

This, in my view, comes near the heart of the matter. The triumph of 'Mr High Mind' was one of the most significant events in recent British history and one with profound consequences for the moderate, reformist nature of British politics and society after 1945 – with both its strengths and weaknesses. There remains, moreover, the difficult question of how far similar developments would have occurred without the war. It is, ultimately, unanswerable. It appears, however, that in most respects we are dealing with a continuation of pre-war developments, but one in which an occasionally decisive political impact was registered by the demands of total war.

Conclusion

What then were the most significant features of British society in the years between 1914 and 1945? One which certainly stands out is the widening role of government which, like some 'new Leviathan', was playing a greater part both in the running of the economy and the provision of social services. Between 1913 and the eve of the Second World War, public expenditure as a percentage of the gross national product rose from an eighth to over a quarter. Both in terms of economic involvement and the provision of social services, central government came to play a major part in the working of the economy and the welfare of its citizens. Moreover, while by 1939 the government had already taken on many new responsibilities, the Second World War led to two lasting changes in the role expected of central government. The acceptance by all major political parties of the general principles expressed in the Beveridge Report for a system of comprehensive social welfare – the Welfare State – implied a much larger commitment by the state to provide minimum standards of health, education and living standards. Equally crucial was the acceptance in 1944 of government responsibility for maintaining full employment after the war, a commitment which implied continuing intervention in the management of the economy. The growing role of government was evident not only in the increasing amount spent by the governments, but also in the numbers employed. Between 1938 and 1950 the percentage of the working population employed in the public sector rose from less than a tenth to almost a quarter, over five and a half million people. Although the nationalization of major industries and the expansion of welfare services accounted for much of this increase its signs were evident much earlier in the growth in the number of civil servants from 282,000 in 1914, to 376,000 in 1938, and to 575,000 in 1950. This was not an even process. The number of civil servants actually fell in the 1920s in response to a relinquishing of responsibilities and commitments undertaken in the Great War and the 'reconstruction' policies which lasted up to the early 1920s. Taking a broad perspective, however, it is clear that the rise of the state was a process which derived from a complex inter-action of social and political forces, evident before 1914 and continuing thereafter. Democratization, collectivism and egali-tarianism all contributed to the greater involvement of the state in the lives of its citizens, part of a process which saw social amelioration and a reduction of privilege as part of the necessary consequence not only of total war, but also of longer-term pressures.

It is difficult to acquire a proper sense of perspective about the performance of the British economy in these years, dominated as much post-1945 writing has been by the theme of decline, encapsulated in concern about structural weaknesses, balance of payments and exchange rate difficulties, inflation, poor industrial relations, bad management, a lack of entrepreneurship and, latterly, the re-emergence of high rates of unemployment. However valid these questions – and the issue of relative economic decline cannot be in dispute – the years we have been considering witnessed major scientific and technical advances, substantial economic growth, an average rise in real incomes of those in work of something in the order of a third, and a major shift of resources towards the provision of welfare benefits and social opportunities. At a basic level, average life expectancy increased by almost fifteen years, infant mortality was more than halved and the incidence of major diseases was much reduced. Although poverty remained, it had been much reduced in the course of thirty years, years which also produced significant improvements in housing, social security and pensions. Whatever the cause of Britain's relative decline after 1945, the legacy of these years was not unpromising. New industries, a significant degree of relocation and rationalization and rapid economic growth, at least by the 1930s, prepared the way for the war effort and export boom which was to save Britain both from Nazi dictatorship in 1940–41 and from bankruptcy in the immediate post-war years. These achievements, however, were inevitably overshadowed by the painful memories of mass unemployment. These can never be ignored in any balance-sheet of the inter-war years: derelict towns, dole queues, poverty and hardship, petty humiliations at the hands of officials, the sheer affront to human dignity in the condemnation of hundreds of thousands of men and women to idleness and uselessness through no apparent fault of their own. Mass unemployment was, like the 'lost generation' of the First World War, to cast a shadow over much of the inter-war years.

It would be misleading, too, to overstate the element of change in the structure of British society between 1914 and 1945. Although there was some redistribution and equalization of incomes over the whole period, the distribution of wealth remained unequal. While there was a reduction in the numbers of the poor, through the coming of full employment, the provision of comprehensive social security and the rise of 'affluence', the pyramid of incomes was somewhat flattened rather than levelled. On the eve of the Second World War there had been only a minor redistribution of wealth, and this mainly amongst the top few per cent of capital owners. Nor, it became apparent later, was the situation very much different immediately after 1945. In 1950, 54 per cent of all capital wealth was owned by a mere 1.5 per cent of the population, while a great mass, 62 per cent, were essentially propertyless.

In some respects such figures have led to a recognition of the more immutable features of the British class system. It was during the 1950s that the term 'the Establishment' became current usage (it was actually coined around 1920) to describe the traditional ruling bodies of British society, the aristocracy, the church, the judiciary, the Civil Service, the older universities, the heads of the armed forces, the City of London and the leaders of business. In fact, the governing classes of Britain did show a degree of differentiation during the first half of this century, increasingly reflecting the long-standing ability of the British upper classes to absorb and assimilate new elements. The rise of the financiers and businessmen, of the top civil servants, administrators and managers, of the recruits drawn through public schools and grammar schools from a broader section of society, reflected both the enduring and the adaptive aspects of the British social structure. At its apex, legitimizing at once the hierarchic and cohesive forces of British society, stood the monarchy, hardly less prestigious in the 1940s than in the 1900s, and possibly even more so through its subtle adaptation to a more ostensibly democratic polity and by the skilful use of publicity and greater public display. The landed aristocracy still in 1945 represented an important component of British society, less through their possession of great wealth than through their powerful hold over its ethos.

These years did see, however, a broadening of the middle class and the increasingly pervasive influence of middle-class values. The growth of the professions, of the managerial and supervisory elements, of scientists and technicians, and of traders and shopkeepers led to an expansion of the middle classes. Although there was a significant amount of movement between classes, or 'social mobility', in real terms this affected only a small fraction of the total population. Most British people in 1945 remained, and were to remain, in the class in which they were born, reflecting that the majority of the population were working-class and stayed within it. Routes of advancement, taken by some, and higher living standards, moreover, led to the increasing absorption of what had hitherto been middle-class values. Although a distinctive working-class culture was still easily discernible in many parts of Britain in 1945, it was increasingly being overlaid by a consumer-orientated society in which 'keeping up with the Joneses' was by no means confined to the middle class. To the often complex elaborations of status and value within the working classes were increasingly added the manifestations of a mass consumer culture. The range and possibility of material improvement developed considerably by 1945, bringing new standards of comfort and status within the reach of ever widening groups of people. The clean and well-appointed home, the bric-à-brac of domesticity and popular culture, smaller families and their better provision, reflected perhaps the most important – certainly the most widespread – social development of the twentieth century, the attainment (or aspirations towards the attainment) by more and more people of the middle and working classes of standards of respectability and comfort enjoyed by a smaller number before 1914. In many respects the experience of the most deprived section of the population bore this out. The most deeply felt reactions to the most serious problem of the inter-war years, mass unemployment, were couched both by outside observers and the unemployed themselves in terms that indicated a scale of values in which notions of self-respect and human dignity were those most grossly affronted by the powerlessness, poverty and petty humiliations of 'life on the dole'. Their impact is perhaps well expressed by one man who, putting his experience of unemployment in the 1930s in a single phrase, said, simply, 'Men were treated like dirt.' That the unemployed of the 1930s were probably, on average, living at a standard no worse than that enjoyed by the average employed worker in 1900, received what were amongst the highest level of unemployment benefits paid in any industrialized nation, and were the subject of genuine and deep concern by writers and social investigators matters less than the perception of unemployment by those who experienced or feared experiencing it as an affront to standards which had become increasingly accepted in the years since the end of nineteenth century. It was remarked upon, for example, that for some unemployment meant little more than reabsorption into a culture of poverty and 'making-do' which they had barely left, but for others the frustration of a lifetime's careful pursuit of respectability. Indeed, one of the most frequently expressed concerns of those worried about the impact of mass unemployment was that it was undoing both for existing and future generations all that had been achieved in the 'progress' of habits and behaviour over the course of a century or more. It was reflected just as much in the fear of 'black-coated unemployment' amongst the professional and salaried classes: *Sorrell and Son* had as much to say as *Love on the Dole* about the pervasiveness of ideals of 'respectability' amongst ever-widening sections of the British population during these years.

These values were also reflected in the styles of life which rising real incomes promised and which, for some, were threatened by unemployment. The privatization of family life increased, a reflection of greater mobility, looser family and kinship ties, and new patterns of housing. This was shown too in smaller families and a greater investment of time and energy in children and young people, greater concern for their welfare and education, and a more 'home-centred' culture. Again, one of the most striking features of British society in the twentieth century has been its high expectations and investment in housing, both on a personal and governmental level. These tendencies reinforced ideals of domesticity and private life which, ultimately, frustrated the fuller emancipation of women dreamt of by some of the early pioneers of women's liberation. None the less, women were often the beneficiaries of expanding opportunities in the labour market, the greater freedom allowed by social convention and a somewhat less arduous round of housework and childbearing, while full equality of opportunity, equal pay and a recognition of equal status awaited a revolution in values more profound than any encountered in these years. In religion and culture, these were years of a confusing, and sometimes bizarre, challenge to older values. As we have seen, much of this challenge had its origins in the incredible ferment of intellectual, artistic and scientific activity which began in the years before 1914. The years between 1914 and 1945 saw a working-out of many of the developments evident at its beginning: the decline of formal religious adherence, experimentation in the arts and new discoveries in science, some of them of quite literally 'earth-shattering' significance. But over the period there was a certain steadying of values and beliefs. It is easy in the seemingly violent fragmentation of styles and attitudes, so marked in reaction to the

Great War, and in the intellectual climate of the 1930s, to underestimate the less obvious qualities of the British intellectual and cultural scene. Vitality for one thing – for ferment always seems to be creative – in which literature, music and the plastic arts flourished, finding both a wider audience and new outlets. Moreover, disenchantment and disillusionment can also be overplayed here. The documentary movement in the arts offered some at least a resolution (often temporary) to the intellectual and artistic dilemmas of the period. Amongst scientists, too, there was no lack of confidence, encouraged by a sense of standing on the threshold of new and exciting discoveries and the growing application of science to more and more aspects of everyday life. No one could ignore the rise of a science and technology which brought faster travel, broadcasting, new medicines and new, more destructive weapons of war. Indeed it was R. V. Jones, one of the war-winning scientists most intimately engaged in the field of radar and radio direction, who noted the irony that in the very universities of the 'climate of treason' and the 'King and Country' debate were also at work the scientists who played such a major role in inventing and perfecting the weapons of eventual victory. So, too, were the economists and social scientists, the 'humane technocrats' whose moment came with the groundswell of 'middle opinion' in the late thirties and the war years. There was no shortage of optimism in the schemes of architects and town planners to refashion the cities, of social scientists to survey and to solve social problems, and of scientists and technologists to provide the fruits of fresh advance.

Two more general developments were the creation of a more uniform 'mass society' which in spite of its regional and social differences had common sources of information and similar awareness. This had already proceeded a long way in Britain by 1914, but was to go still further with the spread of mass consumerism, national radio broadcasting and the cheap press, greater mobility, and the shake-up created by two national emergencies, requiring the mobilization of large numbers of people and their organization and regulation by government.

But a growing 'sameness' can also be exaggerated, for it was balanced not only by continued diversity but in other ways, notably by the increasingly complex network of societies, clubs, pressure groups and organizations. The largest of these, the churches, the major political parties and the trade unions, were already in existence by 1914, but they were to be followed between 1914 and 1945 by a host of new societies and organizations, large and small, reflecting a wide range of political, economic and social concerns. Professional groups, artists, philanthropists and many others were often to create some of the most distinctive organizations of Britain between the wars. At a local level, too, there appeared a still greater proliferation of societies and clubs. This pressure towards association, paralleled in the concentration of business and the specialization of government, represented in part the reaction to an increasingly complex and diverse society, one in which organization for both functional and social purposes was necessary and suited.

Many of these developments were not unique to Britain; they were shared with other industrial and westernized countries not only in Europe but also further afield. Material advance, falling birth rates, the formal emancipation of women, greater state intervention to provide social welfare and management of the economy, to take only the most obvious examples, could be found elsewhere in the world. While a sometimes wilful ignorance and conceit on the part of the British often persuaded them that they had pioneered most things or, if not, perfected their exercise, there was a growing opening-up of British society to wider influences, transatlantic, European or even more exotic. Enthusiasm for 'planning' drew on the examples of Soviet Russia or Fascist Germany; art and culture on the current concerns of central Europe; the 'mixed' economy on the Scandinavian countries; and popular culture and business methods on the United States. English-speaking immigrants from the Dominions, Jewish refugees from Europe, Irish labourers and American GIs brought their own distinctive traits. Moreover, Britain remained in 1945, formally at least, what she had been in 1914, the greatest imperial power in the world. Thousands of men and women — emigrants, administrators, service personnel and missionaries — continued to sustain an Empire of millions. While there was little doubt by the Second World War that this imperial role was under challenge, it continued to exert an important influence upon the ethos of British life and culture. Although under criticism from within, many of the British would still in 1939 have seen the imperial role as a vital underpinning not merely of Britain's power but of its self-esteem and cultural identity.

A still great imperial power also enjoyed in an era of war, revolution and totalitarianism a considerable degree of stability and cohesion. Critically, Britain was not defeated in the Great War, its economic depression was more prolonged but less severe than those of other countries, and she emerged uninvaded and victorious from the Second World War. Moreover, the two most important and potentially, therefore, disruptive forces in British society, the middle classes and organized labour, acquiesced in the maintenance of the *status quo*. In many respects, the middle classes enjoyed a form of heyday in the inter-war years. Rising real incomes and increasing affluence, still relatively plentiful domestic service and a dominant Conservative Party assuaged most of the disruptive effects of war, depression and democracy. Unlike some other countries, where national humiliation, inflation and the threat from the left led the propertied classes to give widespread support to Fascist or totalitarian solutions, the cautious 'Safety First' of Baldwin's and Chamberlain's Britain offered little scope for the growth of the extreme right. No less important was the *de facto* acceptance of the leaders of organized labour and its representatives within the Labour Party of 'gradualism'. Conflicts and confrontations there certainly were — tanks in the streets of Glasgow in 1919, warships in the Mersey in 1921, a mobilization of troops and middle-class volunteers in 1926, baton charges against unemployed demonstrators in the early 1930s, and sometimes partial and politicized use of the law against those deemed to be militants and subversives — but the overwhelming stance was one of accommodation and negotiation, the acceptance of piecemeal advance within the context of parliamentary democracy. Referring to the debate on the social and political repercussions of the Second World War, Paul Addison has written:

> In my own view, one of the most important facts is that the trade union movement, and the Labour Party, were controlled on the eve of the war by a generation of leaders who were essentially moderate social patriots. Working-class politics had suffered numerous defeats. For all the divisions in its social structure, Britain was a small and closely knit community, insular, and bound together by strong patriotic or perhaps nationalistic feelings which no historian has yet fully documented. For five years, an aristocrat steeped in a romantic vision of his nation's role was the undisputed leader of an overwhelmingly working-class nation of whose social conditions and daily concerns he was largely in ignorance. Churchill is a symbol of how little class-feeling counted in the final analysis. The Labour movement's participation in the war effort might have had more radical consequences in a more class-conscious society, but in practice the demands of the leaders were modest, and there is no evidence that the rank-and-file, in the factories or the services, demanded more.

Commentators at the time and subsequently, British and foreign, have attempted to grasp the nature of the forces which have conditioned the distinctive qualities of the British polity. The French social historian François Bédarida has referred to 'an extraordinary cohesive force in the common fund of values which throughout history has been shared by the whole British community, regardless of political, religious or intellectual differences'. Similarly, a sociologist considering the changes in British society in the course of the twentieth century has referred to 'the custom and culture of a most peculiar island'. Custom and culture certainly involve some of the deepest and most obscure forces at work in British society during these years, a complex web of history, tradition and 'myths of ourselves' which are easier to describe than to explain. It was George Orwell, an ex-Etonian and socialist, who came close to expressing the essential quality of British society in these years when he wrote in December 1940:

England is not the jewelled isle of Shakespeare's much quoted passage, nor is it the inferno depicted by Dr Goebbels. More than either it resembles a family, a rather stuffy Victorian family, with not many black sheep in it but with all its cupboards bursting with skeletons. It has rich relations who have to be kow-towed to and poor relations who are horribly sat upon, and there is a deep conspiracy of silence about the source of the family income. It is a family in which the young are generally thwarted and most of the power is in the hands of irresponsible uncles and bedridden aunts. Still, it is a family. It has a private language and common memories, and at the approach of an enemy it closes its ranks. A family with the wrong members in control – that, perhaps, is as near as one can come to describing England in a phrase.

A particular and partial judgement, perhaps, but one which offers a crucial insight into the fundamental character of British society in this period.

Further Reading

•

A comprehensive guide to all the books, leaving aside articles and theses, of relevance to the study of British society in the twentieth century would make up a small volume in itself. I have restricted myself here to those books which have influenced my writing and which amplify what I have said here. In writing about recent history, the line between 'primary' and 'secondary' sources is extremely blurred and I have included both contemporary or near-contemporary works with later writing where they appear to complement each other. For those concerned with the nature of the historical evidence for this period I would strongly recommend C. L. Mowat, *Great Britain since 1914* (1970), a critical review of the sources available for recent history, and P. Thompson, *The Voice of the Past: Oral History* (1978).

General

This is a period which is relatively well served by general works which relate social and economic to political developments. C. L. Mowat, *Britain between the Wars, 1918–1940* (1946), remains a central work, but no less important are A. J. P. Taylor, *English History, 1914–1945* (1965), A. Marwick, *Britain in the Century of Total War: War, Peace and Social Change, 1900–1967* (1968), W. N. Medlicott, *Contemporary England, 1914–1964* (1967), and A. Havinghurst, *Britain in Transition: The Twentieth Century* (revised edition 1979). The anglocentric bias of much writing on this period has now been compensated by two excellent works, C. Harvie, *No Gods and Precious Few Heroes: Scotland 1914–1980* (1981), and K. O. Morgan, *Rebirth of a Nation: Wales 1880–1980* (1981), both of which have useful bibliographies.

An important attempt to write a general social history of England since the mid nineteenth century has been made by the Frenchman François Bédarida in *A Social History of England, 1851–1975* (English translation 1976) and there is a stimulating survey of British social history from 1900 to 1945 by Asa Briggs in R. Floud and D. McCloskey (eds.), *The Economic History of Britain since 1700, Vol. 2: 1860 to the 1970s* (1981). S. Glynn and J. Oxborrow, *Interwar Britain: A Social and Economic History* (1976), offers an able blend of social and economic history, while A. H. Halsey, *Change in British Society* (1978), provides valuable sociological insight into social change in twentieth-century Britain. A. M. Carr-Saunders and D. Caradog Jones, *A Survey of the Social Structure of England and Wales* (1927; revised edition 1937) and (with C. A. Moser) *A Survey of Social Conditions in England and Wales* (1958), provide valuable information on most social aspects of this period. More accessible to the general reader will be R. Graves and A. Hodges, *The Long Week-End: A Social History of Great Britain, 1918–1939* (1940), and R. Blythe, *The Age of Illusion: England in the Twenties and Thirties* (1963). N. Branson, *Britain in the Nineteen Twenties* (1978), and N. Branson and M. Heinemann, *Britain in the Nineteen Thirties* (1971), are more recent social histories of the period. Two worthwhile impressionistic accounts which concentrate upon social history are L. C. B. Seaman, *Life in Britain between the Wars* (1970), and the second volume of *Leslie Baily's BBC Scrapbooks* (1968), covering the years 1918 to 1939. Also valuable are the essays in J. Raymond (ed.), *The Baldwin Age* (1960).

Facts and figures can be found in A. H. Halsey, *Trends in British Society since 1900* (1972), D. Butler and A. Sloman, *British Political Facts, 1900–1976* (1980), and C. Cook and J. Stevenson, *The Longman Handbook of British History 1714–1980* (1983). *The Concise Dictionary of National Biography, II, 1901–1970* (1982) provides the most accessible source of bibliographical information.

There is a wealth of memoir and biographical material

relating to almost every walk of life. Amongst the general appreciations see, for example, M. Muggeridge, *The Thirties* (1940), and J. Symons, *The Thirties: A Dream Revolved* (1960). S. Orwell and I. Angus (eds.), *The Collected Essays, Journalism and Letters of George Orwell* (1968), are a valuable source of comment. Of the travelogue literature of the period, the outstanding contribution is J. B. Priestley, *English Journey* (1934), but see also A. Wilson, *Walks and Talks* (1934). Upper-class life is well documented in *Chips: The Diaries of Sir Henry Channon* (1967) edited by Robert Rhodes-James. The other side of life is described in H. Forrester, *Twopence to Cross the Mersey* (1974), an account of poverty-stricken childhood in Liverpool during the 1930s. An important supplement to the conventional memoir material is the increasingly valuable collection of oral evidence; see especially M. Bragg, *Speak for England* (1977), an oral history of Wigton, Cumbria, C. Forman, *Industrial Town: Self Portrait of St Helens in the 1920s* (1978), and the continuing productions of the History Workshop Series.

Britain in 1914

See D. Read, *Edwardian England, 1901–15* (1972), and P. Thompson, *The Edwardians* (1975), a work based substantially upon oral evidence. R. Roberts, *The Classic Slum* (1971), M. Penn, *Manchester Fourteen Miles* (1947), and M. Pember Reeves, *Round About a Pound a Week* (1913 and 1979), are excellent accounts of lower-class life. C. Oman, *An Oxford Childhood* (1976), is immensely evocative of upper-class life in the period. G. Dangerfield, *The Strange Death of Liberal England* (1936), is the classic exposition of the 'end of an era' view of the period, now much disputed.

The Great War

A. Marwick, *The Deluge: British Society and the First World War* (1965), is the best overall study. The experience of mass soldiering is well conveyed in D. Winter, *Death's Men* (1978),

J. Ellis, *Eye-Deep in Hell* (1976), and J. Keegan, *The Face of Battle* (1976). Amongst the mass of memoir material on the Great War, G. Coppard, *With a Machine Gun to Cambrai* (1969), E. Hiscock, *The Bells of Hell Go Ting-a-Ling-a-Ling* (1976), H. E. L. Mellersh, *Schoolboy into War* (1978), and P. J. Campbell, *In the Cannon's Mouth* (1979), probably offer more typical accounts than the more famous works. None the less, R. Graves, *Goodbye to All That* (1929), and S. Sassoon, *Memoirs of an Infantry Officer* (1930), rightly occupy a major place in the literature of the period.

Domestic experience of the war is movingly portrayed in V. Brittain, *Testament of Youth* (1933), while particular themes can be pursued in A. Marwick, *Women at War, 1914–1918* (1977), and K. Burgess, *The Challenge of Labour* (1980). The cultural impact of the war has been challengingly encapsulated by P. Fussell in *The Great War and Modern Memory* (1975), while J. Stallworthy, *Wilfred Owen* (1974), is an outstanding biography of the war's most famous poet. Something of the flavour of post-war Britain is also caught in P. Gibbs, *Realities of War* (1920), and C. F. G. Masterman, *England after War* (1923).

Economy, wages and living standards

Amongst the clearest expositions of Britain's economic performance in these years are S. Pollard, *The Development of the British Economy, 1914–1950* (1962), and D. H. Aldcroft, *The Inter-War Economy: Britain, 1919–1939* (1970); see also the last sections of P. Mathias, *The First Industrial Nation* (1969). While these works discuss living standards in the context of economic developments see also J. Burnett, *A History of the Cost of Living* (1969), S. Pollard and D. Crossley, *The Wealth of Britain* (1968) and J. Burnett, *Plenty and Want: A Social History of Diet in England from 1815 to the Present Day* (1966). G. D. H. and M. I Cole, *The Condition of Britain* (1937), and J. Hilton, *Rich Man Poor Man* (1944), are two important surveys of social conditions and attitudes, to which should be added A. L. Bowley and M. Hogg, *Has Poverty Diminished?* (1925), B. S. Rowntree, *Poverty and Progress* (1941), and H. Tout, *The Standard of Living in Bristol* (1938).

Population, household and family

Population trends are very clearly discussed in N. Tranter, *Population since the Industrial Revolution: The Case of England and Wales* (1973); see also R. M. and K. Titmuss, *Parents' Revolt* (1942). The development of birth control is examined by A. McLaren in *Birth Control in Nineteenth Century England* (1978), while the starting-point for the wider aspects of sexual relationships is J. Weeks, *Sex, Politics and Society: The Regulation of Sexuality since 1800* (1981). The collection of letters to Marie Stopes, edited by R. Hall, *Dear Dr Stopes* (1978), provides a crucial glimpse into sexual attitudes in the 1920s, but women's role in general can be judged from the collections of material from the Women's Co-operative Guild, edited by M. L. Davies, *Maternity* (1915), *Life As We Have Known It* (1931) and M. Spring Rice, *Working Class Wives* (1939).

Occupation, work and organized labour

A. M. Carr-Saunders and D. Caradog Jones, *A Survey of the Social Structure of England and Wales* (1927), and A. M. Carr-Saunders, D. Caradog Jones and C. A. Moser, *A Survey of Social Conditions in England and Wales* (1958), both provide breakdowns of industrial and occupation distribution; see also G. Routh, *Occupation and Pay in Great Britain, 1906–79* (1980). The experience of manual and other work in the 1920s is included in C. Forman's oral history, *Industrial Town: Self Portrait of St Helens in the 1920s* (1978), and forms an important component of W. Greenwood's autobiography *There Was a Time* (1967). B. L. Coombes, *These Poor Hands* (1939), and G. A. W. Tomlinson, *Coal Miner* (1940), both say something of the nature of mining in the inter-war years. The publications of the History Workshop Series based on oral history are gradually uncovering more of the realities of working life in the recent past, as in R. Samuel (ed.), *Miners, Quarrymen and Saltworkers* (1977), although there is still relatively little work available on clerical and service groups. The major study here remains D. Lockwood, *The Black-Coated Worker* (1958).

H. Pelling, *A History of British Trade Unionism* (1963), remains the most succinct overview of the development of organized labour, but there are some suggestive comments towards the end of D. Kynaston, *King Labour: The British Working Class, 1850–1914* (1976), and there is a more recent contribution in K. Burgess, *The Challenge of Labour* (1980). For the militant movements of the period see W. Kendall, *The Revolutionary Movement in Britain, 1900–21* (1969), R. K. Middlemas, *The Clydesiders* (1965), and B. Pribicevic, *The Shop Stewards Movement and Workers' Control, 1910–1922* (1959). For the General Strike see P. Renshaw, *The General Strike* (1975); G. A. Phillips, *The General Strike: The Politics of Industrial Conflict* (1976), and M. Morris, *The General Strike* (1976). H. Francis and D. Smith, *The Fed: A History of the South Wales Miners in the Twentieth Century* (1980), discusses perhaps the most militant area in Britain during this period, while there is much useful material to be gleaned from S. McIntyre, *Little Moscows* (1981).

Health and health services

F. F. Cartwright, *A Social History of Medicine* (1977), offers a broad perspective on developments, but important contributions in the period were J. Boyd Orr, *Food, Health and Income* (1936), G. C. M. M'Gonigle and J. Kirby, *Poverty and Public Health* (1937), and C. E. McNally, *Public Ill-Health* (1935). C. Fraser Brockington, *A Short History of Public Health* (1966), is admirably condensed; see also D. Hunter, *Health in Industry* (1962), E. H. Ackerknecht, *A Short History of Psychiatry* (1959), and B. Abel Smith, *The Hospitals, 1800–1948* (1951). For some of the wider relationships of disease to environment, see G. Melvyn Howe, *Man, Environment and Disease in Britain* (1972).

Housing and town planning

J. Burnett, *A Social History of Housing, 1815–1970* (1978), is an outstanding general survey, sensitive to both political and social pressures. The origins of mass public housing are discussed in M. Swenarton, *Homes Fit for Heroes* (1981), while E. D. Simon, *How to Abolish the Slums* (1929) and *Rebuilding Britain – A Twenty Year Plan* (1945), offer valuable evidence of the housing enthusiasm of the period. For the private house-building boom see A. A. Jackson, *Semi-detached London: Suburban Development, Life and Transport, 1900–1939* (1973).

The genesis of the town-planning movement is discussed in C. and R. Bell, *City Fathers: The Early History of Town Planning in Britain* (1969), G. Darley, *Villages of Vision* (1978), A. Sutcliffe, *Towards the Planned City: Germany, Britain and the United States, France, 1780–1914* (1981), and P. Hall, *Urban and Regional Planning* (1975).

Childhood, youth and education

J. Springhall, *Youth, Empire and Society: British Youth Movements, 1883–1940* (1977), is a brave attempt to chart relatively unknown territory, as is S. Humphries, *Hooligans or Rebels? An Oral History of Working-Class Childhood and Youth 1889–1939* (1981). The most comprehensive histories of educational provision in this period are H. C. Barnard, *A History of English Education from 1760* (1970), and B. Simon, *The Politics of Educational Reform, 1920–1940* (1974); see also K. Lindsay, *Social Progress and Educational Waste* (1926). J. Gathorne-Hardy, *The Public School Phenomenon* (1977), is an attempt to sketch some broad outlines of development, but on particular themes see R. Skidelsky, *English Progressive Schools* (1969), A. S. Neill, *Summerhill – A Radical Approach to Education* (1962), W. A. C. Stewart, *Progressives and Radicals in English Education, 1750–1970* (1972), and J. Kamm, *Hope Deferred – Girls' Education in English History* (1965).

Unemployment

For a good general survey of the question of unemployment, see S. Constantine, *Unemployment in Britain between the Wars* (1980). Amongst the surveys of the social effects of unemployment, see B. Seebohm Rowntree, A. A. Bowley, et al., *The Third Winter of Unemployment* (1922); J. Jewkes and A. Winterbottom, *Juvenile Unemployment* (1933); The Pilgrim Trust, *Men Without Work* (1938), and the Carnegie United Kingdom Trust, *Disinherited Youth* (1943). H. L. Beales and R. S. Lambert, *Memoirs of the Unemployed* (1934), provides some important first-hand accounts of the experience of unemployment. The great classic of the semi-documentary literature on unemployment is G. Orwell, *The Road to Wigan Pier* (1937); equally well known is E. Wilkinson, *The Town That Was Murdered* (1939). W. Hannington, *The Problem of the Distressed Areas* (1937), and A. Hutt, *The Condition of the Working Class in Britain* (1933), are valuable, but written from a politically committed point of view. W. Greenwood's novel, *Love on the Dole* (1933), remains one of the most moving accounts of the human consequences of mass unemployment. The political and wider repercussions of the depression are discussed in J. Stevenson and C. P. Cook, *The Slump: Society and Politics during the Depression* (1977), R. Benewick, *The Fascist Movement in Britain* (1969), and W. Hannington, *Never on Our Knees* (1967).

Social policy

For social policies and welfare provisions in this period see M. Bruce, *The Coming of the Welfare State* (revised edition, 1968), D. Fraser, *The Evolution of the British Welfare State* (1973), and B. B. Gilbert, *British Social Policy, 1914–1939* (1970). There are some useful essays in P. Thane (ed.), *The Origins of British Social Policy* (1978), and see also J. MacNicol, *The Movement for Family Allowances, 1918–45* (1980). J. Harris, *William Beveridge: A Biography* (1977), and A. Briggs, *Social Thought and Social Action: A Study of the Work of Seebohm Rowntree* (1961), discuss two of the most important figures involved in social investigation during the period. In J. Pinder (ed.), *Fifty Years of Political and Economic Planning* (1981), a group of people involved in PEP from 1931 examine its work and philosophy.

Wealth, class and elites

The wealthy have not had as much research devoted to them as the poor, but W. D. Rubinstein, *Men of Property: The Very Wealthy in Britain since the Industrial Revolution* (1981), offers a pioneering investigation of this group. The last section of F. M. L. Thompson, *English Landed Society in the Nineteenth Century* (1963), has some essential information on the survival of the 'landed interest', while B. Masters, *The Dukes* (1975), is a fascinating set of portraits of the higher nobility. The vexed question of class is discussed comparatively in A. Marwick, *Class: Image and Reality in Britain, France and the U.S.A. since 1930* (1980). R. Hoggart, *The Uses of Literacy* (1958), and B. Jackson, *Working Class Community* (1968), are invaluable sources about the nature of working-class communities both before and after the Second World War. M. Stacey, *Tradition and Change: A Study of Banbury* (1960), remains one of the most important studies of British urban society; see also P. Wilmott and M. Young, *Family and Kinship in East London* (1957).

The study of elites properly begins for this period with R. H. Tawney, *Equality* (1930), but see also the modern studies by W. L. Guttsman, *The British Political Elite* (1968), and P. Stanworth and A. Giddens, *Elites and Power in British Society* (1974).

Religion, crime and police

A. D. Gilbert, *The Making of Post-Christian Britain: A History of the Secularization of Modern Society* (1980), is a highly suggestive work in which the history of individual churches can be put in the perspective of wider changes in religious adherence. R. Currie, A. D. Gilbert and H. Horsley, *Churches and Churchgoers:*

Patterns of Church Growth in the British Isles since 1700 (1977), has the most detailed statistics on fluctuations in church membership. A. Wilkinson, *The Church of England and the First World War* (1980), is an important and sensitive reappraisal of the experience of the established church, while S. Koss, *Nonconformity in Modern British Politics* (1975), examines the wider role of the dissenting churches. R. Currie, *Methodism Divided: A Study in the Sociology of Ecumenicalism* (1968) discusses some of the organizational pressures leading to Christian union.

For crime in this period see H. Mannheim, *Social Aspects of Crime in England between the Wars* (1940), and F. H. McClintock and N. Howard Avison, *Crime in England and Wales* (1968). On the police, T. A. Critchley, *A History of Police in England and Wales, 900–1966* (1967), is a sound guide. Accounts by criminals are rare, but a pioneering effort was W. F. R. Macartney, *Walls Have Mouths* (1936), an account of prison life, and, more recently, R. Samuel, *East End Underworld* (1981).

Leisure, recreation and the media

J. Walvin, *Leisure and Society, 1830–1950* (1978), is a good overview; see also his *Beside the Seaside* (1978) and *The People's Game: A Social History of British Football* (1975). J. A. R. Pimlott, *The Englishman's Holiday* (1947), remains a fine study; see also W. Vamplew, *The Turf: A Social and Economic History of Horse Racing* (1974). B. S. Rowntree and R. Lavers, *English Life and Leisure* (1951), offers a compendium of information on leisure habits around the Second World War. The place and role of the public house is caught by Mass Observation's *The Pub and the People* (1943).

The rise of the press before 1914 has been most ably documented in A. J. Lee, *The Origins of the Popular Press in England, 1855–1914* (1976). A good history of the press after 1914 has still to be written, but R. Williams, *The Long Revolution* (1961), has some useful material and R. Hoggart, op. cit., directly addresses itself to the issue of the quality of popular literature. On radio and television, A. Briggs, *History of*

Broadcasting in the United Kingdom: 1. The Birth of Broadcasting (1961); *2. The Golden Age of Broadcasting* (1965) is the standard work; see too M. Pegg, *Broadcasting and Society, 1918–1939* (1983).

Arts, science and culture

M. Bradbury and J. McFarlane (eds.), *Modernism, 1890–1930* (1976), offers some crucial perspectives on the modern movement as it affected Britain; see especially A. Bullock on The Double Image' and M. Bradbury on 'London 1890–1920'. B. Ford (ed.), *The Pelican Guide to English Literature. 7. The Modern Age* (1961) has much useful introductory material. For classical music, see P. M. Young, *A History of British Music* (1967), and for the popular scene, A. McCarthy, *The Dance Band Era* (1971). D. Farr, *English Art, 1870–1940* (1979), and R. Shone, *The Century of Change: British Painting since 1900* (1976), are useful guides. For individual artists see also J. Russell, *Henry Moore* (1968), J. Rothenstein, *Modern English painters* (1952–74), and Sir Kenneth Clark (ed.), *The Penguin Modern Painters* (1944–9). For architecture, see H. S. Goodhart-Rendel, *English Architecture since the Regency* (1953), and P. Kidson, P. Murray, and P. Thompson, *A History of British Architecture* (1979). G. MacCarthy, *A History of British Design, 1830–1970* (1979), is a reliable guide to the overall framework of design change, but its practical implications are admirably illustrated in M. and N. Ward, *Home in the Twenties and Thirties* (1978). G. Warren and D. Klein, *Art Nouveau and Art Deco* (1976), has some splendid colour illustrations, while the Arts Council catalogue to the 'Thirties' exhibition held at the Hayward Gallery in 1979–80 is an invaluable source of reference for inter-war artistic developments. For cinema, see R. Armes, *A Critical History of British Cinema* (1978).

For science and technology see J. G. Crowther, *Science in Modern Society* (1967), H. and S. Rose, *Science and Society* (1969), and C. P. Snow, 'Rutherford and the Cavendish' in J. Raymond (ed.), *The Baldwin Age* (1960). Broader movements in culture are sketched in R. Williams, *Culture and Society, 1780–*

1950 (1958), R. Williams, *The Long Revolution* (1961), and J.
Clark, M. Heinemann, D. Margolies and C. Snee, *Culture and
Crisis in Britain in the 30s* (1979).

The Second World War

A. Calder, *The People's War: Britain 1939–1945* (1971), and H.
Pelling, *Britain and the Second World War* (1970), are good
general accounts. A. S. Milward, *War, Economy and Society
1939–1945* (1977), has a highly sophisticated account of the
economic and social consequences of the Second World War,
viewed on a comparative basis, while more specifically British
reactions are discussed in T. Harrison, *Living Through the Blitz*
(1976). Reactions to the war are also discussed in A. Marwick,
'People's War and Top People's Peace? British Society and the
Second World War' in A. Sked and C. Cook (eds.), *Crisis and
Controversy: Essays in Honour of A. J. P. Taylor* (1976). A.
Marwick, *The Home Front: The British and the Second World War*
(1976), has a fine selection of photographs of the war years. P.
Addison, *The Road to 1945: British Politics and the Second
World War* (1975), provides an excellent account of the political
repercussions of the war and Nella Last, *Nella's Last Diary* (1971),
of its domestic impact.

Index

Bold *numbers refer to tables*

MORE ABOUT PENGUINS, PELICANS AND PUFFINS

THE PENGUIN ENGLISH DICTIONARY

The Penguin English Dictionary has been created specially for today's needs. It features:

* More entries than any other popularly priced dictionary
* Exceptionally clear and precise definitions
* For the first time in an equivalent dictionary, the internationally recognised IPA pronunciation system
* Emphasis on contemporary usage
* Extended coverage of both the spoken and the written word
* Scientific tables
* Technical words
* Informal and colloquial expressions
* Vocabulary most widely used *wherever* English is spoken
* Most commonly used abbreviations

It is twenty years since the publication of the last English dictionary by Penguin and the compilation of this entirely new *Penguin English Dictionary* is the result of a special collaboration between Longman, one of the world's leading dictionary publishers, and Penguin Books. The material is based entirely on the database of the acclaimed *Longman Dictionary of the English Language*.

1008 pages   051.139 3   £2.50 ☐

A CHOICE OF PENGUINS

☐ **The Complete Penguin Stereo Record and Cassette Guide**
Greenfield, Layton and March £7.95

A new edition, now including information on compact discs. 'One of the few indispensables on the record collector's bookshelf' – *Gramophone*

☐ **Selected Letters of Malcolm Lowry**
Edited by Harvey Breit and Margerie Bonner Lowry £5.95

'Lowry emerges from these letters not only as an extremely interesting man, but also a lovable one' – Philip Toynbee

☐ **The First Day on the Somme**
Martin Middlebrook £3.95

1 July 1916 was the blackest day of slaughter in the history of the British Army. 'The soldiers receive the best service a historian can provide: their story told in their own words' – *Guardian*

☐ **A Better Class of Person** John Osborne £2.50

The playwright's autobiography, 1929–56. 'Splendidly enjoyable' – John Mortimer. 'One of the best, richest and most bitterly truthful autobiographies that I have ever read' – Melvyn Bragg

☐ **The Winning Streak** Goldsmith and Clutterbuck £2.95

Marks & Spencer, Saatchi & Saatchi, United Biscuits, GEC . . . The UK's top companies reveal their formulas for success, in an important and stimulating book that no British manager can afford to ignore.

☐ **The First World War** A. J. P. Taylor £4.95

'He manages in some 200 illustrated pages to say almost everything that is important . . . A special text . . . a remarkable collection of photographs' – *Observer*

A CHOICE OF PENGUINS

A CHOICE OF
PELICANS AND PEREGRINES

☐ *The Knight, the Lady and the Priest*
Georges Duby   £6.95

The acclaimed study of the making of modern marriage in medieval France. 'He has traced this story – sometimes amusing, often horrifying, always startling – in a series of brilliant vignettes' – *Observer*

☐ *The Limits of Soviet Power* **Jonathan Steele**   £3.95

The Kremlin's foreign policy – Brezhnev to Chernenko, is discussed in this informed, informative 'wholly invaluable and extraordinarily timely study' – *Guardian*

☐ *Understanding Organizations* **Charles B. Handy**   £4.95

Third Edition. Designed as a practical source-book for managers, this Pelican looks at the concepts, key issues and current fashions in tackling organizational problems.

☐ *The Pelican Freud Library: Volume 12*   £5.95

Containing the major essays: *Civilization, Society and Religion, Group Psychology* and *Civilization and Its Discontents*, plus other works.

☐ *Windows on the Mind* **Erich Harth**   £4.95

Is there a physical explanation for the various phenomena that we call 'mind'? Professor Harth takes in age-old philosophers as well as the latest neuroscientific theories in his masterly study of memory, perception, free will, selfhood, sensation and other richly controversial fields.

☐ *The Pelican History of the World*
J. M. Roberts   £5.95

'A stupendous achievement . . . This is the unrivalled World History for our day' – A. J. P. Taylor

A CHOICE OF
PELICANS AND PEREGRINES

☐ *A Question of Economics* **Peter Donaldson**   £4.95

Twenty key issues – from the City and big business to trades unions –
clarified and discussed by Peter Donaldson, author of *10 × Economics* and one of our greatest popularizers of economics.

☐ *Inside the Inner City* **Paul Harrison**   £4.95

A report on urban poverty and conflict by the author of *Inside the Third World*. 'A major piece of evidence' – *Sunday Times*. 'A classic: it tells us what it is really like to be poor, and why' – *Time Out*

☐ *What Philosophy Is* **Anthony O'Hear**   £4.95

What are human beings? How should people act? How do our thoughts and words relate to reality? Contemporary attitudes to these age-old questions are discussed in this new study, an eloquent and brilliant introduction to philosophy today.

☐ *The Arabs* **Peter Mansfield**   £4.95

New Edition. 'Should be studied by anyone who wants to know about the Arab world and how the Arabs have become what they are today' – *Sunday Times*

☐ *Religion and the Rise of Capitalism*
   R. H. Tawney   £3.95

The classic study of religious thought of social and economic issues from the later middle ages to the early eighteenth century.

☐ *The Mathematical Experience*
   Philip J. Davis and Reuben Hersh   £7.95

Not since *Gödel, Escher, Bach* has such an entertaining book been written on the relationship of mathematics to the arts and sciences. 'It deserves to be read by everyone ... an instant classic' – *New Scientist*

A CHOICE OF PELICANS AND PEREGRINES

☐ *Crowds and Power* **Elias Canetti**   £4.95

'Marvellous . . . an immensely interesting, often profound reflection about the nature of society, in particular the nature of violence' – Susan Sontag in *The New York Review of Books*

☐ *The Death and Life of Great American Cities*
Jane Jacobs   £5.95

One of the most exciting and wittily written attacks on contemporary city planning to have appeared in recent years – thought-provoking reading and, as one critic noted, 'extremely apposite to conditions in the UK'.

☐ *Computer Power and Human Reason*
Joseph Weizenbaum   £3.95

Internationally acclaimed by scientists and humanists alike: 'This is the best book I have read on the impact of computers on society, and on technology and on man's image of himself' – *Psychology Today*
